AF247613

Separate Schools

Separate Schools

Gender, Policy, and Practice in Postwar Soviet Education

E. Thomas Ewing

NORTHERN ILLINOIS UNIVERSITY PRESS

DeKalb

Library of Congress Cataloging-in-Publication Data

Ewing, E. Thomas

Separate schools: gender, policy, and practice in postwar Soviet education /

E. Thomas Ewing.

   p. cm.

Includes bibliographical references and index.

ISBN 978-0-87580-434-7 (clothbound : alk. paper)

1. Single-sex schools—Soviet Union—History. 2. Sex differences in education—Soviet

Union. 3. Education and state—Soviet Union. I. Title.

 LB3067.7.S65.E85 2010

 371.821—dc22

               2010019100

For Amy and Claire

Contents

Figures

Acknowledgments

My interest in Soviet separate schools in the 1940s and 1950s came about through a complex relationship between a historian's fascination with primary sources that reveal an unfolding array of social practices, a desire to find ways that historical understanding can inform contemporary policies, and a developing concern about the tensions involved in the enactment and enforcement of gender roles in educational contexts. To the extent that this topic is located at these multiple points of intersection, it has always been more than a research exercise; it is also an opportunity to work through a whole series of professional issues that have been as enlightening for me as I hope they prove engaging for those interested in Stalinism, the comparative history of education, and the significance of gender in schools.

A remarkable level of financial support for this project has been generously provided by the Spencer Foundation, and I wish to thank the president, Michael McPherson, and the program officers, Annie Brinkman and Maricelle Garcia, for their assistance. The Spencer Foundation is a rare resource for scholars of the comparative history of education, and I am very grateful for this continued support of my research. Additional financial support for this project was offered by the National Council for Eurasian and East European Research, under authority of a Title VIII grant from the U.S. Department of State; neither NCEEER nor the U.S. government is responsible for the views expressed within this text. I also received funding from the Virginia Tech Department of History, the College of Liberal Arts and Human Sciences, and the ASPIRES program. An earlier version of chapter 4 was published as "The Repudiation of Single-Sex Schooling: Boys' Schools in the Soviet Union, 1943–1954," *American Educational Research Journal* 43, no. 4 (Winter 2006): 621–50.

Research for this project was conducted in numerous archives and libraries, and I wish to express my appreciation to the many archivists and librarians who offered assistance during numerous visits to these facilities: Archive of the President of Kazakhstan; Central Archive for Public Movements in Moscow; Central State Archive of the President of the Republic of

Kazakhstan; Central Archive of the City of Moscow; Russian State Archive of Social and Political History; Russian State Archive for Literature and Art; Research Archive of the Russian Academy of Education; State Archive of the Russian Federation; Russian State Library, Russian State Pedagogical Library, National Library of Kazakhstan, and academic libraries at Stanford University, the University of Illinois at Urbana-Champaign, and the University of Virginia. Research materials from the State Archive of the Republic of Uzbekistan were provided by Khurshida Ismailovna Abdurasulova, who sent copies of documents and transcripts of sources, for which I am very appreciative. At the Library of Congress, Grant Harris and his colleagues at the European Reading Room offered particular assistance with newspapers and other published materials. At Harvard College Library, Hugh Truslow helped to identify the photographs from the Soviet Information Bureau collection that appear throughout this book as illustrations. At Virginia Tech, the staff of the Interlibrary Loan department provided efficient, reliable, and consistent service that facilitated my research.

At Northern Illinois University Press, the encouragement and assistance offered by Amy Farranto, Susan Bean, Julia Fauci, and their colleagues has been much appreciated. I am especially indebted to the careful comments from the two readers solicited by the press. Over the years, this project has benefited from the advice, criticism, and encouragement of many colleagues, and I wish to thank them for their valued professional service: James Albisetti, Mark Barrow, Joseph Bradley, Greta Bucher, Kathleen Canning, Jean Clandinin, Ning de Coninck-Smith, R. W. Connell, Rebecca Friedman, Margaret Gallego, Wendy Goldman, Eva Jeppsson Grassman, Heather Gumbert, David Hicks, David Hoffmann, Sandra Hollingsworth, Larry Holmes, Kathleen Jones, Greta Kroeker, Ann Livschiz, Sara Mead, Amy Nelson, Jan Nespor, Douglas Northrop, Donald Raleigh, Roy Robson, Rebecca Rogers, Christine Ruane, Helen Schneider, Elena Silva, Barbara Ellen Smith, Robert Stephens, Ronald Suny, Daniel Thorp, William Wagner, Peter Wallenstein, Marcus Weaver-Hightower, and Elizabeth Wood. Amy and Claire know better than anyone else what I have invested in this project, and how much I depend on them for support, encouragement, and love. I regret that my research trips and the writing process have taken time away from our family life, even as I look forward to reclaiming that time as this project comes to an end.

Separate Schools

Introduction

Why Single-Sex Schooling?

"WHERE DOES THE IDEA COME from that girls are worse than boys at math, physics, and chemistry?" This question, asked in a 1950 letter by student Liudmilla Chernogubovskaia, responded to the Soviet policy of separating boys and girls in urban schools. Complaining that separate schools assumed "boys understand technology better than girls," Chernogubovskaia traced these patterns to adult influences on the youngest children: "As soon as a baby begins to understand anything, toys are bought: motor vehicles and construction toys for a boy, dolls and kitchen dishes for a girl." Recalling how coeducation challenged her to surpass boys, Chernogubovskaia complained that in an all-girls' school, her younger sister "interacts with boys at evening events at school and in homes [and] judges them, in effect, by how well they dance."[1]

Chernogubovskaia's letter calls attention to the complex factors shaping gender identities even in the authoritarian context of the Stalinist school. Beginning in 1943, separate schools for boys and girls were introduced throughout Soviet cities. A quarter century after the Russian Revolution had introduced coeducation throughout Soviet education, both educational policy and school practices were now divided along sharply defined gender lines. Chernogubovskaia's letter articulated the broad sense of uncertainty prompted by the transition from coeducational schools, which Soviet educators for decades had proclaimed as proof of socialist equality, to separate schools, which were introduced as a new instrument for promoting achievement and imposing order. This letter also anticipated the return of coeducation in 1954, as widespread recognition of the failure of separate schools led educators, parents, and pupils to repudiate this policy. Yet at the core of both the experiment with and the subsequent elimination of separate schools remained the basic question raised by this young woman's letter: how did assumptions about gender differences shape the schooling of boys and girls? Implicit in this question was the issue of whether schools should acknowledge, embrace, and even reinforce gender *differences,* or whether schools should challenge, diminish, or even reject these differences to provide the *same* education to boys and girls.

The Soviet postwar experiment provides a unique example of a large-scale effort to use gender segregation as a tool for social engineering. Although Soviet history includes other instances of social policies aimed at changing the status of women such as marriage laws, employment policy, and reproductive rights, the decision to separate schools clearly and intentionally *gendered* the experiences of girls and boys. For the first time, Soviet children were told explicitly that, although their educational trajectories were supposedly exactly the same, their schooling would occur in different locations, their schoolmates would be exclusively the same gender, and their teachers would take into consideration their "particular needs." During this eleven-year experiment, millions of Soviet children living in major cities became subjects of a wide-scale social reform as they attended several thousand separate boys' and girls' schools. While older pupils, such as Chernogubovskaia, retained some memory of coeducational schools and thus had a basis for comparing their own experiences, younger pupils, like her sister, increasingly knew only separate boys' and girls' schools. In fact, for many city children who began their schooling between 1943 and 1945, their entire primary and secondary education took place in separate schools, as the elimination of the policy in 1954 allowed the final class of tenth graders to graduate from separate classrooms. The significance of the Soviet experiment with separate schools thus lies specifically in the decision to make gender the defining variable shaping the practices and processes of educating children.

The effort to provide the same education to pupils in different schools can be illustrated by two photographs from 1950, the same year as the letter from Chernogubovskaia cited above. Boys' and girls' classrooms shared common traits of educational spaces even as they embodied the boundaries imposed by the gendering of spaces.[2] The two photographs found in figure 1 demonstrate the similarities of separate schools, as rows of pupils write in notebooks while listening attentively to their teachers in

1—Pupils in Moscow boys' school No. 110 and Moscow girls' school No. 100. Soviet Information Bureau photographs, Davis Center, Harvard College Library.

ways that embodied both the instructional and disciplinary purposes of schools. Yet these same photographs also emphasized the visible differences, as the male pupils wear distinctively masculine clothes that range from the open collars of the front-row boys to the more military costume of the seemingly younger boy in the second row. The female pupils wear the customary dark dress, white collar, and braided hair of Soviet schoolgirls, even as subtle differences in material and style reflect the distinctiveness of each pupil. These photographs were staged for production and distribution by the Soviet propaganda service, yet the positioning, presentation, and appearance of pupils indicated how the establishment of gender homogeneity served the Stalinist imperative of collective unity. While photographs concealed far more complicated processes in the execution of policy and interactions of pupils, as is discussed in the chapters that follow, they nevertheless illustrate how educating Soviet children in separate classrooms shaped their experiences, identities, and trajectories.

These tensions between similarities and differences placed separate schools in an anomalous position in the Stalinist context. At a time of rigid ideological controls, the Soviet public voiced concerns, doubts, and even opposition to state policy on separate schooling. The publication of dissenting opinions, like the letter from Chernogubovskaia cited above, demonstrated that even in this dictatorial environment, certain perspectives were allowed within a tolerable range of disagreement.[3] In September 1950, shortly after the publication of numerous letters critical of separate instruction, when minister of education Ivan Kairov told a Communist Party meeting that he too believed coeducation was "advisable," his comments provoked "applause," yet he also told these Communists that he could not express "this point of view" publicly, because Soviet officials must "adhere to the law."[4] Less than a year later, a report from the Academy of Pedagogical Sciences conceded that "there is no single opinion" on separate education, but "the majority" of those expressing views in meetings, letters, and reports "favored coeducation."[5] These statements revealed not only the crystallization of views against the official policy but also the potential for public opinion and everyday life to shape the construction and enforcement of gender roles.[6]

Although discussions of separate schooling were permeated by official Soviet ideology, they nevertheless included careful consideration of substantive educational issues from multiple perspectives. Taking seriously the experiences, attitudes, and objectives of those involved in this experiment reveals how teachers and pupils as agents, and schools as structures, participated in the discursive production of gender, in a dynamic relationship with broader contextual processes such as recovery from a destructive war, the constraints of the Stalinist regime, and the influence of family, cultural, and personal factors on identities. Studying Soviet separate schools thus contributes to a broader understanding of the late Stalinist period as well as the construction, experience, and negotiation of gender roles in distinct social contexts.

The Significance of Separate Schools

The decision to establish separate schools for boys and girls was announced on July 16, 1943.[7] At the time, German forces still occupied vast territories and major cities, yet the Soviet victory in the battle for Stalingrad and the lifting of the Leningrad blockade at the start of the year seemingly ensured an eventual victory for the Allied forces.[8] This policy change resulted from a number of overlapping and intersecting concerns, as is discussed more fully in the first chapter. The war, which began two years earlier with the German invasion in June 1941, exerted a direct influence by emphasizing the gender-specific contributions expected of future generations, as boys were needed to fight and girls were needed to bear and rear children.[9] Yet the fact that discussion of separate schooling actually began in the spring of 1941, months before the German invasion, suggests that the growing militarization of society, rather than the extraordinary costs of the first years of war, led educators to see separate schooling as a viable and even desirable strategy for training Soviet youth for future civic responsibilities.[10] The 1943 decision on separate education also coincided with pro-natalist policies, which began in the prewar decade but saw further extensions during the war, including restrictions on divorce, bans on abortion, and awards offered to mothers with many children.[11]

To the extent that historians have acknowledged the introduction of separate schooling, it has been seen mostly as a response to these broader social trajectories, as the "ultimate expression" of "the normative differentiation of masculinity and femininity," according to Gail Warshofsky Lapidus, and as "a clear repudiation of the principle of equal co-education hallowed by the theories and practices and socialism and sex equality," in the words of Richard Stites.[12] Some contemporary western observers reached similar conclusions, with assertions that separate schooling "represents a new view of the Soviet woman and the place of women in national and social life."[13] As this book argues, however, a broad commitment to gender equality as an ideological promise remained a powerful factor in popular evaluations of separate schooling and would contribute directly to the restoration of coeducation after this eleven-year experiment.[14]

Yet within educational discourse of the time, improvements in classroom order, pupil conduct, and academic achievement—rather than changes in the status of men and women—emerged as the *primary* justifications for the new policy direction.[15] Separate education thus responded to serious shortcomings in classroom discipline, especially in large cities, which persisted in spite of the increasingly severe disciplinary techniques of the Stalinist school.[16] Even some western observers noted at the time that the determination to strengthen school discipline, rather than any desire to "create a barrier between the sexes," explained this abrupt policy change.[17] A central question for this study is why gender segregation appeared as an attractive and effective instrument for disciplining boys and girls at a time when other techniques—such as reinforcing the authority of teachers, monitoring behavior through daily record keeping, or accusing unruly pupils of "anti-Soviet" acts—proved ineffective in maintaining the desired levels of individual obedience and classroom order. More important, as this study will argue in the final chapters, deteriorating discipline in boys' schools throughout this experiment also became the most compelling argument for repudiating single-sex schooling.[18] Approaching separate schooling as a disciplinary technique thus offers new perspectives on Soviet youth as both sites of collective practices and objects of state repression, yet in ways that offer alternative perspectives to recent debates over resistance, conformity, and victimization.[19] By recognizing gender as an instrument of state power as well as a constitutive element of social identities, this study demonstrates how social, political, and ideological processes shaped both the everyday practices of children and the policies implemented, evaluated, and then eliminated by state actors.

Exploring the experiences of Soviet pupils and the policy implications of this experiment focuses attention on the meaning of gender roles and relations in educational contexts. These questions have fascinated educators since the era of the Enlightenment, including generations of progressive Russian reformers.[20] Recent innovations in research methods have brought substantial insights into the ways that gender may shape learning capacities, classroom interactions, socialization processes, teachers' expectations, and educational achievement.[21] Embedded in these different perspectives on personal identity, classroom dynamics, and social interactions, however, lies the unresolved question of whether gender differences are "natural," in the sense of being physiological in origin and essentially fixed, or "social," that is, products of environmental factors and thus potentially susceptible to reinforcement, modification, or elimination.[22]

This study does not claim to resolve this dispute but, rather, explores the ways in which similar questions shaped the Soviet experiment with separate schools. For school director V. Solov'eva, for example, separate schools were justified, because they addressed the "physical and psychological development of boys and girls," especially as they passed through adolescence in the senior grades.[23] Yet other proponents of separate schooling referred to "the social roles of the sexes," which implied constructed, rather than essentialist, definitions of gender roles.[24] As suggested by Chernogubovskaia's letter cited above, opponents of separate schools explicitly challenged assumptions of different gender roles, whether biological or social in origin and enforcement, and argued instead for an egalitarian education that prepared boys and girls for equal roles as adult citizens. Although similar tensions shaped deliberations on employment, military service, and parental responsibilities, separate schools offered a unique example of how gender differences were initially implemented as policy, subsequently contested by participants, and ultimately repudiated as practically ineffective and ideologically inconsistent.

The sources used for this study reflect the conditions of Stalinism during and after the war as well as the particular character of discourse on gender in the Soviet context. The opening of post-Soviet archives makes it possible to examine firsthand descriptions of separate schools found in inspectors' reports, observations by teachers, assessments by school directors, and even letters from parents and pupils.[25] One of the most revealing archival sources is Konstantin I. L'vov's unpublished dissertation on girls' education in Russia and the Soviet Union, which includes extensive firsthand reports on separate schools during the first year of implementation.[26] Although some of this material appeared in L'vov's published articles, the unpublished version includes more revealing examples and critical insights from the perspective of an educator with a long commitment to girls' education.[27] This study also makes use of the internal deliberations by policy makers that are preserved in government archives in Russia, Kazakhstan, and Uzbekistan.[28] At crucial moments during this experiment, educators at various levels, ranging from teachers addressing colleagues at school conferences to successive ministers of education circulating draft decrees, engaged in a serious and substantive discussion of whether and how schools should accept, reinforce, contest, or ignore differences in gender identities while promoting the equal achievements of boys and girls. Even though the Stalinist decision-making process was shrouded in mystery, and the public sphere was dominated by hagiographic statements and formulaic denunciations, a careful reading of archival sources, in combination with published reports, yields important insights into the implementation and elimination of separate schools.[29] These sources make it possible to see separate schools as a kind of dialogue in which the experiences of pupils and the tactics of teachers shaped, and were shaped by, the policies and perceptions of administrators. This sense of an informed exchange between policy makers and the Soviet public emerges most visibly in the collection of unpublished letters, available in the Russian state archive for literature and art, submitted to the newspaper *Literaturnaia gazeta* in response to an article by educational psychologist Viktor Kolbanovskii.[30] While a small selection were published, including the letter from Chernogubovskaia cited above,[31] a review of more than fifty unpublished letters sent by pupils, parents, educators, and officials yields fascinating insights into the experience of separate schooling.

A revealing glimpse of this dialogue emerges in the way certain correspondents responded directly to Chernogubovskaia's published letter. Both supporters and opponents of the government policy commented on her concerns about how attending a girls' school might affect her sister's personal and academic development. A. S. Reiser, a manager in a mining enterprise, drew on his experience in a prerevolutionary coeducational school to declare that "nothing good" came from mixing the sexes. Reacting to Chernogubovskaia's criticism of parents and educators who seemed to exaggerate gender differences, Reiser issued a direct warning to the young engineering student: "Yes, comrade Chernogubovskaia, masculine and feminine profiles are *essential!*" While echoing official policy that separate schools should maintain the same academic standards, and implicitly conceding that some girls' schools lowered standards in math classes, Reiser nevertheless declared that the current policy was justified by the imperative to address the particular needs of male and female pupils.[32] Two other correspondents, K. Kobyzev and N. Lobanov, who identified themselves as military aviators, while initially praising Chernogubovskaia and other "progressive women" for their "natural and logical opposition" to separate schools, nevertheless proclaimed that women must fulfill their "fundamental task" of birthing, raising, and educating the next generation of Soviet citizens. Denouncing critics of separate schooling for "naive idealism" that could lead to "one-sided" and "harmful" outcomes, the authors exposed their own self-interest when they declared that women should never be allowed to "clog up" the ranks of military aviators.[33]

But Chernogubovskaia's views elicited equally strong support from correspondents who shared her concerns that separate schools were reinforcing distinctive gender roles. Mikhail Brodskii, a pedagogical student who also graduated from a prewar coeducational school, praised Chernogubovskaia's "correct" perception that educating girls primarily for motherhood would lead to diminished knowledge of mathematics, physics, chemistry, and other "hard sciences." Brodskii also denounced the "reactionary" view that women's "destiny" was to raise children, because this position discouraged boys from viewing girls as equal partners in schools and society.[34] School director Fedotov seized on Chernogubovskaia's example of her younger sister, who knows boys as dancers but not as academic peers, as confirmation of the harmful effects of separate schools. In his letter to *Literaturnaia gazeta,* Fedotov speculated that if this young girl were to become acquainted with a good dancer, "with dark hair," they might develop a friendship, but what would happen when she learned more about this boy: what if he had been held back to repeat the ninth grade, or if he smokes and is undisciplined? Their friendship would be over, and she would be alone. But if this girl were educated together with boys, Fedotov proposed, then she would know boys as well as she knew her family members, their friendship would be more personal, and all pupils, boys as well as girls, would follow the same path from school to work and into a happy family life.[35]

The strongest support for Chernogubovskaia came from a group of ninth-grade pupils in Moscow girls' school No. 43, who wrote a collective letter after discussing the initial article and subsequent letters. Like Brodskii, they strongly condemned those who refused to acknowledge that conditions had changed since the prerevolutionary *gymnasia* trained female pupils for marriage and maternity. According to the more than thirty female pupils who signed this letter, Soviet girls should be educated to become as socially valuable and physically strong as boys. Asking rhetorically whether female pupils should yield "even a little bit" to male peers, the letter declared emphatically: "No! In our country a girl can and must, shoulder to shoulder with young men, build our beautiful future of communism, and into this beautiful future, she must enter with fully equal rights as an advanced member of the new society."[36]

These five letters illustrate how separate schools exposed the boundaries of gender roles even as they provoked contestations over the location and significance of these categories. Although these letters do not constitute evidence of resistance, they suggest the potential for public opinion to shape both the enactment of educational policies and the experiences of individuals in response to a structure that simultaneously promised gender equality and enforced gender boundaries. The significance of Soviet separate schools is thus located in the ways that education becomes a forum and an instrument for articulating, enacting, and negotiating gender in a specific historical context.

Studying Separate Schools

A comparative approach illuminates the ways that educators, policy makers, and pupils in diverse contexts negotiate similar tensions between, in the words of Rosemary Salomone, "same, different, equal."[37] Soviet educators acknowledged the possibilities for such comparisons, as they simultaneously recognized similarities with gender-segregated schools in other contexts (including prerevolutionary Russia as well as contemporary "bourgeois" countries) and emphatically asserted the uniqueness of the Soviet situation, based on the claim that women's equality had been established as a prerequisite for school segregation. Soviet officials asserted that only in communist society could separate schools guarantee "the equal rights and identical level of general education for boys and girls."[38] Yet these claims were not automatically accepted by the Soviet public, as suggested by letters from Chernogubovskaia, Brodskii, Fedotov, and the more than thirty female ninth graders cited above. As soon as the policy was announced, in fact, some parents questioned whether this "return to the past" violated the Soviet commitment to women's equal rights.[39] Just as Soviet parents and pupils made comparisons to coeducational and single-sex schools in other contexts, this study explores the Soviet experiment in relation to schools across spatial and temporal boundaries.[40]

A comparative approach seeks to draw insights and deepen understanding, not impose categories or evaluate outcomes. This study recognizes the distinctiveness of the postwar Soviet Union as an authoritarian dictatorship, with a totalizing ideology, rigid controls over public discourse, and a population shaped by two decades of systemic repression, devastating war, and personal tyranny.[41] Any comparison between postwar Soviet schools and single-sex schools in any other context, especially in pluralist, democratic, and prosperous societies like the United States and Western Europe, where separate schools are under reconsideration, or even postcolonial states in Africa and Asia, where gender segregation appears to offer new paths to women's educational equality, needs to recognize the fundamental differences in social, political, and ideological structures and opportunities. The similarities in location, appearance, or experience in separate classrooms should not obscure important differences associated with political control over the curriculum, the threat of repression, and the pervasive authoritarian power claimed by the Soviet government and Communist Party.[42] As objects of comparative analysis as well as educational projects, Soviet separate schools were simultaneously the same and different.

These comparisons suggest the possibility of using the Soviet case study to evaluate more recent efforts to deploy separate schools in pursuit of educational as well as civic and individual objectives. In the United States, separate schools have enjoyed a kind of renaissance in the last decade, due to a combination of increased concerns about "sexism" in coeducational classrooms, perceptions of boys and/or girls as "failing" or being "left behind," political support for expanded "choice" in public education, attention to marginalized and disadvantaged youth, and new research on male and female "differences" in cognition. While all these factors are contested and remain controversial, a significant shift in educational policy and practice is under way, given the "resurgence of single-sex schools in the public sector" in the United States.[43] Although the hundreds of separate schools represent a tiny fraction of the nearly one hundred thousand public schools, the shift in public discourse has been far more significant, as policy makers, educational researchers, advocacy organizations, and media outlets have called attention to these significant changes in attitudes, policies, and practices.[44] As was the case in postwar Soviet education, single-sex schools seem attractive because of the perceived failure of coeducational schools to provide appropriate educations for boys and girls, while also contributing to (or at least not resolving) certain kinds of behavioral, social, and academic deficiencies.[45] Like Soviet predecessors decades ago, contemporary advocates argue that the attainment of gender equality in society now makes it possible to segregate schools in ways that more directly address gender-specific needs in terms of sex-role socialization, physiological cognitive capacities, or natural differences in learning.[46] And as in the Soviet 1940s and 1950s, contemporary experiments with separate schooling are often implemented on short notice, in limited ways, by administrative decree, and with considerable publicity, at least during the initial stages of implementation but with diminishing attention over time, especially when the outcome is the restoration of coeducation.[47] Integrating a comparative dimension into this substantive analysis of Soviet separate schools more clearly and fully illustrates the possibilities and the problems of educational transformations.

This study also addresses specific shortcomings that exist in the current understanding of separate schools. Scholarly understanding has been significantly enhanced by recent studies offering serious examinations of the academic potential, organizational structures, and legal implications of separate schools.[48] As these scholars acknowledge, however, their narrow case studies constrain the claims made about separate schooling more generally. Major research studies have been based on observations of a handful of classrooms over a few years, which even these researchers acknowledge to be a limited basis for drawing broad conclusions.[49] By comparison, this study of the Soviet experiment encompasses several thousand schools, enrolling millions of pupils over an eleven-year period. Given the narrow scope of available research, this study makes an important contribution to the scholarly literature.

Research on separate schools has always yielded ambivalent and contested findings. A comprehensive review of scholarship commissioned by the U.S. Department of Education concluded that "the results are equivocal," with some evidence showing advantages for single-sex schooling and other evidence showing advantages of coeducation; for many outcomes, "there is no evidence of either benefit or harm."[50] Other reports concede that research "is slim, and much of it inconclusive," that the results are "controversial," that "the weak and contradictory research evidence which now exists" does not justify changes in policy, that the appropriate response to the question of whether single-sex schools provide better academic results is "a resounding 'Yes,' 'No,' and 'Maybe,'" and that thorough comparisons produce no results "favoring either single sex or coeducational studies, either for boys or for girls, on a broad range of outcomes."[51] A recent report finding that graduates of girls' schools reported higher levels of academic achievement qualifies these distinctions as "generally small," cautions against "over-generalizing," and concludes that "it would be unwise to draw unilateral conclusions about whether single-sex education is superior to coeducation."[52] These ambiguous results lead some researchers to make narrower arguments about the advantages of separate schooling for distinct populations (middle-school grades or certain disadvantaged populations) or for specific subjects.[53] Other scholars have looked to other international contexts where parallel systems of coeducational and single-sex schooling coexist in the public system of education, yet these studies also reach ambivalent conclusions.[54] These unresolved questions about the causal effects of gender separation on academic achievement inform this study of postwar Soviet schools, even as they establish the need for more comprehensive and innovative research.[55] By focusing on school spaces, the interactions of pupils and teachers, and classroom practices, this study contributes to this scholarly field by explaining how the actual experience of separate schools generated widespread opposition to this experiment in gender segregation.

The ambivalence of academic research has left the field open to more popular books that make partisan arguments based on personal engagement in self-selecting schools or simplified claims of biological difference.[56] Interest groups and political activists shape this discourse in ways that promote specific agendas.[57] In the case of the one study cited above for its qualified and cautious results, subsequent reports, especially by proponents of girls' schools, omitted the conditionality of the original research.[58] Echoing these same claims, a number of high-profile articles, often based on limited observations of classrooms, describe new initiatives in separate schooling, while acknowledging only indirectly the uncertain results of academic research.[59] At a time when policy makers, school officials, and parents are considering proposals for significant expansions of single-sex schooling in public education, learning lessons from previous efforts to segregate schools seems especially timely and important.

These issues can be explored with the interpretive tools of gender analysis, which call attention to the structuring of categories of difference, the operation of power through discourses, and the ways that gender is used by institutions and individuals to construct identities and manipulate meanings.[60] For scholars interested in the construction, enforcement, and contestation of gender boundaries, the Soviet experiment with separate schooling provides insights into "gender history in practice," in the words of Kathleen Canning, as the "relentless relationality" of gender was embodied by schools training boys and girls separately for the common purpose of building communism.[61] Devoting attention to "the always complex ways in which relations of power are signified by difference,"[62] as argued by Joan Scott, makes a unique contribution to scholarly and public discourse by examining a large-scale experiment across the full cycle of deliberating, advocating, implementing, experiencing, criticizing, and finally repudiating separate schools. The claim that only 2 percent of more than eight hundred correspondents who wrote to *Literaturnaia gazeta* expressed support for separate schooling provides fascinating evidence of public views about gender roles in the Stalinist dictatorship, as well as the ways in which a large-scale system of gender segregation actually served to deepen and broaden support for coeducation.[63]

Chapter Outline

The structure of this book reconstructs the chronological narrative even as it facilitates examinations of specific themes, topics, and issues. The first chapter, "Disciplining Gender: Making the Case for Separate Schools," explores the factors that led to the 1943 decision to create separate schools, the steps taken to prepare for this school reform, and initial experiences in boys' and girls' schools. Archival records of policy deliberations reveal that separate schooling responded to multiple factors, including the mobilization of society to meet the military emergency, concerns about women's roles in families and society, and especially the problem of discipline in schools. Repeated statements that "the vast majority of teachers" approved the introduction of separate schooling in 1943 reveals a broad receptivity to enhancing gender boundaries as a means of improving the education of boys and girls.[64] This chapter thus addresses contemporary debates by demonstrating how an unexpected transformation in schools built upon existing assumptions about the identities of pupils and the purposes of schools.

The second chapter, "Teaching and Learning in Separate Schools," focuses on teachers' expectations and pupils' experiences. Firsthand observations by educators as well as more theoretical contributions by Soviet pedagogues document specific changes in policy and practice, ranging from the greater emphasis on military training in boys' schools and on domestic skills in girls' schools, to more subtle adjustments in teaching historical topics, analyzing literary characters, or conducting scientific experiments. For boys and girls, these differences in practice and policy shaped the context in which they experienced structured gender categories. Yet these innovations provoked critical scrutiny, as educators consistently affirmed that all schools must adhere to the same standards of achievement even as they addressed the "particular needs" of boys and girls. Anticipating current debates over the "hardwiring" of boys and girls to learn differently, Soviet educators engaged in "scientific" discussions of gender and psychology, even as comparisons of academic achievement suggest that separating schools had little effect on pupils' learning, despite the promises of proponents and the warnings of critics.

The third chapter, "Clean, Warm, and Calm: Girls' Schools in Action," begins with the striking images of girls' schools that immediately filled Soviet newspapers: well-disciplined female pupils walking in quiet hallways, sitting in calm classrooms, listening attentively to teachers, and eagerly responding to their commands. Girls' schools that adapted most enthusiastically to the new policy of providing an equal yet different education added new subjects such as housekeeping, child care, or sewing or emphasized certain themes in lessons such as female characters in literature, women's biographies in history, or domestic applications of natural sciences. But most directors and teachers did not make any changes in the academic program. As a result, personal identities, social relationships, and extracurricular activities became the realms of action most directly affected by gender separation. As suggested by the letters from Chernogubovskaia and the Moscow ninth graders cited above, however, female pupils, as well as educators and parents, also strongly objected to lowered academic standards and pejorative stereotypes. Recognizing how these contradictions emerged in Soviet girls' schools complicates more recent claims, based largely on experience and anecdotal evidence, that separate education protects girls from being "shortchanged" in coeducational schools.

The fourth chapter, "The Problem of Order: Boys' Schools in Crisis," examines the growing emphasis on discipline as a justification for, and then increasingly a challenge to, the effort to make schools more masculine. Soviet officials explained the introduction of separate schooling in 1943 as a measure to prepare boys to be brave defenders of the socialist homeland, but this same policy also responded to perceptions of boys as unruly and thus in need of discipline. Boys' schools received additional resources such as instructors for military training, expanded facilities for physical education, equipment for technology clubs, or the assignment of "strong-willed" teachers. Yet these justifications and modifications reinforced broader perceptions of boys as objects of deviance, instability, and disorder, and as threats to an authoritarian state. Transcripts of school directors' meetings, surveys of educators, and inspectors' reports admitting to worsening discipline "especially in boys' schools" provide clear evidence of disruptive practices and policy failures. The crisis of order in boys' schools led directly to the end of separate schools, for educators came to believe, in direct contradiction to assumptions from a decade earlier, that coeducational classrooms actually provided a better way to discipline boys.

The fifth chapter, "Debating Policy: The Challenge to Separate Education," examines how the experiment with separate schooling indirectly confirmed public support for coeducation. The overall situation in Soviet education, including the rapid expansion of enrollment and the stresses on classroom facilities, undermined the effectiveness of separate schools as did the increasingly blatant contradiction between a policy of gender differences and an ideology of gender equality. Widespread dissatisfaction with the failure of separate schools, which even appeared in the popular press, significantly undermined both governmental and public support for this experiment. After just a few years, pupils, parents, teachers, and even educational officials were calling openly for a return to coeducation. For parents and educators contemplating separate schooling in a contemporary context, this chapter provides a remarkable story of how initial enthusiasm for separate schools faded in the face of actual experiences of boys and girls in separate schools.

The final chapter, "Restoring Coeducation: The End of an Experiment," explores the serious efforts by educational policy makers, school directors, teachers, parents, and pupils to bring this obviously unsuccessful experiment to an end. The context was not favorable for major educational reforms, as difficult living conditions, the final waves of Stalinist repression, and the void in leadership that followed the dictator's death created obstacles that delayed the widely desired restoration of coeducation. Yet these conditions also allowed for a remarkable level of public engagement, as demonstrated in the spring of 1954, when thousands of teachers and parents attended meetings in Soviet cities and expressed strong opposition to separate schooling. In the Ukrainian republic, more than twenty thousand parents and teachers attended meetings in thirty cities, with the "overwhelming majority" of speakers favoring coeducation.[65] In Tbilisi, the capital of the Georgian republic, 98 percent of more than a thousand speakers at similar meetings called for a return to coeducation.[66] In the Kazakh capital of Alma-Ata, where more than five thousand teachers and parents attended meetings, only four of more than three hundred speakers argued in favor of separate education.[67] Although the change in policy, finally announced in July 1954, created certain administrative difficulties in the merging of schools, transfer of pupils, and assignment of teachers, certainly the most important result was the decisive repudiation of the principle that education could be simultaneously separate and equal for boys and girls.

In her letter, Chernogubovskaia appealed to policy makers to "listen to our voices, the voices of former pupils in coeducational schools," as they decided how to end this failed policy. Four years later, her appeal to policy makers was seemingly legitimized, not only by the restoration of coeducation but also by the opening phrase of the Council of Ministers' decree: "Taking into consideration the wishes of parents and the opinion of teachers . . ."[68] This book makes a similar argument for "listening" to the "voices" of those who experienced this remarkable experiment with separate schools. The history of Soviet schools offers important lessons about the possible difficulties and potential consequences of imposing gender segregation in educational contexts, as revealed by this substantive examination of the short-term effects and long-term implications of using separate schools as a strategy of social engineering.

1

Disciplining Gender
Making the Case for Separate Schools

ON SEPTEMBER 1, 1943, children in the city of Ufa entered separate boys' and girls' schools for the first time. According to the Bashkir regional newspaper, pupils in girls' school No. 45 "looked over each other with curiosity," as almost all were newly transferred to this school. In nearby boys' school No. 64, by contrast, "noise filled the courtyard" on the first day, as "boys chased and fought with each other." Teachers and school directors set the tone for the new school year, using strikingly different approaches. Boys' school director P. A. Matveev's entry into the yard "quickly brought calm," and teachers and pupils began lessons "practically, calmly, and confidently." Girls' school director A. A. Karataeva greeted pupils with "warm words of welcome" and exhorted them to study as successfully as the Soviet army was fighting against the German enemy. Pupils eagerly surrounded their teacher, E. M. Trefilova, telling her about their summer activities, each hoping the teacher would "look her way, recognize her, and then smile." Once inside, girls "quietly" walked through the school to their desks. During lessons the pupils, especially the new transfers, were generally quiet, as "shyness and embarrassment" prevailed. As pupils grew more comfortable with one another, the newspaper predicted, the school would become "their beloved second home." The narrative of the first day at boys' school No. 64 ended in a different tone, however, with a description of teachers fanning out into the neighborhood to determine why so many pupils were absent from school.[1]

This description of Ufa schools, like many other reports celebrating separate schooling in September 1943, illustrated key themes that dominated the first stages of this experiment. Most obviously, this article, as a product of the Communist Party and Soviet government apparatus, presented the policy as a necessary, positive, and progressive step toward further improvements in mass education. Because all of the media were controlled, these sources must be read critically and carefully to uncover the layers of experience, practice, perceptions, policy, and propaganda embedded in these accounts. Although director Karateeva's exhortations to emulate the Soviet army was the most obvious example of this propaganda, other elements of these narratives, such as the emphasis on order, the authority of directors, the dedication shown by teachers, and especially the imperative to enroll all children, should also be seen as elements of the broader political processes of education.[2] Interpreting layers of meaning embedded in Soviet educational discourse reveals schooling as a complex process shaped by both the policies of the state and the practices of educators and pupils.

Yet this article about Ufa schools is perhaps even more revealing of how separate schools involved the construction, reinforcement, and manipulation of gender boundaries. For probably the first time in their young lives, boys and girls were *officially* sorted by gender through their assignment to different schools. The announcement of the new policy in the summer of 1943 was a sudden and seemingly unexpected change, not only in the administration of schools but also in the expected roles of men and women. Yet this article in *Krasnaia Bashkiriia* illustrates how easily the division of pupils by gender adhered to, confirmed, and even reinforced underlying assumptions about the boundaries that divided—and defined—boys and girls. Describing pupils in Ufa girls' school No. 45 as quiet and calm, engaged in social relationships, and attuned to the emotions of classmates and teachers was simultaneously a narrative of girls' behavior, a rhetorical construction of preferred female identity, and a justification of an educational policy that reinforced gender distinctions. The description of boys' school No. 64 served a similar pedagogical purpose, yet with different implications, as the unruly behavior of boys in the courtyard and their absenteeism were problems to be identified, managed, and eliminated by a disciplinary regime specifically attuned to transforming masculinity from disorderly to efficient. The gender boundaries imposed by separate schooling thus preceded the new policy, as they existed not only in the established categories of boys and girls, but also in the presumptions of appropriate attitudes, behaviors, relations, and intentions. Recognizing how the implementation of separate schooling built upon, while also confirming and expanding, these gender boundaries yields insights not only into the introduction of this policy but also into the unresolved tensions that would lead to the restoration of coeducation eleven years later.

Exploring these issues traces the transition from the total commitment to coeducation in the 1920s and 1930s, through preliminary discussion of separate schools on the eve of war, to the adoption of a new policy in the summer of 1943, and finally to the rapid creation of boys' and girls' schools, enrolling more than a million pupils in September. Uncovering the steps that led to this decision is complicated by the opacity of the Stalinist policy process, the turmoil caused by total war, and the absence of detailed, consistent, and reliable archival materials. The lack of records from the very top circles of the Communist Party and Soviet government means that it is possible only to speculate about the personal motivations and interventions of individuals, particularly Joseph Stalin but also his associates and the leading figures in the educational administration. A close analysis of materials from the Ministry of Education, regional educational departments, and pedagogical meetings does illustrate how these issues were discussed and debated prior to the policy change and how they were subsequently implemented, but the immediate process of decision making is only partially illuminated by these materials. As soon as the policy was announced, however, the implementation process became more visible, in sources such as meeting transcripts, inspectors' reports, and newspaper articles. While these records and reports have obvious biases and limitations, they also provide an essential "on-the-ground" perspective, as they illustrate how this policy had an immediate effect on where pupils studied, what teachers taught, and how schooling was experienced.

Researching separate schools is further complicated by the administrative structures of Soviet education, which involved a combination of government and Communist Party authorities. The educational branch of the government (the People's Commissariat of Enlightenment [*Narkompros*] until 1946, and then the Ministry of Education) administered elementary and secondary schools. Because government ministries adhered to the geographical boundaries of the Soviet Union, ministries located in Moscow had jurisdiction only over schools in the Russian Republic (RSFSR), while schools in other republics were administered by their own ministries.[3] Throughout this period, in other words, the Soviet Union did not have a single educational ministry responsible for all schools, although in practice the decrees issued by Narkompros RSFSR were simply replicated across the Soviet Union. While in theory this system allowed for regionally specific applications of policy, the most significant result was not any degree of autonomy or flexibility but, rather, replication of administrative layers and inefficiencies in executing policy.[4]

The centralization of educational control was enforced through Communist Party involvement at every level of the apparatus: the School Section *(Otdel shkoly)* of the Central Committee, Communist Party organizations in the Ministry of Education, and republic, regional, and city Communist Party organizations that controlled educational offices at the equivalent levels. Within schools, Communist Party school directors and teachers assumed particular responsibility for implementing political instructions, while Communist Youth *(Komsomol)* leaders and students served a similar function among pupils.[5] All government and Communist Party organizations were subject to Stalin's intervention and manipulation, yet the available evidence reveals little concrete information about his involvement in the decision to separate schools (as discussed below).[6] Although the decision-making process remains almost as invisible to the historian as to participants at the time, tracing the discussion of separate schools preceding the 1943 decree and a close reading of responses make it possible to understand how perceptions and preferences produced a dramatic break with established policies and practices.

Although Soviet policy makers responded to unique circumstances, their approach to separating schools anticipated similar processes in other contexts, including examples in the contemporary United States where coeducation has been replaced by separate schooling. The notable similarities across different policy-making processes include the following steps: the idea of separate education was raised as a possible solution to perceived problems, this seemingly radical proposal found support among key constituents, limited experiments in the classroom as well as positive applications elsewhere were cited to justify more widespread applications, and the end result was a policy decision to teach boys and girls separately, either by classroom in a single school or more systematically in separate schools. As with the coverage of the first day of school in Ufa in the article cited above, this transition from the articulation of separate schooling as a viable option to its implementation in the classroom seems to attract the most media attention and, thus, lends itself to this kind of comparative analysis.[7] Looking at similar processes in different contexts suggests that separate schooling attracts supporters in times of social change or cultural anxiety, when schools seem to be failing in their ascribed mission and thus in need of fundamental transformations.[8] This comparison also suggests, however, that this process of implementation introduces tensions that undermine the principles and practices of separate schooling and may contribute to the eventual restoration of coeducation.[9]

Separate schools were particularly anomalous in the Soviet context, as most educational discourse before, during, and after the experiment with separate schools did not acknowledge either the influence of gender on education or the influence of schooling on gender identities.[10] The title of this chapter, "Disciplining Gender," refers to the duality inherent in this shift in public discourse, as gender became both a marker of identity and a technique of classification. By separating schools, the Soviet government declared that gender differences were important enough to justify two distinct categories of facilities, classmates, and experiences. At the same time, separate schools were expected to teach the same curriculum, thus asserting that all pupils would pursue the same goals and be measured by the same standards. The disciplinary functions of separate schools thus found expression in this tension between imposing boundaries between genders and overcoming differences in pursuit of the same educational objectives. As will become clear in the chapters that follow, these disciplinary purposes were never fully realized, as the contradictions of this policy undermined the goals of providing the same education in different schools.

The Decision to Separate Schools

Although exploratory discussions of separate schooling occurred as early as 1939 within the educational apparatus and had reached the level of policy proposals by early 1941, these discussions remained essentially invisible, not only to the Soviet public but even to most educators. According to a former teacher, the announcement of the "very strange and unexpected" policy in July 1943 "took everyone by surprise."[11] The separation of schools was shocking to Soviet educators because coeducation seemed like an essential component of mass schooling in a revolutionary society. During the last decades of the Tsarist era, progressive educators supported demands that coeducation, which existed mostly at the primary level, be extended into secondary and higher education. According to reformers, educating girls and boys together would promote equal opportunities in professions and public service, diminish the harm associated with traditional forms of masculinity and femininity, and contribute to healthier relations in society and at home.[12] Although most secondary schools remained separated by gender, the expanding system of primary schooling enrolled girls as well as boys; already in the 1890s, girls made up nearly one-half of enrollment in the elementary schools of Moscow and St. Petersburg.[13] By 1911, girls accounted for approximately one-third of elementary-school enrollment in rural schools.[14] In 1918, less than one year after the October Revolution brought the Bolsheviks to power, the new government announced that all schools would become coeducational. The government decree went so far as to mandate priority enrollment of pupils of the opposite sex into formerly single-gender institutions.[15] This action firmly established the principle of gender equality in Soviet education, even if the enrollment of girls, especially in so-called non-Russian regions, continued to lag behind that of boys.[16]

During the 1920s, Soviet educators praised coeducation for improving relations between men and women and strengthening mass support for women's equality.[17] Recognizing that simply putting boys and girls in the same classroom had not changed attitudes and practices, however, some educators advocated further steps toward equality, such as requiring boys and girls to share the same desks, as a way to achieve full integration.[18] Underlying these policies and practices was the consensus that gender equality was a desirable objective pursued most effectively by educating boys and girls together, even as these same educators acknowledged that school practices and social attitudes had not yet achieved this ideal. Although coeducation shared an idealistic approach with other experiments of this revolutionary era, the significant expansion in all school levels that accompanied the "revolution from above" meant that the composition of elementary and secondary classrooms continued to change significantly, even as the politics of Soviet education became more constrained. By the fall of 1935, more than 11 million girls accounted for almost 47 percent of enrollment in all Soviet elementary and secondary schools.[19]

Toward the end of the 1930s, two contradictory interventions occurred in the discourse of gender and education. In the only direct discussion of coeducation in Soviet schools in a decade, Moscow educator A. Savich stated that educating boys and girls together would encourage "mutual recognition," first in the classroom and then in life. While Savich repeated ideological affirmations of educational equality in education, his declaration that coeducation allowed boys and girls to exert positive mutual influences involved distinctly different gender attributes: the softness and emotionality of girls could "smooth out" the sharp and even rude features of boys, and girls could learn from the "liveliness, vivacity, and enterprise" of boys. Even with this attention to differences, Savich's article nevertheless affirmed that "complete real equality of the sexes" could be maintained only by educating boys and girls together.[20]

At the same time as Savich wrote in support of coeducation, however, the Communist Party Central Committee solicited proposals for the separate instruction of boys and girls. While the text of the instructions has not been located, thus leaving their scope and intent unclear, the Moscow educational department responded by endorsing this remarkable proposal. In an unpublished message, Moscow city educational department director Aleksei Orlov supported the separation of boys and girls in urban schools, for all grades, but he also stated that the upper grades should be assigned to their distinct school, which would avoid a "mechanical separation" of boys and girls.[21] Although the absence of further documentation makes it difficult to evaluate these instructions, Orlov's response anticipated key elements of subsequent policies, including the focus on urban schools, the inclusion of elementary and secondary grades, and promises that rather than just creating a "mechanical" separation, these steps would improve schooling. These instructions thus reveal that at least some policy makers were contemplating separate schools as early as 1939 even as public rhetoric, as demonstrated by Savich's article, resolutely endorsed coeducation as an essential step toward gender equality.

Significant changes in the late 1930s shaped the context in which separate schooling emerged as a viable strategy to address chronic problems. Enrollment expanded dramatically, doubling to more than 31 million pupils in elementary and secondary schools by the end of the decade. While rural schools accounted for more than two-thirds of all pupils, urban schools also saw significant increases. Enrollment in urban secondary schools rose from less than one million in 1929 to over five million in 1939, thus demonstrating the increasing significance of this highly concentrated sector.[22] The ethnic diversity of the Soviet Union, combined with the government's commitment to providing some measure of equality in opportunity, meant that schools offered instruction in more than seventy different languages.[23] The growth in schooling, together with increasingly conservative tendencies in political and social policies, led the Soviet government to charge fees for secondary schooling.[24] The mounting threat of war furthered the militarization of education.[25] Throughout this same period, Soviet educators were increasingly concerned about the lack of discipline, as the increasingly strict regulations imposed during the 1930s had not resolved problems of truancy, insubordination, and disobedience.[26] Although these policy changes did not differentiate between boys and girls, educators seemed receptive to new approaches to training disciplined youth willing to serve the Communist state.

Policy makers began increasingly practical discussions of separate schools during the 1940/1941 school year. In late 1940, the Moscow city educational department proposed to separate boys and girls into different classrooms as "a necessary measure" to improve military training.[27] In May 1941, Communist leaders instructed commissar of education Vladimir Potemkin to "work up the question of separate instruction for boys and girls in the secondary grades."[28] Republic and regional educational departments were instructed to "look thoroughly" at this question, consider school conditions, discuss the issue with Communist Party organizations, and then respond, in less than ten days, with proposed steps toward implementation.[29] Responses to these instructions indicate that separate schools were discussed broadly, and in general positively, across the Soviet educational system, but only within the apparatus.[30]

A detailed report from the Uzbekistan Commissariat of Education is suggestive of the ways that separate education appeared to resolve multiple problems yet could also be reconciled with ideological promises of women's equality, which were especially important for the Soviet project in Central Asia. Separate instruction was praised as a "very useful measure" that would strengthen discipline, improve instruction, organize "the correctly differentiated education of pupils," train boys for military service, and prepare girls for "useful practical activity in socialist development" as well as for assisting in the home and family. Separate schools had particular value in Central Asia, according to this report, by providing a new approach to the chronic problem of decreasing female enrollment, especially in more senior grades. If girls acquired "practical skills" such as gardening, caring for livestock, and needlecrafts in addition to their academic instruction, parents would look more favorably on schools and permit daughters to keep studying. Separate schooling would also prevent "unhealthy relations" between girls and boys as well as between female pupils and male teachers. According to this report, deliberations by Tashkent and Samarkand city educational departments revealed that the majority of educational officials, "especially Uzbeks," supported gender separation in urban secondary schools.[31]

Although any request from Communist Party leaders should have prompted an obedient and compliant response, the range of responses by educational departments at the regional and city levels also suggest that uncertainty, ambivalence, and reluctance characterized reactions to this abrupt change in policy. Based on these preliminary responses, the Central Committee conceded that "it is not possible" to recommend separate schools as a measure to improve Soviet education.[32] Despite this equivocation, educational policy makers continued to take steps toward this new policy. In May 1941 Potemkin, with Central Committee endorsement, announced the following changes: girls and boys in grades eight through ten would be separated into "girls' *gymnasia*" and "boys' *gymnasia*," while girls and boys in grades one through seven would be separated into "girls' *progymnasia*" and "boys' *progymnasia*." This separation would begin with the 1941/1942 school year in the largest cities, while all other schools would remain coeducational. Additional materials, including suggestions of what kind of schools to create, in what time period, and where to maintain coeducation, were requested from regional Narkompros organizations, with a deadline of June 1, just three days away.[33] Referring to these separate schools as "gymnasia" and "progymnasia" drew directly from the prerevolutionary terminology, thus revealing how closely separate schools resembled other reforms, such as school uniforms or instructional fees, with deep roots in Russian educational traditions.[34]

Even as plans for separate schooling were limited to urban areas, these same deliberations suggested that the reform might eventually be extended to rural schools despite the obvious logistical problems of separating smaller schools, often with just one room and one teacher, serving widely scattered populations. The draft instructions conceded that, "in the short term, it is possible in practice to implement this measure only in urban schools," and thus coeducational instruction should be "temporarily preserved" in rural locations.[35] At this preliminary stage, the long-term goal seemed to be separation of all schools, not just those in large cities, as would be the policy implemented in 1943. The draft proposals were thus ambitious in their scope—and, judging by the implementation of separate schools in 1943, also quite unrealistic. The proposed time line called for separate schools by September 1941 in twenty-three cities, and then a year later in all cities with populations above twenty thousand, a total of more than five hundred cities.[36] Given that the 1943 policy applied to only seventy-two cities with populations over fifty thousand, the 1941 instructions certainly anticipated a more expansive reform. Convinced that separating schools "will not create special difficulties," the only logistical change was to expand the radius served by each school.[37]

Although the instructions issued in late May called for the rapid implementation of separate schools, the German invasion on June 22, less than a month later, dramatically shifted the attention of educational authorities, who assumed the burden of evacuating children, expanding military training, and dealing with the staggering human costs of invasion and occupation.[38] The significance of the May 1941 instructions emerged only two years later, when similar proposals were implemented as official policy. Yet the fact that discussions were under way as early as 1939, and more extensively by early 1941, demonstrates that the decision to separate schools was more than a reaction to the crisis of wartime. These deliberations also illustrate how readily educational administrators accepted these seemingly anachronistic proposals that contradicted more than two decades of commitment to coeducation. Although the authoritarian structures of Soviet education ensured that proposals from the center should elicit positive approval and even enthusiastic endorsements, the tone and content of the responses certainly suggest widespread acceptance of the underlying premise that separating boys and girls could promote important educational objectives. This enthusiastic acceptance of gender separation has been attributed to persistent sexism in Stalinist political culture, thus associating separate schools with other conservative shifts in the prewar period.[39] Yet educators in other contexts, including democratic systems with ideological and legal commitments to gender equality, when faced with seemingly intractable problems of classroom management and personal development have also embraced gender segregation as an appropriate instrument for achieving desired results.[40] As the next section will demonstrate, these early discussions illustrated both the immediate advantages of gender segregation and the unresolved tensions that led to the restoration of coeducation more than a decade later.

Experimenting with Separate Classes

According to the May 1941 report cited above, proposals for implementing separate schools across the Soviet Union were based "loosely" on experiments in Moscow and nearby smaller cities.[41] In other words, educational leaders were contemplating a reform that could affect potentially eight million pupils in more than five hundred cities based "loosely" on experiments in a handful of schools in and around the capital city.[42] After this implementation was put off by the German invasion, the experiments resumed in February 1943, when a small number of Moscow schools separated boys and girls. In a sequence that anticipated the reform process seven months later, this experiment was announced suddenly, with little time for preparation. Some school directors were given just a few days to reassign boys and girls. The sudden transfer of pupils in the middle of the school year, with little advance notice and during a wartime emergency, had "a negative effect on pupils, teachers, school directors, and parents." It is not surprising that this experience led to recommendations that any separation be implemented after the school year ended, "so pupils know where they are going to be studying."[43]

When educators gathered in April 1943 to assess these experiments their comments, as recorded in an unpublished transcript, were mostly positive, even as they suggested nuanced evaluations of gender segregation.[44] Inspector Zaslavskii offered this summary of participants' attitudes: "All teachers favor separate education, and no one made any objections." Inspector Borisov reported: "Teachers unanimously (I did not hear a single comment in opposition) supported this measure." These teachers believed that separation was "wholly acceptable," and some recommended separating pupils as early as the first grade.[45] Whereas teachers were convinced, "not just externally and formally, but in substance," that this measure would improve schooling, at least some parents and even children were more skeptical, or perhaps less immediately compliant, as they expressed concerns about alienation from friends or siblings and the loss of a close connection to "their" school. In a few cases, parents were so upset that district officials needed to "calm down" the situation. But inspectors also declared that parents generally supported the experiment. One mother's remark that "things are better, if you like, with boys and girls separate" was reportedly echoed by "the majority of parents who say that it is better to have boys separated from girls, especially in the senior grades."[46]

Yet other remarks during this same meeting revealed a certain ambivalence, caution, and even doubt about separating boys and girls. An inspector could not detect any difference in instruction or discipline in boys' or girls' classrooms and reported conflicting assessments by teachers: "one said it was easier to work with boys, while another said that it is easier to work with girls." At first, boys and girls "secretly" competed for the best discipline and the highest achievement. After a short time, however, boys seemed less well behaved because they were no longer as "self-conscious" as in coeducational classrooms. With the encouragement of educators, pupils maintained connections with their opposite-sex peers by studying together after school or participating in extracurricular activities.[47]

Even as these statements were generally positive, reports of a conversation with schoolgirls revealed a more complex response to both the direct experience and the underlying assumptions involved in separate schools. When inspector Zaslavskii asked some girls if they missed boys, they responded: "Oh, bother with them, we are doing fine." Asked if the boys also were doing fine, the girls said: "We don't have anything to do with them now." When asked who studies better, boys or girls, the pupils got into an argument, first about which school was better equipped and then about whether the girls would "leave them behind."[48] Although Zaslavskii refrained from offering his own interpretation, the conversation suggests that these girls were happy to be apart from boys, even as they were ambivalent about the implied competition and concerned about inequities that might result from separation.

As this policy moved toward implementation, assessments of the Moscow experiments became increasingly positive. Thus, Moscow educational department director Orlov declared that this "great experience" led to improvements in academics, discipline, and even pupils' behavior: "Girls are not doing their preening and fixing their hair, but rather are focusing on school work." Speaking "frankly" to other educators, Orlov stated, "We should have done this a long time ago—brought up our boys to be men," and that "vice-versa, our girls, our young women, should be brought up to be women." Anticipating the language used in policy decrees and instructions just a few months later, Orlov praised separate schools for devoting attention to "the specifics of gender."[49] A later published report cited other "positive evaluations": instruction was more organized, pupils obeyed classroom rules, lessons were more serious, military and physical education was improved for male pupils, and subjects were taught in more depth and with more laboratory work.[50]

The limited Moscow experiment with separate schools and, just as important, the subsequent interpretations suggest that this seemingly sharp break from coeducation was surprisingly acceptable to school directors, teachers, and even pupils. The logistical complications concerned some parents, and the disruption of social relationships worried some pupils, but gender separation itself did not seem especially alarming. To some extent, this acceptance may have resulted from the ways that Soviet schools were already informally gender-segregated spaces, as boys and girls tended to sit separately, play apart, and identify differently, at least until adolescence, when they began to socialize in mixed-gender groups.[51] Yet these comments are also suggestive of similar patterns of schools in diverse contexts, where the initial separation of boys and girls—especially when presented as strategy to improve teaching and learning—often led to strikingly positive assessments by participants, including those with no previous interest in—and sometimes even suspicions of—gender-segregated education.[52]

A speech given by Potemkin in February 1943 but apparently not published until the summer provided a more extensive explanation of the factors that converged to effect a dramatic change in policy just a few months later. After describing Stalingrad as a turning point toward victory, the costs of the war, the importance of universal education, the significant role of the teacher, and the priority assigned to military training, Potemkin suddenly referred to ongoing experiments with separate education in Moscow schools:

> Military physical training of pupils occurs with the separate instruction of boys and girls. This principle has a very positive meaning. In Moscow, it is applied to all subjects of school instruction. However, in my opinion, the Moscow educational department has stopped halfway. Boys and girls remain in the same building. I consider this to be a half measure. In the fall, it is necessary to implement separate education completely by dividing boys and girls into their own buildings.[53]

In this indirect way, Potemkin announced plans for separate schooling at the very time the limited experiments were still under way. According to the published transcript, these remarks provoked "warm applause," prompting Potemkin to thank his audience of activist teachers for their support. Potemkin provided further details of this initiative, including a warning that this change should not be implemented "mechanically" but, rather, should follow the development of educational programs, with particular attention to teaching girls about anatomy, hygiene, and pedagogy. Taking a position seemingly at odds with Soviet ideology, which condemned the mindless drudgery of housekeeping as a factor maintaining women's subordination, Potemkin declared that girls should be taught domestic skills such as needlecrafts because otherwise schools would turn out "young noble ladies" who were so helpless around the house that they hired working women to clean for them. The "highest priority" was "to increase discipline among young people," according to Potemkin, by expanding military training, imposing rigorous demands, eliminating liberal approaches, and punishing rule breakers.[54]

Even though neither the Moscow experiments nor Potemkin's speech were publicized at the time, the content and especially the tone of these evaluations revealed the basis for further implementation of separate schooling.[55] The promised advantages in instruction and discipline were apparently already visible in classrooms, while logistical issues such as the reassignment of pupils or the disruption of friendships were dismissed as inconsequential. By promising practical improvements while also accepting, rather than challenging, existing gender boundaries as succinctly described by the Moscow girls cited above, the new policy seemed to generate a generally favorable response, at least at this early stage of experimentation and deliberation.

Steps toward Separation

The exact process by which Soviet leaders decided to separate schools remains obscured by the lack of reliable records as well as the complexities of the Stalinist decision-making process, especially in wartime conditions. The factors described above—the gender differentiation that resulted from militarization, the search for more effective disciplinary tactics, the favorable recommendations from regional educational departments, and positive experiments in Moscow schools—certainly prepared the ground for further steps, even as they remained mostly invisible to the public. Soon after the speech in February cited above, Potemkin issued instructions to separate schools in Moscow, beginning in September 1943. These instructions were then extended to other cities, as policy makers began gathering information about the number of schools, teachers, pupils, and resources involved in making this transition.[56]

The change in national policy was adopted in July 1943, although the public announcement was delayed and then disclosed only gradually.[57] A resolution, issued by the Council of People's Commissars of the RSFSR and approved by the Communist Party Central Committee on July 11 and by Stalin on July 16, ordered the creation of separate secondary schools for boys and girls in Moscow, Leningrad, and other large cities.[58] This opening phrase criticized coeducational schools for failing to prepare boys and girls for distinct roles in Soviet society:

> Taking into consideration that coeducational instruction of boys and girls in the secondary school creates certain difficulties in instructional and educational work with pupils, and that with coeducational instruction it

is not possible to take into consideration the particularities in the physical development of boys and girls, the preparation of one and the other for labor, practical activities, and military matters, and does not ensure the required discipline of pupils. . . .[59]

The opening statement located the justification for separate schools in the alleged shortcomings of coeducational schools, thus building upon, but also amplifying, recommendations made by educators during the previous two years of deliberations and experiments. The most significant omission was any statement that girls should be trained for motherhood, housekeeping, or other domestic responsibilities. The phrase "particularities in physical development" could have implied these responsibilities, but this passage included both boys and girls and referred specifically to military, labor, and other practical activities. This silence illustrates the ambivalence of Soviet maternalism, which simultaneously assumed girls would become mothers and expected them to fulfill the same roles as boys.[60] If anything, this preface implied that girls too were being prepared for "military matters," a goal consistent with wartime mobilization.

The final clause of this statement—coeducation's failure to discipline classrooms—was clearly an important factor in the policy-making process. Concerns about disciplinary shortcomings found a more direct expression in a statement later attributed to Stalin, who reportedly told Potemkin, as he signed the decree: "Creating separate boys' and girls' schools in the large cities is likely to make things calmer."[61] Although Stalin's comment, which was not publicized at the time, says little about the policy-making process, it does reveal how the instigation of separate schools responded to multiple concerns and promised divergent outcomes. Stalin clearly believed that restoring order was a primary concern, not so much in the formula of "conscious discipline" but, rather, in the more pragmatic sense of controlling students in classrooms, hallways, and other public spaces. Stalin's comment did not specify how things would be made "calmer," but his remark was consistent with a shared belief among educators that gender separation would lead to better behavior by boys.

The main focus of this decree was on implementation. Separate instruction would begin on September 1, 1943, which meant that a major transformation in educational policy would be implemented in less than six weeks' time. Separate schools would be established in the two largest cities, Moscow and Leningrad, as well as in regional capitals and major industrial cities; a list of seventy-two cities was attached to the decree (but not widely publicized). Separate schools would cover "existing plans and programs," thus denying any kind of gender-specific curriculum. Regional educational authorities were allowed just three weeks to assign buildings, teachers, and even pupils to the new separate schools. All these steps were prefaced with the phrase "recognizing the great government significance," thus implying that this reform was a major shift in policy.[62] As the subsequent discussion of separate schooling would show, a recurring tension, right up until the decision in 1954 to restore coeducation, was whether this reform was "purely" pedagogical or whether "political" issues were involved as well.

Public announcement of the new policy was apparently delayed for almost three weeks, until early August, when Potemkin, speaking at the All-Russian Conference on Education, announced that "a distinctive feature" of the new school year would be the introduction of separate schooling. Quoting from Potemkin's speech to the conference and repeating phrases from the still unpublished decree, *Pravda* explained that separate schools would enhance teaching, strengthen discipline, and consider "particularities" of boys and girls in ways that improved preparation for adult roles.[63]

During the three weeks between approval of the decree and this public announcement, additional instructions were issued by government and educational agencies, although still not in any way visible to the public.[64] In addition to detailed guidelines and time lines for assigning buildings, personnel, and students, these instructions exposed key tensions in the transition to single-sex schooling. The requirement that boys and girls be located in different buildings, which precluded the model of divided classrooms applied in some Moscow schools, complicated the logistics of implementation but asserted more emphatically the underlying purpose of dividing boys and girls into their own instructional spaces.[65] By contrast, the repeated statement that schools would follow the same instructional program reaffirmed that all pupils would adhere to the same standards, thus avoiding the inequities associated with prerevolutionary *gymnasia*.

The considerable attention devoted to pupil assignments acknowledged the logistical challenges involved in redistributing children from the same geographical space into different schools. School directors working in consultation with district, city, and regional educational departments were supposed to assign "personally" pupils, after taking into consideration distance from schools and the "living, family, and other conditions."

District educational departments were instructed to "personally" examine pupils' assignments, "accept and review appeals from parents," and begin "explanatory work." Each school should post a list of pupils, so parents knew where sons and daughters would enroll. School directors should assign pupils to specific classrooms, and teachers should assume responsibility for enrolling pupils, checking medical examinations, obtaining files, and creating class lists.[66] Even as this policy attached unprecedented significance to gender as a boundary, the process relied upon key elements of the Stalinist approach to educational administration, including sudden interventions, accelerated implementation, and personalized obligations.[67]

These instructions partially resolved the question raised in earlier deliberations about whether to start separation when pupils began the first grade or later, when they reached adolescence and gender differences became more significant. Even as the decision to separate urban secondary schools meant that pupils as young as seven or eight years would be divided by sex, the policy also affirmed that all elementary schools, even in cities with separate schooling, remained coeducational.[68] Elementary schools thus remained an obvious inconsistency in this definition of gender boundaries. To compound this distinction, parents whose young children lived more than three kilometers from an assigned boys' or girls' school could request a transfer to an elementary school, and then their children would enter a separate school starting in grade five.[69] The inconsistency among urban schools, combined with the numerically larger discrepancy between separate schools in large cities and coeducational schools in rural regions, at all levels, ensured that the effort to achieve the complete separation of male and female pupils was never fully achieved, even at the planning stages.

The instructions also addressed resource issues such as the teaching of foreign languages and the allocation of buildings, equipment, and materials. Soviet secondary schools, especially in large cities, were committed to teaching foreign languages, to prepare students for higher education and employment. Whereas a single teacher might be sufficient for each language offered in a coeducational school, the division of schools required either the appointment of a second teacher or the same teacher's offering classes in two different schools, or a school dropping one or more foreign languages. In fact, these instructions specified that, if it was not possible to fill a class with pupils studying the same foreign language, schools could offer "parallel lessons" in two foreign languages in the same classroom.[70] These accommodations thus produced additional complexities in the seemingly straightforward policy of gender segregation.

The instructions also specified that equipment, libraries, and laboratories be kept in the same school, without any "redistribution of equipment and instructional materials," except as needed for military and sports training or, more broadly, "in cases where a school lacks equipment."[71] This provision may have been designed to facilitate the smooth transition to single-sex schooling, but it also prevented schools from making further claims on equipment. Yet the two exceptions suggest potential complications, especially when boys' schools began to demand additional equipment and facilities for military training and sports activities, as will be discussed in subsequent chapters. While the instructions sought to maintain equality, these adjustments also opened up possibilities for preferential treatment for certain schools and pupils.

The significance of gender boundaries could be seen in the instructions stipulating that men be appointed as directors in boys' schools and women as directors in girls' schools. Yet the fact that no such requirements were imposed on the assignment of teachers also illustrated the permeability of gender boundaries. The first priority in selecting teachers was to maintain existing staffs, but these appointments should also "take into consideration not only the sex of a particular person, but also traits of personal character that determine suitability for boys' or girls' schools."[72] Although the assignment of educators was a crucial step in preparing for the new school year (as discussed in the next section), these instructions offered contradictory statements about gender boundaries, as directors (but not teachers) were supposed to be the same sex as pupils.

The decree on separate schooling was just one of several major educational changes implemented in 1943, which a later western account called "a most eventful year in Soviet education."[73] Other significant changes included the "Rules for Pupil Behavior," the formation of the Academy of Pedagogical Sciences, new policies on grades and examinations, and evening schools to prepare adolescents for employment.[74] The wartime context shaped all these reforms, yet each policy built upon prewar precedents and deliberations, even if these connections were often distorted or concealed not only from the Soviet public but even from educators. According to former teacher Dora Shturman, separate schools seemed so contradictory to official Marxist-Leninist ideology on women's equality that the new policy "was rumored to have been personally inspired by Stalin." Yet Shturman also made a direct connection to the wartime context when she wrote that, "if we exclude Stalin's personal views and whims," then the main factor shaping this new policy was "the intention to militarise the schools as much as possible."[75] Potemkin seemingly reinforced this association in his statement that educational officials "began considering this question in the first year of the war," even though proposals for separate schools were circulated in the spring of 1941, months before the German invasion.[76] Western observers also focused on the military implications, repeating statements from Soviet educators (which were not in the official decree or instructions) that the goal was to prepare boys to be soldiers and girls to be mothers in response to the wartime emergency.[77]

The limited evidence of the internal character of policy deliberations provides further insights into the factors that produced this decision. According to a later recollection by minister of education Kairov, many in the educational administration were opposed to separate schooling. In fact, at one Narkompros meeting, "everyone spoke unanimously against separate instruction." Yet when the decision was announced, "there was a 180-degree turnaround," and these same educators demanded separate schools not only in the cities "but everywhere."[78] The tensions exposed by this new policy also found expression in one educator's recollection of listening to Potemkin's speech to activist teachers in 1943. In contrast to the enthusiastic response reported in published materials (as discussed above), Zolotova remembered listening with a "very grim" feeling to the promise to train boys to be soldiers and girls to be homemakers.[79] The recollections of Kairov and Zolotova, both expressed only years later as part of a growing criticism of separate schools, suggests that beneath the deliberately homogeneous discourse of public Stalinism, a broader range of perspectives and certainly a more complicated set of responses also shaped the process of separating schools.

Transmitting the New Policies to Schools

The new policy had to be explained to educators, parents, and pupils, who were often surprised and sometimes skeptical of this sudden change in gender arrangements. Within weeks of the government decree, and even before it was announced at the August conference, educational departments began to discuss division of schools, assignment of teachers and pupils, and public explanations of the reform, in addition to the regular administrative tasks already complicated by the stresses of total war.[80] Even the public record demonstrated the abrupt effects of this policy change. In the Tatar republic, a newspaper article at the end of July on preparations for the new school year made no mention of the new policy, but just two weeks later, the same newspaper announced that separate schools would open at the start of the new school year.[81]

Explanations and preparations drew directly from the instructions cited above, including the commitment to go beyond the "mechanical" reassignment of schools, teachers, and pupils to a more complicated "elaboration" of new approaches to administering schools, developing teaching methods, and devising rules for appropriate conduct.[82] Although the designation of boys' and girls' schools often involved little more than renaming schools and reassigning pupils, these efforts did sometimes result in more substantial consequences, such as extending the distance traveled by pupils or integrating pupils drawn from multiple schools.[83]

The assignment of school directors and teachers further illustrated the effects of gender perceptions and policies on the allocation of resources. As stated above, men were supposed to be appointed as directors of boys' schools and women as directors of girls' schools.[84] In strictly numerical terms, this division seemed feasible, as men made up a sizable majority of secondary school directors.[85] Initial reports reveal efforts to adhere to these gender categories.[86] In Tula, all nine boys' schools had male directors, while eleven of the twelve directors of girls' schools were female.[87] In this context where propaganda images mattered as much as policy statements in shaping public responses to government actions, the most visible examples of successful directors usually, but with notable exceptions, adhered to gender boundaries. A glowing report on the male director of Tula boys' school No. 9 praised his formal qualifications, membership in the Communist Party, and extensive efforts to prepare the school for the new year.[88] An article about a new girls' school opening in Vologda offered a very flattering description of the female director.[89] Yet other reports indicated that even these seemingly straightforward instructions were not consistently implemented. A December 1943 meeting of boys' school directors included three men, two women, "and others," whose gender was not specified.[90] A January 1944 article describing the purposes and advantages of girls' schools was authored by a male director.[91] When the educational newspaper ran parallel reports on a Sverdlovsk girls' school and a Moscow boys' school in early 1944, both directors were women, yet this deviation from the instructions did not provoke any commentary.[92]

Even as they coped with the logistical challenges of making these appointments, therefore, the underlying justification for enforcing gender boundaries often did not generate further endorsements. An inspector evaluating separate schools devoted considerable attention to the appointment of teachers, class leaders, and school directors yet made no claim that the gender of school directors should be the same as pupils."[93] A subsequent report by the same inspector conceded that the "relatively small number of experienced school directors who were men" meant that many boys' schools still had women as directors, and thus educational departments did not "uphold the principle of appointing men" as boy's school directors.[94] As discussed in later chapters, however, it was the leadership of boys' schools that attracted the strongest criticism, in terms not only of the limited number of men but also of their effectiveness and reliability. The inability to adhere to instructions on the appointment of school directors illustrated the complex nature of school as gendered spaces, as men occupied a disproportionate share of administrative positions, yet the quantity, and particularly the quality, of male directors fell short of the demands of boys' schools.

Although not explicitly required by government policies, the increasing emphasis on feminine and masculine aspects of separate schools led to recommendations that assignments of teachers "take into consideration the specifics of working with boys and girls" and "the particularities of boys' and girls' schools."[95] When Moscow schools began their experiments in early 1943, the director of a new boys' school "began to pick out teachers who were men."[96] Prior to the new school year, director Kasperskii declared that "men teachers should have a significant role in the leadership of boys' schools," and the same was true for women teachers in girls' schools.[97] These practices received a kind of official endorsement in August 1944, when Potemkin declared that boys and girls responded to teachers "of the same sex," who better understand their mentality, morals, and life needs.[98]

Yet the gendered structure of the teaching profession complicated the realization of these unofficial aspirations. In 1939, even before the wartime mobilization of men for military service, women were 56 percent of all Soviet teachers, with even higher proportions in urban schools.[99] By 1950, women made up 70 percent of all Soviet teachers, including 84 percent in grades 1–4, 74 percent in grades 5–7, and 67 percent in grades 8–10. By 1955, women made up 85 percent of all teachers in urban schools, thus demonstrating this continuously upward trajectory.[100] As men made up only one-fifth of urban teachers, it was obviously difficult to fill all the positions in boys' schools. An observer of Moscow school No. 318 conceded that the teaching collective did not match the gender of pupils: "Of course, the majority of teachers are women."[101] In Uzbekistan, recommendations that only men teachers be assigned to boys' schools and only women teachers be assigned to girls' schools were not supported by either educational departments or "the mass of teachers," who recognized that qualifications and personality, not gender, determined effectiveness.[102] In Armenia, Erevan officials attempted "as much as possible" to assign men teachers to boys' schools and women teachers to girls' schools, but these efforts were later disowned as mistakes made by "zealous proponents of separate instruction."[103]

The assignment of school directors and teachers thus revealed that the underlying claim of the advantages of homogeneous gender composition conflicted with both the actual composition of the teaching corps and the assertion that qualifications, character, and experience mattered more than gender. By allowing many women to continue teaching in boys' schools, and a smaller number of men to teach in girls' schools, the practices of separate schools demonstrated that gender was not the sole, and not even the most important, factor shaping schooling.

The Soviet commitment to providing native-language instruction to so-called non-Russian children further complicated the division of schools along gender boundaries. More than one-third of all Soviet schools provided instruction in languages other than Russian.[104] The vast majority of these schools were located in rural regions, but administrators in multiethnic cities also had to consider native language instruction in the distribution of teachers and pupils.[105] In Uzbekistan, the overlap between gender and ethnic categories resulted in the creation of forty-two separate schools with Uzbek language instruction, sixty-two separate schools with Russian language instruction, and fourteen separate schools for "other nationalities," with instruction in one or more languages other than Russian or Uzbek.[106] In some cases, the need to provide instruction in multiple languages led to a higher proportion of coeducational schools, thus mitigating the demand for teachers and concentrating pupils sharing the same abilities.[107] Reflecting both the demographics of urban population and the preferences of parents, the number of Russian schools frequently exceeded their share of the urban population. In Alma-Ata, for example, only two of all forty-three secondary schools, and just one of twenty girls' schools, taught in the Kazakh language.[108]

The new policy further complicated ongoing efforts to prepare for the new school year, which also included tasks such as repairing buildings, enrolling children, providing fuel, and implementing the new rules on pupil behavior.[109] All these measures, including separate schools, further tightened state control of education. Separating schools was "not just the mechanical separation of boys and girls, but a government reform of tremendous principled importance."[110] Reaffirming a constant element of Stalinist politics, Communist Party committees were instructed to "control" separate schooling, to ensure that changes were implemented "in the best, most organized, and disciplined way."[111]

The process of considering, deciding, and then proclaiming separate schools followed a characteristically Stalinist pattern, in which a perceived problem—the lack of discipline in schools—generated an interventionist and administrative response. After a limited trial with a small number of Moscow schools and narrowly circumscribed deliberations by a few policy makers, the policy was decreed on a national level, with instructions prepared only after the policy was approved. Although the decision-making process remains obscured, separate schools went from a small-scale experiment to a national policy in just a matter of months, to the surprise and even shock of some school directors, teachers, and especially parents.

Mobilizing Participation

In the few weeks between the policy announcement and September 1, school directors, teachers, and parents attended meetings devoted to explaining "the meaning of separate education."[112] The goal was described in a totalizing manner: every school director, teacher, pupil, and parent must understand the new policy, so that no one has "even the least doubt about the expediency and necessity of this reform."[113] The tone of public discourse clearly specified no possible hesitations about the policy, no exceptions to total implementation, and no deviations from imposed gender boundaries.

School directors and teachers became subjects of these explanatory campaigns as they assembled in late August to prepare for the new school year.[114] A teachers' conference in the Bashkir region heard predictions that separate schools would improve discipline and instruction.[115] Reflecting the new imperatives of gender differences, Iaroslavl' teachers in girls' school No. 6 listened to a presentation on "The Education of Girls," while in boys' school No. 44, teachers discussed "Measures of Discipline."[116] At Moscow girls' school No. 57, a teachers' assembly adopted the goals of educating girls with the knowledge and skills needed to enter various professions or higher education, preparing girls for future family responsibilities as mothers, and developing the moral qualities of a Soviet woman, including patriotism, commitment to the motherland, love of labor, selflessness, honesty, and modesty.[117] In a Sverdlovsk school, teachers and the school director discussed the question, "What should the girls' school be?" An approved resolution, said to express their "common opinion," declared that "a well-rounded education" for girls would "develop the qualities and traits of the Soviet woman patriot: pride, courage, skillful hands, seriousness, thoughtfulness, honesty, truthfulness, moral purity, restraint, modesty, and the skillful fulfillment of the obligations of a mother, the creator of a domestic hearth."[118] Although consistent with the stated objectives of separate instruction, these goals clearly emphasized the academic preparation and public contributions of girls; motherhood was included, but as just one of many elements of a holistic training for adult roles. From their very inception, therefore, girls' schools reflected the tensions between the new policy emphasizing "particular duties" related to motherhood and the academic preparation needed for civic and professional responsibilities.

Preparations for the new boys' schools immediately identified discipline as the main challenge. On August 24, Orlov told Moscow school directors that "it would be a great mistake to underestimate the difficulties that confront us in connection with organizing work in boys' and girls' schools." Yet his comments about separate schools in general were accompanied by a more specific warning that "it will not be easy to regulate discipline in boys' schools." Orlov also cautioned against "disturbing" comments from teachers that "it would be better to end up in a girls' school, where it will be easier to work, because girls are calm and quiet, whereas boys are less disciplined and so there will be more trouble in boys' schools." Orlov issued a direct warning—"do not make this argument"—because no one knew which school would be the easier assignment, and more important, teachers with sufficient training and correct methods could properly educate boys or girls.[119] Yet responses to Orlov's comments only reinforced associations between masculinity and discipline. School director Roshchin called for "special attention" to discipline in boys' schools: "Our pupils have not acquired even the most elementary habits in this area. We have not inculcated in them the habit of submitting to the instructions and demands not only of the school director, but also the teacher."[120]

Educators expressed a range of reactions to the new policy, many of which revealed a more complicated reality underlying the formulaic phrase that the new policy was "warmly welcomed and supported by teachers."[121] Adopting typically indirect language, a report on the Urals region complained that "not all teachers sufficiently understand and clearly explain to children, in age-appropriate ways, the resolution on separate instruction."[122] During the meeting cited above, Orlov reported the following "absurd" comments overheard from educators:

> "Why have they decided to educate boys and girls separately 25 years after the revolution?" . . . "Is this not a return to the past?" . . . "Is this not a violation of a woman's rights?" . . . "Why introduce subjects such as needlework, homemaking, and child care?"[123]

Although Orlov dismissed these reactions, in the decade that followed, the same questions were raised repeatedly and ultimately contributed to the repudiation of separate schooling.

The issue of separate schools also "attracted a lot of interest from the population."[124] According to a later report, officials encountered "significant difficulties" as they "explained the meaning of the reforms to the population."[125] Despite deliberate efforts to "explain the difference between Soviet boys' and girls' schools and prerevolutionary *gymnasia*," many parents reportedly believed the new policy simply meant "a return to the old school." At a meeting in late summer 1943, parents concerned about "this return to the past" asked whether the new schools would be called "gymnasia," and even whether Soviet schools would resume the prerevolutionary practice of teaching religion? Faced with these challenges to Soviet ideology, an educational official worked hard "to explain the true meaning of this reform." The skeptical response of parents also led to concerns that separate schools would accentuate the differences between boys and girls, stimulate pupils' interest in members of the opposite sex (as some remembered from prerevolutionary separate schools), and spark dissension between brothers and sisters within a single family.[126] The seeming paradox of these concerns—that boys and girls would simultaneously seem more different, more interested in each other, and more alienated—revealed the intensity and variety of public views on gender roles in education.

Initial reactions to separate schooling thus revealed a spectrum of perspectives, including compulsory support, cautious skepticism, guarded criticism, wary acceptance, and enthusiastic approval. The Soviet system required that educators in particular and also the public accept new policies without questions or objections. A close analysis of these responses suggests that separate schools adhered to broadly shared perceptions of the "particular needs" of boys and girls, while the promise of specific improvements in discipline, physical education, and preparations for adult roles were consistent with deeply embedded assumptions, norms, and aspirations. Yet this discussion also revealed concerns about the regime's commitment to gender equality. These responses were mostly invisible in the public record but were articulated during meetings with school directors and teachers, and even in conversations with parents and pupils. Although these concerns would persist throughout the eleven-year experiment, in the short term they were overshadowed by celebrations of the new boys' and girls' schools in September 1943.

The First Day of Separate Schools

The start of school on September 1 illustrated striking changes in the structure, composition, and practices of Soviet education. Newspapers graphically displayed these differences. The educational newspaper showed S. M. Tsipina meeting her new first-grade pupils in a Kazan girls' school.[127] The Tatar newspaper published photographs of a third-grade geography lesson in a boys' school and a second-grade math lesson in a girls' school.[128] A photograph in the Kazakhstan newspaper depicted a woman teacher surrounded by eight female pupils.[129] Alongside the accounts of Ufa girls' school No. 45 and boys' school No. 64, as described in this chapter's introduction, the Bashkir newspaper published a photograph of first-grade teacher L. I. Kachkaeva standing before rows of boy pupils (almost thirty were visible in the photograph, and the number may have been even higher).[130] These images of well-ordered boys and girls, affectionately obedient to their teachers and eager to learn in their own classrooms, provided a compelling vision of the desired experiences and outcomes of separate schools. Yet the image of a woman teacher in a boys' classroom also revealed complicated tensions in gender boundaries, for this boys' school was not an entirely masculine space.

From the first days, the appearance and especially the tone of boys' and girls' schools moved along different trajectories. A report on the first day in Leningrad schools described the exemplary order and efficiency of a boys' school and the cozy classrooms of a girls' school. As boys wrote essays about their role in defending their city from the German siege, girls began lessons in child care and needlecraft.[131] In Kazan, all pupils arrived at school "with happy and joyous faces, on time, neatly dressed, and wearing Pioneer neckties." At their school, girls listened attentively to honored teacher M. Mikhailovskaia explain school policies and appeal for contributions to the war effort. After a quiz on the "rules for pupil behavior," Mikhailovskaia began the first day's poetry lesson. While this girls' school began "in an organized way," as "teachers did everything to make sure pupils have a good feeling about the school," the same article provided a different account of a boys' school. Although school No. 24 made "a pretty good impression," the "real deficiency" was that many male pupils did not come to school. In fact, the only pupils with perfect attendance were those who had been in this same school the previous year, whereas just a small fraction of transfers found their way to the new school. The director could not explain this unexpected deficiency and refused to accept responsibility for the absences.[132] The contrast between the well-ordered pupils in a girls' school and the absence of so many pupils from the boys' school illustrated the complex effects of structuring schools along gender boundaries.

Already at this first stage, girls' schools seemed to receive more attention than boys' schools, perhaps reflecting how the process of feminization facilitated the depiction of separate schools as idealized models of order. In Leningrad, pupils in girls' school No. 47 appeared on September 1, 1943, "with bright faces and dressed as for a holiday."[133] A description of Vologda girls' school No. 3 praised the "tastefully decorated office" of director A. I. Mukhina, who declared that "we will undoubtedly have excellent cleanliness in the school."[134] At Tashkent girls' school No. 110, as columns of pupils waited in the courtyard for the school director, the "animated and loud voices" of fifth graders contrasted with the "sedate" tenth graders. After praising the Soviet army for its victories, and workers for their contributions to the war effort, director E. F. Ermolaeva issued the following call: "Be worthy of your fathers and older brothers, study in an excellent way, and be examples of discipline and love of labor in school and at home." After some physical exercises, the girls, "in a solemn, elated mood," began their first lessons. Within minutes of the bell ringing, "an atmosphere of efficiency settled over the classrooms," and lessons began with high standards of academic rigor. When biology teacher S. I. Lisova asked questions about the classification of invertebrates, Bogunova "answered the teacher's questions as if she had studied the textbook just the night before." E. V. Sazonova's eighth-grade literature class began to read poetry, stories, and epics that celebrated heroes, whose descendants were now winning victories for the Soviet people.[135]

All accounts of the opening of separate schools in September 1943 need to be read with an awareness of "the difficult conditions resulting from the war."[136] In fact, many educational departments extended the summer break until October 1 to allow older pupils to assist with the harvest.[137] A different delay occurred in a few cities, where separate schools opened in January 1944 to allow for more time to implement the new policies.[138] The war also complicated the lives of pupils, especially children of frontline soldiers or those whose parents had been killed, and encouraged efforts to make the school feel like a "second home."[139] Even as educators declared that pupils understood "the need to behave better than they did before the war," they also acknowledged that the war complicated efforts to enroll, retain, and educate children, especially in cities where organizing a new "collective" was difficult because so many pupils had been evacuated. The new policy compounded this dislocation by reassigning pupils and teachers.[140]

These problems were especially significant in the Soviet context, where issues of collective affiliation, obedience, and subordination were central to Stalinist pedagogy.[141] Moscow school director I. Novikov proclaimed that boys' schools should "make the class into a friendly collective," develop a sense of "collective work," and work together toward "common goals."[142] Rather than "mechanically" assigning pupils simply by gender, directors and teachers were expected to take many factors into consideration to ensure that classrooms were "more or less homogeneous" in terms of ability and activism: "Of course, assignments to classes must also pay attention to already formed collectives, and consider comradely unions and established friendships."[143]

During the implementation phase, separate schools were credited with addressing chronic problems involving youth and education. Ongoing efforts to overcome juvenile delinquency received a new impetus, as steps to enroll and retain pupils in boys' schools focused attention on male adolescents who were homeless, orphaned, or otherwise beyond systems of supervision or control.[144] Girls' schools also offered a new approach to increasing enrollment and reducing attrition, but with different kinds of emphasis. Sverdlovsk officials looked for girls who had dropped out to care for their younger siblings.[145] Additional attention to "particular" needs reinforced campaigns in Central Asia and the Caucasus to increase retention, especially of older girls. In Groznyi, the director of school No. 3 claimed that all 682 girls who enrolled in September 1943 were still attending school in the spring, marking a significant improvement from previously high attrition levels.[146] Although these measures had been part of Soviet education prior to the war, the separation of schools amplified efforts to identify gender-specific factors that impeded or disrupted the education of boys and girls. Yet these same strategies also perpetuated and reinforced gender distinctions: boys were perceived as undisciplined and therefore were subjected to tightened mechanisms of control, while girls' schools sought to compensate for the loss of education due to family responsibilities or traditional prejudices. As is discussed in subsequent chapters, the disciplinary functions of boys' schools and the nurturing potential of girls' schools remained powerful themes throughout the experiment, even as the difficulty of reconciling these particular strategies with shared expectations prepared the way for the restoration of coeducation in 1954.

These descriptions of new schools illustrate the complications of transforming education in a wartime context, yet the available sources confirm the widespread implementation of separate schooling in designated cities during the 1943/1944 school year. Perhaps just as important, the discourse of schooling changed, as boys and girls occupied separate spaces and pursued educations designed to advance their particular needs. The process of implementation encountered some obstacles and even some resistance, but the transformation of urban secondary schools was executed in a remarkably short time. However, the tensions, inconsistencies, and shortcomings of separate schooling, glimpses of which were already visible in the fall of 1943, would become only more obvious as this experiment became part of everyday practices.

Conclusion

Soviet educators were eager to proclaim the successes of separate instruction. At a meeting to discuss the Moscow experiments, director Borisov declared, "I have never seen the kind of discipline that now exists" in boys' classrooms. In another boys' school, according to Borisov, teachers "never have to raise the question of discipline, which was not the case before the war."[147] City educational department reports on the first year of the new policy praised the "positive effect on all instructional work" and the "undeniably" positive changes, and concluded that separate schooling "had certainly proven itself."[148] In August 1944, commissar of education Potemkin praised separate schools for their greater efficiency, the "serious" attitudes of pupils, and the elimination of "coarse" relations seen in coeducational schools. Based on this assessment of the first year, Potemkin called for "broadening and deepening" this policy beyond the list of cities designated for initial implementation of separate schooling.[149]

Positive evaluations were also attributed to teachers, parents, and pupils. According to a 1944 report, "pupils quickly understood the essence of the reform's implementation and valued the positive aspects of separate instruction," as "the vast majority of teachers responded positively to the introduction of separate schooling."[150] Moscow educational department director Orlov declared that teachers in single-sex schools found everything "to be so clear" that they could no longer imagine teaching in any other situation.[151] Inadvertently exposing the multiple discourses embedded in Stalinist education, the director of Groznyi girls' school No. 3 stated: "All the parents spoke only positively. Even in our private conversations we did not hear any negative comments."[152] This admission that real attitudes were expressed "in our private conversations" is a striking comment on the truth claims of public discourse yet also suggests that separate schools did not provoke the "negative comments" heard about other educational policies and practices.

These initial assessments of separate schooling tended to reproduce and reaffirm gender boundaries. A Iaroslavl' educational department report criticized boys' schools for failing to establish order and maintain discipline, whereas the "increased discipline, order, and diligence in lessons" in girls' schools produced a "striking impression."[153] An Uzbek report praised boys' schools for training pupils for professions requiring great physical strength, endurance, or prolonged absences from home, while girls' schools prepared pupils for motherhood and traditionally feminine occupations.[154] A teacher in Dagestan observed that girls were "very glad" to be studying without boys, because they "felt more free" in their quieter classrooms.[155] When Moscow boys' school directors met in December 1943, a few schools earned praise for "establishing firm school order and discipline," but most had "a very low level of discipline."[156]

As suggested by the comments from Moscow boys' school directors, these same assessments revealed more complicated, ambivalent, and even critical evaluations of the first year of separate schooling. Perhaps the most intriguing aspect of this same report on the meeting of Moscow boys' school directors was the admission that disciplinary problems prompted "an animated discussion."[157] Given the context of personal dictatorship, communist ideological imperatives, and a wartime obsession with loyalty and obedience, this reference to an "animated discussion" suggests that school directors were willing to express a range of perspectives. A different departure from the assertive certainty of Stalinist discourse could be seen in this startling admission from girls' school director Mukhina: "To tell you the truth, it has been necessary to move gropingly, relying mainly on an internal pedagogical feeling." To make sense of the policy, according to Mukhina, educators drew upon memories of their "own school years," while "rereading books on psychology." Thus, even an experienced school director saw the implementation of separate schooling as a moment of uncertainty, with practices shaped as much by personal feelings as by official policies. Later in this same article, Mukhina combined a similar ambivalence with a positive statement of educational objectives, yet in a way that evoked gender-neutral goals that could easily be pursued in coeducational schools: "Maybe not everything will come together as I have imagined, but my goal for the school is to produce educated people, with strong souls, prepared for life and public activity, and who will work for the good of the motherland."[158] As discussed in the chapters that follow, separate schooling remained the subject of contentious debates and divergent views, a pattern that led to a decisive shift in public opinion in favor of coeducation.

The question of public support for separate schooling is difficult to answer using the evidence presented in this chapter, as official discourse left little room for individual perceptions, evaluations, or interpretations. Yet the available descriptions of the internal dynamics of classrooms, the responses of boys and girls to their new schools, and even the ambivalent assessments of educators like Mukhina are all suggestive of attitudes in agreement with, but not determined by, this shift in official policy. This ambivalence found expression during the first Moscow experiments in one educator's judgment that separate schools "had more positive than negative elements."[159] Despite representing a substantial break with educational practices, the introduction of separate schools seemed to adhere to "commonsense" perceptions of gender boundaries in education. Whereas coeducation had mostly ignored and at times even sought to eliminate the differences between the sexes, the new policy permitted educators and pupils to acknowledge, and even celebrate, these established boundaries in school communities, cultures, and attitudes. Although separate schools were certainly unexpected, the initial implementation and public response seem to have been both surprisingly affirmative and relatively smooth, given both the scope of the change and the extent to which it contradicted previous policies and ideology.

Separate schools further complicated the tension between homogeneity and difference in Stalinist education.[160] For the first time, the Soviet government gendered the experience of childhood: boys and girls would have the same experiences in nursery and preschool facilities, then would attend separate schools until they completed the tenth grade or dropped out, and finally as adults would assume the same obligations in higher education, employment, and public service. Implicit in separate schools, therefore, was the statement that gender mattered as much as, but also in different ways from, other factors such as age, ethnicity, location, aptitude, or achievement. The socialization function of schooling emphasized the boundaries between male and female as well as the distinctive traits, inclinations, and trajectories of girls and boys. The emphasis from the very first day of school on the discipline of boys and the relationships of girls illustrated how powerfully, yet also how subtly, these gender boundaries permeated Soviet education.

Along with these positive assessments, however, the first stages of implementation revealed underlying issues, concerns, and contradictions that would, in the decade to follow, undermine support for separate schooling among educators, policy makers, parents, and even pupils. These tensions include the challenge of teaching the same curriculum in different schools, concerns that girls' mental ability and educational potential were being undervalued, the logistical problems of teachers' assignments, perceptions of the relative advantages of different schools, the inconsistency between separate schooling and an ideology of gender equality, anxiety about the norms of masculinity and femininity cultivated in schools, and the administrative challenge of maintaining three separate systems in cities as well as a different structure outside the main cities. These tensions would accumulate, expand, and intensify in the years to follow. As the novelty of separate schooling faded, this policy attracted heightened criticism for failing to deliver on promised improvements, leading eventually to the decision in 1954 to repudiate this experiment and restore coeducation in Soviet schools.

These early stages of the Soviet experiment with separate schooling offer revealing parallels—and thus potentially significant lessons—for the implementation of separate schooling in other contexts. The Soviet example illustrates how the idea of single-sex schooling gradually attracts adherents through a combination of appealing to accepted views of gender differences, offering an alternative to failed disciplinary strategies, and promising to provide an education that is simultaneously equal yet different.[161] Initial experiments with separate schooling are perceived as successful when they achieve limited goals—improving discipline, confirming gender roles, and promising better academic outcomes—while concerns or doubts about the implications for gender equality are postponed, obfuscated, or ignored.[162]

Initial reports on the first experiences with separate schooling in many of these situations, as in the Soviet Union in the fall of 1943, tend to be quite positive, as all children seem more engaged, girls take on new roles, and boys seem more disciplined.[163] This positive impression, as suggested by the comments by Soviet educators, seems to reflect the ways that separate schools confirm gendered identities, thus promoting the idea that schools can offer the same education by addressing the different needs and interests of boys and girls. As gender segregation changes from an innovation to a structure, however, these same schools seem to take on a different character, for the common challenges of teaching and learning are exacerbated by the ways that these schools, almost by definition, depend on reinforcing gendered boundaries between boys and girls. As the next chapters argue, further experiences with separate schooling would continue to generate positive assessments yet would also increasingly disappoint policy makers, educators, and parents seeking to improve the education of all Soviet children.

The potential for dissatisfaction with separate schooling was already in place as this experiment began, as illustrated by the pointed questions about "a return to the past," concerns about the equal education of girls, and doubts that the policy would achieve the desired disciplining of boys. The boys and girls who entered a first-grade class in September 1943, like the Ufa children described above, probably spent their entire education in separate schools, as their tenth grade ended just a year before the policy was repudiated in 1954. But it was their experiences in boys' and girls' schools, in combination with those of millions of classmates across the Soviet Union, that increasingly persuaded the public as well as the educational establishment that separate schools did not fulfill the promises anticipated in the summer of 1943.

2 Teaching and Learning in Separate Schools

THE PURPOSE OF SEPARATING SCHOOLS, as announced by the government decree and echoed by educators, was to improve the education of both boys and girls. This stated objective raised questions about the possible effects of gender separation on the processes and outcomes of education. Should separate schools offer the same curriculum taught by the same methods and with the same results, or should attention to the "particularities of boys and girls" also shape the content, strategies, and outcomes of the instructional process? What standards should be used to evaluate the means and ends of instruction, and would these measures reveal significant differences between schools? Most important, could separate schools successfully overcome the "deficiencies" of coeducation, as identified in the 1943 decree, or would these problems actually be compounded by new challenges associated with gender segregation? Exploring these questions provides a basis for evaluating the Soviet experiment with separate schools while also identifying the potential advantages and complications of this educational strategy.

The new policy challenged educators to identify the specific ways that boys and girls should be taught differently in their separate schools. A revealing perspective came from a physics teacher who taught simultaneously in two schools, and whose observations were recounted to a 1948 meeting by girls' school director Perstova:

> He says that while working at the same time in a boys' and a girls' school, he has realized that in a girls' school, and in particular in our school, when he comes to teach a lesson, he can be certain that very many girls have conscientiously learned the material and will talk about what they know. But when he starts to explain new material, he does not see that interest and that keenness of thought which he observes in a physics lesson in a boys' school. But the opposite phenomenon also occurs. There [the boys] may catch fire during a lesson, become interested, try to get to the bottom of something, but by the next class they have not learned their lesson, and it seems that half his efforts have been for nothing. In the most broad sense, when discussing knowledge of physics in a girls' and a boys' school, he says: there [in the boys' school] they grasp it better, but here [in the girls' school] they know it better.[1]

This statement illustrates how personal observations based on experience tended to confirm gender stereotypes: boys were intrinsically more interested in science, quicker to grasp material, and more willing to challenge the teacher but were also unable to sustain this interest and were undisciplined in their work habits. Girls were less interested in science and not as dynamic or stimulating to teach but worked more consistently. This teacher's distinction between "grasping" and "knowing" demonstrates how separate schools were responding to, but also encouraging, distinctively different perceptions of masculine and feminine interests and abilities.

This teacher's observation also revealed the complexity of evaluating educational outcomes. Was it better to "grasp" the instructional material quickly, enthusiastically, and keenly or to "know" it through diligent work but with little enthusiasm?[2] This comparison focuses on the question of how children learn, as well as an obvious corollary and complication, which is the recognition that different children learn in different ways. By separating boys and girls, Soviet policy implicitly made one of two claims: either the differences in the learning processes of boys and girls were sufficiently important to justify their separation, or else other objectives such as imposing discipline, cultivating social relationships, or preparing for adult roles were so important that boys and girls should be separated, regardless of the academic effects. The comments from this physics teacher reveal the tensions embedded in the new policy. Even as perceived differences in male and female learning influenced the ways that teachers related to students, the curriculum remained the same for all pupils. As discussed more fully below, some educators did call for adaptations in the curriculum, but these recommendations were always questioned, challenged, and ultimately repudiated as being contradictory to the goals of preparing pupils to become fully equal Soviet citizens.

Whereas the preceding chapter focused on policy deliberations, decisions, and implementation, this chapter looks specifically at what happened in boys' and girls' schools, beginning with the important question of how many pupils studied in separate schools. The instructions issued in 1943 listed the cities that were supposed to separate their secondary schools, but not all schools in these cities were separated, even as more cities beyond this initial list implemented separate schooling. Understanding *how many* pupils attended separate schools thus sets up analysis of *what happened,* or more specifically what was *supposed* to happen, in these schools. The prescriptive statements of Soviet pedagogues drew upon multiple perspectives, including the historical legacy and personal memories of prerevolutionary single-sex schools, the experience of Soviet coeducational schools, perceptions of intrinsic male and female traits, the tenets of communist ideology, and social conditions during and after the war. A critical reading of these programmatic statements illustrates the assumptions, expectations, and perceptions that shaped classroom practices.[3] These texts were intended to guide the practices of teachers, yet they also became objects of debate and even contestation, as their promises of achievement and transformation were contrasted with the actual practices and outcomes of separate schooling. In addition to published articles, this chapter draws upon observations, recommendations, and criticisms by educators, cited in inspectors' reports or in educators' meetings, such as the comments from director Perstova cited above. These materials, which often went unpublicized at the time, provided the frank evaluations and critical assessments necessary to understand classroom dynamics, social interactions, and pupil development.[4] A careful analysis of both published and archival sources reveals how the attempt to "gender" teaching and learning led to significant changes in classroom practices and educational objectives yet also exposed the inherent contradictions of pursuing the *same* outcomes in *different* schools.

Exploring educational goals and classroom practices in separate schools makes a direct contribution to contemporary debates on gender and schools. Research on the educational outcomes of separate schooling produces consistently ambivalent and equivocal conclusions.[5] As a result, both advocates and opponents of separate schools tend to emphasize nonacademic outcomes, such as personal development, social behavior, or peer interactions as preferred outcomes of schooling.[6] The contribution of this study, therefore, is to focus attention on the instructional practices of separate schools as the basis for evaluating their effects on pupils. As this chapter demonstrates, examining these questions reveals the limited, and even contradictory, effects of gender separation on academic outcomes.

Given that the Soviet Union had a centralized school system, with decisions about the curriculum, textbooks, and even pedagogy made by the top leadership and then transmitted by Communist Party organizations and the educational apparatus directly to teachers and pupils, the statement that boys' and girls' schools taught the same curriculum should have been definitive. Yet the very system of separate schooling posed implicit challenges to this policy, because if the content and outcomes of schooling were the *same,* how were educators supposed to consider the "particularities" of boys and girls, as specified in the 1943 decree? For director Perstova, whose summary of a physics teacher's impressions is cited above, these tensions emerged in subtle yet significant ways as she described teaching practices in a girls' classroom. Speaking to her colleagues, Perstova declared that her girls' school taught the same curriculum as coeducational or boys' schools in all subjects, with the exception of physical education, where some adaptations were made for female pupils. Perstova also stated that biology was now easier to teach, as "certain themes" could be discussed more calmly and practically with a class of girls. Although there had been some "talk" about teaching housekeeping during the first stages of the reform, her school "did nothing," because she did not receive precise instructions.[7] According to Perstova, therefore, teaching in a girls' school meant covering the same curriculum, yet also acknowledging small differences in physical education, affirming the advantages of a single-gender classroom for biology, and rejecting gender-specific lessons tied to traditionally feminine roles. This statement adhered to official Soviet policy, which promised educational equality, yet her judgment of what could be different and what should be the same demonstrates the tensions at the center of separate schools.[8] Exploring the practical negotiation of this balance in Soviet boys' and girls' schools thus suggests issues to be acknowledged and evaluated in other contexts where separate schooling promises the same education to different genders.

Enrollment in Separate Schools

This evaluation of how gender segregation affected teaching and learning begins with a seemingly simple question: how many boys and girls attended separate schools? The best estimate is that between three and four million Soviet children, approximately 13 percent of total enrollment, attended separate schools each year from 1943 to 1954.[9] This figure is an estimate because neither published works nor archival sources offered comprehensive statistics on separate schools.[10] Yet the question remains significant, despite the lack of complete information, both as a measure of the scope of this experiment and as a gauge of the comparative implications of the Soviet experience.[11]

The number, size, and composition of separate schools were shaped by enrollment patterns before, during, and after the war. Whereas elementary and secondary enrollment reached nearly 35 million pupils by the end of the 1930s, this number fell by one-fifth during the war and then only gradually recovered, reaching a high of 33 million by 1950.[12] The postwar expansion placed new strains on Soviet education, as more schools, classrooms, and teachers were needed to meet growing demand. This structural context is important for understanding the increasing dissatisfaction with separate schools, as the new policy coincided with more demands on Soviet education.

Separate education involved only a small fraction of Soviet schools. Because the vast majority of all schools were classified as "rural," they were not eligible for this policy.[13] Of course, the concentration of populations in the largest cities where this policy was most widely implemented meant that these schools enrolled higher proportions of children.[14] Approximately one-third of all Soviet pupils attended urban schools and thus were potentially affected by this policy.[15] Not even all "urban" schools were separated. Elementary schools, which enrolled grades 1–4 and composed approximately one-third of urban schools, were usually not separated.[16] Taking all these factors into consideration, the urban secondary schools eligible for separation composed perhaps 8 percent of all Soviet schools.

The available evidence on enrollment provides further evidence of a range of patterns. By the spring of 1944, according to reports on more than seventy cities in the Russian Republic, separate schools enrolled more than three-quarters of all pupils, with a higher percentage (45%) in girls' schools than in boys' schools (33%).[17] Eight years later, a report on a smaller selection of cities indicated a slightly lower ratio, as just over two-thirds of pupils attended separate schools: 32 percent in boys' schools, 37 percent in girls' schools, and 31 percent in coeducational schools.[18] While these figures are incomplete, they suggest that significant numbers of children were involved annually in this experiment. Yet the policy was never totalizing in its scope, as coeducational schooling always coexisted with separate schools even in the designated cities. Most important, the lack of detailed, reliable, and consistent statistics illustrated a more general reluctance to acknowledge the full scope or implications of separate schooling. While these issues are discussed more fully in subsequent chapters, the important starting point remains the scope of the Soviet experiment, which far exceeded more recent efforts in other contexts to separate schools in the public sector.

These measurements of enrollment were complicated by the absence of an all-Union ministry keeping track of schools. The 1943 instructions listed 71 cities in the Russian Republic that should implement separate schooling. Later reports indicate that an additional 96 cities also separated schooling, bringing the total to 167 cities.[19] Reports from other republics suggest a similar distribution. In Uzbekistan, Turkmenistan, and Kazakhstan, separate schooling was implemented first in the capital cities of Tashkent, Ashkhabad, and Alma-Ata, and then in other cities.[20] In Uzbekistan, 136 separate schools functioned in eight cities by the fall of 1944; a decade later, 75 separate schools in Tashkent enrolled approximately forty-five thousand boys and girls.[21] In Armenia, three cities implemented separate schooling in the first year.[22] In Azerbaijan, by contrast, only Baku schools implemented this policy during the first year, although at least eight more cities followed in the next eleven years.[23] In Georgia, 194 schools were separated by the spring of 1954, including 98 schools in Tbilisi.[24] Kirgizia had twenty-five separate schools by 1954, enrolling eight thousand pupils in just Frunze.[25] In Ukraine, as many as thirty cities implemented separate schooling.[26] In the Russian republic, a partial list of cities accounted for over two thousand schools and more than two million pupils.[27] While all these numbers are incomplete, they are consistent with the estimated total of between three and four million pupils a year in separate schools across the Soviet Union.

The distribution of pupils between coeducational and separate schools varied considerably in these same cities. The highest proportions, according to a partial list from 1952, were in the largest cities: 97 percent in Moscow and 93 percent in Leningrad. The lowest proportions were 7 percent in Sevastopol and 10 percent in Stalingrad. Almost one-half of the twenty-eight cities on the list reported that separate schools enrolled approximately one-half (40–60%) of pupils.[28] Separate schooling was thus implemented incompletely and inconsistently, despite the context where educational policies and practices were supposed to conform to uniform and absolute standards.

Moscow schools consistently reported the highest proportions in boys' and girls' schools. The first year saw the creation of 156 boys' schools and 173 girls' schools.[29] By the third year, 192 boys' schools and 216 girls' schools vastly outnumbered five coeducational schools. Three years later, separate schools in Moscow accounted for 99 percent of 445 secondary schools.[30] By 1954, 524 separate schools in Moscow were divided exactly in half between boys' and girls' schools.[31] Each year, more than a half million boys and girls studied in Moscow's separate schools, a total that accounted for at least one-sixth of all pupils enrolled in all Soviet separate schools.

By contrast, the two cities in the Russian Republic reporting the lowest proportion of separate schools, Sevastopol and Stalingrad, were also among those most damaged by the war.[32] Neither appeared on the initial list of cities to implement separate schooling in the summer of 1943, and it is not clear when they began this reform. Five years after the war, however, only six of the eighty schools in Stalingrad were single-sex.[33] Three years later, when the total number of Stalingrad schools had increased to more than ninety, the number of separate schools remained the same, suggesting that factors beyond war damage accounted for the higher proportion of coeducational schools.[34] In Sevastopol, just one girls' school and no boys' schools functioned in 1951, and 93 percent of the nearly thirteen thousand pupils studied in coeducational schools.[35] Yet the effects of the war were clearly not the only factor, as shown by the example of Leningrad; the three-year siege by German armies ended just months after separate schooling began, yet this city recorded the second-highest proportion of pupils enrolled in separate schools.[36] By 1950, boys' and girls' schools enrolled 94 percent of the more than two hundred thousand pupils in Leningrad.[37]

Enrollment levels in separate schools also did not adhere to obvious regional patterns. In Khabarovsk, located far to the east of Moscow, just 20 percent of pupils studied in separate schools in 1952.[38] While distance from the political center might explain this very partial implementation, other cities located in comparably remote regions—including Novosibirsk, Krasnoiarsk, Omsk, Kazan, and Irkutsk—reported enrollments of one-half of pupils in separate schools.[39] Similar variation occurred in regions with high proportions of "non-Russian" pupils. In Groznyi, the capital of the Chechen region, three-quarters of pupils studied in separate schools, with girls' schools enrolling a slightly higher proportion than boys' schools. In Nal'chik, the capital of the neighboring Kabardin region, fewer than one-quarter of pupils studied in separate schools, and the proportion in girls' schools was just one-half the proportion in boys' schools.[40] In the latter city, the total number of pupils had doubled since 1943, yet enrollment in separate schools had fallen by one-half.[41] In Alma-Ata, the 39 separate schools educated more than 25,000 pupils, thus accounting for the overwhelming majority of secondary enrollment.[42] In Tashkent, separate schools accounted for 88 percent of more than 130 schools.[43] In Kiev, approximately one-half of more than 100 schools offered separate instruction for boys and girls.[44] In Ufa, the setting for the newspaper report on the new school year discussed in the previous chapter, separate schools enrolled just 37 percent of pupils by 1950, with boys' schools enrolling just two-thirds as many pupils as girls' schools.[45]

Even cities located near the political center with predominantly Russian populations reported considerable variation. In Vologda, where girls' school director Mukhina earned praise for exemplary order (as discussed in the next chapter), slightly less than three-quarters of pupils studied in separate schools.[46] In Gor'kii, where boys' school teachers called attention to "crude violations of discipline" (as discussed in chapter 4), some 77,000 pupils attended separate schools, while 21,000 attended coeducational schools.[47] In Saratov, where girls' school director S. Razvinova authored a flattering yet controversial report (see chapter 3), 31 percent of pupils studied in girls' schools, 25 percent studied in boys' schools, and 44 percent studied in coeducational schools.[48] In Rostov-on-Don, where boys' school director V. Tiapkin provoked controversy when he publicly endorsed gender-specific instruction in a 1950 letter (see chapter 5), almost three-quarters of pupils studied in separate schools.[49]

These patterns—the variation across cities, the clustering of rates in the 40–60 percent range, and the absence of clear connections with geographic location, the impact of war, or ethnic composition—all suggest that regional and/or district educational departments were mostly, but not totally (with the obvious exception of Moscow and Leningrad), fulfilling instructions on separate schooling. Even with this variation, these numbers indicate that a substantial proportion of pupils and schools in most major cities had shifted to separate institutions. Although a very large proportion of pupils and schools were separated, the remaining coeducational schools ensured that different kinds of schools coexisted within the same geographical space.

Soviet boys and girls in postwar urban society were thus statistically quite likely to attend separate schools, even as most of their generational peers attended coeducational schools in villages, towns, and even the same cities. Although the establishment of separate schools was a significant effort of gender engineering, this experiment was always incomplete, and thus inevitably subject to contestations, negotiations, and transformations. Even in the authoritarian context of postwar Stalinism, the binary division of gender proved unattainable and unsustainable in practice. Yet the inconsistency in implementation revealed how attempts to define gender boundaries conflicted with the totalizing aspirations of the Stalinist regime, as partial and inconsistent implementation ensured that Soviet pupils followed very different educational trajectories. The Soviet experiment with separate schooling illustrated a persistent tension between gendered experiences of boys and girls in separate schools and the common experiences of boys and girls in the authoritarian context of postwar dictatorship.

Gender Equality as an Objective

One of the principles of Soviet ideology was the commitment to recognize, sustain, and promote the equality of women.[50] The implementation of coeducation in all Soviet schools in 1918 was cited as proof of this commitment to gender equality.[51] Soviet educators in the 1920s acknowledged that promises of gender equality had not been fully realized, especially given regional and cultural variations that shaped connections between education and social status. Yet a combination of ideological principles, changes in practices, and substantial advances in girls' enrollment confirmed the promise, if not the full realization, that children were learning about "correct relations between the sexes."[52] Articles 121 and 122 in the 1936 "Stalin" Constitution, promising respectively "the right to education" and "equal rights" for men and women, provided further confirmation of this commitment to coeducation and to gender equality.

Attempts to explain how the policy of separate schools was consistent with the ideology of gender equality revealed the tensions embedded in a system that differentiated pupils by gender yet promised the same educational access and achievements.[53] The argument that coeducation was "no longer necessary in present circumstances," as Soviet women had achieved complete equality, was articulated as early as 1941 by proponents of a new policy. From this perspective, only separate schools could recognize the different developmental stages of boys and girls, strengthen school discipline, increase enrollment, and still uphold "unshakable" principles of equal rights to education and an identical level of knowledge for both sexes.[54]

After the policy was announced in 1943, educators offered more extensive explanations of how separate schools would ensure gender equality, even as they developed a revised narrative of the path to this objective. The introduction of coeducation in 1918 was still described as "a huge step forward," because it advanced universal education, broadened women's access into higher education, and ensured equal rights in professional training.[55] Now that women's equality had been achieved, according to this argument, boys and girls could be educated separately without any danger of returning to the inequality characteristic of prerevolutionary Russian society. Based on this foundation of fully realized equality, schools could more effectively "educate boys to be future fathers and courageous fighters for the socialist homeland and girls to be the conscious mothers and educators of the new generation."[56]

Offering an early version of this new narrative, Moscow educational department director Orlov told school directors in August 1943 that "coeducational instruction had played its historical role" of eliminating the "centuries-long inequality between a man and a woman." Now that Soviet schools were training women to become scientists and engineers, "there is no need to put up with the shortcomings" of coeducational schools. Orlov asked rhetorically: "Does this mean that the introduction of separate instruction means the re-examination of the question of the equality of women and of their political and civil equality? Of course not."[57] Echoing this same argument, a Leningrad city official, E. Fedorova, praised coeducation's contribution to achieving full equality for Soviet women, but then she asserted that "in these conditions, coeducational instruction is no longer a necessity, and it is even impeding further improvements of schools." Coeducational schools did not take into consideration "the particularities in the physical development of boys and girls," whereas separate schools, according to Fedorova, provided "new opportunities" for instruction and upbringing, including training boys into "skillful, firm, brave, hardy, and physically strong future fighters."[58] In a 1945 article, M. G. Timofeev declared that the main objective of the coeducational school was to promote the equality of women, but now the task had essentially been accomplished: "Educated by the new school, the woman of our country has not only legally, but also factually, become equal in rights with men."[59]

Soviet educators thus justified separate schools as actually doing more than coeducational schools to ensure gender equality. According to L'vov, although coeducation encouraged "a feeling of value" among Soviet women, promoted girls' political activism, and spread "the idea of equality among men and women," it had not eliminated a persistent view of girls as unequal and thus not deserving of the same education.[60] But some justifications of separate schooling went even further, by criticizing coeducation for promoting a kind of "leveling" that ignored or denied gender differences, as in this statement from M. Tsuzmer: "But social equality does not mean ignoring the particularities created by the physiological and psychological features specific to the two sexes. Social equality is by no means leveling." Warning that coeducation involved "a certain suppression of typical features of masculinity and femininity which have a certain social value," Tsuzmer predicted that separate schools would provide "some differentiation of school knowledge and habits" appropriate for the "natural" and "social" roles of boys and girls.[61] More particularly, Tsuzmer charged that coeducation inadequately prepared a girl for "the extremely important function of being a mother-teacher," whereas a separate school could develop "the knowledge and habits" of taking care of an infant, educating children, and maintaining a healthy home, thus contributing to the "new and no less important" task of "the all-around strengthening of the primary cell of our society—the socialist family— on the basis of the fully valued development of the traits of masculinity and femininity of the father and mother, the heads of the family with fully equal rights."[62] Writing in anticipation of the opening of separate schools, director Solov'eva predicted that the new policy would better "prepare boys to be future fathers and courageous fighters for the socialist motherland and girls to be fully conscious mothers." Whereas coeducation might not "fully prepare a girl to fulfill the important functions of being a mother-educator," a girls' school could teach skills needed to raise children in a hygienic home, while a boys' school offered the "physical and moral hardening" necessary to enter military service.[63]

As this rhetoric became policy, however, pupils as well as teachers and parents struggled to make sense of this new criticism of coeducation and the promised advantages of separate schools. Orlov cited the following exchange with a female student as evidence that "vulgar" equality had been taken too far. According to Orlov, a young woman responded strongly to his question about becoming a mother: "Curse that tongue of yours, for I am a citizen with equal rights." Speaking to an August 1943 meeting of educators, Orlov warned that this girl revealed "an incorrect interpretation of equality" by her virulent reaction: "Think about it, or don't think about it, but a woman must give birth to children, and if we say 'a,' then we need to say 'b.' If this is so, then the education of girls should be different from the education of boys."[64] In other words, women's role in reproduction meant that their education should also be different, and thus this girl's forceful assertion of equality was really a rejection of her natural gender role.

These promises that separate education would ensure full equality continued to provoke substantial challenges, even if the wartime dictatorship ensured that they remained muted and indirect. Less than a year after dismissing this girl's assertion of her equal status, Orlov conceded "there has been some talk" expressing "the opinion of some comrades" that "the introduction of separate education would reduce certain rights of women." In a context where it was almost inconceivable—and certainly potentially dangerous—to suggest that educational policies were contradicting a key principle such as women's equality, his admission suggests more widespread concerns about the implications of separate schooling. Perhaps anticipating the further spread of these critical views, Orlov reassured school directors that "separate schooling not only does not decrease women's rights but, on the contrary, actually strengthens these rights."[65]

Further evidence of dissenting views came from L'vov's unpublished study, which stated that the new policy caused "considerable agitation" among pupils, "and especially girls," who worried about limits on their education and reductions in their rights. One girl, described as "an activist," drew upon historical memory to declare: "If they want to lock us up in a tower, it will not work."[66] While both Orlov and L'vov dismissed these objections and anxieties by declaring that separate schools were consistent with gender equality, other evidence suggests that these girls were not alone in their reactions. A 1944 report on Nal'chik schools stated that boys were "indifferent" to the announcement of separate schools, but "girls were upset and ran for explanations" to the city educational department.[67] These responses, while anecdotal, suggest that at least some pupils, and especially girls, believed that coeducation was more favorable to women's positions in society. Separate schools were seen as more of a threat to girls than to boys, even as policy justifications emphasized the "particular needs" of girls more than those of boys.

Discussion of separate schools and gender equality continued, even as the terms of this discourse changed. By 1950, at a time of increased criticism of separate schools (see chapter 5), the newspaper *Literaturnaia gazeta* asserted that separate schools were delaying the "final *equalization*" of women. Whereas this policy had been introduced with the promise that equality could be advanced by separating the sexes, this editorial now declared that separate schools were incompatible with ideological promises of women's equality.[68] One year later, in response to such criticism, the Academy of Pedagogical Sciences rejected as "completely unfounded and mistaken" the perception that separate schools contradicted the "principle of the equal rights of women."[69] Yet the very fact that such a view had to be refuted suggests that separate schools, and girls' schools in particular, raised basic questions about gender equality. As will be seen in the final chapter, the return of coeducation in 1954 was justified in part as the best way to ensure equality for men and women.

The implications of separate schools for principles of gender equality are still debated in other contexts with comparable ideological as well as legal commitments. In the contemporary United States, for example, both advocates and opponents of separate schooling base their arguments on a commitment to gender equality. Supporters of separate schooling point to the inequities of coeducation and assert that addressing different capacities can promote equal opportunities; opponents declare that separate schools are inherently unequal and that the only way to ensure equality is in a coeducational classroom.[70] These arguments were anticipated from the very beginning of the Soviet experiment, as acknowledged, however indirectly, even by the proponents of the new policy.

Gender Differences

All these policy statements and rhetorical justifications for separate schools implicitly endorsed the significance of gender differences. Educating pupils separately made sense only if there were meaningful gender differences in learning, cognition, behavior, or outcomes.[71] While the commitment to gender equality persisted as an overarching principle of Soviet education, the identification of gender differences became an essential, yet always deeply ambivalent, part of this discourse. Exploring the rhetoric of gender differences in separate schools thus provides insights into the broader processes of constructing and contesting gender identities in Stalinist discourse.[72]

Gender traits were usually defined as psychological, physiological, or biological, but rarely as natural or innate, as the latter terms contradicted Soviet ideological premises that all human traits and social behaviors were socially determined. In a rare exception to the dominant discourse, school director Butkevich wrote in early 1944 that only separate schools could "take into consideration natural particularities."[73] More commonly, the Marxist and materialist foundations of communist ideology affirmed that the position of women was determined by a socioeconomic infrastructure and an ideological superstructure but was completely independent of any biological determination.[74] Separate schools directly challenged these premises, for the new policy elevated a biological category into a defining boundary of the educational system. The only possible justification for separate schooling was to assert the significance of gender differences in education.

As with the discussions of women's equality cited above, explanations of the importance of gender differences usually began with charges that coeducational schools could not "take into consideration the particularities in the physical development of boys and girls," as in this statement by school director Solov'eva: "The identical level of education for boys and girls is necessary, with some differentiation in school knowledge and habits appropriate for the nature of the two sexes," based on "the physical and psychological development of boys and girls."[75] Phrases such as the "physical particularities" or the "particularities of the psycho-physiological development of the sexes" were repeatedly invoked to justify implementation of the new policy.[76] According to Timofeev, even though teachers in coeducational schools observed significant differences between the sexes (girls showed more diligence, conscientiousness, cleanliness, orderliness, and punctuality while boys tended to be more energetic, mobile, decisive, and determined), only in separate schools could teachers specifically revise their approaches to consider these differences.[77]

The longest published discussion of how separate schools would address particular needs appeared in September 1943, just weeks after the new policy was implemented. Two psychology professors from Moscow State University, A. Smirnov and N. Levitov, wrote, as the title stated, "about the psychological particularities of boys and girls."[78] They began with the assertion that differences between boys and girls did exist, the results not only of biological factors but also of social position and historical conditions. Although the psychology of men and women was the same, and variations within sex categories were extensive and sometimes even more significant than between the sexes, "certain specific features" were nevertheless "more characteristic" of one sex or the other. Yet the authors also warned against making comparisons. Any suggestion that girls were less capable had been "completely disproven by our schools," while the war clearly demonstrated that girls possessed self-control, initiative, courage, and determination. Thus, the differences between the sexes were found not in relative levels of development but, rather, in the "qualitative particularities" of boys and girls. Examining masculinity and femininity could reveal "the special, *equally positive*" qualities of boys and girls, but without making any "comparative evaluation."[79]

The psychological features described by Smirnov and Levitov were seemingly based on ideal-type descriptions of inclinations, behaviors, and aptitudes, as in these blanket comparisons: boys liked to work with wood and metal, while girls preferred cloth and paper; girls undervalued their own strengths, while boys had lots of self-confidence; girls expressed emotions more openly, quickly, and frequently, without being ashamed of them, while boys were more restrained in their expression and kept strong emotions "under conscious control." Yet these psychologists also qualified their comparisons. After describing boys' desire for strong-willed, knowledgeable, demanding, and fair teachers, the authors offered this clarification: "Of course, girls also value these qualities, but boys express these desires especially sharply, and it is really boys who are inclined to catch the teacher in inconsistencies, ignorance, mistakes, or slips."[80]

Only after describing these psychological particularities, sometimes illustrated by impressionistic anecdotes or individual examples but never with quantitative measures or documented observations, did the authors explain why separate schools would "best fulfill" the task of educating Soviet youth, as teachers could consider the "psychological particularities" of boys and girl in designing methods and assignments. Girls tended to prefer exercises that offered easier solutions, while boys were not good with exercises that required precision and accuracy. Boys needed variety and sometimes a faster tempo, as they could not stay on one subject for too long, while girls were more stable and thus could work with more focus as well as more patience. In separate classrooms, the authors asserted, the "homogeneity" of pupils would enable teachers to pay close attention to "differences" in the inclinations of boys and girls.[81]

This call for more awareness of gender differences was echoed by other educators as they implemented separate schooling. After schools were separated, teachers met to discuss "the particularities of boys and girls."[82] Affirmations that "the psychology of boys and girls in lessons is different," as displayed by their levels of concentration, led to instructions on modifying lesson plans.[83] School director Solomakha declared that girls were "more diligent" than boys, while director Butkevich warned that girls were more "excitable," and thus teachers should "take into consideration" these attributes by emphasizing self-discipline and self-control.[84]

An unresolved tension in these assertions was the question of whether these differences were psychological, physiological, or environmental in origins and influence.[85] School director Bessanova declared that any discussion of "physiological particularities" must address "psychological particularities," because "surely the physiology of the boy is different than the physiology of the girl, and if the physiology is different, it means the psychology is different."[86] According to L'vov, both sexes followed the same paths of psychological development, yet the cited examples of "physical differences" involved striking differences in aptitudes, attitudes, and interactions. Boys reportedly had "a greater attraction to adventure, to risk, to overcoming danger, to activities which demand good physical training." Girls, by contrast, exhibit "gentleness and thoughtfulness," and they delight in caring "for children" and becoming involved with "their small needs and griefs." After declaring that boys were more interested in "adventure literature" while girls preferred books that "vividly expressed the fullness of personal experience, the whole internal world of the person," L'vov concluded by emphasizing the essential similarities among Soviet youth, who are "captivated by the heroic spirit of the struggle of the person for a better life for all humanity, the heroic spirit of the revolutionary struggle, the magnificence of socialist development, the great achievements of the simple Soviet people for their Homeland, and the demonstration of the best qualities of the human spirit."[87]

This discussion of physiological and psychological differences assumed gender-specific trajectories during adolescence. According to Tsuzmer, boys ages ten to thirteen experience "a certain halt in physical development and a time of accumulating strength," while girls of the same age experience "rapid physical development." By contrast, girls age fourteen to seventeen years undergo a similar "period of delay and a time of rest," while boys "develop rapidly." These periods of physical variation coincided with psychological developments associated with adolescent sexuality. Echoing nineteenth-century arguments against coeducation (although without any acknowledgment), Tsuzmer also claimed that "the cyclical periods of adolescent girls' sexuality" were connected with "a certain indisposition" in work capacity each month, but these conditions were "unlikely to be taken into consideration in coeducational classes."[88] Criticizing coeducational schools for ignoring questions of sexuality, thus leaving pupils "either ill-informed or misinformed" and "not adequately prepared for life," defenders of the new policy asserted that pupils attending separate schools "during the years of sexual maturation" would acquire "the most rational instructional and educational influence" as they learned about their "rights and obligations both as citizens of the great socialist country and as friendly builders of Soviet life, the most progressive in the entire world."[89]

These efforts to manage proper development of sexuality suggest that supposedly physiological attributes were also shaped by environmental factors. This tension was especially evident in explanations of distortions in behavior and attitudes. According to Smirnov and Levitov, boys exposed to harsh and crude actions by others would themselves use bad language, express cynicism, inflict senseless cruelty on animals, show indifference to others, disdain neatness and punctuality, act aggressively toward girls, and demean so-called women's work. The solution to these distortions of masculinity, according to these authors, was to change the environment, as "only military service" proves the importance of discipline and order, as well as the importance of "real chivalrous behavior toward a woman."[90] Girls were also said to be susceptible to environmental influences, such as "false views of femininity," as parents who emphasized wearing fancy dresses or other kinds of appearances stimulated feelings of empty sentimentality, passivity, and superficiality. Too much time spent reading romance novels could also lead girls to show heightened interest in "love" and thus behave differently toward boys—all before the age where "the biological basis of love" was in place. Smirnov and Levitov thus conceded that much of what was considered "specific to boys and girls" was "in fact created by the environment," characterized by "still not eliminated false views of masculinity and femininity."[91]

These references to gender differences in development led to explanations of the purpose of separate schools that were both emphatic and vague, as in this statement by L'vov: "The girls' school should contribute to the more fruitful development of the qualities of a woman, just as the boys' school should educate the qualities of a man." Even as L'vov emphasized the common goal of developing "a well-rounded person," a builder and defender of socialism, he conceded that gender differences did matter: "While educating the Soviet citizen with a well-rounded developed character, we are simultaneously educating a man—a future father and courageous fighter for the Homeland, and a woman—the future public activist and educator of children."[92]

The tension between the *same* education for all pupils and the *different* education of girls and boys was thus embedded in the discourse on separate schools. In a rare acknowledgment of this dilemma, L'vov challenged the proponents of both single-sex and coeducational schools for their affirmation and denial of similarities and differences:

> Some advocates of coeducation emphasize what is common in the development of men and women, and deny situations where differences are evident in their development. Proponents of separate schooling emphasize first and most of all this difference, forgetting what is common in the development of men and women.[93]

Yet these efforts to assert both common and unique objectives nevertheless left in place the tension over what kind of schooling would address both the commonalities and the differences in the education of boys and girls.

The practices of separate schools thus involved different perceptions of the roles of boys and girls. While the rhetoric of preparing pupils for citizenship provided the overall framework, these authors also invoked specific traits, characteristics, and qualities associated with men and women as the desired outcomes of separate schooling.[94] Such efforts would be made easier by separate schooling, according to this argument, because educators could cultivate the specific features desired in a man and a woman, yet these schools would prepare children for the same duties as adult men and women. Separate schooling was thus promoted as a better way to achieve both gender-specific objectives and the shared objectives of education more generally. Yet this same tension between common goals and separate spaces would ultimately contribute to the full restoration of coeducation, because the failure to meet these shared objectives exposed the limitations of gender-segregated schooling.

Classroom Strategies

These descriptions of male and female psychology, attributes, and inclinations shared the same purpose of defining a pedagogy appropriate for separate schools. All these discussions occurred in the framework of a Stalinist pedagogy that required political indoctrination, reinforced the authority of the teacher, and attached primacy to the collective.[95] The concept of "classroom strategies" extends the analysis beyond the formal category of pedagogy to include teachers' management of pupils, interactions between students and teachers, and the ways that identities responded to these practices.[96] This approach is especially useful for exploring the gendering of classroom spaces, for it calls attention to the ways that gender can reinforce but also distort or undermine practices of authority and expressions of identity.[97]

The specification that all schools teach the "existing program" was stated in the initial announcement of the new policy and then repeated by proponents. Not only would separate schools teach the same curriculum, but boys and girls would "obtain identical knowledge" and "a completely identical level of general education." Yet the policy also allowed for "differentiation" in content and methods, as "appropriate to nature and certain distinctions in the social roles of the sexes." Separate schools should require mastery by boys and girls of the same instructional program, while also "paying attention to the aspects of the content that fully satisfied the needs of boys and girls."[98]

As educators began to implement the new policy, they sought to balance covering the same curriculum with recognizing the particular needs of boys and girls. In Samarkand, boys' schools taught "military physical skills," while girls' schools taught "skills needed for the role of mother and housekeeper."[99] In the far North, girls' schools prepared "the future conscious and cultured mothers and educators of the new generation" while "boys learned to be brave and skilled defenders of the motherland."[100] In Baku, boys' schools emphasized military training and trade skills, while girls' schools taught "pedagogy, housekeeping, child care, personal hygiene, and so on."[101] In Uzbek separate schools, girls engaged in sewing, knitting, and other needlecrafts with domestic applications, while boys took part in shoemaking, carpentry, and metalworking with military applications.[102] Separate schools thus allowed educators to reinterpret a traditional theme of Soviet pedagogy—training youth to serve the communist cause—by emphasizing gender-specific attributes, needs, and contributions.

A similar perception of gender differences led some educators to proclaim that the favorite subjects in girls' schools were literature, foreign languages, biology, and geography, while preferred subjects in boys' schools were math, physics, chemistry, history, geography, and military science.[103] Reports on separate schools also emphasized differences in the behavior and even the personalities of pupils. In Moscow, girls were said to be more diligent, conscientious, and efficient but also dependent, passive, introspective, and less confident.[104] In Alma-Ata, boys were praised for "eagerly" working on complicated algebra formulas and mastering physics problems related to technology, while girls were encouraged to use graphic methods for problem solving.[105] Even reading preferences were subject to gender differentiation. Although one observer claimed that boys were "more active readers,"[106] a report from librarians concluded that girls were less interested in reading scholarly texts but were better at "analyzing books and identifying the substance." Citing the librarians' conclusions that girls saw reading "as a means of filling up leisure time" but not "as a source of knowledge," girls' school teachers were exhorted to promote reading, especially on "practical subjects," to foster "intellectual curiosity among girls," broaden their range of interests, and develop "real independence of thought."[107] These statements demonstrate how perceived boundaries between masculinity and femininity were both confirmed and reinforced by affirmations of different academic orientations for boys and girls.

As educators began to reflect on classroom strategies, the effort to balance promises of an equal education with consideration of differences revealed the inherent tensions and obvious contradictions of the new policy. In early 1943, as Moscow educators discussed their first experiments with separate classrooms, they all embraced the premise that separate schools must provide the same academic preparation, as summed up in the goal that girls "should be able to enter higher education on an equal status with boys." Even as they made this commitment to equal educational outcomes, these same educators called for modifications in military training, physical education, labor, hygiene, anatomy, and physiology that examined "certain questions" with "greater elaboration," as deemed appropriate for boys and girls.[108]

One of the easiest adaptations took place in biology classes, as teachers devoted more attention to "male and female organisms," reproduction, anatomy, physiology, personal hygiene, and sexual education, but without any compromise in the scope or rigor of the materials. Yet the new policy also encouraged teachers to respond differently to pupils who "were not embarrassed to ask questions, as they were in coeducational classrooms."[109] In physics classes, by contrast, teachers were expected to adapt to perceived differences in aptitude, not attitude. Thus physics teachers in boys' schools should take advantage of pupils' interest in technology to deepen their understanding, while girls' school teachers should emphasize "purely methodological approaches," make greater use of visual explanations, and ensure that girls were not "overburdened" with specialized problems.[110] Yet images of male and female pupils in classrooms with scientific equipment emphasized the academic rigor, not gendered expectations, of separate schools. In a pair of photographs published at the midpoint of this experiment, the intense focus of male and female pupils on their science lessons reinforced the common academic content of gender-segregated classrooms (see figure 2).

History classes also adapted to separate instruction in revealing ways. A teacher observed that boys could spend a long time analyzing battles against the Mongols, while girls focused on a princess who blessed Russian forces in this same battle.[111] Yet other reports emphasized the similarities in history classes. Both boys and girls reportedly showed great interest in history when it was taught well.[112] In Moscow girls' school No. 29, the history curriculum covered war heroes, famous mathematicians, poets, and artists; the only gendered topic was the war heroine Zoia Kosmodem'ianskaia, but her image as a martyred partisan was neither maternalist nor traditionally feminine. History teacher E. A. Fersova pursued goals, such as acquiring a profound understanding of contemporary life, awareness of international events, and knowledge of historical facts, that did not include any elements specific to female character and future roles as women.[113]

Literature classes also prompted consideration of gender in terms of both topics and approaches. Observations of teachers leading discussion of the same Mikhail Lermontov poem revealed striking differences, as boys focused on the courage of the main character and could describe in graphic terms his battle with a leopard, his heroic achievements, and his love for freedom. But girls were better as describing the main character's "love of nature" and emotional relations in the poem.[114] During discussions of a female character in an Ivan Turgenev story, girls tended to approve of her actions, while boys expressed "bewilderment and condemnation."[115] In a lesson on Turgenev's poem "How Fair, How Fresh Were the Roses," girls reportedly understood the lyricism of the words, whereas boys found the poem uninteresting. One boy announced that he would rather read a poem "How Wonderful Were the Tanks." Even as he reported these perceptions and practices, L'vov exhorted teachers to prevent male pupils from "impoverishing" literature courses, because they too should understand "complex psychological characters" in ways that more closely emulated the approach of female pupils.[116] These comments were unusual in the Soviet context in their taking a feminine approach as the norm to which male pupils should aspire, rather than assuming that girls should aspire to a masculine standard. Despite L'vov's implied criticism, however, these perceptions were certainly consistent with both the rhetoric and practices of teachers in separate schools.

Other comments on literature lessons illustrated how differentiation penetrated classrooms with varying levels of intentionality and intensity.

2—Science classrooms in a boys' and a girls' school. (Top): Ninth-grade physics lesson, Tallinn boys' school No. 20. "Na puti k attestatu zrelosti," *SSSR na stroike* 4 (1949): 11. (Bottom): Chemistry lesson in a girls' school. "The Road to a Big Life," *Soviet Union* (September 1950): 30.

Girls could understand the experiences, feelings, and actions of literary characters, whereas boys were more inclined to examine the "world outlook" of characters, the philosophy of the text, and descriptions of the environment.[117] A literature teacher encouraged colleagues to "set themes differently." A lesson on Turgenev in a boys' school would examine "parents and children," while in a girls' schools, the topic would be "Turgenev's female characters." Another teacher told the same meeting that, in the teaching of Leo Tolstoy's novel *War and Peace,* girls read chapters about peace and boys read chapters about war.[118] Although it is difficult to know how representative these practices actually were, the fact that these same examples were criticized by commissar of education Potemkin in a 1944 speech suggests that both the practices and the underlying assumptions were widespread in schools. More significant, however, was Potemkin's declaration that these differentiated approaches had been "appropriately rebuked" and "relegated to the past."[119] Gender-differentiated instruction was thus one of the main justifications for separate schools, even as it was also a controversial aspect of this policy.[120]

Even military training, initially invoked as one of the main rationalizations for separate schooling, involved similar tensions between differentiated approaches and common objectives.[121] According to Potemkin, military instructors were "unanimously supportive" of separate instruction.[122] Not surprisingly, the practices associated with military training were perhaps most revealing of biases embedded in separate schools. Boys' schools deserved "the strongest, firmest, and tactically literate" military leaders, sufficient space for training drills, and appropriate weapons. Once the needs of boys' schools had been satisfied, one instructor announced in August 1943, whatever was left could be allocated to girls' schools. Expressing a similar preference for military training in boys' schools, Orlov declared: "We should educate our boys to become resolute, courageous fighters, who can fight with enemies, and who would take up arms to repel the attacks of the enemy." Girls, by contrast, should be trained to care for the wounded. Orlov's invocation of gender distinctions in education and character could be seen in his warning that a fighter (that is, a man) would be impeded by the development of traits such as softness, tenderness, and warmth, whereas a woman caring for the wounded needed precisely these traits.[123] Thus, the justification of separate schooling connected the natural attributes of women (as mothers) to the social roles of men (as soldiers).[124] Initial reports indicated that boys were very interested in their expanded opportunities for military training, especially involving weapons and martial arts, but girls were less excited about their nursing lessons.[125] Although all Soviet children were expected to defend the homeland, the particular obligations of boys thus seemed to justify the additional attention they received in their separate schools.

Every discussion of separate schools exposed the more complicated question of how boys and girls should be taught differently. Speaking in early 1943, Gel'mont echoed Soviet ideology by declaring that "of course separate instruction cannot and should not violate the equality of women or deny them any paths to education or practical activity." Gel'mont then identified a key tension by stating that "even with the same curriculum and textbooks," separation into different schools "raises serious questions about possible differentiation and variation." As Gel'mont deliberated on this new policy, he also speculated on possible connections between the education of girls and the life trajectories of women, asking whether it was "coincidental" that women were engaged overwhelmingly in certain occupations, such as secretaries, drafters, stenographers, laboratory staff, nurses, and so on: "Is there something specific in the life course of women which should be cultivated in the educational process, given that we do not want to smooth out or somehow eliminate the feminine in women and the masculine in men?" Gel'mont then declared that "we have not fully thought through these questions," and it is easier to "brush them aside, rather than resolving them correctly in accordance with socialist principles."[126] This seeming contradiction was repeated by the meeting chair, who stated that participants were in "unanimous agreement" on providing "identical levels and dimensions" of education, yet they also acknowledged that having "special subjects" in girls' schools meant reducing "certain subjects in the general educational program."[127]

During this same meeting in April 1943, however, Parmerov asked why girls "should be given an education with a humanities orientation." Asserting that the achievements of female telegraph and telephone operators proved that a humanities orientation was neither inclusive of women's interests nor sufficient for their preparation, Parmerov also pointed out that so-called women's professions were actually reflections of socioeconomic factors, such as salaries and training.[128] Other speakers denied that girls' schools should have a humanities focus and declared emphatically that curricula and textbooks "must be identical."[129] Declaring that "any orientation of girls toward the kitchen, etc. is harmful," and thus "separate programs should not be created for boys' and girls' schools," Solomon Rives asked: "Why shouldn't girls know about military physics, defense chemistry, the history of war, etc.?"[130] The educators at this Moscow meeting in early 1943 were reportedly "unanimous" in their conviction that the "knowledge given to girls should not be less than that given to boys," the math curriculum "should remain the same in all schools," and "the physics curriculum in girls' schools should not be inferior to that in boys' schools."[131] Even when one science educator affirmed that the only differences should be in physiology and hygiene, with girls learning more about child development and nutrition, it was clear that these differences should not appear in textbooks or programs but, rather, be conveyed "through conversations."[132] Initial deliberations thus illustrated how two key principles of Stalinist education, the promise of women's equality and the academic emphasis on core subjects, were difficult to reconcile with separate schools. For educators, gender differentiation might be tolerable elsewhere in the schools, but not at the expense of these core principles.

One response to this dilemma was to emphasize personal traits, rather than academic content, as the most important outcome of separate schooling.[133] In 1943, for example, Orlov responded sharply to doubts about changes in teaching:

> Can our school be organized in a way to take into consideration the particularities of sex? We should not be surprised that girls' schools offer needlecrafts and child care, as if those were demeaning to a Soviet girl. Is it really so bad that after completing her education, our girl can do what is necessary not only for herself, but also for children?

Orlov called on separate schools to teach boys to be more respectful of girls and to teach girls to acquire "the sacred feeling of maternity," as well as the "modesty, diffidence, and, if you like, elegance" that should be the distinctive traits of Soviet women.[134]

These comments on potential adaptations in curriculum, pedagogy, and purpose illustrate how educators considered "both *common* and *distinctive* elements" of the education of boys and girls.[135] Implicit in both assertions of difference and concerns about deficiencies, of course, was the same fear that girls would receive less of an education than boys, thus replicating the historical experiences of earlier eras when female students were excluded from elite programs, the curriculum of girls' schools was less rigorous, and assumptions about female inferiority justified limits on educational accomplishments. Even as educators affirmed the promise of educational equality, the gendering of schools created differences in the content, purpose, and outcomes of education. The shift in emphasis for certain subjects, the addition of new subjects for boys and girls, and the connections between teaching methods and educational outcomes all reveal how this new policy produced greater differentiation. Even as these new school arrangements challenged established policies and previous ideologies, however, the redrawing of gender boundaries appeared consistent with commonsense perceptions of important traits of masculinity and femininity. After more than two decades in which Soviet pedagogy told teachers to ignore or deny differences, now schools were separated in ways that promised to better address these differences, but only if they also provided a fully equal and identical education for all. A later observation that, during the first phase of their experiment, Moscow teachers "came gropingly to the task of separation" offers a vivid image of the challenges inherent in this transformation in schooling.[136]

Even as educators initiated, implemented, and questioned these steps toward gender differentiation, others emphasized the similarities and continuities in separate schools. In 1948, Moscow girls' school director Pokrovskaia recalled that, in the first years of separate education, teachers in girls' schools tried to find themes in literature and history that illustrated women's roles, but they soon gave up on this effort, and now they taught the same curriculum as in other schools.[137] In the spring of 1954, on the verge of the complete restoration of coeducation, minister of education Kairov emphatically denied that different programs were ever created for separate schools.[138] As will be seen in subsequent chapters, the uncertainty about academic differences increasingly cast doubts about the necessity and advantages of separate schools.

Evaluating Academic Outcomes

Separate schools were supposed to raise pupils' levels of achievement.[139] Stalinist education emphasized quantitative measures such as exam results, final grades, and promotion or retention rates, which were used to evaluate not only individual pupils but also teachers, school directors, and even educational departments.[140] According to teacher Zhiguleva, who taught in Alma-Ata boys' school No. 33, exams demonstrated the level of work done by pupils and teachers during the entire year.[141] Teachers faced expectations that all students would pass final examinations, or else they were accused of falling short of outcome targets. These expectations generated very high passing rates. In urban schools in 1951, for example,

83 percent of pupils were promoted to the next grade, 9 percent were held back to repeat a grade, and 8 percent took examinations again in the fall.[142] In Moscow girls' school No. 29, more than 98 percent of pupils earned promotion each year.[143] Despite the emphasis on quantitative measures, however, academic outcomes received surprisingly little attention in the public discourse on separate schools.[144]

Even with this notable silence, however, available figures on exam scores and passing rates provide important insights into classroom strategies. During the Moscow experiments in spring 1943, improved exam results were attributed "to a certain extent" to gender separation.[145] Occasional reports in subsequent years revealed additional evidence of differences in academic performance, although all this evidence was limited and incomplete. In 1944 in Nal'chik, the proportion of pupils with the worst grades was the same in boys' and girls' schools (20%), but girls' schools had a higher proportion earning the highest grades (25% of girls and 18% of boys), while boys' schools had a higher proportion of pupils kept back for a second year (15% of boys and 8% of girls).[146] In 1947, a district in Arkhangel'sk reported that passing rates were slightly higher for the boys' school (85%) than in the two girls' schools (83%).[147] In 1953, graduation rates were higher in separate schools (97%), as compared to all schools (94%), while the proportion of pupils earning the highest honors was also higher in separate than coeducational schools.[148] In Leningrad, the five schools in 1949 with highest grades in math were all girls' schools, while five of the six schools with the lowest scores were boys' schools.[149]

Even as these results suggested slight academic advantages for separate schools, these same reports provoked concerns about declining performance specifically in boys' schools. In the case of the Arkhangel'sk schools cited above, the fact that passing rates in the girls' schools had increased by up to six percentage points, while the rate in the boys' school remained the same, prompted concerns that academic performances were lagging in the latter schools.[150] A more detailed report on the Moscow experiments raised similar concerns, as five pupils did not pass in five girls' classrooms, but twenty-one pupils did not pass in three boys' classrooms.[151] In Moscow schools in 1952, the passing rate was 91.4 percent in girls' schools and 88.5 percent in boys' schools, a difference of three percentage points. Yet the data that should make educators "anxious," according to a school inspector, were that, of fifty schools with low achievement rates, three were coeducational, eight were girls' schools, and thirty-nine were boys' schools.[152]

But other measures of academic success seemed to favor single-sex schools and even boys' schools. In Stalinabad, the exam results for a boys' school and a girls' school in 1949 were compared to the last year of coeducation. Girls' achievement began at a high level and rose only gradually, from 80 percent to 87 percent, while boys' achievement began at a lower level but increased more quickly, from 74 percent to 86 percent. According to the school directors who compiled this data, separate schools saw increased achievement levels, especially for boys, who were almost making up the gap that existed even in coeducational schools.[153] Somewhat ironically, but also deliberately, the strongest evidence for the academic advantages of separate schools was presented even as this policy was widely repudiated. A 1953 Ministry of Education report indicated that for the previous three years, separate schools had approximately twice the proportion of students earning top academic distinctions as coeducational schools. In Cheliabinsk, nine separate schools awarded gold or silver medals to thirty-four pupils, compared to twice as many coeducational schools that made awards to just half as many pupils. Yet this report did not draw any conclusions from these numbers but, rather, cited these numbers only to counter the so-called undervaluing of separate schools.[154]

"Who Studies Better — Boys or Girls?"

Despite the obvious limits of this comparative evidence, educators generally perceived girls' schools as being academically stronger than boys' schools. In some cases, these claims reflected the determination to prove that Soviet girls' schools, unlike their prerevolutionary antecedents, did not presume that girls were academically less capable than boys. Even statements that separate schools should take into consideration "well-known particularities" of boys and girls denied that there should be any difference in academic outcomes: "these particularities are not influencing and should not influence either the scope of the material, or the quality of its mastery, or the range of its content, or the general level of development of pupils of both sexes." This view was then generalized and amplified by L'vov: "the vast majority of teachers zealously protest against the absolutely incorrect assertion" that girls were not equal to boys in their scholarly capacities.[155] Yet these affirmations of the academic quality of girls' schools also provoked a strongly defensive reaction on behalf of boys' schools. Thus boys' school director Mostovoi complained that his colleagues "feel awful" at conferences, because achievement rates of 96 percent in girls' schools and 95 percent in boys' schools made them seem "second-rate."[156] This sense of favoritism could also be seen in a complaint that published reports on "excellent teachers" were exclusively about girls' schools, "as if boys' schools did not exist."[157]

The absence of reliable quantitative measures meant that subjective perceptions influenced evaluations of separate schooling.[158] Reviewing the first year of the new system, Potemkin declared: "from the start we encountered cranks who in all seriousness proclaimed that the capabilities of boys and girls are not equal, that boys were more inclined to precise sciences and girls were more interested in questions of social life and even—just imagine—less honest."[159] Even as they admitted "it is too early to tell" whether separate classrooms produced different outcomes, observers of the first experiments nevertheless declared that girls were more successful in languages and literature (boys were apparently afraid to make speeches), while boys were more successful in physics and military science (they wanted to study technological applications).[160] The tension between school practices and educational outcomes found expression in the seemingly obvious question cited by Borisov at an April 1943 meeting: "Who studies better—boys or girls?" Among senior-level pupils, boys seemed to complete assignments better, but parents and teachers offered an obvious explanation: older girls were "distracted" by domestic duties, especially with parents at work or in military service. While "girls do more housework," boys stayed late at the school to work with classmates on finishing assignments. Even as Borisov conceded that "it is difficult to say whether girls complete assignments or perform in school better or worse," he invoked the belief of teachers that boys and girls "worked more quietly when they sat separately." Observing that "it is interesting that now most teachers think along these lines," Borisov referred to one school director who had been an opponent of separate schooling, but "now he is a supporter."[161] For these educators, the answer to Borisov's question was that *both* boys and girls studied better when they studied separately.[162]

For other educators, however, even slight variations in achievement became evidence of significant gender differences. In 1950, Moscow director Liukhin said, "I'm not surprised that girls receive more medals," because female pupils were "conscientious and diligent," and their teachers were "at a high level."[163] Yet a different conclusion was offered in a manuscript submitted to *Literaturnaia gazeta* in 1950, by two Stalinabad school directors, Mushat and Remukhov.[164] Reaffirming the standard line, these directors declared that the "particularities" of boys and girls were not only physical, "but also to some extent psychological," yet this "does not mean that a woman is intellectually not equal to a man." Proclaiming that all pupils "can and should" master the same academic program, the authors declared that boys and girls have different levels of interest. As evidence, the directors cited exam results from prewar schools, when boys earned higher grades in math and physics, girls earned higher grades in literature, and pupils earned similar grades in history and chemistry. Based on these comparisons, the authors concluded that boys and girls have definite inclinations that appeared from the youngest ages and lasted throughout adulthood: "Already from the age of two, girls love to play with dolls and boys are drawn to hammers (even if no one is teaching them do so)." Boys like to run, throw rocks, jump, play football, shoot arrows, and fight, while "girls develop their own interests." Even in a coeducational school, Mushat and Remukhov declared, "this specificity exists, even if we do not mention it." Yet their recommendation that schools pay more attention to "natural differences" between the sexes drew heavily on projections regarding gender roles:

> Practice has proven to us that in the separate school, work is more interesting, and in its own way, easier, than in a coeducational school. The life of the school pulses more intensely, with energy, inventiveness, a smart appearance, and precision. Just look at the morning lineup, observe boys during a military-physical inspection, go with them on a 20 kilometer hike, and you will recognize the accuracy of this statement.[165]

Even as this argument for separate schooling invoked quantitative measures such as exam results, this final comment demonstrates that support for separate schools came from a subjective, even emotional, commitment to reinforcing gender differences between boys and girls.[166]

This discussion of measuring achievement is thus suggestive of the broader contours of classroom practices in separate schools, as a significant change in policy produced little measurable change in outcomes. Although it is possible that these data may have been concealed, lost, or destroyed, the lack of internal references in reports or deliberations suggests that educational officials were not seeking out or collecting this information. In fact, educators themselves complained about the lack of careful study of separate schools, as the absence of such research meant it was impossible to make "fully and completely grounded" statements about boys' and girls' schools.[167] A similar lack of evidence demonstrating causal connections between separate schools and academic results has occurred in other contexts that are not subject to Stalinist censorship or propaganda.[168] Given the lack of such data, Soviet educators invoked other explanations of the educational objectives advanced by separating boys and girls.

The Value of Homogeneity

The greatest advantage of separate schools, according to Kazakhstan commissar of education A. Sembaev, was "more homogeneity" in instruction and a more "homogeneous regime" in schools.[169] Educators frequently and consistently declared that "homogeneity" would facilitate class management, "make the teachers' work easier," allow classes "more deeply and more fully to cover certain sections of the curriculum, depending on the interests of pupils," make it easier "to find a common language," and "create the possibility for more profound instructional and educational influence on pupils of both sexes."[170] Photographs of rows of male or female pupils taught by a male or female teacher vividly illustrated the realization of homogeneous instructional spaces (see figure 3).

Explanations of these advantages also became a rare opportunity to discuss sexuality in schools. According to L'vov, whereas in coeducational schools girls were ashamed even to say the word "pregnancy" during a discussion of the constitution's guarantee of maternity leave, pupils in a girls' school "devoted a lot of attention to this topic." The "homogeneity" of girls' schools also promoted sincere and natural discussions of love, marriage, chastity, "the appearance of a baby in the family," and parental obligations. After referring to improved teaching of military topics in history and geography in boys' schools, L'vov linked, although tenuously, stages of sexual development with forms of intellectual engagement: "The homogeneity of the classroom helps the teacher to answer the pupils' questions both in more detail and in more concrete ways, because pupils are situated, basically, at the same stage of sexual development, with interests close to each other, possessing or lacking the exact same knowledge and information."[171]

Affirmations of the advantages of homogeneity at times elevated classroom composition above other key features of Stalinist pedagogy. In a homogeneous class, according to Orlov, "conversations can be more intimate, and pupils can express themselves more freely."[172] In a time of military emergency and repressive dictatorship, both "intimacy" and

3—Pupils in a girls' classroom and a boys' classroom. (Top): Moscow girls' school with teacher S. Ivannovna, February 1954. From author's personal collection. (Bottom): Moscow boys' school, with teacher. From Soviet Information Bureau.

"openness," it seems, contradicted a discourse dominated by instrumental and political language. The potential for homogeneity to redefine gender roles could also be seen in the claim that girls' school teachers had an "opportunity" for "free discussion" and could take up "questions that would be risky" in coeducational classrooms.[173] This heightened confidence among girls would "raise consciousness of the value of their sex," which would prepare them to deal with "crudeness and bravado" on the part of boys.[174]

The value of homogeneous classroom spaces was also expressed by a seventh-grade pupil of Moscow boys' school No. 665:

> Separate instruction is better because during lessons you become more confident and you are not embarrassed, because previously if a boy said something incorrectly, girls would giggle, and the boy would be embarrassed, and vice versa. Now this does not happen. In general, the class has become more friendly and cohesive. In my opinion, this is the greatest advantage of separate schools.[175]

Even as his assessment differed from the more common perception that girls lacked confidence in the presence of boys, this statement offered the same conclusion that pupils felt more comfortable when their classmates were of the same gender.

The term "homogeneous" exposed a key tension in Stalinist education, for it expressed an ideal condition much more than the realities of offering instruction in literally dozens of languages to pupils of different ages attending school in multiple shifts. Given the emphasis on the collective in Stalinist pedagogy, this value assigned to gender as a boundary seems inconsistent with the broader emphasis on students' attributes such as discipline, political obedience, and intellectual capacity, which were supposed to be the same for both genders. Defining the collective in terms of a single category, gender, in effect undermined the relative significance associated with other traits, practices, and outcomes.

The emphasis on homogeneity also provoked objections that separate schools were too defined by distinct male and female attributes. Teachers who "set one sex off against the other," as in remarks that mocked pupils as "not real boys" or "not real girls," were blamed for "biologizing" the instructional process and undermining the equal value of all pupils.[176] Yet the experiences of pupils demonstrate that separation reinforced differentiation. In a 1950 letter, tenth-grade female pupils complained that separate schools promoted a "harmful" division into male and female "profiles," which in turn produced "profoundly mistaken" views on roles and responsibilities.[177] A. V. Idel'son warned that separate schools encouraged boys to look at girls as "noble ladies," and girls to look at boys as "young gentlemen," thus interfering with "correct communist relations" between the sexes.[178]

One common response to concerns about increasingly rigid gender categories was to encourage interactions between boys and girls outside schools.[179] Teachers and school directors asked for guidance in organizing extracurricular activities that recognized the particular needs of the sexes but also maintained "healthy, comradely friendship between boys and girls."[180] Criticizing "some comrades" who believed "incorrectly" that "boys and girls should not meet with each other," Markov provided a list of appropriate extracurricular activities for boys and girls: nature study clubs, Pioneer events, getting together in parks and skating rinks, school celebrations, and the theater, "so they can work together and enjoy themselves."[181]

Assessments of interactions between boys and girls offered new insights into the construction of gender roles and relations. During extracurricular literature circles involving pupils from separate schools, which were explicitly designed to encourage "normal" relations between boys and girls, "what really caught the attention" of teachers was that "boys spoke with more maturity." Girls did a good job of raising questions, although sometimes too "effusively," but boys pursued more "fundamental" examinations of key issues. At a 1948 meeting, school director Perstova admitted that these patterns might have been "accidental," but she nevertheless praised the experience for its positive effect on female pupils. Yet the next speaker, Moscow boys' school director Gorbunov, repudiated Perstova's claims that boys were somehow "more mature," by suggesting that these pupils simply came from a more senior grade. Gorbunov then diverged from official guidelines and emerging consensus by declaring that extracurricular study circles should not be coeducational but, rather, should involve pupils and teachers from a single school. Yet a third perspective came from director Pokrovskaia, speaking at the same meeting, who also expressed concerns that girls were more cautious and boys more assertive when participating in coeducational groups. After she had a talk with her pupils, Pokrovskaia reported, "things are now going differently."[182]

The experience of separate schooling thus seemed to deepen the divisions between boys and girls, even as educators attempted to foster positive relations. In the case of two schools located close enough that boys and girls got together before or after school, separation did not initially result in any "alienation," nor did it stimulate "heightened interest" in the opposite sex. Over time, however, boys and girls began "to move apart," as they seemed more embarrassed in the presence of the others and as organized activities took the place of "simple, friendly relationships."[183] Yet another educator warned that organized coeducational "events" did not promote "healthy comradely relations" but, in fact, encouraged flirtatious behavior between boys and girls.[184]

These assessments of out-of-school interactions drew simultaneously, but also unevenly, on memories of prerevolutionary separate schools, direct experiences with coeducational schools, observations of experimentally separated classrooms, and projections of desired trajectories in boys' and girls' schools. The significance associated with "homogeneity" exposed the tensions of gender separation in heterogeneous schools. Soviet education already sorted children into categories: by age, with a standard school entry age; by achievement, as partially determined by promotion benchmarks based on ability, but also involving formal and informal tracking of high- and low-capacity pupils; and by language of instruction, with pupils divided by ethnicity even within the same school districts. By separating boys and girls, however, this new policy affirmed the primacy of homogeneity based on gender.

Conclusion

Teachers and school directors struggled on a practical level to implement an educational policy based on shifting combinations of physiological, psychological, cultural, historical, social, familial, and developmental causes. Thus, Timofeev concluded his article with a seemingly straightforward, yet also self-contradictory, statement that gender differences should shape the separate schooling of boys and girls: "It is essential to distinguish clearly which aspects of the psychology and behavior of boys and girls are manifestations of masculinity and femininity in conditions of our society and which are derived more fundamentally from survivals of the past, when the man occupied a dominant position and the woman was excluded from many aspects of public life." Declaring that "boys and girls bear some still not yet eliminated legacies of the past," Timofeev concluded that "different attitudes" toward various subjects produced "different traits" in educational activities.[185] The next two chapters expand on the observations of Timofeev and the other educators regarding the education of boys and girls in separate schools, with particular attention to the ways that gender differences were initially encouraged, but then increasingly contested and ultimately repudiated in both policy and practice. Timofeev's prediction that separate schooling could improve teaching and learning became the focus of an intense debate (discussed in chapter 5) over the apparent failure to realize these outcomes. The articles, comments, and observations discussed in this chapter fueled this debate, as critics of separate schools compared the broad promises made initially by proponents with the actual realities of schools as experienced by teachers and pupils.

Like many Soviet educators, contemporary advocates of separate schools offer a combination of observation, evaluation, speculation, and projection. Differences observed within a single class or among a small selection of pupils are generalized to apply universally to all boys and girls. Gender differences situated in biology are simultaneously overdetermined by those seeking justifications for specific methods, and underestimated by those who promise an equal education regardless of the composition of classrooms. The tension between a school system structured along lines of difference and a broader social, political, and legal discourse of equality frame contemporary debates, just as they did in postwar Soviet discourse, because observable patterns and practices of separate schooling are difficult to reconcile with the principles and promises of gender equality.

The fact that materials in this chapter mostly come from the first stages of separate schooling is also suggestive for drawing lessons for contemporary situations. Although all Soviet publications of this era functioned as propaganda, these articles should also be seen as propaganda in favor of separate schooling. They echoed official justifications for the new policy, mostly cited positive evaluations of practices, and rationalized problems or deficiencies as results of the transitional period, with the promise of eventual improvement. The declining number of articles about pedagogical theories or physiological attributes after 1945 could be explained by the overall tightening of discourse in the postwar period but may also have reflected a shift in thinking about separate schools as a result of the growing gap between promise and practice. The Soviet case study thus provides a cautionary lesson for evaluations of separate schools that focus only on this implementation stage, where the novelty of the approach may produce significant changes, and any difficulties or shortcomings can be blamed on the transition from coeducation. By contrast, studies that evaluate separate schooling over a longer period of time offer more complicated, balanced, and generally, but not always, critical assessments.[186]

The Soviet case study also demonstrates that, from the very first stage of experimentation and implementation, some educators, even in the context of a dictatorship, raised serious questions about the efficacy of this policy. These doubts were mostly raised in closed meetings, yet some appeared in published articles or shaped the pronouncements of policy makers. School directors and teachers questioned the impact of separate schooling on pupils' learning and classroom discipline, reaffirmed the principle of an equal education for boys and girls, and made positive arguments for coeducational instruction. This counterdiscourse prepared the way for increasingly critical assessments of separate schooling (as discussed in the chapter 5), which began in closed meetings of school directors in the late 1940s and then burst into public view with an influential article by an educational psychologist in the spring of 1950. In addition to preparing the way for the restoration of coeducation in 1954, these critical voices exposed the tensions embedded in promises that schools could be separate and equal. These competing views of the purposes and practices of teaching and learning contributed to this movement along this trajectory from initial enthusiasm through a more cautious and critical evaluation to, eventually, a wholesale repudiation.

3 Clean, Warm, and Calm
Girls' Schools in Action

IN 1949, RAZVINOVA, director of Saratov girls' school No. 3, described how her literature teachers used nineteenth-century female characters to illustrate the circumscribed roles of elite women and the difficult living conditions of working women before the revolution. Themes and methods deemed appropriate for girls were integrated into other subjects as well. History lessons devoted particular attention to famous women in the past, such as Nadezhda Durova, Sofia Kovalevskaia, and Nadezhda Krupskaia. Even the sciences, Razvinova asserted, were adapted to the special needs of girls' schools. Physics lessons taught girls how to connect electrical wires, install a switch and socket, and repair an electric stove. Chemistry lessons emphasized practical applications such as removing spots from fabric; a girl also learned "how to make a mirror or do repairs on her own." In art classes, girls made "beautiful and elegant decorations" for the school and the home. Senior pupils learned about female anatomy, personal hygiene, motherhood, and childrearing.[1]

The education of Soviet girls also occurred out of the classroom. In discussion circles, students debated the characteristic features and appearance of a "cultured person." Dances taught pupils "to eliminate clumsiness and awkwardness of movement," while musical evenings enhanced the "simple and beautiful" atmosphere of the school. Teachers invited parents to lectures on "physics in everyday life," "the upbringing of girls in the family" or "the development of a girl's will and character." According to Razvinova, attention to the latter topic was necessary to counter the view of some parents that girls, with their "exceptional sensitivity and nervousness," should be protected from "real life."

As discussed in previous chapters, the implementation of separate schooling responded to intersecting concerns, some of which related specifically to women's position in Soviet society. This chapter focuses on the implications of policy changes, pedagogical practices, and ideological issues for girls who attended separate schools. As illustrated by Razvinova's article, educational practices, from the selection of lesson materials to the organization of social activities, responded directly to the imperatives of teaching girls. The school instructed pupils not only in academic subjects but also about the meaning of being female in Soviet society. Separating schools thus reinforced gender boundaries, as pupils were reminded on a daily basis by classmates, teachers, and school officials that their presence in this school resulted from their gender position. Even as this school added content, methods, and activities specifically for girls, however, the overall structure, curricular content, and educational objectives adhered to the requirements for Soviet education as a whole.

The steps taken to adapt schools to the perceived needs of girls, like those outlined by Razvinova, also revealed the limits of such adaptations. In particular, the process of making girls' schools more "feminine" provoked concerns, objections, and even resistance, particularly from the pupils who were the intended beneficiaries of separate instruction. Careful attention to girls' "voices" demonstrates that, despite the perceived effectiveness of girls' schools in maintaining discipline and promoting social relations, these achievements were overwhelmed by growing objections to separate schooling. Understanding girls' schools thus further demonstrates how the Soviet experiment with separate schools actually reinforced support for coeducation.

The Soviet policy on separate schools has generally been interpreted in terms of the history of women during and after the war.[2] Although the policy of separate schools affected all urban pupils, focusing on the position of women suggests that changes in gender roles were especially significant for girls, even when these same policies also applied to boys. While the 1943 decree referred to training boys and girls for "particular" roles as defenders of the fatherland and mothers of the next generation respectively, the policy change also coincided with new pronatalist policies, including restrictions on divorce, bans on abortion, and awards offered to mothers with many children.[3] Yet the claim that girls' schools represented a "conservative" reassertion of "traditional" women's roles, as argued recently by Ann Livschiz,[4] overlooks important countercurrents in Soviet discourse on separate schools, which not only challenged seemingly anachronistic visions of girls' education but directly addressed practical questions such as the content of the curriculum, the actions of school administrators, the conduct of pupils, and even the tone of teachers.

Girls' schools were expected to provide an education simultaneously different from yet equal with that of boys. In the words of an educational official, speaking in early 1943, girls' schools "cannot and should not violate the equality of women."[5] Discussion of girls' schooling in other contexts often emphasizes the advancement of female equality in terms of the culture of schools, the objectives of educators, and the experiences of pupils.[6] Yet studies that concentrate on well-established girls' schools involve a different narrative from that of the Soviet postwar condition, where girls' schools resulted from an abrupt transition from coeducational institutions. To a certain extent, the Soviet trajectory bears more resemblance to the recent "resurgence" of girls' schools, where a combination of concerns about sexism in classrooms and awareness of girls' developmental needs has broadened support for this option.[7] While recognizing the important differences in historical context, this comparative literature can be used to explore the ways that Soviet schools, teachers, and female pupils navigated this policy transformation.

These issues can be explored using sources that provide insights into school practices and gender roles, even as they reflect the constraints of the postwar Stalinist context. Positive accounts, like the article by Razvinova, describe the objectives of separate schools, but these sources must be read critically, "against the grain," to identify tensions in the practices of schools and experiences of pupils.[8] Contrasting perspectives can be found in archival transcripts of educators' meetings, inspectors' reports on schools, and especially in unpublished letters, many written collectively by female pupils reflecting on their experiences and articulating dissenting views. The latter sources make it possible to listen to the "voices" of girls, which serves as both an analytic method and an affirmation of female agency.[9] Exploring these sources in terms of perceptions of difference and assertions of identity makes it possible to "highlight the workings of gender as ideology *and* as material and cultural practice."[10]

Soviet girls' schools were part of the communist system of education, which dictated the content of textbooks, constrained the options of educators, and aspired to determine the adult roles of children.[11] Soviet girls' schools thus balanced gender-specific purposes with totalizing political claims. All schools had common tasks of preparing cultured and educated people with good practical skills as well as patriotic commitment, yet girls' schools were guided by their own imperative, according to Razvinova: "The woman in our country is a great force, to whom much has been given, but from whom a great deal also is demanded." Girls' schools thus fulfilled a complex mission: "to educate pupils to work successfully, engage in public activities, and carry out scientific research, while combining all this with the organization of family life and the upbringing of children, for these also are tasks with great political importance."[12] This approach ensured that girls' schools fulfilled their "particular task" of teaching "those qualities that life will require from a future woman and mother." This tension between the common goals of training children to be public citizens and the "particular tasks" of preparing girls to be women illustrates the dual purposes that transformed girls' schools from an abstract educational policy into a lived experience that in turn shaped the practices of gender identities.

Making Girls' Schools Feminine

From the first days of the new educational policy, descriptions of girls' schools called attention to the new conditions of gender separation.[13] Obvious improvements were described by one Moscow pupil, as quoted in a later report:

> From the beginning of the school year we began to study in a new way, boys in certain classes, girls in others. In my opinion, this is better. Previously, when we all studied together, discipline in the school was bad. Boys disrupted lessons by shooting catapults, pulling hair, talking all the time, and other kinds of pranks. We still have many conversations during lessons, but nevertheless it has become better. Previously we did not have such interesting subjects as needlecrafts, we were not really friendly with boys, and we did not participate equally with them in common activities, because they fought all the time. They did not consider our interests.[14]

The standards by which this girl decided that the current arrangement was "better" were suggestive of gender dynamics in coeducational and single-sex schooling. Whereas boys disrupted lessons, girls could talk without disturbing others. New activities, such as needlecrafts, matched both her interests and normative gender roles. The last sentence is most revealing, for it contrasted the memory of being marginal in a coeducational school with her own experiences in a separate school, where girls received the entire attention of teachers and classmates.[15]

Important changes in school practices were noted by other girls, who predicted that "no one will be tripped up, braids will not be pulled, and no one will interfere with lessons." Teachers could easily "establish normal, natural relations" in a "calm, efficient" classroom, where pupils "do not laugh at some mistaken word or action." While this report omitted the agents of these actions, it was obvious that *boys* tripped girls, pulled their hair, and interfered with their lessons. One of the most significant steps toward making girls' schools feminine, therefore, was the removal of boys, which meant also removing the kinds of behavior associated with masculinity in schools.[16]

Moscow girls' school director Perstova reaffirmed the importance of protecting girls from disruptive boys when she declared in 1948 that girls, "even with their well-known playfulness," had begun to act "completely calmly" inside their school. Whereas previously, in the coeducational school, "a whole series of childish conflicts took place, sometimes braids were pulled, even jerked, and complaints were made," now that misbehavior was gone. Perstova was especially enthusiastic about field trips, as "we hear only positive comments" and "not a single complaint" about girls' behavior. If there had been problems during excursions, Perstova declared, "we would have heard about them."[17]

Educators thus consistently described improved discipline and order in girls' schools.[18] According to one observer, "discipline in girls' school improved from the very first day."[19] In Gor'kii, "almost no violations of school rules were seen in girls' schools."[20] In Moscow girls' school No. 29, violations of discipline were "rare and incidental."[21] Moscow director Nekrasova stated that "because this is a girls' school, the question of discipline did not come up," and thus she could focus on other aspects of administration.[22]

The absence of disciplinary problems seemed to generate a new sense of identity, as girls became "more active in lessons and recesses," related to one another and to adults "more softly, with greater restraint, politely, and obediently," and acquired "ever more sense of their merit, feelings of modesty, and elements of femininity."[23] Echoing similar themes, the Groznyi educational department offered this assessment: "Politeness and sensitivity in relations among girls create a soft tone for the entire class. The words 'thank you' and 'excuse me' are heard ever more often. There is a growing desire to create comfort and cleanliness in the classroom, and no one ridicules or denigrates this natural striving of girls."[24] Iaroslavl' girls' schools were marked not only by improved order and discipline but also by a "friendly" atmosphere and "comfortable" lessons.[25]

The theme of cleanliness permeated descriptions of girls' schools. Alma-Ata girls' school No. 15 had clean and comfortable classrooms, hallways decorated with patriotic slogans and portraits of leaders, and flowers in the windows.[26] The stairs and floors in Moscow girls' school No. 29 were so clean that visitors were ashamed to wear their outside shoes: "cleanliness is everywhere."[27] In Vologda girls' school No. 3, the "doors, floors, and walls all shine with cleanliness."[28] In Fergana girls' school No. 2, "cleanliness, comfort, and order prevailed."[29] A published report on school No. 36 described first-grade pupils sitting at desks where their snacks had been placed on "white embroidered napkins."[30] Some teachers praised pupils for voluntarily cleaning the classroom: "They take care of this on their own and then report the results of their work."[31] These descriptions thus offer a striking combination of girls' "natural strivings," such as politeness, obedience, and cleanliness, with a school system and political ideology that identified conformity, order, and discipline as necessary conditions and desirable outcomes.

Only rarely did educators recognize that cleanliness and order required deliberate effort and did not happen just because all the pupils were female. In 1944, director Fomina stated that pupils initially resisted new expectations, and only "after protesting" did they begin cleaning the school.[32] According to Moscow girls' school director Solomakha, "We demand that girls respect the labor of others and that they labor themselves." In anticipation of major holidays, pupils "do everything themselves," including washing windows and desks. Solomakha concluded with a remarkable statement of how girls' schools transformed perceptions of appropriate duties: "Girls, who do nothing at home, eagerly work at the school, and by doing this work themselves, they acquire greater respect for the work of cleaning women."[33] Although some parents complained that daughters had to work at school in ways they did not at home, others reportedly supported these new expectations of girls.

The emphasis on the appearance of schools was reinforced by comparable attention to the appearance of pupils. While uniforms were not compulsory in Soviet schools, a normative style for girls included a dark dress, white collar, and hair in braids.[34] In Sverdlovsk girls' school No. 36, pupils earned praise for paying attention to their appearance, dressing simply and beautifully, closely adhering to the rules of hygiene, and remembering such "trifles" as a handkerchief.[35] In Moscow girls' school No. 516, pupils were expected to keep their hair in braids and come to school in neat clothing; a mending corner was available for pupils with torn clothes, but "since girls are so proud," they do their mending at home rather than using the materials provided by the school, according to director Butkevich.[36] In Alma-Ata girls' schools, pupils strove to wear the same brown dresses with white collars and kept their hair in long braids.[37] In Gor'kii, the importance of physical appearance was illustrated by the story of Liudmila Zerchinova, who initially "came to school dirty, in torn clothes, and was rude to the teacher, sitting with her back turned and ignoring all the teacher's comments." By the end of the year, however, Zerchinova had turned "in a positive direction," as she finished the seventh grade and now planned to enter pedagogical training because of her "strong interest in working with children."[38] In this transformative narrative, a dirty, disorderly, and disobedient girl matured in directions consistent with gendered expectations. This same objective was stated explicitly in a profile of Moscow girls' school No. 29, where educators viewed the "external appearance" of pupils as a "serious pedagogical task," demanding constant, thorough, and intrusive attention, including compulsory inspections of faces, hands, and clothing each morning.[39] In Alma-Ata girls' school No. 37, "not a single girl" wore makeup on her face, but instead girls had neatly cut and braided hair, modest clothing, and white collars.[40] These girls' schools pursued the goal of producing neat, attractive, and beautiful students by waging "a major struggle" against unacceptable practices and inclinations, such as slovenliness, dissipation, coquetry, pretentiousness, and extravagance in clothing, hairstyles, or behavior.[41]

Attention to culture carried over to other kinds of everyday behaviors. In Leningrad, one "typical" girls' school was "clean, warm, and calm," with well-behaved pupils, "walking the corridors in groups, without commotion, running, or shouting."[42] V. D. Matekin described how his daughter and her classmates walked together in small groups, quietly discussing lessons.[43] According to director Butkevich, teachers helped pupils develop "a taste for everything beautiful," which included flowers in corridors, paintings on walls, tablecloths and curtains (many sewn by the pupils themselves), and holiday decorations.[44] Moscow director Solomakha praised the "bright decorations" in her school for "creating a certain level of comfort and culture."[45] Moscow boys' school director Khrushchev observed, perhaps contemptuously, that female pupils "walked around in pairs," without the sound of a "human voice."[46]

Descriptions of well-ordered classrooms were illustrated by photographs showing rows of attentive pupils sitting in orderly desks, small groups surrounding teachers, or a couple of girls reading or talking together. The pose of honored teacher Ol'ga Leonova,[47] with one hand on the shoulder of a young pupil while her other hand pointed to the book, emphasized this combination of affectionate and instructional relationships between pupils and teachers (see figure 4). The appearance of pupils reaffirmed the purposes of the girls' school. In addition to providing an appropriate education, as discussed in the next section, girls' schools became a symbol of efficiency and discipline. By separating girls from boys, Soviet officials found a way to achieve the desired goal of perfect order, a school where being "clean, warm, and calm" marked the convergence of pupils' behavior and state objectives.

Yet this ideal assumed certain behaviors that girls themselves did not always choose to practice. An illustrative account of the tension between expectations and experiences came from a Moscow teacher early in 1943. In anticipation of a school holiday, girls made diligent plans to decorate their classrooms with flowers, posters, and pictures. The boys in a nearby school did nothing in preparation—until the day before the holiday, when they went into the girls' classrooms and simply took everything they needed. Enraged, girls demanded that the boys return all the decorations.[48] This incident involved just a few pupils and occurred even before separate schooling was implemented across the Soviet Union, yet it illustrated the importance of external appearance, the diligence of female pupils, and boys' indifference to both school rules and the feelings of female peers. Although these elements appeared to conform to clearly differentiated gender roles, the girls' outrage about this violation of their space led them to assume a confrontational position. This self-assertion anticipated the increasingly critical attitude that girls themselves developed toward separate schools in the decade to follow.

Educating the Soviet Girl

Soviet educators defined the goals of girls' schools as "preparing female patriots to participate in public activities and political development and at the same time to fulfill the obligations of future mothers and educators."[49]

4—Teacher Leonova in a Moscow girls' school. "Pervye shkol'nye gody," *SSSR na stroike* 4 (1949): 7.

These objectives thus combined academic goals with desired personal traits (such as initiative, confidence, will, and independence) and political ideals (civic responsibility, communist morality, and patriotic obedience).[50] Particularly in the first stages of this reform, Soviet educators emphasized the need to cultivate feminine identity. Director Butkevich defined the task of the Soviet girls' school as the preparation not of "proper young ladies" but, rather, of brave patriots dedicated to serving their homeland, as well as loving and skilled mothers and educators of children. Girls' schools were supposed to offer the same curriculum as boys' schools, yet should also train pupils in femininity, modesty, and a sense of "female dignity and honor." Girls must learn how to think, work with boys, and acquire the practical habits needed in daily life and in the family, because the future of the country depended on the education of girls as future mothers. In pursuit of these goals, Moscow girls' school No. 516 introduced a one-hour lesson dedicated to explaining the rules of behavior, proper conduct in public, and how to deal with adults and children.[51]

As suggested by Butkevich's comments, the separation of schools focused educators' attention on gender-specific traits, such as softness, sensitivity, sympathy, emotional warmth, tenderness, and thoughtfulness. According to a 1944 article by Smirnov and Levitov, schools should reinforce distinctive inclinations of girls, whose character was evident in the ways they related to adults, cared for children, empathized with fictional characters, enjoyed "artistic emotional experiences," showed sympathy for animals, especially kittens and puppies, and played with dolls, "the unfailing objects of their care, attention, and concern."[52] A year later, pedagogue Timofeev defined the "basic positive features of female character" as "*sensitivity* to the emotional experience of others, *responsiveness* to this emotional experience, softness in relation to surroundings, along with *tenderness* and *care*, especially in relation to the weak, those needing assistance, and children."[53] Timofeev then offered an even broader statement of girls' particular capacities, needs, and potential:

> Thus the majority of girls on the basis of their own qualities—femininity, a softness of nature, great concern for other people—show heightened interest and intellectual curiosity toward events from the life of people, their internal world, with all the variety of their experiences, strivings, and activities, both in the present and in the past, which find expression primarily in the humanities subjects: literature, language, and history.

Contrasting girls' great interest in "certain spheres of human activity—family relations, housekeeping, questions of daily life and culture" to their diminished interest in "the struggle against powerful forces of nature and the triumph of the will of man," Timofeev concluded that girls were less engaged with fields of study, such as geography, physics, chemistry, botany, zoology, and mathematics, directly connected to "technology and production." In recognition of these distinct interests, girls' school teachers should "devote special attention to the use of visual methods" and to making "connections between scientific laws and living practical activities of people," including the lives of scientists "involved in some discovery or law studied by the children." Even as Timofeev called for greater consideration of the particularities of girls, he also declared that the academic program would not be diminished in any way.[54] By framing this comparison between fields of study that girls found more or less interesting, Timofeev implied that girls' schools should devote special efforts to making up for their deficient engagement with sciences and other disciplines with technological, economic, or social applications.[55]

This emphasis on gender-specific schooling also appeared in unpublished materials. Following the January 1944 article by Butkevich on girls' schools,[56] *Izvestiia* editors received "many letters" from Soviet soldiers praising the new policy for preparing girls to be good mothers, with essential domestic skills and able "to love and value all that is good." One letter bluntly defined the purpose of girls' schools: "Educate for us a good housekeeper, a mother able to bring up children, and a wise friend–public activist."[57] These statements clearly assigned the greatest value to women's domestic and maternal roles, with the only mention of civil equality in the last phrase, the "wise friend–public activist." This role was clearly far from that of the equal citizen envisioned by communist ideology and reaffirmed by proponents of separate schooling.

Similar objectives were visible in the ways that some girls described their own separate schools. During a literature discussion, pupils concluded that being a "real woman" meant becoming not only an equal patriot devoted to the homeland but also "a deserving friend of a deserving man," able to support his labors, and "an affectionate and sensible mother."[58] Although the promise to become "affectionate and sensible" mothers lacked the sentimentality of the soldiers' letters, the girls appeared to accept that women's occupational and civic identities should be coordinated with familial roles.

But other descriptions of the academic goals of girls' schools tended to deemphasize gendered traits, inclinations, or capacities. In his 1946 report,

L'vov stated that girls' schools should train pupils to exercise mature judgment, use proper scientific methods, develop critical thinking, apply knowledge in practical ways, understand terms precisely, and acquire skills of independent work.[59] Even more emphatic (and public), a 1948 profile of Moscow girls' school No. 29 praised teachers for fostering active participation during lessons, developing thinking skills, and enhancing capacity for independent work. In mathematics classes, pupils solved problems independently; in science classes, pupils did more laboratory exercises than the curriculum required; in foreign language classrooms, pupils went beyond formal comprehension to a real mastery of the language. Director Mart'ianova encountered some criticism for giving "too much free will to pupils," but she contended that allowing pupils "broad independence" within the structure of school rules was the best way to train pupils to take initiative and assume responsibility for their actions.[60] Given the general tendency to emphasize girls' emotions and empathy and to diminish reasoning and knowledge, these affirmations of academic potential countered this increasingly binary perception of the interests and abilities of boys and girls.[61] Photographs of female pupils engaged in serious academic pursuits, such as the sixth graders in a mathematics lesson at a Tajik girls' school (figure 5), conveyed the same message that separate schools maintained high expectations even as they recognized gender categories.

Definitions of Soviet femininity also provoked debate and even consternation. In a 1944 meeting, director Nekrasova offered to read excerpts from essays about girls' "moral character." Even before she began reading, however, the audience of school directors responded negatively: "enough already, that's plenty." Nekrasova's selection of quotations from the essays reflected the contradictions of Soviet discourse on gender roles. One girl described the ideal traits of the Soviet woman as modesty, accuracy, courage, patriotism, and the ability to keep a home neat, clean, and comfortable. Another girl, however, wanted to be a doctor, and she aspired to be considerate, tender, observant, loving, and attentive. To acquire these traits, this girl pledged to fulfill the ubiquitous Soviet slogan: "study, study, and study."[62]

As the latter comment suggests, girls' experiences in separate schools were not confined to acquiring the feminine traits appropriate for home and family. In fact, some reports called attention to the ways that girls assumed new roles that transcended, even as they reinforced, traditional gender boundaries. Director Mukhina praised her pupils for good manners and

5—Mathematics lesson in a Tajik girls' school. Soviet Information Bureau photograph, Davis Center, Harvard College Library.

polite behavior: "We would like for girls to be well brought up, disciplined, punctual, and respectful with each other and with adults."[63] Within days of entering their new separate school, girls began to thank cafeteria workers for food, asked permission before entering the director's office, used proper forms of address when talking with the staff, and became attentive in the hallways, even apologizing for inadvertent bumps. To ensure that girls were learning to become "their mother's primary helpers in the family," teachers "check closely on behavior in the family." Acquiring habits of "self-reliance," including washing floors, darning socks, and sewing clothing, also made girls more useful in schools. Through "sincere discussions" about modesty, appearance, feelings, passions, and honor, girls learned that "an honest Soviet person" should "subordinate" personal interests to the public need.

Reports on separate schools emphasized positive changes in attitudes, relations, and aspirations of girls, who studied "intensively and actively," asked questions of their teachers, "demonstrated a desire for self-expression," took more responsibility for learning, and approached their work more seriously.[64] Both implicitly and explicitly, these changes in practice were compared to gender dynamics in coeducational classrooms. Whereas boys in coeducational classrooms acted so confidently that even the best female pupils "were sometimes ashamed to answer, because boys might make fun of them," the pattern was different in separate schools: "girls become independent more quickly," allowing teachers to cultivate a passion for the sciences, appreciation of a good book, skill in handling technology, and interest in competitive games.[65] This shift in attitude was revealed during biology examinations, according to director Maksimova: "I listened with great satisfaction to the explanations offered by female pupils during biology examinations for the sixth grade. Whatever happened to the previous shyness and constraint caused by the presence of boys?"[66] A teacher in Dagestan contrasted a coeducational classroom, where boys "hold back a confident girl," with a single-sex classroom, where girls display "more independence."[67] A 1944 report in Alma-Ata declared that separate schools encouraged independence, which was "especially notable among girls." Whereas girls had acted shyly in the presence of boys, unwilling to express their opinions or undertake practical work, "now they feel themselves more free," as they "bravely and confidently" make speeches, engage in discussions, and conduct laboratory experiments.[68] Praising teachers for encouraging girls to "feel greater independence and show more initiative," teachers drew comparisons to coeducational classrooms, where "girls are more diffident and recede into the background, because they are afraid of saying or doing anything that will make boys laugh and bother them."[69] Echoing these themes, but also invoking more subtle associations with perceived feminine traits, another teacher from Dagestan made the following comparison: "Girls feel themselves more free now. They eagerly take up any kind of work. With coeducation it was difficult to make pupils keep clean notebooks. Now, in spite of paper shortages, all the girls keep daybooks. They treat them very carefully and even make them artistic."[70] A published evaluation of the first year of separate schooling praised "an especially notable increase in the independence of girls," as female pupils were "boldly and confidently making reports," participating in discussions, and carrying out laboratory work.[71] According to one school director, "girls themselves" assumed responsibility for making repairs in the absence of boys, and soon they no longer turned to the neighboring school for mechanical assistance to repair fuses, switches, and projectors. This shift in attitudes and behaviors was cited as evidence that girls in separate schools were becoming more "independent."[72]

Yet even these positive accounts demonstrated girls' subordinate positions. While evaluations implicitly acknowledged the "shortchanging" of girls in the coeducational school,[73] this perspective also omitted crucial questions: would the confidence girls acquired in separate schools carry over to coeducational environments in higher education and employment? Would separating boys into their own school make them more or less respectful of girls? Did the emphasis on building girls' self-esteem come at the cost of academic rigor or breadth? As the next sections will demonstrate, even these seemingly positive trajectories provoked questions, concerns, and criticism—particularly among the girls who were both the subjects and the objects of this experiment.

Lessons for Girls

In 1948, director Perstova recalled that when separate schooling had been implemented five years earlier, teachers understood immediately, without any hesitation or disagreement, that girls must acquire the fundamental knowledge essential to pursue higher education and become specialists in useful occupations. Reflecting a core tension in separate schools, however, these same teachers also understood the need to consider the "particular features of girls" and "their extremely responsible obligations as future mothers, as future teachers of children."[74] This tension between providing an equal education and considering the "particular needs" of girls permeated discussions of how to teach specific subjects, what modifications to make in instruction, and how to evaluate the achievements of female pupils.

Girls' schools modified instruction to address perceived needs and interests. One of the most common adaptations was increased attention to female characters in literature and history.[75] At Razvinova's school, as cited above, pupils examined images of male and female friendship from various literary epochs, with the goal of "developing correct ideas about mutual relations between boys and girls, young men and women." Girls were expected to "imitate the best qualities" of Russian literary women, such as sensitivity, attentiveness, and politeness.[76] In Sverdlovsk girls' school No. 13, pupils discussing the question "What should the Soviet girl be?" prepared by reading works by Tolstoy, Turgenev, and other Russian and western authors.[77] During discussions of Ivan Goncharov's novel *Oblomov* in a Sverdlovsk girls' school, ninth-grade pupils spent more time than usual on the character Ol'ga Il'inskaia. Whereas lessons in coeducational schools usually ignored this character, now female pupils could discuss her ideas, curiosity, strong will, deep understanding, musical talents, and "alluring femininity!" Through their animated discussion, girls learned a lesson "they will never forget."[78]

Other educators echoed this perception that teaching girls to "understand people" could be achieved by devoting more attention to female characters, who tended to be ignored in coeducational school.[79] In a discussion of Mariia Ivanovna in Alexander Pushkin's story *Captain's Daughter,* a teacher in an Ashkhabad girls' school called attention to the "modest-heroic traits of the Russian girl," who remained faithful to "the voice of her heart," respectful of elders, and restrained in her passion.[80] In Alma-Ata girls' schools, literature teachers contributed to the goal of educating pupils who were "patriotic, strong-willed, and at the same time truly feminine."[81] In Sverdlovsk girls' school No. 36, a literature class organized an all-school conference that explored the moral strength, selflessness, commitment, and duty exhibited by Turgenev's female characters.[82]

History lessons in girls' schools also provided examples of women for emulation. A fourteenth-century Russian princess who resisted Mongol invaders became a historical antecedent for Soviet women fighting German invaders.[83] In a Molotov school, "naturally, when they selected essay themes, most girls examined the heroic character of Russian women in the past and Soviet women in the present."[84] In a Sverdlovsk school, eighth-grade students wrote research papers, prepared displays, and created exhibition rooms dedicated to such famous women as Krupskaia, Kovalevskaia, Joan of Arc, and Marie Curie, as well as explorers, war heroines, artists, and "common Soviet women" working in factories, fields, and institutes.[85]

Asserting that girls' schools should devote particular attention to female characters implied that single-sex schools should compensate for male bias in coeducational schools. Yet the overall objective of this preferential attention was to prepare literate girls with advanced knowledge and analytical skills. Gender-specific means were thus designed to achieve seemingly universal ends. Discussions of literary and historical women did focus on emotional and familial themes, yet students also explored the narrow constraints of domestic roles as well as patriotic devotion to the homeland. Strikingly, none of the historically prominent women were identified by maternal, familial, or domestic duties. Even the exhibit on "common Soviet women" emphasized economic, cultural, or political contributions. Girls' school lessons celebrated women for their creative expression, devoted patriotism, and ideological commitment, not their "particular" roles as wives or mothers.

Teaching domestic skills emerged as one of the most significant—and contested—features of girls' schools. Instruction in needlecrafts, cooking, housekeeping, home decorating, and child care had a long historical legacy in female education, starting with mothers preparing daughters for marriage and motherhood. In Russia, the ornamental crafts taught in elite *gymnasia,* the Tolstoyan emphasis on communal self-sufficiency, and the communist labor school provided durable, yet also controversial, examples of this aspect of education. During the 1930s, however, Soviet schools had largely eliminated polytechnical education, particularly in urban secondary schools.[86] Teaching domestic skills to girls thus drew upon historical antecedents yet also marked new gender boundaries in schools.

As soon as separate education was introduced, girls' schools began to offer lessons in knitting, sewing, housekeeping, decorating, preparing meals, making clothes, and child care.[87] In Samarkand, lessons in "handicrafts, pedagogy, and household management prepared Soviet girls for the responsible and honored role of mother and housekeeper."[88] Director Perstova connected civic values such as diligence and patriotism to girls' duty "to help in the family." While the latter obligation had been regarded as "an abstraction" in the coeducational era, now pupils learned to darn stockings, cook dinner, and clean their room, all "utilitarian skills" essential for family roles.[89] At Nal'chik girls' school No. 1, teacher M. B. Boldyreva praised needlecraft lessons for teaching dexterity, accuracy, and artistic taste, which were considered essential traits for both employment and housekeeping.[90]

These activities were part of a broader commitment to shaping attitudes and practices. Expanding the "general cultural outlook" of pupils included opportunities to make speeches at public assemblies, get involved in school organizations, participate in needlecraft circles, and decorate schools with artificial flowers. Pupils at one girls' school were so enthusiastic that they filled the building with flower arrangements, made wreaths for military tombs, and gave bouquets to teachers and mothers on International Women's Day.[91] According to Moscow director Solomakha, "we train girls for housekeeping" through activities such as flower arranging, yet she also admitted "it is surprising how much resistance occurs." Criticizing the "stubborn attitude" displayed by "some pupils," Solomakha described how girls neglected to water and care for flowers—but "just try to remove those flowers," and see what kind of tears and agitation follow. At this same Moscow school, nineteenth-century paintings hung in hallways to "teach children about the need for cleanliness, comfort, and beauty in the classroom," with the hope that "these habits are carried into the family."

Yet here too educators realized the difficulty of their task: "Do you think it is possible to change girls quickly? No, a great struggle is needed to make classrooms clean and comfortable." These efforts extended beyond the school, as teachers went to pupils' homes, where "they do not always find things in order." Despite the great efforts of teachers, "it cannot be said that we have resolved everything." Rather than assuming that pupils on their own would beautify classrooms, educators encouraged, and even compelled, efforts to maintain the appearance expected of a girls' school. As suggested by Solomakha's statement, teaching domestic skills was occasionally justified as remediation for perceived deficiencies in families. Director Perstova recalled that when a girl applied to join the Komsomol, the admissions committee asked whether she could cook a simple meal of pasta. She said yes but, when pressed, could not explain how, a response that prompted "general laughter" and a recommendation that she reapply after she had learned how to cook. At the next meeting, she announced that now she cooked occasionally, even though she had both a housekeeper and a grandmother at home.[92] This anecdote illustrates not only the growing interest in domestic skills in girls' schools but also the perception that schools had to compensate for the fact that many girls lacked even basic housekeeping or cooking skills.[93]

Yet these same deliberations exposed strikingly different views on this aspect of teaching femininity in girls' schools. Although many parents praised girls' schools for teaching basic skills such as sewing, embroidery, and crocheting as part of the core curriculum, some handicrafts instructors complained that their lessons were relegated to secondary status, even within girls' schools. Teacher Sarintseva from Kirov taught needlecrafts as an extracurricular activity, but it was not included on the regular lesson schedule. Teachers Rakitina and Gorodetskaia from Kharkov also called for special measures to train teachers with these skills, concluding that it was "obvious" why girls' school should teach needlecrafts.[94] At the same 1948 meeting cited above, soon after one speaker declared that needlecrafts instruction took place "in all schools," director Pokrovskaia warned against "wasting time" on these skills and recommended devoting more attention to language and literature instead of "required instruction in housekeeping, sewing stockings, preparing food, etc." Expanding on this point, Pokrovskaia described her school's "different path": "Our primary task is to educate a Soviet citizen, a new person who should, just as much as a boy, acquire a high degree of culture, an advanced general education, a resolute sense of purpose, and great courage." Pokrovskaia drew on her experience in a girls' *gymnasium,* where handicrafts instruction was "so distorted, worthless, and unnecessary" that the girls did not learn anything. Declaring that she learned "to sew, knit, and do everything necessary for my family" from her experience of living, Pokrovskaia offered this blunt conclusion: "Teaching housekeeping is an unnecessary waste of time and effort."[95]

The practice thus remained controversial. Responding to these objections to teaching domestic skills, one pupil wrote in her diary that the word "homemaking" should not provoke negative responses, when "a homemaker is, first of all, a mother."[96] Illustrating the unresolved tensions in the perceived purposes of girls' schools, a 1952 article on a Moscow school made no mention of housekeeping or needlecrafts as even extracurricular activities (they were mentioned only in relation to girls' responsibilities in their families), while discussion of lessons and assignments emphasized high academic expectations.[97]

These concerns about diluting academic requirements led some girls' schools to offer domestic skills outside regular classroom instruction. Director Butkevich called for courses in pedagogy, psychology, and housekeeping, but without any reduction in the general curriculum. Yet even this enthusiastic advocate conceded that housekeeping was introduced in 1944 as an extracurricular activity rather than as part of the academic program.[98] Often sewing, knitting, and child care were offered along with a range of academic, athletic, artistic, and service activities. In the Bashkir republic, every girls' school had afterschool needlecraft activities, but girls also participated "eagerly" in academically oriented activities devoted to literature, history, and math, as well as sports.[99] Director Mukhina also listed a range of afterschool circles that included literature, history, math, chemistry, geography, drama, and art, as well as handicrafts such as embroidery, crochet, knitting, and sewing.[100] In Alma-Ata, pupil Zhubusova praised afterschool activities that encompassed mathematics, chemistry, history, native language, Russian literature, handicrafts, and sports, all designed to prepare "active builders of communist society."[101] In this discourse, handicraft skills were clearly associated with girls' presumed interests and activities, even as these accounts also revealed how domestic roles were connected to the public service expected of all Soviet citizens. Housekeeping activities were also conspicuously absent from some reports. A flattering profile of Moscow girls' school No. 29 listed only academic circles (math, physics, geography, and botany), with no mention of handicrafts, maternity, child care, or housekeeping. The only specifically gendered activities at this school were occasional dances, with invited boys, which the director called "useful" for the development of female pupils.[102]

The attention devoted to maternity in girls' schools revealed a similar balancing of public and personal roles, as well as the complex, ambivalent, and often contradictory messages of Soviet gender ideology.[103] While separate girls' schools were maternalist, in the sense that preparing girls for motherhood was an explicit goal, this objective was always integrated into, and at time eclipsed by, efforts to train girls for further study, employment, and public service.[104] Some schools offered instruction in child care and maternal hygiene, either in existing courses (such as biology) or as afterschool activities.[105] Other schools addressed the same issues in terms of communist development. One girls' school organized lectures, discussions, and speeches "about the Soviet girl, the Russian woman, and what the motherland requires from youth," with the goal of promoting "a culture of deep respect for the mother." Yet when director Mukhina listed the notable portraits hanging in her girls' school, all the women were famous for reasons other than familial or reproductive roles—as war heroines, public activists, or cultural figures. In an exhortation seemingly devoid of maternalist content, Mukhina proclaimed that these exemplary women would "constantly summon our pupils to a persistent, steadfast, hardworking, and active participation in building a new life." Mukhina also praised her "best pupils" for good grades, excellent discipline, extensive reading, public engagement, and helping at home. While the latter attribute involved a familial role (although not necessarily gendered female), Mukhina's goal of stimulating girls' desire to "know more, read more, and become physically strong and morally steadfast" did not include specifically maternal traits.[106]

Practices and rhetoric explicitly connected to maternal and domestic objectives provoked especially critical responses. Most prominently, in August 1944, Potemkin condemned the idea that separate schools should "prepare women to create female comfort and domestic coziness" as an example of "petit bourgeois" thinking that had provoked "a deserved rebuke" and had "already been relegated to the past."[107] L'vov also warned that teachers who emphasized "the education of future mothers" risked compromising the overall goals of Soviet education. Girls needed "first of all" to acquire "a complete, well-rounded education," leaving subjects related to preparing for motherhood to occupy "an appropriately secondary place."[108]

By contrast, efforts to train girls for gender-specific professions seemed less controversial. To prepare girls for teaching, schools incorporated pedagogical lessons into the curriculum, provided experience in child-care activities, or added an eleventh grade devoted to teacher training. In some schools, pupils interested in the "noble" profession of teaching joined "pedagogical circles," whose participants worked with pupils in the primary grades, organized lectures, and developed resources for classrooms.[109] The promise that girls' schools were training "a future educator" illustrated the convergence of personal and public roles, as the term *vospitatel'nitsa* could refer to a maternal or an educational role.[110] In most cases, however, these activities were extracurricular rather than an integral part of the school program.

Nurse training began in girls' schools in the wartime context of preparing all pupils for military service. Girls learned to care for the wounded, assist with medical operations, maintain sanitary conditions, and pay attention to personal hygiene.[111] The emphasis on nursing skills certainly diminished after the war. In 1948, director Solomakha stated that girls' schools initially taught first aid, "but now these lessons have been eliminated." Solomakha recalled that the prerevolutionary girls' *gymnasia* emphasized personal hygiene, family health, and child care, but Soviet girls' schools covered these topics only "incidentally" in biology classes.[112]

Girls' schools displayed an equally strong, yet seemingly more consistent, commitment to physical education, as part of the effort to develop "a cultured, sensitive, and physically strong girl."[113] One girls' school offered daily calisthenics, marching exercises, and military training, such as grenade throwing, all designed to train pupils to "harden their bodies."[114] In some cities, girls' schools fielded sports teams to compete against each other.[115] Physical training was said to have a "positive effect" on girls' "external appearance," while also improving skills such as dexterity, accuracy, and consistency.[116] Invoking a potent historical legacy, director Solomakha declared that while schools should be careful not to "educate pretentious young ladies," they should teach a sense of rhythm and motion, so that girls would be "feminine, and not crude."[117] Schools that cultivated a "healthy" concern about appearances could offset the awkward movement and "boyishness" perceived among some girls.[118] While these objectives challenged gender boundaries by depicting girls as physically active, personally competitive, and socially engaged, they also confirmed gender roles, however indirectly, by connecting physical education to specific qualities, such as physical appearance or fluid motion, associated with femininity, even in this communist context.

From the first deliberations about this policy innovation, Soviet educators struggled to maintain the correct balance between meeting the "particular" needs of girls and maintaining the same standards as coeducational and boys' schools. In February 1943, just as Moscow schools began their experiment, one educator warned that adding housekeeping, pedagogy, psychology, hygiene, and aesthetics would mean "an inevitable reduction in lesson hours for other subjects." This chemist declared that the science curriculum must not be reduced in girls' schools, especially when so many Soviet women worked in laboratories. Yet these affirmations of equality in education were immediately undermined by the same speaker's concession that, first, women needed knowledge of chemistry to perform household duties, and second, reducing lesson hours could be accomplished by "compressing" content, but there was not any explanation as to how girls could acquire the same knowledge in less time.[119]

Similar debates occurred elsewhere during this first phase of deliberation and implementation. At Tashkent teachers' meetings in the summer of 1943, "isolated voices" expressed concerns about girls' capacity to master the entire science curriculum, but later reports claimed that girls could complete the program if they were taught effectively.[120] Moscow educational department official Orlov also denounced as "incorrect" any proposal to limit or modify science and math in girls' schools by imposing "narrow family and everyday functions," adding "artificial" methods, or invoking "girls' diminished mental capacities."[121] This list is striking, because the last point addresses, and to some extent confirms, warnings that eliminating coeducation would lead to a devaluing of women's education and girls' potential.[122] As will be seen in the final sections of this chapter, Soviet girls responded especially negatively to any suggestion that they were academically less capable than boys.

Contesting Feminization

Even if the policy promised equality in education, the practices of girls' schools conveyed the impression of lower expectations, less rigor, and narrower interests. As described in the preceding sections, the process of "feminization" went beyond the formal separation of the sexes to changes in appearance, expectations, interactions, attitudes, and academics, all of which contributed to making girls' schools seem fundamentally different from coeducational and boys' schools. At each step, however, this feminization provoked concerns, resistance, and outright repudiation, not only from educators but also from girls themselves. As recalled by director Fomina, some girls immediately objected to needlework courses. They wanted to be doctors, builders, architects, and pilots, and they found needlework boring. Fomina told the girls that, while not all of them would enter these professions, they would all become wives and mothers, and thus they must learn to sew.[123]

Although Fomina's account described an unusually direct confrontation between two contrasting perspectives, other reports describe more complex patterns, where girls' perceptions were mediated by the school's adjustments to new policies. At a 1948 meeting, for example, director Pokrovskaia praised pupils for their "remarkable enthusiasm for literature," yet she also conceded that "they study physics poorly and without enthusiasm" and that they were "not especially attracted to mathematics." As her school devoted more attention to the latter subjects, however, girls responded enthusiastically, with marked improvements in achievement and great involvement in afterschool activities. But Pokrovskaia also conceded that it was "quite difficult, and we were not successful during the first years."[124] Even as Pokrovskaia described positive efforts to engage female pupils, her statement reproduced assumptions of girls' disinterest in subjects such as math and science.

These assumptions were rarely stated explicitly, but the underlying perceptions were often disclosed indirectly. Speaking at the same meeting, boys' school director Khrushchev described a mathematics lesson in a girls' school and then concluded that "things are done poorly," as pupils have "a great deal of difficulty." Although Khrushchev prefaced his comments by saying, "I do not intend to defame the female half of mankind," he also declared that even the best girls' school teachers were not "strong" enough for boys' schools.[125] In an earlier published report, girls' school director Butkevich declared that, "as a rule," most girls do not find instructional materials exciting, and different methods were needed, particularly in sciences.[126]

The perceived need to modify the curriculum shaped the content, tone, and purpose of girls' schools. Chemistry lessons connected scientific concepts to household tasks such as salting vegetables, cooking meat, making soap, dyeing clothes, and fermenting fruit.[127] Physics and math instruction made use of visual aids and emphasized practical applications.[128] A girls' school director in Groznyi went even further, by calling for "significant reductions" in physics, chemistry, biology, geography, history, and literature in order to introduce new subjects such as pedagogy, hygiene, and housekeeping.[129] Despite assertions that "a small, insignificant number" of educators shared these views, their reaffirmation suggests the extent of their dissemination in separate schools.

Even positive statements of girls' capacities in the sciences evoked underlying perceptions of gender differences. Director Bocharova declared that girls had great potential to succeed in all fields, "not only in the humanities but also in physics and chemistry," as long as requirements remained the same: "Look at newspaper photographs of Stalin Prize winners, and you will see many women."[130] Celebrated examples of successful instruction in math, physics, and other sciences provided models of intellectual potential and academic success that transcended the usual gender boundaries. E. I. Iur'evaia taught female pupils about the latest advances in physics. Rather than emphasizing domestic applications, Iur'evaia explained how physics made possible the radio transmissions used to coordinate large-scale agriculture. She also took her pupils to see science laboratories at the pedagogical institute. According to a later report, it was "no accident" that these girls became interested in physics, for Iur'evaia was "a good propagandist for science," who could "inspire passion" in her students, and "a model for emulation in the acquisition of knowledge, industriousness, and unselfish creativity."[131]

Other science teachers earned praise for engaging, innovative, and demanding instruction.[132] Moscow physics teacher Sigodin designed experiments and demonstrations, "so that pupils can repeat in practice the lessons learned from the teacher."[133] Teachers who required pupils to complete laboratory experiments, or in some cases even to design and build instructional equipment, provided further evidence of high expectations.[134] In a 1944 report, Alma-Ata girls' school No. 36 pupils were praised for making their own physics equipment and setting up radio transmitters.[135] Nine years later, many tenth graders in this same school sought admission into an institute for precision instruments and into the math-physics program in higher education, thus following in the footsteps of their favorite teacher, a man named N. A. Avramov.[136] Sverdlovsk chemistry teacher Orlova overcame girls' initial disinterest in the topic of solvency by assigning them to grow crystals. As girls became involved in this project they assembled a classroom display, and "every pupil prepared her work thoroughly and attentively."[137]

A published report on physics and mathematics in girls' schools devoted considerable attention to the way that pupils demonstrated their knowledge in examinations as well as to efforts such as organizing conferences, leading discussions, attending lectures, and constructing laboratory equipment.[138] When teachers noticed "a cold attitude" toward mathematics, as pupils avoided difficult problems, confined themselves to memorizing rules, and refused to apply lessons in practice, they implemented "more active methods of instruction" that led pupils "to love mathematics."[139] Photographs of female pupils with microscopes, as shown in chapter 2, encouraged these same associations between girls' schools and scientific knowledge. Profiles of effective teachers and images of engaged pupils challenged tendencies to adapt science teaching to girls' schools by narrowing the scope, emphasizing domestic applications, or diminishing the rigor.

The transformative potential of teaching found expression in reports that recognized the causes of girls' relative interest in different subjects. A report on Kursk girls' school No. 8 found that pupils "really love lessons on literature" but also "demonstrate great interest in studying and solving chemistry problems." The "quality of instruction in these two subjects" explained pupils' high levels of interest and achievement, whereas the "disinterested and listless" methods of the physics and mathematics teacher discouraged these same pupils. In Kursk girls' school No. 3, by contrast, pupils showed the same high level of interest in physics and mathematics as in history, language, and literature: "Many girls from this school, having completed the tenth grade, seek to enter the mathematics department of the university."[140] While refuting assumptions that girls were interested only in humanities subjects, this report asserted that teachers who engaged, excited, and challenged their classes could overcome any presumed lack of interest or ability.

These deliberate attempts to emphasize girls' potential in the sciences were accompanied by other reports that simply assumed girls' more "lively interest" in literature, language, and history. Teachers "skillfully used the inclination of girls toward emotional experience" to teach biographies of great historical figures and the psychological attributes of fictional characters, with the goal of preparing "girl-patriots, strong-willed yet truly feminine."[141] Director Perstova claimed that humanities subjects evoked greater interest than the sciences. In math classes, for example, girls might learn the assigned material, but "they are not captivated" by the subject. In an unusually candid statement, Perstova admitted that these trends could result from the character of girls' schools or because humanities teachers used especially lively methods.[142]

Perceptions of girls' interests and abilities in sciences were often compared to boys' aspirations and achievements. One report claimed that girls' limited understanding of technology made them ignorant of applications already "familiar" to boys. When a physics teacher used a specific term, many pupils did not understand, so he made sure to provide a detailed explanation, to which pupils devoted careful attention. This teacher declared that the situation would have been different in a coeducational classroom, as boys already familiar with the term would not have listened to his explanation and instead would have distracted the girls by mocking their ignorance.[143] Boys' school director Khrushchev made a similar comparison, although in a more dismissive manner, when he claimed that girls did not grasp the significance of the steam engine in a physics lesson on friction.[144] Other reports claimed that many boys perceived girls' schools as less rigorous, and female pupils as academically inferior.[145] These reports exposed the core tension of separate schools, because they assumed that effective teaching was needed to overcome girls' inherent limits in physics and math; in the absence of dedicated teaching and supplementary activities, girls would presumably remain at a lower level. Teaching physics and mathematics in girls' schools thus acquired a remedial character even in these generally sympathetic reports.

Presumptions of girls' "particular interests" shaped teaching in fields beyond the sciences. The best geography teachers engaged female pupils by encouraging independent work, out-of-school excursions, and map exercises.[146] Sverdlovsk girls participated actively in geography circles, researched explorers, and corresponded with pupils in other cities, including London.[147] Nothing in this account suggested that girls were constrained in their range of interests and activities, which by itself made an important statement about the potential for equal interests and achievement. Photographs of girls examining globes, like the images cited above of girls in laboratories, provided a distinct image of academic rigor that challenged traditional gender boundaries (see figure 6).

A spring 1944 article about examinations in girls' schools directly refuted "the exaggerated nonsense" proclaimed "by certain educators" that physics and mathematics were "masculine" subjects, that girls were less capable of abstract thinking, or that girls had no interest in technology. The answers that tenth-grade pupils gave during physics examinations, according to the author A. Levshin, had a clarity, accuracy, and certainty that many young men would have envied. This firsthand account of examinations thus praised the rigorous standards of teachers and the excellent knowledge and inquisitive thinking of pupils in a girls' school.[148]

6—Geography lesson for elementary pupils. "The Road to a Big Life," *Soviet Union* (September 1950): 29.

This emphasis on feminization also obscured significant differences between girls' schools. In one unusual account, director Solomakha stated that "thank goodness," not all girls' classrooms were peaceful and quiet, as illustrated by two hypothetical classes, 7A and 7B. Although the latter was "dull in its development and intellect," it was quiet and made few demands on the teacher, whereas the former seemed more "emotional," as clever, bright, and energetic pupils sought more engagement and activities. Even though class 7A was potentially more difficult to teach, it was also more interesting, especially if the teacher directed pupils to use their energy and interests in productive ways.[149] Although Solomakha did not make this point explicitly, her two hypothetical classes evoked masculine and feminine modes of learning, which assumed that boys, like the 7A class, were both more challenging and interesting to teach, whereas girls, like the 7B class, were almost too obedient. Solomakha's affirmative argument for separate schools implicitly conceded that conformity might also mean an undesirable level of passivity.

Educators who sought to reconcile these competing claims exposed the delicate balance between difference and equality in separate schools, as illustrated by Timofeev: "Work in a girls' school acquires its own coloring, so that female pupils develop the characteristically feminine features necessary for cultured women of our society, in combination with the general characters of the fully developed person of the Stalinist epoch." Yet

Timofeev went a step further in the following proclamation: "All lessons in girls' schools demonstrate the barely perceptible but, nevertheless, peculiar approach that girls use in perceiving and mastering instructional material, reflecting the peculiarity of their historically conditioned interests, needs, and aspirations." Rather than citing examples from lessons, however, Timofeev referred to afterschool clubs on scientific and artistic pursuits, needlework, housekeeping, toy-making, military training, sports, and political activity.[150]

These reports thus offered a contrasting and to some extent contradictory impression of teaching and learning in girls' schools. Introducing subjects such as handicrafts, sanitation, or pedagogy, devoting more attention to female characters in history or literature, and adapting science lessons to teach basic housekeeping skills were evidence that girls' schools provided an education different from coeducational or boys' schools. Yet these efforts were always limited in scope, involved marginal rather than substantive adjustments, and often occurred outside of classrooms. Instruction thus seemed to change little in girls' schools. Yet even these limited efforts, as will be seen in the next section, prompted concerns, objections, and even resistance.

Gender Boundaries

Although the girls' school was by definition exclusively for female pupils, it was not an exclusively female space. Some men worked as teachers or directors in girls' schools, although as a distinct minority, given both the majority of women among urban teachers and the preference for assigning men to boys' schools. Alma-Ata teacher Avramov, as cited above, was one exception to this general pattern, as was a Moscow physics instructor praised as "a very good teacher," an expert in his field, and "a favorite of pupils."[151] Yet the fact that these male teachers taught the sciences actually reinforced the impression of a feminized teaching corps in girls' schools. Women teachers also earned praise for their work in fields, such as the sciences, usually dominated by men.[152] Most girls' schools had women directors, although some evidence suggests a few men also served in this role, including Butkevich, author of an influential article in early 1944.[153] Whereas boys' schools had a visible representation of women as teachers and directors, the pupils and staff of girls' schools tended to adhere to designated gender boundaries.

In response to this policy of gender segregation, girls' schools created opportunities to interact with boys, especially in the more senior grades.

A Saratov girls' school established "friendly relations" with a boys' school. Rather than being "guests" in each other's schools, boys and girls worked together to plan combined events. On March 8, as "a gift to girls on Women's Day," the boys' school organized celebrations for female pupils.[154] Some accounts claimed that separate schools actually improved relations between boys and girls. An early report claimed that when invited to girls' schools, boys behaved tactfully and attentively, for "being courteous and respectful was the duty of every cultured person."[155] A Moscow pupil also observed that boys behaved more politely when dances occurred at girls' schools.[156]

Yet these arranged activities also attracted sharp criticism. Ninth-grade Leningrad pupils complained that they interacted with boys only at "really boring" school events.[157] Tenth-grade Moscow pupils had three years of complete isolation from boys before their school finally arranged "combined events," but without any experience to draw on, girls had no way to talk with boys, and these events actually worsened their "estrangement."[158] Other pupils lamented that "boys and girls [were] never together," except at school dances, when boys were too shy to ask girls to dance, so they just "stand along the wall." These experiences led to charges that "there is no friendship between boys and girls, that is, no real friendship."[159] A different tone was struck by tenth-grade pupils, who charged that at dances, half the girls stood by themselves, while the other half was "too familiar (to put it mildly)." After attending such events, these girls declared, the only reasonable decision was "to stop going."[160] Similar complaints about dances led Leningrad eighth-grade pupils to support a return to coeducation, where boys and girls shared interests and "relate[d] to each other differently."[161] A mother of an Alma-Ata girls' school pupil complained that some girls were "unnecessarily bashful" around boys, while others displayed "coquetry," and they all had negative attitudes about classmates who spent time with boys.[162]

Although these criticisms certainly reflected an adolescent sense of alienation, school officials echoed these denunciations of practices that "set boys against girls and girls against boys" or created a "high fence" between children.[163] Yet educators themselves seemed ambivalent about appropriate kinds of interactions between the sexes. Thus, Moscow boys' school director Mostovoi recalled how a neighboring girls' school called three times in a single day to complain that "your boys are in our courtyard." When Mostovoi went to the girls' school, however, he found just five pupils, who told him that no one had even asked them to leave.[164] Girls' school officials found other ways to restrict interactions with boys' schools.[165] When pupils at a Novosibirsk school proposed to invite boys to play male roles in a theater production, they were "scolded" for "dissoluteness" and "freethinking." According to a newspaper report, their "schoolmarms" engaged in "sanctimony" unacceptable in a Soviet school.[166] Perhaps as a result of such restrictions, male pupils allegedly referred to girls' schools as "nunneries" or "womanish schools," thus showing contempt for female peers.[167]

Underlying all these concerns, of course, was anxiety about adolescent sexuality. Girls' school pupils were allegedly preoccupied with appearances, relationships, and status, rather than the utilitarian and ideological values desired by Soviet educators.[168] Discussions of the desired traits of the Soviet girl reportedly devolved into talk of hairstyles, cosmetics, and jewelry.[169] A teacher in a boys' school charged that girls feared boys but also dreamed about them. When girls came to the boys' school for events, they stood separately, while boys looked at them "in undesirable ways."[170] Director Perstova admitted that female pupils received mixed messages, as they were told that interest in boys was natural and appropriate, yet they also faced interrogations about their activities and warnings about consequences from distrustful supervisors.[171] Many activities arranged with boys' schools such as literature circles, drama groups, athletic competitions, and political celebrations demonstrated this effort simultaneously to acknowledge and to control female sexuality.[172]

Parents echoed complaints about proper interactions between boys and girls. The mother of a fourth-grade pupil contrasted the strong friendships forged in her own coeducational school to "petty bourgeois" relations observed in her daughter's school.[173] A father complained that girls were not interested in "comradeship and friendship with boys their age," which he blamed on their lack of "daily interactions" with male peers.[174] A mother warned that girls perceived boys "as somehow alien, and not as comrades with whom they can have a conversation, so they keep away from boys and vice versa."[175] A father warned that his daughters thought in terms of "us" and "them," which meant that all boys seemed alien, even hostile.[176]

Separate schools could thus either diminish or exacerbate underlying concerns about female sexuality. Director Perstova claimed that female pupils were spared the "difficulties" of coeducational schools, when children became sexually aware in a mixed setting. In five years, her school had only one incident of inappropriate sexual expression, which was resolved "without any fuss," and "now we do not see any of this kind of behavior." Yet later at the same meeting, director Pokrovskaia exclaimed that teachers found "pornographic" notes everywhere, and especially during dances. Girls' sexuality, according to Pokrovskaia, "was not solved during coeducation, and it has not now been solved."[177]

According to director Bocharova, sexuality had been "the most acute challenge" in coeducational schools, yet at least with the presence of boys, teachers could take a more direct approach. In separate schools, by contrast, relations were "so far from comradely!" A drama group at her school invited pupils from a boys' school to play the male parts. Although just four boys came for rehearsal, their arrival provoked a mass reaction. Every girl gathered in the commons room, all shouting: "Boys! Boys!" While this incident may have been an excited, and perhaps enthusiastic, response to a rare event, Bocharova followed up the story with some highly critical remarks. Whereas in the coeducational school, pupils exchanged inoffensive notes, now "you should see how banal is the correspondence between pupils in boys' and girls' schools." Even more ominously, Bocharova warned, her older pupils were no longer looking to boys' schools for romance but instead spent time outside the school looking for older men, seeking to find an admirer, "or perhaps even a fiancé." Whereas coeducation allowed a balance of femininity and comradeship, these girls were behaving like noble ladies, displaying "airs and graces" inconsistent with socialist morality.[178] Evoking a similar nineteenth-century discourse, another educator warned that girls displayed "excessive sentimentality, nervousness, and amorousness" during rare encounters with boys.[179] Yet other accounts suggest a more subtle balance between desire and control in girls' schools. Director Pokrovskaia conceded that boys could provoke "extreme sexual excitement," as girls started screeching, running around, and displaying "unhealthy attitudes." But when events were carefully organized, "comradely relations" were possible, if these combined activities were "based on healthy foundations."[180]

In contrast to these anxious and even alarmist warnings of heightened adolescent sexuality, most accounts of girls' schools emphasized the calm, relaxing, and even boring character of the academic environment. Some girls' school directors and teachers did not even bother discussing "the question of discipline."[181] Yet educators also warned against the misleading ease of maintaining discipline in girls' schools.[182] According to director Groza, while girls' schools achieved "a certain formal order," they needed "a more profound and serious discipline" than just "external behavior and appearance."[183] Although this statement confirmed perceptions that girls' schools had better discipline, it also expressed concern about threats lurking beneath the surface of public conformity. Other directors and teachers who thought it was "somehow easier" to manage a girls' school were denounced for tolerating "the absence of firm internal order," with absenteeism and tardiness cited as obvious shortcomings.[184] In Alma-Ata, teachers who thought it was easier to work in a girls' school were urged to look beyond the "superficial order," because a girls' school required the same "strength and effort" as a boys' school, even though the most common "violations of discipline" were seemingly mild: running in the hallways, whispering and writing notes during lessons, and absenteeism from class.[185] Criticizing teachers for believing that only boys could commit transgressions, a director called attention to misbehavior in girls' schools: "At the start of the school year, girls came late to school, were absent, left lessons, deceived the teacher, acted crudely, and wrote bad words on the walls."[186] As an example of how the appearance of order concealed disobedience, a school director in late 1943 described the insolent and disengaged behavior of a ninth-grade pupil during a physics lesson, about which the teacher did nothing, because the classroom remained quiet.[187]

Even these warnings of disciplinary lapses thus reinforced impressions of well-ordered schools. Tardiness, absenteeism, disrespect, and petty vandalism represented significant infractions, but certainly nothing compared to what was happening in boys' schools (as will be discussed in the next chapter). In fact, when the Alma-Ata city educational department reported on the highest levels of discipline and organization, it listed "the girls' schools," and then just three of the eighteen boys' schools.[188]

Girls' Voices

According to a later report, the most senior girls, who had the longest experience in coeducational schools, also objected most strongly to the new policy, asking "what kind of school they found themselves in and what it meant." One girl openly declared she was "a Soviet girl," not a female character from a Turgenev story. Her teacher responded to this challenge by organizing a debate about the role of girls in the nineteenth century and in the Soviet era. While pupils willingly discussed the meanings of culture, politeness, and femininity, as soon as they asked for their teacher's opinion, she responded with only vague statements about girls doing what was proper and right.[189]

Positive evaluations of girls' schools were often accompanied by, and sometimes directly contradicted by, assessments that revealed deeper tensions in gender roles. Some observers noted that in a single-sex classroom, girls initially seemed reluctant to speak up or participate. In a Moscow school, girls waited for "prompting" from the teacher: "At times, it seemed like a girl knew the answer, but instead of answering the question, she would think more about what might happen if she gave a wrong answer than about the problem itself." When teachers asked "leading questions," pupils answered more confidently.[190] A different concern about the reticence of girls was articulated by director Davydova, who described some apparently "remarkable girls" who earned excellent grades, never violated classroom rules, and were honored for their public service yet behaved selfishly at home and made insulting comments to their mothers. Teachers had trouble identifying these problem girls, however, because no pupil would speak against her classmates, whereas in a coeducational school boys would turn on each other "and drag the girls along behind them." Urging her fellow directors to "speak honestly," Davydova concluded with a remarkably negative list of traits attributed to pupils in girls' schools: "Falsity, hypocrisy, lies, egoism, hysteria, and petty bourgeois!"[191]

Educators thus expressed anxiety about negative practices hidden by a veneer of obedience.[192] Moscow girls' schools pupils were disciplined, punctual, efficient, organized, and diligent, according to one report, but also passive, petty, capricious, fainthearted, and emotional.[193] Another report claimed that girls tended "to withdraw from contemporary surroundings and retreat into their own individual experiences," a pattern of behavior illustrated by seventh graders playing with dolls.[194] Concerns about hidden misbehavior led to dire warnings about religious expression, which ranged from attending church to telling fortunes.[195] In the militantly atheistic context of postwar Soviet education, these dire warnings were no gauge of activity, let alone faith, yet they revealed anxiety about behaviors and beliefs concealed within communities of girls.

These observations also indicated that not all girls adhered to the ideals of Soviet femininity. In 1944, director Fomina complained that girls no longer displayed a desirable sense of modesty and even shame. But her comments provoked an immediate response from other directors: "This is not true." To illustrate her point, Fomina recalled when she told pupils that boys were not invited to an afterschool event, a girl declared: "Well, we will not come, it will not be interesting." Whereas Fomina saw evidence of girls' rude behavior, another school director clearly saw it differently:

"Why was it not possible to invite boys?" Acknowledging implicitly that separate school pupils had a legitimate need for interaction with the opposite sex, Fomina immediately denied that her school was a nunnery and complained again about girls' immodesty and rudeness.[196]

Discussion of "the complexities and difficulties" of controlling female pupils focused attention on disputes among girls, the formation of cliques, and other kinds of interpersonal behavior.[197] In 1954, boys' school teacher Kul'nitskaia complained that a "feminine environment" encouraged worrisome behaviors. Although the youngest pupils looked cute, with their bows and hankies, already they "whispered secrets" to one another. Any time five girls played together, Kul'nitskaia claimed, two would always be left on the side, while the other three talked about them.[198] Director Perstova stated that while "external discipline" was fully achieved, girls' schools needed to work on "internal discipline, conscious discipline." Perstova tried to ban "the writing of notes" by making girls pledge that they would always speak openly to one another, as a way to eliminate tendencies toward "any kind of grouping" or "separatism."[199] The same tension between visible conformity and underlying conflicts could be seen in the recollections of former girls' school pupil Guzel Amalrik: "We were supposed to walk quietly, and at a measured pace, but at least we were allowed to talk with each other, though not loudly." The most common form of disobedience, according to Amalrik, involved disputes between pupils, which provoked a specific kind of disciplinary response: "If any pair misbehaved, they were separated, the pairs were changed, and the new pairs walked around the circle together pouting."[200] Girls were clearly expected to conform to high standards of behavior, while also subordinating any desire for either physical exertion or interpersonal conflict, to adhere to norms of harmonious and cooperative interactions.

Director Solomakha exposed this same tension between visible conformity and hidden disobedience in her warning that quiet corridors and classrooms did not mean "all is calm." A surface level of discipline concealed "moods, conversations, groupings, and passions." Whereas boys' open challenges to discipline could be addressed directly, girls acted "in the deeper pool where, as they say, the devil plays." Solomakha warned about a certain type of female pupil: "She is very respectful and well brought up, saying 'how do you do' while bowing from the waist, but at the same time she displays petty bourgeois inclinations, egoism, and pettiness, and maybe would not mind gossiping a little." These "survivals of capitalism" presented real challenges to teachers: "If you just look at how girls walk along the corridors, it seems okay, but if you worm your way into the secret places, sometimes we find out very unpleasant things, and we have to think a great deal about correcting these deficiencies."[201]

These stereotyped feminine behaviors were amplified by school directors who warned about girls' "falsity," "absence of truthfulness," and tendency to "look after themselves."[202] Boys' school director Gorbunov criticized teachers in girls' school who became entangled in "squabbles, gossip, and so on."[203] Sverdlovsk educational officials declared that "girls were less likely than boys to develop their own ideas bravely, to challenge the textbook or the teacher's opinion," but "more likely to conceal everything, be deceptive, and allow factions and mutual ill-will in their midst."[204] Director Davydova said that the "balance" of coeducation yielded in girls' schools to "excessive femininity, weakness, tears, and hysteria." When a fourth-grade girl received a bad grade, for example, she would burst into tears in an all-girls' classroom, whereas she might be "ashamed" to cry in front of boys.[205]

Yet descriptions of deceptive, emotional, or petty behaviors were always contested and even directly refuted. Responding directly to the expression of such views as soon as schools were separated, Potemkin denounced educators who described girls as politically disinterested or personally dishonest.[206] An extended debate over these stereotyped perceptions took place at a meeting of school directors. According to Davydova, girls' schools seemed so orderly: "external discipline is perfect, as girls walk around during recess, greet each other politely, and maintain a smart appearance." But "lifting the cover" to look under "surface discipline" exposed the "hypocrisy" of pupils: "a girl is one thing at a school, a second thing on the street, and a third thing at home." Yet the next speaker, Pokrovskaia, stated that while she sympathized with Davydova's "cry from an aching heart," it was wrong to say only "bad things" about "good girls." But even Pokrovskaia conceded that girls were too "passive" and "reticent," as even "the smallest remark" prompted "tears, sobbing, and all kinds of reactions."[207]

Although these comments focused on the emotional dimensions of separate schools, they also reinforced concerns about academic interests and capacities. According to the Leningrad educational department, girls demonstrated "a certain diminished intellectual curiosity," a "narrowing" of interests to "ordinary everyday matters," decreased engagement with political affairs, and "less honesty" in comparison with boys.[208] The "narrowing" of interests seemed to converge on precisely the "everyday" concerns that received "particular" attention in girls' schools. Separate schools thus subverted their intended purposes, by emphasizing "feminine" behaviors that, in effect, excluded girls from "masculine" spheres of activity. According to one girl accused of joining an "unofficial group" at a Cheliabinsk girls' school, the appeal of this nonconformist practice was "the fact that we didn't discuss politics, which didn't appeal to us."[209] The perception of girls as "less honest" was especially complicated in a political context composed of secrecy, manipulation, and intimidation. The policy of separating the sexes seemed to have a contradictory effect of reinforcing stereotypical gendered behavior.

The ambivalent purposes and contested effects of girls' schools were revealed most clearly in pupils' own evaluations. "Girls' voices" reveal the complex ways that female pupils, through their articulation of experiences, shaped practices in separate schools.[210] These comments, like all expressions of public opinion in the Stalinist context, were circumscribed not only by censorship but more broadly by the subordinate position of girls in both school structures and the gender order. Yet even in this context, listening to girls' voices directs attention to unique perspectives on practices and policies and also to the ways that girls themselves shaped separate schools and thus contributed to the repudiation of this increasingly unpopular policy.

During the first year of separate schools, a group of Moscow girls offered a multilayered assessment of their passage:

> We have studied in school for five years. We studied together with boys for four years, and only in the last year did girls and boys study separately. We think there are positive and negative sides. Studying together with boys can be uncomfortable, as girls have their opinions and views, and boys have different ones. Without boys, behavior improves in lessons and during recess. Girls became more modest. Previously some girls imitated the behavior of boys: they began to whistle, make insults, and push each other. In girls' schools, sewing lessons were introduced. Every girl should learn to sew, and coeducational schools did not offer such lessons. But boys have a sophisticated newspaper, make and repair things, and really love arithmetic. We look at them and try to act in the same ways. But all the same, we like separate schools, and want to keep studying apart from boys.[211]

Even as they appreciated the advantages of their school—common interests, quiet classrooms, and useful skills—these girls also realized what had been lost from the coeducational school. This endorsement of separate schools was thus accompanied by awareness of missed opportunities that anticipated the increasingly critical assessments that accumulated during the experience of separate schooling.

These perceptions of a limited social environment also informed girls' frequently expressed desire for "real friendship between boys and girls." Leningrad tenth graders complained about "deformed, unnatural relations" between boys and girls, who lacked any "common interests and shared matters" and thus could not spend time pleasurably with each other.[212] Ninth-grade pupils from Sverdlovsk declared that "real friendship between boys and girls is very rare."[213] Two eighth-grade pupils in Ivanovo called attention to their classmates' "incorrect" views of boys, as some feared them, others looked for possible "admirers," and very few could "understand and relate correctly."[214] Ninth-grade pupils praised coeducation as a model for the collectivism, patriotism, and comradeship displayed by the Soviet people during the war: "Would they really have fought as friends for the freedom of our Motherland, if they had not been united by many years of friendship in the school?"[215]

While these comments addressed social interactions, other girls objected specifically to the academic character of separate schools. Directly challenging the assumption that girls were interested only in humanities subjects, Leningrad pupils declared that "many girls are very interested in subjects such as mathematics, physics, and chemistry."[216] A seventh-grade pupil named Tat'iana Goriaeva wrote, "I really love physics, geometry, algebra, chemistry, and zoology." She was offended by claims that sciences are "specifically masculine subjects," especially when such opinions were "unfortunately" expressed by teachers.[217] Other pupils rejected the view attributed to male peers, but also articulated in published reports, that only boys could be fascinated by physics or mathematics.[218] A former pupil, Galina Zaitseva, affirmed that she, like many of her schoolmates, was more interested in physics and mathematics than in history and literature. Girls dreaming of becoming physicists, chemists, and engineers needed more than training only for the duties of motherhood: "I am in favor of the girl receiving the exact same knowledge as the boy, so I support coeducation, and I am sure that this is not only my personal opinion, but the opinion of all Soviet girls."[219]

Adult women also challenged assumptions about girls' inability or disinterest in scientific fields. Recent graduates of a Molotov girls' school declared that female pupils should never be limited to studying the practical applications of science.[220] A mother with two daughters in girls' schools recalled that her favorite subject was chemistry, while many of her female classmates preferred mathematics.[221] Another woman described being fascinated with both mathematics and literature, thus challenging the idea that girls' supposed preferences for certain subjects justified separate schooling.[222] Even a male pupil warned that girls' schools lowered academic achievement, worsened discipline, promoted "vulgar" dancing, fostered "love" adventures, and weakened pupils physically, all leading to his emphatic warning that girls should not be educated in "the spirit of needless sentimentality and femininity."[223]

Girls also challenged the practice of using female literary or historical characters as objects for emulation. A letter signed by thirty-five pupils in Sverdlovsk girls' school No. 12 declared emphatically that, "We, Soviet female pupils," did not aspire to be like Natalia Rostova or Dolly Oblonskaia, two of Tolstoy's characters noted for their devotion to home, husband, and family. After comparing quotes from Tolstoy ("a woman should be a strong, beautiful, and fertile female") and a Soviet boys' school director ("a girl should be educated to become a mother"), these girls rejected the "obsolete" beliefs used to justify separate schools and then affirmed a more ambitious educational purpose: "We want to become not just mothers, but also public figures and scientists; in a word, we want to serve wherever we can be most useful to our country."[224] Other female pupils questioned how Tolstoy's views on motherhood could possibly be embraced by Soviet teachers, when the purpose of schooling was to prepare women who could "make the same contributions to society as will men!"[225] Kazan pupils declared that whereas Tolstoy's women wanted to be happy wives and caring mothers, Soviet girls sought education to become dedicated fighters for Vladimir Lenin, Stalin, and communism.[226] Galina Popova, a tenth-grade pupil, declared that her ideal literary women were not in the novels of Tolstoy but, rather, among political radicals committed to gender equality in Nikolai Chernyshevsky's novel *What Is to Be Done?*[227]

Girls thus objected most emphatically to perceived limits in single-sex schools. Moscow ninth-grade pupils responded defiantly to the idea of being trained for motherhood: "No! Now times are different, and Soviet girls have different dreams."[228] Echoing this sentiment even more vehemently, fifteen recent graduates of a Molotov girls' school asked: "Are we, the new generation of young Soviet women, really supposed to be satisfied with just motherhood? No!!! Never!!!"[229]

Conclusion

These letters demonstrate that girls were active participants in defining, enacting, and interpreting the meanings of separate schooling. By comparison to coeducation, separate schools devoted an unusual amount of attention to girls' perceived interests and offered opportunities and resources that would otherwise probably have gone to boys. These schools thus fulfilled the promise made by Soviet officials, and one shared by advocates of girls' schools in other contexts, that girls can succeed in their own space in ways that are more difficult in coeducational schools. To a great extent, Soviet girls, as well as educators and parents, seemed to accept that separate schools could become an alternative space where the dominant messages of society about gender roles could be mediated by practices that valued the academic potential, personal development, and social relations of girls. Rather than reverting to an anachronistic model of a convent or finishing school, Soviet girls' schools challenged gender roles through measures to improve pupils' preparation for adult roles.[230]

Yet this history also revealed widespread, passionate, and thoughtful objections to the policies and practices of girls' schools. Critics pointed to the prioritization of domestic identities, weakening of academic standards, and compromises in gender equality. Concerns about girls' schools never reached the alarm apparent in complaints about boys' schools (as will be discussed in the next chapter), yet these views certainly contributed to the shift in public opinion in favor of coeducation.[231] Girls' schools did not fail on an everyday level as boys' schools seemed to do, but they appeared as an ideological failure, as an institutionalized practice that compromised principles of gender equality.

These concerns also suggest that girls' schools were perhaps working too well to train conformist, loyal, and compliant children. Girls' schools, more than coeducational and boys' schools, approached the Stalinist ideal of a well-governed system.[232] By walking quietly in hallways, conversing calmly, and behaving dutifully, female pupils put into practice a model of Soviet subjectivity consistent with the ideals of the communist system. A 1948 article about Moscow girls' school No. 29 even referred to the "pedagogical gaze" that "followed pupils everywhere," as "teachers control every step taken by pupils." According to this report, "nothing special" was done to maintain exemplary order, which seemed to occur "on its own, without any special effort," as if "some kind of intelligent, efficient hand" was ruling the school discreetly and unobtrusively. The behavior and appearance of pupils was so uniform that they appeared as "children from the same family," all demonstrating the same unfailing politeness, respect, and cultured behavior. This school embodied the dual goals of Stalinist pedagogy: to control the individual's behavior by a strict regime of rules and to encourage the realization of individual productivity. Pupils internalized these rules and expectations and began to correct one another even in the absence of actions by teachers and the school director. The appearance, language, and behavior of pupils were subjected to constant observation, evaluation, and correction, all within the context of the Stalinist girls' school.[233]

Yet letters from girls also called attention to a level of practice sharply at odds with this disciplined space. By discussing their shared concerns with one another, inscribing their complaints in a collectively signed letter, and seeking possible publication in a national newspaper, these girls challenged the rigid constraints on public discourse enforced at the height of the postwar Stalinist dictatorship. Girls who denounced separate schools for excessive femininity had learned an important lesson from their Soviet education. By affirming an alternative vision of girls learning in a coeducational environment, these girls proclaimed that their interests would be better served by emphasizing what they had in common with boys. While leaving the underlying tensions unresolved, this determination to compete, achieve, and excel at the same level as boys in a coeducational setting remains perhaps the most significant lesson from the Soviet experiment with girls' schools.

The Problem of Order

Boys' Schools in Crisis

IN 1952, NINE YEARS after single-sex schooling was introduced, the Moscow city educational department heard this stark report on one boys' school:

> In school 558, during a physics lesson there is unbelievable noise, shouting during the lesson, and thus the complete absence of any kind of organization or order. As a result, pupils simply do not study physics at all. Or take the example of a teacher of foreign languages who works in conditions such that almost no one can ever hear her voice, so she has to shout all the time in order to quiet the pupils. I asked for her plan of work, and she said that no plan had been created: "It doesn't matter," she said, "we are not really even studying foreign languages in this lesson."[1]

Using terms like "alarming," "sickly," "abnormal," and "catastrophic" to characterize boys' schools the speaker, Peter Kholmogortsev, described one classroom so noisy that it was impossible to tell that a teacher was even present—until it became clear that the teacher's shouts were also part of the clamor. In another school characterized by "massive disciplinary violations," boys ran through the halls, whistling and shouting, yet the director seemed oblivious to the "unchecked avalanche" of commotion and disruption. While recognizing that many boys' schools were following "the correct path" by creating an orderly environment, Kholmogortsev also drew attention to schools where a virtual "civil war" was ongoing between teachers and male pupils, between those who wanted to impose order and those who sought by whatever means to evade or disrupt that order.[2]

In addition to demanding measures to strengthen discipline, improve instruction, and organize classrooms, Kholmogortsev also recommended transferring a number of teachers from girls' schools to boys' schools. Recognizing that such transfers would be "difficult," Kholmogortsev nevertheless argued that boys' schools had to be staffed with the best teachers who could handle the particular demands of disciplining and instructing male pupils.[3] Other speakers attending this meeting organized by the Moscow city education department echoed this call for transfers yet also called attention to the debilitating effects of teaching in boys' schools. One official, Lutskova, described an excellent woman teacher, Gordilenko, who taught literature in a boys' school and was very successful in her academic and disciplinary efforts. Before her first year was finished, however, she declared that she would quit rather than remain in a boys' school. Warning that many teachers suffered from nervousness and exhaustion, Lutskova declared that boys' school teachers should be "younger in age, more energetic, and primarily men, the majority of whom are now teaching in girls' schools."[4]

These statements transformed a seemingly disadvantageous situation in boys' schools into a relative advantage for boys. By creating disciplinary problems and failing to achieve at the desired levels, boys attracted the attention of school administrators, who responded by escalating disciplinary measures. But these officials also recommended that a scarce resource (experienced and effective teachers) be reallocated to boys' schools. By causing disruptions in classrooms, defying school authorities, and creating disorder in the hallways, boys were constructed not only as objects of disciplinary regimes but also as recipients of special pedagogical investments.[5] By contrast, girls who conformed to disciplinary and academic requirements stood to lose their best teachers. The failure of boys' schools, in other words, was being transformed into a loss inflicted on girls' schools. Separating the sexes had not provided a better education for boys and girls but, rather, had reproduced in another context—and thus legitimized and reinforced—the patterns of masculine privilege that structured gender inequality more generally in Soviet society.

An examination of Soviet boys' schools offers new perspectives on current theories and arguments about the advantages of single-sex schools in the United States and other countries. Focusing on the question of order, as in the examples cited above, demonstrates that discipline actually worsened in Soviet boys' classrooms, especially in a context where neither the infrastructure nor the teaching staff was adequate to meet additional demands. A careful examination of Soviet boys' schools also indicates that the expected benefits of fewer distractions, gender-specific pedagogy, and a more "masculine" environment were largely unrealized or ineffective. At the same time, more obviously harmful effects—some anticipated, others clearly unexpected—revealed deeper tensions between the emphasis on masculinity in schools and the ideological commitment to gender equality in Soviet society.[6]

Recent research has explored the meanings, practices, and implications of the complicated relationship between masculinity and education.[7] The "boy turn," in the phrase introduced by Marcus Weaver-Hightower,[8] is a further elaboration on efforts to understand gender-specific differences in academic achievement, social relations, and personal development.[9] Even as researchers began in the early 1990s to ask, "What about the girls?" other scholars have now asked, "What about the boys?" Both questions have the potential to enhance understanding of gender in schools, yet the latter approach has also generated considerable controversy. Some scholars pursue a research agenda of eliminating sexism by focusing on the more problematic behavior and attitudes of boys, but other advocates for boys can be openly hostile to the feminist research that has shaped this field and look instead for evidence of boys' disadvantages as a way to resist gender equity programs. While this polarization has attracted the most public attention, asking the question of how to educate boys has nevertheless yielded considerable insights into broader issues of student achievement, classroom organization, and pedagogical strategies.[10] By pursuing R. W. Connell's appeal for research on "gender arrangements in the midst of change,"[11] this analysis of the historical experience of Soviet boys' schools can deepen and broaden discussion of similar issues and perspectives today.

Focusing on boys' schools demonstrates how the imperatives of improving the education of boys shaped both the implementation of separate schools in 1943 and the restoration of coeducation in 1954. Even though girls' schools provoked certain kinds of criticism and dissatisfaction (as discussed in the previous chapter), boys' schools provoked much stronger criticisms (as suggested by the above comments by Kholmogortsev) and thus drove reform efforts. Despite a seemingly complete reversal in Soviet policies over an eleven-year period—from coeducation to single-sex schooling and back to coeducation—the one constant remained the ways that schools, in conjunction with other structural conditions, preserved and promoted masculine privilege.

Disciplining Boys

The 1943 decision to separate schools continued Soviet campaigns to discipline pupils. Measures implemented in prewar schools included strengthening the personal authority of teachers and directors, emphasizing pupils' collective responsibility to obey rules, maintaining daily records of pupils' transgressions, and punishments that included reprimands, demotions, isolation, and expulsions, depending on the severity of the violations.[12] The implementation of the "Rules for Pupil Behavior" in August 1943 signified intensifying efforts to regulate every behavior of each pupil at all times.[13] All these measures illustrated the escalating anxiety of policy makers, educators, and parents, yet they all seemed "gender neutral," with no explicit consideration of whether boys or girls were more or less at fault for discipline problems.[14] Separate schooling thus marked a dramatic shift in approach. Gender was now identified as both a cause for current problems and an instrument for desired changes.

Initial reports on separate classrooms emphasized the immediate improvements in discipline. One observer of the first Moscow experiments declared that prewar schools never saw the excellent discipline achieved with separate instruction.[15] Just three months after the school year began, however, Moscow school directors met to discuss "order and discipline" in boys' schools. Arnantov, from the Moscow city educational department, praised the leading schools and the best directors for "establishing firm school order and discipline," but he also charged that "discipline is on a very low level" in many boys' schools, as pupils were disorderly, lessons were noisy, homework was not finished, and other "crude violations of school rules" occurred frequently. At the end of the meeting, participants pledged to "mobilize the strength of teachers and all school organizations for the fortification of discipline in the school."[16] A different trajectory could be seen in a report that discipline initially declined in boys' schools, as pupils experienced "a feeling of confusion" and teachers revealed their "inability to deal with boys." Over the course of the first year, however, teachers learned how to handle male pupils, and a more demanding "style of work" emerged.[17] In a 1944 speech, minister of education Potemkin conceded that boys' schools failed "to establish the necessary discipline immediately," but by the end of the first year, "the situation had more or less evened out" and no longer provoked "any particular anxiety."[18]

Discipline remained a primary concern for educators, even as separate schooling led to increasingly sharp distinctions between girls and boys. While the former often appeared as models of exemplary deportment, appearance, and relations (as discussed in the previous chapter), boys were increasingly depicted in far more negative terms. Educational departments called for more attention to "the question of discipline," as "the behavior of pupils at many boys' schools is worse than in girls' schools," conduct was unsatisfactory "especially in boys' schools," disorder was "a more serious problem in boys' schools," and the greatest problem was "the unsatisfactory state of discipline in many boys' schools."[19]

This trend continued, and for the next decade the discussion of order in separate schools was really about disciplining boys. Describing boys' schools primarily in terms of disciplinary problems was a discursive practice that associated masculinity with disorder and disobedience, but also with the exercise of power and the assertion of privilege.[20] The end of coeducation enabled the misbehavior of boys, who were no longer "self-conscious" in front of girls.[21] In Penza, boys' school teachers declared that behavior was "significantly" worse than in coeducational schools before the 1943 decision, and thus discipline was "the primary and fundamental difficulty in the school."[22] Prokhorova, a Leningrad teacher with more than twenty years of experience, complained that two years of teaching in a boys' school led her to feel "extremely distressed," and she expressed the "unanimous" opinion of Leningrad educators that discipline was worse in boys' schools than in girls' schools.[23] Reports from educational officials, the Academy of Pedagogical Sciences, and even the Ministry of Education reached the same conclusion that discipline was "significantly worse" in boys' schools.[24] A 1951 report concluded: "One of the main reasons for inadequate achievement in many schools is *the unsatisfactory level of discipline, especially in boys' schools.*"[25]

Reports on boys' schools included examples of theft, smoking, fighting, cursing, vandalism, rude treatment of teachers, entire classes walking out during lessons without permission, frequent running in the hallways and staircases, noisy behavior in the entryway, and improper attitudes toward adults.[26] School director Gordunov declared that teachers felt directly threatened by pupils, as "extraordinary incidents," including violent assaults, had occurred in ten or more boys' schools in Moscow.[27] Knife attacks in or around schools were the most extreme acts attributed to the lack of discipline in boys' schools.[28] At Moscow boys' school No. 706, "one of the best pupils in the sixth grade" attacked another pupil with a knife, and although the wound was not serious, the victim went to the hospital. Speaking to his colleagues, the director conceded that both pupils were among the best in terms of both achievement and discipline, but conditions in the school had changed because enrollment had nearly doubled in less than a year.[29]

As boys' schools became virtually synonymous with disciplinary problems, they were discussed primarily, and sometimes seemingly exclusively, in negative terms. At a 1950 meeting, Moscow directors described discipline in boys' schools as "a serious question that is very disturbing to all," with "violations of basic rules of behaviors, standards, and order in the schools."[30] Director Liukhin complained that several meetings had been convened to address disorder in boys' schools, but "nothing concrete has been done," so teachers "cannot act decisively," and boys "do anything they want." According to Liukhin, when boys' school directors where asked, "How are things?" their most likely response was "The fight goes on," thus illustrating the sense of crisis permeating schools. Teachers routinely gave their classes "a pause," to allow them to "calm down," before undertaking any instructional activity.[31] When teacher Krein returned to a boys' school after teaching elsewhere, he thought there had been a fire or a pogrom, because his classroom was in such disrepair: "one-tenth of the windows were broken, the desks were mutilated."[32] In Ural'sk boys' school No. 6, classroom walls were torn up, desks were covered in knife marks, and windows were broken. Yet when pupils misbehaved, the school director and teachers did nothing, as "sheltering pranksters and hooligans was typical in this school."[33]

Parents echoed these perceptions of boys' schools. When a father visited his sons' schools, he encountered "such a din, with noise, shouting, and screeching" as soon as the classroom doors opened for recess.[34] Zaitov, whose sons were enrolled in Alma-Ata school No. 25, complained about the lack of discipline, the misbehavior of pupils, and even the cursing directed at teachers.[35] Parents at Leningrad boys' school No. 281 complained that the "hooligan behavior" of certain pupils had intimidated their sons into keeping silent about bad behavior at school. In response, two women teachers admitted that they could "do nothing" with the older pupils causing the trouble, and in turn they complained about the lack of support from district officials. Despite the director's promise to "take all measures," the disruptions continued, as pupils were beaten up, boys ran freely in classrooms, and teachers left classrooms unsupervised for long periods of time.[36]

This perception of boys' schools in disciplinary crisis persisted throughout the eleven-year experiment. In May 1954, a newspaper report described a Ural'sk school with a "bad reputation," where pupils assumed that the rules of behavior did not apply to them, and so they did whatever they wanted—wandered around the classroom, disobeyed the teacher, and even set fires in their desks, all without apparent punishment. In some grades, the worst-behaved boys ordered classmates to "boycott" teachers by refusing to answer questions, and their peers obeyed, even if it meant receiving lower grades. According to a published report, the inaction and helplessness of the school director and teachers allowed boys to threaten, intimidate, and even beat up their more obedient classmates, leading to parents' complaints that their sons were afraid to go to school.[37] The lurid description of these deficiencies in a published report as late as the spring of 1954 reveals the intractability of disciplinary problems in boys' schools. Yet this report did not ascribe these problems to the separation of boys and girls but instead blamed the lack of effective leadership by teachers and directors, thus indirectly calling into question the underlying premise that gender segregation would improve discipline.

Measures of Order

Widespread perceptions of disorder provoked demands for "a clear, concrete, and precise system," in the words of director Serova, to eliminate "delinquent" behavior.[38] Already in December 1943, boys' school directors offered "concrete proposals" for the "struggle for exemplary order."[39] Both published accounts and reports at meetings described necessary steps to achieve the desired order. Teachers were exhorted to work "more intensely" on establishing discipline, including using "more severe punishments."[40] In Moscow boys' school No. 470, pupils moved around the building with a good sense of order, lining up to leave the classroom, yielding to adults, keeping passageways clear, and obeying instructions properly. When asked if he liked this emphasis on order, one boy answered: "Of course, it will be useful later in life." In this school, according to an observer, order was maintained not by the director or the teachers but by pupils themselves, who organized meetings, assigned duties, and enforced the rules.[41]

Even formulaic reports with a transformational narrative, in which initial challenges were overcome by the determined, skilled, and persistent efforts of school authorities, began with the assumption that boys needed particular kinds of discipline.[42] In Nal'chik, a 1944 report on boys' schools described how teachers' conscientious and deliberate measures, including making pupils responsible for cleaning schools and maintaining grounds, ensured that discipline improved along with achievement. According to this report, pupils routinely greeted teachers by standing up and removing their hats.[43]

Other stories of transformation revealed a greater sense of desperation, as measures to enforce strict control became both a means and an end. Gor'kii educators pursued a particularly purposeful approach to the "especially difficult" problem of discipline: "From the very first day, the entire teachers' collective was mobilized, guards were posted in the hallways and lunchroom, and a unified order and unified demands were imposed." This intensified strategy brought the desired results, and soon schools reported "almost no violations of the rules."[44] According to Moscow director Liukhin, his entire school administration spent all day "at their posts," trying to maintain discipline in their overcrowded school. Even as he addressed a meeting at the Ministry of Education, Liukhin admitted: "I am thinking: what is happening at my school right now?"[45] Speaking to the same meeting, Khrushchev declared that boys' school directors were preoccupied with "police responsibilities" such as maintaining order and disciplining pupils.[46]

Disciplinary strategies often involved "creating order by watching over the school."[47] At Iaroslav school No. 3, boys remained under constant observation throughout the day. As a result of this pervasive accountability, more troubling behaviors such as theft, fighting, and truancy ceased, so that educators could deal with lesser infractions such as loitering, talking, and tardiness. An inspector's report combined a positive assessment of the current approach with warnings against any decrease in vigilance: "For a majority of pupils, it has become a habit to greet older comrades, yield the path, apologize, and express gratitude. As soon as control of pupils is weakened, violations of discipline and the established order resume."[48] A similar ideal of total discipline shaped efforts to teach male pupils to obey the "Rules of Behavior" even "in the absence of constant external controls."[49]

In the best boys' schools, according to a 1950 inspector's report, the disciplinary strategy was totalizing in both aspirations and implications:

> The way to achieve a high level of discipline is through a high ideological-political level of teaching, clarity and persistence of demands from the administration, unity, active efforts by pupils' organizations, help from teachers to maintain order, thoughtful efforts by class leaders, reasonable extracurricular activities for pupils, and work on an individual level with parents. Not a single incident in the school occurs without leaving some kind of trace—parents are immediately summoned, everything is uncovered, and both the pupil and the parents are educated.[50]

Improving discipline thus required an integrated approach that brought the full powers of administration, teachers, parents, and pupils' organizations to pursue this specific goal. The fact that "not a single incident" went uncorrected illustrates the totalizing aspirations of Stalinist disciplinary regimes. Yet the need for intensified control confirms the perception that lack of discipline in boys' schools was a crucial deficiency in separate schools.

Stricter disciplinary methods could also provoke new challenges, generate new forms of disobedience, and lead to even more desperate methods.[51] In some Moscow schools, teachers began to lock their classrooms immediately upon leaving, making sure that no pupils were left behind, and then unlocking the room to allow pupils into the next lesson. This practice created occasional problems when teachers forgot their keys, but it also generated resistance by pupils. If a boy jammed a coin into the keyhole, for example, the entire lesson would be spent waiting for the locksmith, or if a pupil found a spare key, then all the classrooms might be unlocked. According to inspector Kholmogortsev, "this whole absurd system encourage[d] pupils to engage in all sorts of crimes."[52] Boys' school directors and teachers were also criticized if they grabbed children or forced them to stand at attention, thus violating Soviet prohibitions on corporal or humiliating punishments.[53]

Whereas reports on girls' schools frequently commented on the clean, attractive, and consistent appearance of pupils and facilities, only a few boys' schools received similarly positive attention. A February 1944 report on Moscow boys' school No. 358 began, like many accounts of girls' schools, by emphasizing the sense of order, cleanliness, and calm: pupils walked through hallways without lots of shouting or unnecessary movement, good order in the building "signified that pupils were disciplined," children treated adults with appropriate deference, and clothing was clean and tidy.[54] "Complete quiet" prevailed during lessons. In a ninth-grade math classroom, twenty boys worked diligently on problems set by their teacher, who went beyond textbook requirements to make pupils think for themselves. When they got the right answer, their faces would "light up," as an atmosphere of "successful work" enveloped the classroom. A physics lesson, taught by a woman teacher, provided examples of electrical wiring in an apartment; pupils responded conscientiously and enthusiastically, for they understood the importance of applied electrical mechanics. A chemistry lesson included descriptions of explosives and gas masks. In a history classroom, the traditional impassive narrative of events yielded to lively stories about battles, the examination of maps, and tales of border guards. The cited examples of poor discipline were strikingly minor: one pupil wearing street shoes in a hallway and one pupil throwing sunflower seeds on the floor. Discipline was "real, strong, and judicious," under the "inexorable, severe, and demanding" supervision of director V. S. Konovalova. Pupils knew that they would be punished for any transgression, but they also knew the punishment would be appropriate and fair. Thus, the student who forgot to remove his shoes was banned from the sports hall for three days, and the student who threw sunflower seeds had to pick them up himself. Encouragement, rather than punishment, was the preferred method for cultivating proper behavior and thus creating "a real *boys'* school."[55]

A later account of comparably positive experiences emerged in a report on Tashkent boys' school No. 18, which had the "extraordinary" distinction of having "no serious violations of discipline" during the 1951/1952 school year. Teachers paid careful attention to where pupils were seated, making sure they were constantly visible, and exerted a positive influence on each other. Pupils and teachers were always punctual, to ensure that every minute of working time was valued. A "businesslike silence" persisted throughout the day. During recesses, strictly enforced rules confined running to the courtyard, prevented acts of bullying, and kept all pupils under surveillance by teachers. Every week, teachers met with almost a thousand parents, grandparents, and other relatives seeking advice about the behavior and achievements of boys. Teachers also visited pupils' homes, so they could, in the words of director Sdobnikov, "individualize" their approach. Yet even in this exemplary school, pupils did not always live up to these high expectations: they moved around freely in the classroom, chatting with one another and ignoring the teacher, thus revealing a lack of self-control. Despite these problems, the school director and teachers earned praise because achievement levels were high, lessons were organized, and boys were behaving according to communist standards.[56]

7—Teacher Maria Maliutina teaches a geography lesson in Moscow boys' school No. 135. Soviet Information Bureau photograph, Davis Center, Harvard College Library.

Some descriptions of disciplinary methods suggested a complex relationship between masculinity and order. Moscow teacher E. A. Parsanova described how her second-grade boys decorated their classroom with flowers, put up busts of Stalin as well as nineteenth-century military leaders, washed windows, posted school rules, and placed rags to clean the blackboard in little bags. These steps, which encompassed "everything necessary, however trifling," provoked "real satisfaction" among pupils. Some of the most difficult pupils contributed to creating "this celebratory appearance," thus demonstrating (at least according to their teacher) their eagerness to be part of the collective. Pupils who understood responsibility for maintaining order began to reprimand one another for violations of rules. As evidence of how pupils internalized this pedagogical mission, a mother thanked Parsanova for rescuing her son "from the street," so that "whatever you say in class, he does it all."[57]

Boys' schools thus prompted a range of disciplinary strategies, including those that revised, rather than reinforced, the borders of masculinity. Moscow boys' school director Gogoleva expected pupils to become her "most trusted helpers" in maintaining the school building. Rather than being "a captain standing on the bridge," whose main concern was discipline, Gogoleva affirmed the goal of a collective working well together on common tasks.[58] One of the most successful teachers in a boys' school was cited as proof that the best teachers must "love the school, love children, and live according to the interests of pupils."[59] These accounts emphasized, rather than intensifying surveillance or escalating sanctions, the productive outcomes of a nurturing pedagogy.[60] Photographs of women teachers offering lessons in geography or science, like those of Maria Maliutina in Moscow boys' school No. 35 (figure 7) and of an unnamed teacher in a senior-level chemistry class (figure 8), juxtaposed the femininity of women teachers with the masculinity of their subjects. Even as they offered a romanticized view of engaged learning, these images were seemingly at odds with the effort to make boys' schools more masculine.

Other accounts illustrated the broad range of desirable behaviors exhibited by male pupils. A 1951 article praised a pupil for assuming all the responsibility for housework while his mother worked: "It's nothing, I can do it all," he told his grateful mother.[61] Boys also earned praise when

8—A teacher with senior-level pupils in a chemistry laboratory. Soviet Information Bureau photograph, Davis Center, Harvard College Library.

they assumed jobs, such as preparing the classroom for lessons or cleaning up school facilities, that had, in the coeducational school, been performed mostly by girls.[62] According to other reports, "even boys" were cleaning classrooms and other school facilities, which were jobs that had "previously been borne exclusively by girls."[63] This praise for the conscientious behavior of boys was striking, however, because it assumed that cleaning the school was the responsibility of girls, whereas only the absence of girls led boys to assume responsibility for these undesirable tasks. Given the primary emphasis in boys' schools on the preparation of fighters with traits such as courage, determination, and strength, it seemed unlikely that much positive value would accrue from decorating classrooms or cleaning school facilities, at least as long as these were still seen as "women's work."

As with girls' schools cited in the previous chapter, some boys' schools conveyed a sense of order through pupils' exemplary appearance (see figure 9). At Moscow boys' school No. 218, all pupils had neat haircuts and clean collars (which they washed and ironed themselves).[64] In "tidy" boys' schools in Leningrad, clean faces and red Pioneer neckties symbolized "mutual respect and trust." Boys' school No. 82 had "good external order," pupils respected school property, furniture was not broken, walls were clean, and library books were in good condition.[65] Using terms more commonly applied to a girls' school, a newspaper praised Tashkent boys' school No. 98 for being bright, comfortable, and attractive.[66]

Photographs of pupils working diligently and listening attentively at their desks reinforced claims that masculinity could be disciplined effectively in a separate school, yet descriptions of disorderly pupils and messy schools undermined these more positive images. In a Moscow boys' school, "absolute filth" precluded any kind of effective instruction.[67] According to teacher Aramian, male pupils came to school "in slovenly clothes, without even brushing their hair," a practice that would "never happen" in a coeducational school. The deteriorating standards for appearance were associated with problem behaviors, as these same pupils were late for lessons, skipped school, did not complete homework, and engaged in hooligan behaviors.[68] Moscow boys' school director Serova complained in 1954 that her school was in a terrible state, with "nothing that is educational," as all the desks were ruined and classrooms lacked decorations. After observing many boys' schools, Serova admitted that just one "made a positive impression on me," mostly because some maps were posted on walls.[69] In the Ural'sk boys' school with the "bad reputation" cited above, criticism of undisciplined behavior was amplified by descriptions

9—Pupils in boys' schools. (Top): Ninth-grade pupils, Moscow boys' school No. 135. Soviet Information Bureau photograph, Davis Center, Harvard College Library. (Center): First-grade pupils, Moscow school No. 172. Soviet Information Bureau photograph, Davis Center, Harvard College Library. (Bottom): "Pervye shkol'nye gody," *SSSR na stroike* 4 (1949): 7.

of broken windows, vandalized desks, and other problems that made classrooms seemingly unsuitable for any effective teaching.[70]

Disciplining Masculinity

As discussed in the second chapter, neither published reports nor archival materials provided extensive discussion of how perceptions of psychological differences actually shaped teaching and learning in separate schools. In a 1947 report, however, an inspector complained that "poor knowledge" of masculine development prevented some teachers in a Gor'kii boys' school from providing an appropriate education. This evaluation was illustrated by a comparison of two women teachers, Ovchinnikova and Pasternak. While teaching pupils in grades five, six, and seven, Ovchinnikova cultivated a warm relationship with pupils, who "responded eagerly," studied successfully, and were disciplined. But as the years went by, Ovchinnikova did not change her methods, as she used diminutives with boys, such as "sweet dears" and "dear little children," even patting them on the head. Ovchinnikova did not notice that her "little children" were increasingly rough (some had even taken up smoking), were laughing at her, and were no longer showing any signs of affection: "they do not follow her to the theatre or crowd around her at recess." Whereas Ovchinnikova failed to adapt as pupils matured, her colleague Pasternak "made a serious study of the psychology and physiology of boys." Although elementary pupils saw Pasternak as "a strict teacher to be feared," older pupils appreciated that she knew them well, understood their "interests and particularities," and directed them "on the path to become an honest Soviet man."[71]

Although the main point of criticism of Ovchinnikova and praise for Pasternak was to illustrate the need for teachers to understand pupils as a means of controlling them, this report also obscured the chronology of separate schooling. If the pupils of Ovchinnikova and Pasternak were in the eighth grade in 1946/1947, then this transition from successful, obedient, and affectionate "little dears" to rude, physical, and disobedient youth, on the one hand, or from boys frightened of a strict teacher to adolescents appreciating a teacher's close attention, occurred in the very same years as the transition to separate schools. The sequence described in these two examples was thus suggestive of a broader pattern, as initial improvements in discipline following the separation of pupils were not sustained, except where rigorous and expert teachers maintained tight control. Rather than acknowledge that separation of schools may have contributed to these patterns, this report focused on the skills of teachers, in particular, and on the need for more understanding of adolescent psychology, in general, to explain changes in behavior, attitudes, and relationships.

The transformative power of exemplary teachers could also be seen in the article cited above by Parsanova, who described the rehabilitation of a troublemaker identified only by his initial, K. According to Parsanova, this second-grade pupil behaved very badly, as he made lots of noise, disrupted lessons, defied teachers, beat up classmates, smoked, gambled, swore, stole school property, and was frequently arrested. As Parsanova began to impose order, in part by making pupils responsible for their classmates' transgressions, pupil K began to behave in more desirable ways, including decorating the classroom and helping to compile an album in honor of the Soviet army. Most important, according to Parsanova, K understood the imperative to earn acceptance from classmates and the teacher before he could be included in the collective.[72]

This narrative of disobedience, discipline, obedience, and redemption illustrated the broader promises and potential of Stalinist pedagogy. This 1945 article was remarkable, however, because it simply ignored the issue of gender separation. Neither the behavior of the pupil nor the approach of the teacher was connected to separate schooling. The key to this redemptive process, according to Parsanova, was the "sensitive, maternal attitude of the teacher toward the children," along with engaging lessons, a range of assignments, and especially interesting stories. The emphasis on the maternal approach of a woman teacher in a boys' schools seems inconsistent with more emphatic demands for "police responsibilities," as cited above. Although this difference could reflect the fact that Parsanova was teaching second-grade pupils, who were younger than the problem boys provoking the most concerns, this silence illustrates how gender-specific elements could be subordinated to the imperative of disciplining boys.

As discipline became the central preoccupation of the schools, boys were defined primarily as objects of the school's disciplinary regime. Both "negative" accounts of disciplinary "problems" and "positive" accounts of "successful" discipline shared—and reinforced—a consensus view of masculinity that was inseparable from the gender and disciplinary regimes of the school. In a 1951 resolution passed by Moscow teachers, the only reference to separate schools dealt with discipline problems specifically in boys' schools.[73] In a 1950 report from the Leningrad educational department, a few positive examples of orderly boys' schools were cited precisely to refute the "theory" that it was "impossible" to maintain order in boys' schools.[74]

Educational officials conceded that boys' schools grew worse, not better, each year. According to educator Kholmogortsev, whose critical comments were cited at the beginning of this chapter, schoolteachers, public officials, and even Communist Party leaders acknowledged that "the situation in boys' schools was becoming more unfavorable with each passing year."[75] In a sweeping statement, a 1953 article declared: "There is not a single teacher in the country who would not say with alarm that discipline in most boys' schools is broken and it is difficult to work there."[76] The failure of boys' schools to deliver improved discipline would ultimately undermine the policy of separate schooling.

Outlets for Boys

Confronted by this growing crisis in boys' schools, educators searched for appropriate and effective methods to manage male pupils. Creating opportunities to play games, work with technology, and engage in physical activities were common strategies. Frequent statements that boys' schools needed technology clubs or crafts rooms illustrate how taken-for-granted assumptions about masculine interests shaped allocation of space, the activities of pupils, and purposes of schooling.[77] In Nal'chik boys' schools, students' circles were organized for the manufacture of physics instruments and for the repair of school furniture. Druzhinin enriched physics lessons by guiding students' efforts in building tables, collecting equipment, and repairing desks.[78] According to director Bessanova, male pupils helped to assemble radio equipment for girls' schools, thus reinforcing assumptions about boys' technological skills.[79]

Radio transmitters and receivers were in particular demand, as the interests of boys followed advances in communications technology. The Moscow educational department promised a radio transmitter for every boys' school.[80] Yet the pragmatic efforts of educators encountered the impoverished conditions of postwar schools. Most boys' schools lacked the necessary resources, including equipment, facilities, and qualified supervisors. Directors complained that even though most male pupils "love technology," their schools lacked the resources and facilities to satisfy this demand. Many educators cited the lack of such outlets for boys' interests in technology as a major contribution to worsening discipline.[81]

Chess and other games also provided for the release of the presumed masculine need for competition.[82] School director Serova described how some especially difficult boys began to play board games after school: "They became ennobled under our influence, and they began to talk with us as friends and no longer saw us as enemies."[83] As with the attention to technology, an underlying assumption about boys' innate characteristics led schools to adopt gender-specific programs. This emphasis on competition was restricted to extracurricular activities, with no suggestion of changes in the curriculum or classroom.

These assumptions about the inherent needs of boys also found expression in the widespread belief that boys' schools needed more outlets for physical activities. Reports referred to boys as "lively and loud" and possessing "greater mobility," thus requiring "physical releases" into "correct channels," which would in turn produce "hardened, physically strong, and patriotically minded young men."[84] Physical exercise was thus perceived as an essential and highly effective measure to improve discipline, by ensuring that "boys have a place to get some release."[85] In Moscow school No. 358, physical activities such as gymnastics, skiing, and target shooting made pupils more interested in their school. The director of physical education, who was also the military instructor, demanded "strict discipline" and "unconditional obedience" from a "friendly collective" of pupils.[86] Particularly during the war years, physical education and sports competitions were designed to prepare boys to become "good fighting men."[87]

The need for additional space in boys' schools for both military training and physical activities received particular attention. Boys' schools were supposed to have gymnasiums, which many schools (more than fifty, according to a 1953 report) created by demolishing the walls between classrooms to create larger spaces.[88] Director Mostovoi declared that if boys had "more space," they would refrain from destructive actions, such as breaking windows.[89] These claims reinforced widespread perceptions that boys' schools were materially deprived. One Moscow educator complained that girls' schools had "everything necessary," while boys' schools were "on the verge of collapse."[90] Director Krein declared, "I am not against having well-equipped girls' schools, but it does not have to be this way."[91] More pointedly, another school director declared unequivocally at a 1950 meeting: "Without a doubt, boys' schools should be much better equipped than girls' schools."[92]

These complaints illustrate how separate schools reinforced structures of gender inequity. Invoking disorder in boys' schools to justify reallocating resources away from girls' schools confirmed the broader system of male privilege in Soviet society. Indirect confirmation of this pattern came in a 1953 Ministry of Education complaint that "preferential attention to boys' schools" had not only failed to produce desired results but had "inappropriately" distracted attention away from girls' schools.[93]

Embedded in all these discussions, of course, was the question of whether these problems were the result of creating separate boys' schools or a consequence of general school conditions, with gender exerting only a minor, or perhaps even insignificant, influence.[94] A 1951 report asserted that "many deficiencies" in schools, "and particularly in boys' schools," do not result "from the very essence of separate education" but, rather, were the result of overburdened school buildings, the lack of trained teachers, and insufficient methods.[95] This report thus blamed problems in boys' schools on structural conditions, rather than on any aspect of gender-separated schooling. As will be seen in the next chapters, however, many educators, as well as parents and pupils, came to see the system of separate schools as the cause for many of the problems—and the restoration of coeducation as the best cure for these same deficiencies.

Constructing Masculinity

The practices of boys' schools emerged in a dialectical relationship with masculinity, as assumptions about boys shaped, and were shaped by, the kinds of education offered in separate schools.[96] Director Tiapkin, of boys' school No. 32 in Rostov-on-Don, stated that the education of "young Soviet males in a boys' school should have its own specific character." A boy needed to develop traits such as discipline, hardiness, and dexterity, as well as other qualities that would make him "a good subordinate and an excellent leader." These outcomes could be realized in a school where order was strict, the tone was correct, the demands on pupils were consistent, and discipline was good.[97] Male pupils earned praise for neat clothing, good behavior, and "active and conscious" discipline in and out of the school, as the practices of boys should adhere to cultural norms of masculinity, including "the qualities of a man and the qualities of a fully valued Soviet citizen and patriot."[98]

According to Timofeev, schools offering activities such as technology clubs, gymnastics, and military training, all accompanied by "practical works, experiences, and devices designed by the pupils themselves," produced "exceptionally positive results." Boys "are so carried away that they lose track of the time and express heated dissatisfaction when they hear the bell that announces the end of the lesson." Without specifying what, if any, personal experiences or classroom observations provided the basis for such claims, Timofeev nevertheless asserted that these positive outcomes resulted when "the teacher considers boys' psychological particularities: liveliness, energy, dexterity, organizational particularities, and more." Echoing the heroic narratives cited above, Timofeev promised that this pedagogical approach would transform "disorganizers" into "the best" pupils, "enthusiasts in their academic work."[99]

Extending this emphasis beyond sports, the military, and technology, Timofeev called on teachers to acknowledge boys' "particular interest in heroism, and demonstrations of courage, bravery, and so on." History and geography lessons should emphasize great individuals who "clearly demonstrate the heroism of the Soviet people." Boys would "strive to complete the same accomplishments" and become as "persistent and fearless" as soldiers fighting against Germany. Calling for schools to develop "capacities and characteristics that are boys' natural traits," Timofeev emphasized the need to "educate our male pupils with the qualities of a Soviet man."[100]

Even as he offered these idealized statements, Timofeev acknowledged that boys' schools, more than girls' schools, tolerated deficiencies in pupils' attitudes and behavior, including "lack of discipline, disorganization, laziness, slovenliness, irresponsibility, perversions of friendship and comradeship, especially toward people of the opposite sex, occasional acts of hooliganism, and more." These attitudes found "concrete expressions" in "sharpness, crudeness, carelessness, disorganization, and indiscipline," as well as "poor achievement, absence of order, organization, and discipline, litter and dirt in the classrooms, slovenly clothing, occasional swearing, smoking, fighting, disobedience, poor completion of homework assignments, and more."[101] These remarkable lists of negative traits, behaviors, and attitudes illustrated the complicated relationship between masculinity and education, as both the preferred and the lamentable attributes imagined among boys proved just as powerful as observed and experienced behaviors in boys' schools.

Most descriptions of boys' activities adhered to these normative masculine identities, but in exceptional cases, separate schools did facilitate behaviors that cut across gender boundaries. Whereas, in coeducational schools, girls dominated singing, drama, or dancing ensembles, the separation of schools encouraged the formation of boys' choirs, to the evident pleasure of directors, who praised the gender homogeneity of performers and audience.[102] Just as female pupils took on new roles and responsibilities in girls' schools (as discussed in the previous chapter), at least some male pupils pursued interests that transcended usual gender categories.[103] As the next section argues, however, these tendencies were neither as durable nor as pervasive as the prevailing trend toward forms of masculinity that emphasized discipline and order.

The Problem of Cadres

Echoing the opinion that only the best teachers could teach boys, some school directors declared that their teachers preferred working with male pupils. One director announced that none of her teachers would even consider working in girls' schools.[104] These generalizations about teaching boys were often illustrated by the contrasts drawn with female pupils. A Moscow researcher reported that boys spoke more "freely" and did not require the prompting that girls expected.[105] Expressing a more negative view, a Penza teacher stated that boys lacked desirably feminine traits such as diligence, discipline, neatness, and conscientiousness.[106] Moscow girls' school director Mart'ianova complained that boys were "somewhat undisciplined," as shown by a male pupil who whistled at her when she was invited to speak at a joint event.[107]

Similar assumptions shaped accounts of desirable teaching methods. Moscow boys' school director Gorbunov warned that even the most qualified and experienced teachers had trouble maintaining order if they did not understand that "boys love a strong-willed teacher, boys love to work at a fast tempo, boys love for the teacher to be a conductor and not to leave any pupils without activity; when a boy finishes a task, give him something else to do." According to Gorbunov, pupils might approach more sensitive teachers "with all kinds of personal matters, emotional things, and so on," but these teachers were actually contributing to the deteriorating conditions in boys' schools.[108]

Gorbunov's appeal for "a strong-willed teacher" was frequently echoed by other educators. Moscow director Liukhin stated that it did not matter whether teachers were men or women, "but they should be strong-willed cadres."[109] The Moscow educational department recommended that boys' school directors be "strong-willed people who are knowledgeable about their work," while teachers should "possess the necessary qualities of strong will and organizational ability."[110] In Uzbekistan, "firm and strong-willed teachers" were supposed to be assigned to boys' schools.[111] According to Gorbunov, "even the most qualified, most respected, and most beloved" teachers would have bad discipline "if they did not possess a strong will."[112] The desired qualities of boys' school teachers often involved the negation of traits attributed to girls' school teachers, as in the example of a woman mathematics teacher who taught very well but had a "weak character" and a "gentle nature," and "naturally she turned out to completely unsuited for a boys' school."[113]

These assumptions about the "particular traits" led to demands that the "best" teachers and school directors be assigned to boys' schools, as seen in the proposals cited at the beginning of this chapter.[114] The Moscow educational department recommended that new teachers assigned to boys' schools be the best pedagogical students who possess the necessary "organizational and strong-willed qualities."[115] The common perception among educators, according to one report, was that the boys' school teacher should be "a highly cultured person," with a "lively interest" in current politics, who can "respond to the demands of male pupils." Yet after citing these criteria, inspector L'vov immediately declared that the "requirements" of teachers in boys' schools were also "absolutely necessary" for teachers in girls' schools.[116] Already in August 1943, "some educational officials" in Leningrad were criticized for "the tendency to transfer the best teachers to boys' schools." This approach was called "incorrect," because "girls' and boys' schools provide an equal amount of knowledge to pupils, and the quality of instruction and upbringing should be at the same level in both."[117] Yet seven years later, boys' school directors continued to request that the strongest cadres be assigned to their schools.[118]

As the problems of boys' schools became increasingly obvious, the selection of teachers and school directors emerged as a common explanation for persistent and pervasive problems. Some reports suggested that gender should be one factor, but not the only and certainly not the most important one, involved in appointing staff to boys' schools. According to a 1951 report, many educational departments failed to consider the ways that gender as well as personal character determined the suitability of teachers for different schools.[119] According to inspector Kholmogortsev, when schools were first separated, the teachers were approximately equal in quality, but as more boys' schools opened, they were mostly staffed with new trainees lacking experience or with teachers transferred from elsewhere. As a result, staffing of boys' schools was lower quality than in girls' schools.[120] The 1951 report cited above stated bluntly that "the best teachers" worked in girls' schools.[121] In 1954, director Verbitskii complained that boys' schools "did not have good teachers," which contributed to poor discipline and weak achievement.[122]

In spite of the policy adopted in 1943, boys' schools had difficulty appointing and retaining men as directors. A 1951 report complained about the failure to appoint "qualified and strong-willed" school directors, "recruited from men teachers."[123] By 1954, sixty-nine Moscow boys' schools, approximately one-quarter of the total, had women as directors.[124] According to educator Piun, this policy failed because of the shortage of men qualified and able to serve as directors and also because "experience demonstrates" that many women were "no worse, and in many cases even better" than men.[125]

Assertions that the "best teachers" should work in boys' schools built upon, but also reinforced, perceptions that teaching staffs were "weaker" in girls' schools.[126] Moscow director Khrushchev, whose dismissive comments about teaching in a girls' school were cited in the previous chapter, declared that boys' schools needed "good, strong cadres," and while he conceded that girls' schools had some good teachers, even the best girls' school teachers lacked the "moral firmness" needed in boys' schools.[127] The spread of these attitudes was revealed in the comment that a teacher who could not cope with boys might be told, "Go work in a girls' school."[128] Teachers in boys' schools came to see girls' schools as a kind of "health resort," where "second-rate" teachers found that conditions were "easier."[129] Even as L'vov condemned as "fantastic" and "completely false" the opinion that it was easier to teach in girls' schools,[130] this same perception was confirmed in directors' statements that teaching in boys' schools was so much more difficult "that there is no comparison" with girls' schools, that "it is clear to all of us that working in a boys' school is more difficult," that "it is more difficult to maintain discipline in a boys' school," and that it was "very difficult" to teach in a boys' school, where "many of our best teachers have turned into invalids."[131]

This perception found a more affirmative expression in the claim that the best teachers actually preferred to work in boys' schools. Moscow director Mostovoi declared in 1950 that most of his teachers would not want to be transferred to a girls' school.[132] According to another boys' school director, none of the more dedicated and responsible teachers would willingly work in a girls' school.[133] Some teachers preferred to work with boys, because "you can do anything with boys."[134] First-year physics teacher Kondrat'ev in Penza stated that boys "have a more practical way of grasping the material" and were more likely than girls to ask interesting questions.[135] Many teachers conceded that working with boys was more difficult, because of the challenge of maintaining discipline, but many teachers found these schools more interesting, because boys were intellectually more curious.[136] In April 1954, educator Kul'nitskaia agreed with those who complained about the difficulties of teaching boys, yet her own experience working with male pupils convinced her that she would not want to work in a girls' school.[137] In early 1943, during the first Moscow experiments, some teachers preferred working with boys, who were "more lively" and "absorbed" in their studies.[138] Moscow director Pavlenko said that, of his forty years of teaching, "the best years have been when I worked with boys."[139] School director Khrushchev conceded that girls' schools were much quieter—making it seem as if the pupils were "on a deserted island"—but then he stated his preference for the "inquisitive, energetic, and mobile" character of boys. Drawing on his four of years teaching physics in a girls' school, Khrushchev pointedly questioned teachers who worked in similar conditions: "You know, by the end of my fourth year of teaching in a girls' school, I had reached the point of prostration. I thought that my abilities as a teacher had been lost. There they do not smash the lightbulbs, but there is whispering, the writing of notes, there is what you know takes place in girls' schools." Declaring that he would not work in a girls' school "for any amount of money," Khrushchev went so far as to question the integrity of a teacher who "avoided the robust work of the boys' school to pursue the seemingly easy life in a girls' school—I do not approve of this teacher's conduct."[140]

The most important issue related to staffing boys' schools, however, was the widespread and determined effort by teachers to avoid these assignments. At the end of 1943, just a few months into the new school year, some teachers had already expressed their fear of boys' schools.[141] In the Bashkir region, many women teachers assigned to boys' schools immediately requested transfers to girls' schools.[142] Later reports warned that good teachers were trying to leave boys' schools "under any pretense," usually because of the difficulty of maintaining discipline.[143] A 1951 report on the increasing "pull" of teachers away from boys' schools cited the increasing, rather than diminishing, obstacles to the recruitment and retention of teachers.[144]

Efforts to get the best teachers were thus obstructed by teachers themselves, as those with the most experience either refused to work in boys' schools or tried to leave for coeducational or girls' schools.[145] In the

Altai region, "many teachers [were] afraid to work in boys' schools, and in some cases they requested transfers to girls' schools."[146] Moscow boys' school teacher Amosov made his feelings quite clear: "I would like to be transferred to a different school, because I can't do anything with these pupils."[147] A 1953 article referred to the "spontaneous rush" of teachers to girls' schools, in spite of "the repeated strengthening of boys' schools by transfers of experienced and strong-willed teachers."[148] In 1950, school director Krein asked, if the best teachers were transferred to girls' or coeducational schools, "who will be left to work in boys' schools?"[149]

Repeated complaints about the shortage of experienced teachers in boys' schools further indicate that the negatives outweighed the positives in this category of schools.[150] In 1950, more than one-half of teachers at a boys' school were in their first or second year of teaching; Moscow boys' school director Verbitskii declared that the "great majority" of the eighty teachers in his school had "very little experience."[151] Complaints about teachers often linked inexperience to ineffectiveness. A 1951 report by the Academy of Pedagogical Sciences included the statement that "often those teachers with less experience are working in boys' schools," which contributed to their "extremely unfavorable" situation.[152] Moscow boys' school No. 151 had seventeen "young teachers," two of whom had already been replaced due to "complete maladjustment."[153] Moscow director Rogovskaia reported that most of her twelve new teachers could not maintain discipline, and three teachers would immediately need to be replaced.[154] "Bunches of young teachers" were sent to boys' schools, where they were often assigned to "the most difficult classes, the fifth grade."[155] Director Bessanova complained that young teachers were "completely unprepared" for teaching, and she cited the "lack of training of young cadres," particularly regarding "the psychology of the adolescent boy," as contributing to difficulties in boys' schools.[156] Moscow director Khrushchev denounced graduates of pedagogical institutes as "simply ridiculous," lacking basic literacy or teaching skills.[157]

Yet criticism of boys' school teachers was not limited to young and inexperienced cadres. During the first year of separate schooling, a regional educational department warned that many teachers in boys' schools could not provide the "strong leadership" needed to maintain "discipline and order."[158] In a Sverdlovsk school, "not all teachers were appropriate for boys' schools."[159] Of the thirty-five teachers in another boys' school, almost one-quarter were judged to be barely competent. When school director Krein inspected one classroom, he wrote, "What a nightmare," as the teacher came in, "hid in a corner," and did not know what to do with the children.[160] Krein ended a strong plea for better staffing, stronger teachers, and more support by warning that everyone was "holding on tight," hoping that "the windows are not all smashed."[161]

These concerns about inexperienced and ineffective teachers led to further erosion of gender boundaries, as men lacked both the numbers and the abilities to meet the demands of teaching in boys' schools. The education department in the Riazan region assigned "women teachers possessing firm and decisive personalities" to boys' schools.[162] In Moscow boys' school No. 330, just six of seventy teachers were men.[163] In many cases, teaching staffs with many women earned praise from officials. In Nal'chik, a list of seven teachers effectively managing all-male classrooms included at least five women.[164] In Gor'kii, a report on discipline in boys' schools criticized two women and two men for allowing violations of discipline in their classrooms and praised four women for excellent methods and strict discipline.[165] In 1954 director Mostovoi stated that, when his school was converted to a boys' school, he kept his "female staff" (only nine men, among more than fifty teachers), despite a "rebuke" from the district educational department, yet his school was "on a firm footing" from the very first days.[166]

Excellent women teachers also earned praise for their work in boys' schools. In the report cited above, Mostovoi praised a woman teacher, Konchalovskaia, for maintaining excellent discipline.[167] Moscow teacher Godiaeva had a difficult first year in a boys' school, but over time she earned the respect of male pupils.[168] In Tashkent boys' school No. 98, honored teacher E. P. Leont'eva effectively taught first-grade pupils to acquire literacy skills and labor discipline.[169] In Fergana, a decorated woman teacher, Aleksandra Iakovlevna Begunova, looked over her boys "with a demanding eye," while her colleague Orzhevskaia demanded a high level of knowledge and skill.[170] Their boys' school actually had a majority of women teachers, whose qualifications, passion, and dedication, under the supervision of male school leaders, ensured a high level of discipline.[171] In Novosibirsk, Mariia Feliksovna Monenko taught literature so successfully that many graduates pursued this field into higher education. Monenko maintained close relations with all twenty-six graduates of the previous year, who wrote letters conveying "the most secret and intimate thoughts, which can be shared only with close friends."[172] Monenko thus transcended multiple gender boundaries: she was a woman teacher in a boys' school, whose pupils became passionate about a "feminine" subject like literature, and who reciprocated by maintaining nurturing relations with former pupils.[173]

Not all stories of struggle, endurance, and accomplishment were endowed with the same "heroic" narrative. School director Zolotova recalled working for two years in a coeducational school. When the new policy was implemented in 1943, enrollment suddenly grew to 1,200 boys, and she was appointed as the director (despite having no experience). In a strikingly modest phrase, she summarized her experience over the last decade in the simple statement: "I managed."[174] Zolotova's perspective confirmed that whatever policies and principles may have been in effect, the assignment of school directors as well as teachers often depended on availability, regardless of gender.

Teachers and directors deemed unsuited for boys' schools were often transferred to girls' schools. In Moscow boys' school No. 330, where women made up more than 90 percent of teachers, as cited above, some men teachers had been "exchanged" for better women teachers.[175] In 1952, the Moscow educational department recommended the transfer *to* boys' school teachers of as many as three hundred of "the best teachers," and transfer *from* boys' schools of teachers "who are not managing the discipline and organization of classes."[176] The latter strategy was presented more bluntly in a 1953 Ministry of Education statement that "teachers clearly unable to maintain discipline in boys' schools should be transferred to work in girls' schools."[177]

While educators recognized that it was much easier to call for transfers than actually to find experienced and effective teachers willing to work in boys' schools, they rarely addressed the fact that such a strategy would have a negative impact on girls' and coeducational schools by replacing the most experienced and effective teachers with the least experienced and effective teachers. One exception to this silence was Mostovoi's statement at a meeting that transferring teachers to boys' schools "should be done in ways that do not harm girls' schools."[178]

The complicated relationship between teachers' gender and their work in separate schools found expression in a Bashkir educational department report on how teachers, including women who had initially requested transfers to girls' schools, "adapted" to boys' schools: "Experience showed that if the teacher possesses the necessary strong-willed virtues, then work in the boys' school will be within the teacher's own powers and interesting, regardless of sex." Noting that even some men were "incapable" of maintaining discipline in all-girls' classrooms, the report offered this "conclusion" based on observed practices: "a good teacher, whether a man or a woman, works well in either a boys' or a girls' school; a bad one is bad everywhere."[179] This report provided a striking inversion of the presumed association between the gender of teachers and the gender of pupils. Not only did the claims that any teacher could discipline male pupils, and that even some men teachers could not discipline female pupils, reverse the usual associations and assumptions, but the statement "regardless of sex" actually undercut the basic premise of separate schools—that gender was the most important boundary in schools.

Gendered assumptions about masculinity in education thus led to diametrically opposed conclusions. Proponents like Kul'nitskaia, Serova, Pavlenko, Kondrat'ev, Tiapkin, Gorbunov, and Khrushchev transformed the challenges of teaching boys into an affirmative case for separate schools, but critics like L'vov, Amosov, Krein, and Kholmogortsev invoked the same challenges as evidence of the shortcomings of boys' schools. This tension left educators in a difficult position, as the glaring shortcomings of boys' schools forced educators to search for factors other than the innate character of masculinity to explain persistent problems. The practices of teachers, the administration of schools, and the availability of facilities were all presented as alternative explanations for the problems of boys' schools. Even though various short-term solutions were proposed, such as building gymnasiums, enforcing tighter rules, and reassigning teachers, the ultimate solution came only with the restoration of coeducation, which resolved (or disguised) the problem of misbehaving boys.

Social Relationships

A report on the end of the 1943/1944 school year in Nal'chik included the intriguing statement that tenth-grade boys did not want to leave their school until the morning after their graduation.[180] While this extended revelry was a common experience for secondary-school graduates, especially given the emotionally heightened atmosphere of total war, these pupils had experienced an unusual educational trajectory: after spending nine years in coeducational classrooms, they now celebrated their graduation from a separate school. Expressing an equally powerful sentiment almost a decade later, boys' school director Mostovoi said that he would be "sad" when "boys and girls begin to share the same classroom."[181]

These expressions of a sentimental attachment to same-sex groupings stand in striking contrast to the more widespread complaints about "undesirable" and "uncomradely" attitudes fostered by boys' schools.[182] Some educators pointed to "unhealthy" behaviors associated with the "old" *gymnasia,* including ribald jokes, deliberately unkempt appearance, disparaging views of girls, and "false" loyalty to classmates, especially among those seen as "leaders of the street."[183] S. Platonova recalled that her older son attended coeducational schools until fourth grade but then began the fifth grade in a boys' school, where "the absence of the softening influence of girls" encouraged undesirable behaviors: smoking, lax discipline, a "scornful and even contemptuous" attitude toward girls, and a decline in educational quality. By contrast, Platonova reported, coeducational schools promoted "completely comradely competitions" between boys and girls in the academic sphere.[184] Platonova conceded that recent years had seen improvements in discipline and academics, but the "alienation from girls" persisted, which produced the contradictory manifestations of either greater shyness or intensified interest.

This "alienation from girls" was actually encouraged by some educators, who seemed to believe that even inviting girls to visit a boys' school was a violation of regulations.[185] Stalingrad boys' school teachers complained that when male pupils spotted a girl in their school, they would "correctly or incorrectly" try to make her leave, because girls had no reason to be in their school. These same teachers reported that parents often complained that boys treated girls in an unfriendly way outside the school, thus implying that boys unaccustomed to dealing with girls as classmates were unable to behave appropriately in mixed-gender settings.[186] The mother of a son enrolled in an Alma-Ata boys' school warned that boys looked at girls only as future housekeepers, not as "people who are equally valued like men."[187] A senior pupil, K. Rototaev, blamed fighting, hooliganism, and poor conduct on the lack of regular interactions with girls in schools.[188]

By contrast, more positive accounts of boys' schools emphasized the improvements in attitudes and behaviors that followed from establishing gender boundaries. In 1950, pupils from Novosibirsk boys' school No. 41 "attentively, respectfully, and courteously" hosted classmates from a neighboring girls' school, thus fostering real friendship, respect for women, and appropriately restrained interactions.[189] An even more enthusiastic report came from Lukin, director of Moscow boys' school No. 265, who praised his pupils for their enthusiastic preparations to host girls for a celebration of the Komsomol anniversary: "Boys put the school into an ideal order, cleaned the floors themselves, and worried that the curtains were not well ironed: what will the girls say!" During the event itself, the boys were exceedingly attentive and polite, which Lukin contrasted to coeducational schools, where boys rarely behaved so respectfully or courteously.[190]

Yet other reports offered more conflicting assessments of interactions between male and female pupils, as suggested by girls' criticisms cited in the previous chapter. Moscow director Mostovoi complained that when he invited 60 girls from another school to a mathematics competition, "120 came, and they were interested only in dancing."[191] In Armenia, girls invited to a boys' school dance "kept to themselves" the entire time, dancing only with each other. The tension between boys and girls meant that the event was "listless, uninteresting." When it was over and the girls had departed, the boys announced: "Now, let's really have some fun."[192]

Despite this range of perceptions, it became increasingly clear that growing support for coeducation (a topic for analysis in the next chapter) was directly connected to the "unsatisfactory" situation in boys' schools.[193] School director Il'in declared in the spring of 1954 that, while he would prefer to improve boys' schools rather than restore coeducation, the current situation was so bad that working "from morning to night" made no significant improvement in schools.[194] Later that summer, a boys' school director anticipated that the "great difficulties" of maintaining discipline and achieving order would diminish with the transition to coeducation.[195]

Conclusion

A recurring theme in these deliberations was the lack of information about boys' schools, even within the educational apparatus. Although several articles about boys' schools appeared in the first year of the policy, no further articles specifically on these schools have been located in these same publications (although articles on discipline often included examples from boys' schools).[196] Educators themselves complained about this lack of attention. School directors at a 1950 meeting heard that the lack of guidance on teaching methods was due in part to the fact that pedagogical researchers were "afraid" to venture into boys' classrooms. Even as Ministry of Education official Lutskova conceded that researchers "preferred" to observe girls' schools, she promised that subsequent studies would include both boys' and girls' schools.[197] An official from the Academy of Pedagogical Sciences confessed that he was "afraid" to present a model lesson in a boys' school.[198] A plea that educational researchers "go where it is difficult" provides further evidence of the lack of knowledge about the inner workings of boys' schools.[199] According to Moscow boys' school director Khrushchev, boys' schools were studied very little, and when there was public discussion, it was "only to criticize the bad situation in these schools."[200] As a result of this combination of preferences and fears, most pedagogical training took place in coeducational or girls' schools, thus compounding problems with inexperienced or unqualified boys' school teachers.[201] Even educators in relative positions of power and privilege exhibited similar tendencies. At a 1948 meeting, director Pokrovskaia lamented that no one had spoken about boys' schools, as "female voices" dominated the session, and she asked that at the next meeting, the "voice of the boys' school be heard."[202]

The preferences evident in the Soviet case study are visible in other contexts, where deliberations about separate schools primarily emphasize the education of girls.[203] Yet this silence is misleading, for it perpetuates the assumption that attention to gender really means attention to girls, as the "other" to the normatively defined masculine. Focusing specifically on boys' schools reveals both the potential appeal and the serious problems of separate schools. In the Soviet Union of the 1940s and 1950s, as in contemporary contexts, separate schools were attractive in part because they promised to nurture, assert, and even glorify established norms of masculinity, as they would "let boys be boys." At the same time, boys' schools enjoyed a more instrumental appeal, as a means to bring discipline to a social group perceived as dangerous, unreliable, or deviant. Although some boys' schools, in the Soviet Union as elsewhere, successfully managed these contradictory impulses by allowing greater freedom to pupils to learn to adhere to the school rules, the dominant pattern seemed to push in the opposite direction, as boys became more unruly and schools became more authoritarian.[204]

In this situation, educators faced with an escalating disciplinary imperative came to see coeducation as a strategy for restoring order in schools. This trajectory was observed by Kholmogortsev, whose critical comments about boys' schools introduced this chapter. While refraining from any open criticism of Stalinist policy, Kholmogortsev nevertheless concluded that separate schooling led to many negative outcomes: complicating enrollment patterns, forcing boys and girls into an "unnatural" separation, and creating harmful distinctions among teachers based on the dubious criterion of capacity to teach effectively in boys' schools. Kholmogortsev concluded that "this experiment" yielded "nothing positive," and while it "did not cause any damage, it has not justified itself." Declaring that the situation in boys' schools was "extremely urgent" and "critically acute," as indicated by parents' frantic appeals to "restore order," Kholmogortsev concluded that separate schooling was a failed experiment, and he proclaimed himself "an unconditional supporter of coeducation."[205]

Debating Policy
The Challenge to Separate Education

IN NOVEMBER 1948, at a Moscow meeting to discuss the "peculiar features" of separate schools, girls' school director Disson issued the following warning: "When I was invited to this conference, I warned comrades that my remarks might not be appropriate, because I hold definite views: I am becoming a more and more convinced supporter of coeducational instruction." Because of her positive memories of a girls' school before the revolution ("I loved my *gymnasium*"), Disson had greeted the introduction of separate schools "enthusiastically." She initially hoped that the deficiencies of coeducation "would go away with separate schools," and that Soviet schools would be more like "excellent" prerevolutionary institutions. But her recent experience directing a girls' school created a sense of being at an impasse, as so much that could be done in a coeducational school failed to work in a girls' school: "You offer some kind of idea, propose some kind of measure that you think should be implemented, but in a girls' school, you cannot just do anything, you must demand, you must insist, and, if you do not show sufficient persistence, that effort, no matter how valuable, will fail." Echoing the dismissive attitudes cited in the previous chapter, Disson charged that many teachers viewed their girls' school as "a sanatorium where they can get some rest." As further illustration of the failure of this policy, Disson lamented that "everything negative" about the coeducational school "flourishes" in a girls' school, including religious practices, fortune-telling, romances, concerns about appearance, and heightened sexual interest in boys. Vividly describing the implications of gender separation, Disson compared the mere presence of boys in a girls' schools to the impact of an exploding bomb. Her pupils were shrieking so loudly one day that she rushed out of her office, only to learn that just a few boys had come to plan an event. It was "incredible," she recalled, as if the girls had no boys in their families or in their apartment buildings.[1]

Repudiating her previous stance as "a fervent supporter of separate schools," Disson concluded that her teachers were divided, some for and some against separate schooling, and then she ended with this remarkable statement about both perspective and process:

> If you asked me about my position, I would give you a straight answer: I favor coeducation, without any doubt. Boys receive a concentration of certain qualities, and girls receive a concentration of others, but without any kind of positive results. It seems to me that if a referendum were held [laughter], I have no doubt that the majority of teachers, other than those who just want to work passively and calmly, would say that coeducation is better. We are for coeducation.[2]

Disson's comments offer both a uniquely personal and broadly representative assessment of single-sex schooling at the halfway point. Her memories of a prerevolutionary girls' school had allowed her to see the possibilities of the new policy, yet the actual experience of directing a girls' school produced only disillusionment, as these early hopes as well as the mandates of state policy yielded to despair regarding pupils' attitudes and practices. Separate schooling was not achieving its desired results, Disson affirmed, and these shortcomings were increasingly obvious to those at work in schools. In contrast to discourses described in the previous two chapters, which depicted girls' schools as calm communities and boys' schools as disorderly spaces, Disson's female pupils were badly behaved. Perhaps the most revealing aspect of Disson's comments, however, was the assertion that most teachers favored coeducation and would indicate their support were they asked in a referendum. The "laughter" that follows, as recorded in the transcript, suggests that even in this time of dictatorship, rigid censorship, and personal vulnerability, at least some school directors found the proposed referendum on educational policy to be funny—but it is not clear whether this response expressed amusement, irony, despair, or fear.

Disson's comments and the response of her colleagues locate the debate on separate education in relation to current historiography on the postwar Soviet Union. Western scholars traditionally viewed this period as a time of rigid dictatorship and escalating repression, until Stalin's death in March 1953.[3] A widely circulated book, published under the ominous title *The Country of the Blind: The Soviet System of Mind Control,* identified "education as a weapon" in the hands of a totalitarian regime.[4] More recently, however, the late 1940s and early 1950s are interpreted not just as the final stage of Stalin's dictatorship but also as a time of "transition and negotiation," involving "a dialogue between authorities and individuals," and "a debate between official norms and the people affected by them," in the words of historian Juliane Furst.[5] Disson's comments are certainly suggestive of the latter trajectory, as she, along with many other educators discussed in this chapter, spoke quite critically about the current policy. Her criticisms were framed not as failures to implement Party resolutions, as was the most common style of Stalinist self-criticism but, rather, aimed directly at the failure of separate schooling to deliver a better education for boys and girls.[6] Whatever factors might explain the "laughter," the fact that Disson openly proclaimed a preference for coeducation illustrates how even the rigid structures of the party-state apparatus also contained points of fissure and expressions of disagreements.

Exploring the emerging debate about separate schools thus offers insights into postwar Soviet political culture. Transcripts of meetings with educators reveal a critical dialogue among those directly involved in separate schools. Although these meetings rarely prompted public notice, and most published reports emphasized positive aspects of schooling, this facade cracked open in the spring of 1950 with the publication of an article by educational psychologist Kolbanovskii in *Literaturnaia gazeta,* the national literary newspaper.[7] This article provoked a flood of letters written by pupils, teachers, parents, and school officials. A few letters were published in two subsequent issues of the newspaper, but a much larger number are preserved in the Russian state archives. A careful reading of these letters, especially the unpublished collection, provides numerous insights into the experiences of boys and girls, the expectations of parents and teachers, and the emerging perception of separate schools as an experiment that produced "only negative results," in the words of one correspondent.[8] These important shifts in public discourse demonstrate that the end of separate schooling was anticipated, and certainly influenced, by the ways that pupils, teachers, and school directors debated—to an extent remarkable in a dictatorship—the deficiencies and deformities of this policy.

This approach offers new perspectives on the evaluation of separate schooling as a viable option in public education. The existing literature on separate schools devotes little attention to exploring how educators, as well as pupils, parents, and the public come to realize that separate schooling may not achieve the desired or promised improvements. In the contemporary United States, for example, school systems that introduce separate schooling for boys and girls attract far more public attention, mostly positive but also critical, than do school systems that bring such experiments to an end by restoring coeducation.[9] The broader question of public support for single-sex education has also received surprisingly little attention in either scholarly or popular texts, but the available evidence suggests a comparable spectrum of potential support, skeptical evaluations, and practical concerns.[10] Examining the arguments that Stalinist educators made for the return to coeducation reveals not only the shortcomings of Soviet policy but also the perceived connections between school practices and gender roles in society. As is discussed in the final chapter, Disson and other critics had to wait another six years for the full restoration of coeducation, but their criticism of separate schools certainly contributed to this shift on gender roles in education.

The Problem of Overcrowding

The experiment with separate schooling occurred even as enrollment increased significantly throughout Soviet education. The potent symbolism of rapid growth was illustrated by a 1951 article on a Leningrad girls' school, under the headline "980 pupils sitting at desks," which called attention to a "significant increase" from the previous year.[11] During the war, enrollment decreased, especially at the secondary level, as adolescents left schools for work or the army, while occupation and evacuation caused more general interruptions and disruptions. During the postwar recovery, elementary and secondary enrollment in Soviet cities increased from 18.4 million to 25.5 million, a growth of almost 40 percent.[12] Campaigns to achieve universal education were most widespread in rural regions, where many children still attended only a few years of elementary school, but parallel efforts in cities sought to achieve universal seven-year compulsory education.[13] Enrollment expansion and separate schooling were directly connected, as new structures and methods were implemented in rapidly growing facilities.[14] Enrollment in urban secondary schools, the category designated for gender segregation, more than doubled in the postwar decade, from 4.3 million to 8.9 million.[15]

Overcrowded classrooms resulted from enrollment expansion. Anecdotal reports list classrooms with forty or more pupils.[16] Moscow boys' school No. 110 had a third-grade classroom with forty-seven pupils, with no indication that this exemplary school had excessively high enrollments.[17] Alma-Ata schools reported as many as forty-five pupils in a classroom.[18] Continuing practices begun before the war, many schools operated in two or more shifts, to accommodate all the pupils.[19] As late as 1949, some Moscow schools "had to work in three shifts to meet demand."[20] Boys' school director Mostovoi ran lessons from early morning until midnight as the only way to accommodate multiple shifts.[21]

The lack of comprehensive data makes it difficult to assess how enrollment affected separate schools, but directors frequently expressed concerns about these trends. Mostovoi recalled that the introduction of separate schooling in 1943 meant he "gave up 400 girls and received 1,127 boys."[22] Other directors reported postwar enrollments of 1,500 to 2,000 pupils, as facilities did not keep up with rising enrollment.[23] A Moscow boys' school saw enrollment increase from 800 to 1,300 pupils in just one year.[24] In Penza boys' school No. 1, enrollment rose in just a few years from 500 to more than 1,600 pupils.[25] In Fergana boys' school No. 10, enrollment rose by 25 percent in just one year, reaching 1,153 pupils by September 1949.[26] Enrollment in Alma-Ata boys' school No. 55 more than doubled, from fewer than one thousand to nearly two thousand pupils, in the first five years of separate schooling.[27]

The emphasis on enrollment in boys' schools illustrates the ways that overcrowded classrooms and disciplinary problems were associated with masculinity. Directors of boys' schools complained that they no longer knew every pupil individually.[28] Moscow director Khrushchev declared that a school of 1,600 boys was "pedagogically absurd," because the director could not "guide" each pupil individually. Khrushchev admitted that even he could not recognize his own pupils outside the school. If a boy shot a catapult, he added, then "I should know if this boy is from our school."[29] Moscow director Gordunov admitted that of the almost one thousand boys in his school, he knew only about one-quarter on an individual basis.[30] Moscow school director Liukhin observed that the prerevolutionary *gymnasium* had maybe 300 pupils, whereas his boys' school enrolled 1,500 pupils, and he asked: "Isn't this a lot for just one person?"[31] Teacher Beliaev in Penza lamented that as the number of pupils in his school more than tripled (from 500 to 1,620), neither the director nor the teachers understood their pupils as well as they had in coeducational schools.[32] Moscow director Velitskii complained that in a boys' school with 1,400 pupils, functioning in multiple shifts with overcrowded classrooms, teachers could monitor only 1 percent of what was happening among pupils.[33] Reports on overcrowded urban schools often used the phrase "especially in boys' schools" to connect perceptions of overcrowding with persistent educational challenges.[34]

Many problems in boys' schools were attributed to overcrowding, which was called "one of the main reasons for poor discipline" and "the most terrible question."[35] Moscow director Il'in listed as the first "negative" the "huge army of boys," who were more difficult to teach than girls.[36] Moscow director Gorbunov declared that "it was more difficult" to work in a boys' school than a girls' school, as teaching more than forty pupils was "too much" where pupils were "more mobile and, I would say, more active," whereas a class of forty or more pupils might be manageable in a girls' school.[37]

These complaints often made the additional point that boys' schools were larger and more crowded than girls' schools. Mostovoi declared that all five boys' schools in his district were jammed full, while five girls' schools had vacant classrooms during their second shift.[38] In districts where the number of girls' schools exceeded the number of boys' schools, these perceptions of imbalance seemed especially troubling. Moscow director Liukhin declared that his boys' school and three girls' schools served the same district, which meant that all the boys attended one school, while "of course, the girls' schools are less crowded."[39]

Yet statistical reports indicate that girls' schools were on average actually slightly larger than boys' schools.[40] In the more than seventy cities providing detailed figures, average enrollment at the end of the war was 638 pupils in boys' schools and 710 pupils in girls' schools.[41] Six years later, although the average size of schools had increased by more than one-third, the distribution remained similar: 963 pupils in boys' schools and 1,015 pupils in girls' schools.[42] The real difference, perhaps surprisingly, was the smaller size of coeducational schools, with an average enrollment of approximately 500 pupils.[43] More detailed reports on specific cities provide further confirmation of this pattern.[44] Even in Moscow, where many boys' school directors articulated the complaints cited above, average enrollment was 1,130 pupils in boys' schools and 1,205 pupils in girls' schools.[45] Of the twenty-six cities on this same list, eighteen reported higher average enrollment in girls' schools.[46] In Alma-Ata, girls' schools had a slightly higher average enrollment than boys' schools. Of the six largest schools, each with more than one thousand students, however, four enrolled boys and just two enrolled girls, which might have contributed to perceptions of overcrowded boys' schools.[47]

Only a few cities reported different distributions. In Arkhangel'sk, three girls' schools averaged 1,009 pupils each, compared to the much higher average of 1,325 pupils in two boys' schools.[48] Three cities in the Voronezh region also reported higher average enrollment in boys' schools. The reason for this disparity was obvious, as the educational departments in these cities allocated only one-half of school facilities to boys, who made up two-thirds of the enrollment. In Borisoglebsk, one very large boys' school that enrolled 930 pupils was almost twice the average size of four girls' schools.[49]

Given this discrepancy between shared perceptions and statistical patterns, complaints about overcrowded boys' schools suggest the influence of pervasive anxieties about masculine disorder as well as underlying assumptions that boys deserved better facilities than girls. A perceived deficiency in boys' schooling was transformed into a justification for preferential treatment of boys. Proposals "to relieve the strain on boys' schools" included reducing class sizes, building new schools, and converting girls' schools into boys' schools.[50] Articulating the consequences implicit in proposed remedies, director Bessanova endorsed the "unburdening" of boys' schools by "burdening" girls' schools.[51]

The pressure created by overcrowding and the search for solutions exposed the logistical disadvantages of separate schooling. If a boys' school and a girls' school operated with different levels of enrollment, combining these schools seemed a logical way to restore balance. In one Leningrad district, for example, a boys' school worked in two shifts, with eleven classes, and a girls' school had nine classes. As educators proposed expanding facilities, the current policy required construction of a boys' school and a girls' school, whereas a single coeducational school would immediately relieve overcrowding in both schools.[52] Yet even as parents and educators began to contemplate coeducation as a response to overcrowding, others questioned assumptions of an easy fix. After complaining about difficult conditions in his school, where 1,500 boys were crowded in multiple shifts into just thirty-seven classrooms, Liukhin speculated that even if the school were made coeducational, the noise level would remain the same: "Maybe it would be somewhat quieter and easier, but we would not have resolved the most important thing—the crowding—and thus we still would not have normal conditions."[53]

Both the subjective perceptions of directors and the actual statistical evidence indicate that enrollment patterns created problems for separate schools. Increased enrollments meant more pupils in each school and classroom, thus exacerbating problems such as lack of discipline and the threat that disorder would spill out of schools. Problems attributed to overcrowding contributed directly to the perceived crisis in boys' schools (as discussed in the previous chapter), despite the fact that average enrollment was actually higher in girls' schools. This tension between perception and numbers reveals an important aspect of the gendering of separate education. A school of a thousand or more boys or a classroom of thirty or more boys may have seemed more unruly, disobedient, or even threatening than a comparable number of pupils in a girls' or coeducational school, simply because of assumptions that more active boys needed stricter discipline. Implementing separate schooling at a time of educational expansion posed a direct threat to this experiment, as the goals of disciplined pupils and orderly classrooms seemed ever further from realization. Enrollment patterns thus contributed to increasingly critical evaluations of separate schooling.

Criticism of Separate Schools

Throughout this period, educational departments and other Communist Party and government organizations occasionally convened meetings to discuss separate schools. While some criticism greeted the policy's initial announcement (as discussed in the first chapter), both published articles and archival documents suggest that the first few years saw relatively little debate about this experiment. By the late 1940s, however, after five years of separate schools, Soviet educators became increasingly concerned about conditions in girls' and, especially, boys' schools. The comments from director Disson, as cited at the beginning of this chapter, illustrate how meetings summoned to discuss the "peculiarities" of separate schools provided a forum for increasingly critical evaluations. Even as these meetings illustrated changes in perceptions, this critical discourse remained invisible in published reports from this period.

At this same meeting, the chair, E. I.Velichovskii, called for "serious attention to compiling and generalizing the experience of the hitherto unfamiliar work" of separate schools. Praising certain schools and teachers for devaluing "special methods" and "appropriate traditions," Velichovskii also called for more attention to "unresolved problems." Interestingly, his opening remarks did not differentiate between boys' and girls' schools, thus implying that separate schools were somehow gender neutral, despite the fact that the whole premise of this reform was to differentiate the education of boys and girls.[54]

Other participants at this 1948 meeting echoed Velichovskii's call for more guidance on methods yet also expressed increasingly critical evaluations of separate schools. Moscow girls' school director Bocharova began by telling colleagues, "Comrades, I came here in order to be convinced of the advisability of separate instruction." Bocharova had been following developments closely since 1943, talking "not only with teachers but also with pupils and many parents," trying to find out what was new and effective in separate instruction. "And, speaking openly, I have many doubts about whether this reform has offered real results, whether there are more pluses or minuses, more that is positive or more that is negative, and what are the most important pedagogical ideas." After criticizing the ways that pupils viewed opposite-sex peers as something other than comrades, Bocharova offered this frank assessment: "I eagerly awaited this meeting, I wanted to be convinced by the speeches. But the preceding remarks did not convince me that I was mistaken. I consider that separate instruction has not resolved the main questions and has not created anything specific in instruction and upbringing." Asking for "a demonstration of positive results," Bocharova concluded that her work in schools led her to see "only negative results. What is positive?" Bocharova then offered a sweeping challenge to claims that separate schools should prepare girls to become housewives:

> It has been said here that we are teaching girls to cook and clean. These tasks are so simple that the school does not need to teach them. They should be learned through daily life. And if this is happening, why should boys not master them also? They are going to be soldiers, and will have to cook their food. My husband helps me a lot with daily tasks, and it makes me so happy! He works and I work, and we bear the same responsibilities, since we are in the same situation with a large family with children, and he does not consider it shameful to take my place. Why is this so strange? Why do we consider that this is just the woman's duty?

The only "particularity" of being a woman, according to Bocharova, was caring for an infant, which could not be "entrusted" to a man. Although this assertion of gender role reversals was strikingly unusual in Soviet discourse, it vividly revealed how the assumptions and expectations underlying separate schools provoked educators to see educational practices as antithetical to Soviet values. Directly challenging official policy, Bocharova concluded that "these issues can be resolved only with coeducation."[55]

A similar position was articulated by girls' school director Davydova, whose scathing criticism of pupils' behavior, as discussed in the third chapter, led to a declaration that educating youth for communist society could be done better in a coeducational school.[56] Toward the end of the same meeting, director Pokrovskaia offered a more equivocal assessment, concluding that "it was too early" to decide this question, that the "pros and cons" should be studied, and that "the government, which approved the division into boys' and girls' schools, certainly has plans for a well-grounded resolution."[57] Other participants echoed this ambivalence, while also calling for more research to guide further deliberations. Moscow boys' school director Gorbunov recalled that he had initially supported coeducation and "for a long time thought separate education was distasteful," but now he felt that "it would be strange if girls came to a boys' school." Gorbunov concluded that this "serious problem" required a "profoundly scientific" approach, and while educators could discuss "operational" aspects, educational researchers must complete "scientific studies."[58]

Even as this meeting seemed to invite candid evaluations, however, participants also seemed reluctant to take a strong position. Girls' school director Perstova stated that neither she nor her teachers had discussed the particular challenges of separate schools, and thus she was relaying "nothing more than observations," because "we have not studied" the curriculum and methods. Expressing this ambivalence more pointedly, Perstova admitted that teachers were "sharply divided" between those who saw separate schools as "unnecessary" and those who saw them as a "positive development." Perstova then added the "interesting" point that proponents of coeducation included "the better, the more lively, and the more strong-willed teachers," using the term for the latter—*volevyie*—that was the most frequent attribute ascribed to teachers in boys' schools, as discussed in the previous chapter. Perstova was then interrupted by inspector Kholmogortsev, who pressed her to share her own opinion. Rather than taking sides, however, Perstova remained equivocal: "The director, if you please, occupies a middle position, I do not have a point of view grounded in scientific studies, but I also realize that in strong-willed hands, with a talented teacher, whether pupils are studying separately or together, there will be order, whereas the teacher who lacks mastery in the classroom will follow the line of least resistance, but such a teacher does not fully understand this question."[59]

Despite this equivocation, these comments reveal a surprisingly critical view of separate schools. Even as educators like Perstova, Gorbunov, and Velichovskii called for more study, school directors like Bocharova, Davydova, and Disson questioned the experiences and outcomes of separate schools. A summary of these comments, revealing that "the majority" did not believe that separate schools "justified themselves," was drafted by the School Section of the Central Committee, but apparently had no impact on policy makers.[60] Even as these judgments were articulated at educators' meetings, however, public reports remained uniformly positive. Just six months before this meeting, for example, the newspaper *Uchitel'skaia gazeta* published a full-page report on Moscow girls' school No. 29 that emphasized the strongest features of this exemplary school.[61] Less than a year later, an equally positive account by girls' school director Razvinova praised the achievements of her separate school.[62] Yet when this public silence on separate schools was broken in the spring of 1950 (as discussed in the next section), it built upon the increasingly negative assessments already articulated by educators.

A considerable proportion of the discussion of separate schools during this era either implicitly or explicitly denied the significance of gender. A report on Moscow girls' school No. 610, while consistently referring to female pupils, identified only singing and music as special features of girls' schools.[63] A report on Birobidzhan schools explicitly stated that boys', girls', and coeducational schools "differ little from each other." The only curricular difference was that girls' schools taught needlecrafts. Even as this report denied any significant differences, however, it also concluded that discipline improved in separate schools.[64] A 1945 article on teaching in a boys' school offered recommendations for teachers that made no mention of gender-specific approaches but could easily have applied to all schools, by emphasizing preparation of lessons, organization of instructional activities, and individual knowledge of pupils.[65] A list of more than seventy-five topics for literature and history classes in a Moscow boys' school included no gender-specific topics, other than the propaganda standard, "the heroism of the Soviet woman."[66] On the first day of school in September 1951, Moscow boys' school director Mostovoi described disciplinary challenges without ever addressing the question of how gender affected teachers' approaches or pupils' responses.[67]

The discrepancies between comments at meetings and published reports reflected the power of the propaganda state to determine which issues received any measure of public attention. Yet these discrepancies also reflected deeper tensions embedded throughout the policies and practices of separate schools, as the lack of acknowledgment of problems inadvertently fueled the already eroding base of support for separate schools. Educators acknowledged that many problems, "particularly in boys' schools," did not represent "the very essence of separate instruction" but instead resulted from poor instructional methods, insufficiently qualified teachers, and unsatisfactory conditions for extracurricular work. Yet the failure to make improvements discredited "the very idea of separate schools in the eyes of many parents and educators."[68] Separate schools elevated gender to an unprecedented level as a means of differentiating pupils yet also made gender differentiation into an obvious factor contributing to educational outcomes. When the public silence on separate schools was broken in the spring of 1950, the shift toward negative assessments accelerated, even as the policy remained in place for another four years.

"A Troubling Question"

In an April 1950 article published under the provocative, but also ambiguous, title "A Troubling Question," educational psychologist Kolbanovskii offered a detailed, and very critical, examination of the underlying principles and actual practices of separate schools.[69] Over the next few months, the same newspaper published nine letters, some written collectively and others signed by individuals, responding to this article. All but two of the published letters supported the restoration of coeducation. A follow-up editorial on the eve of the new school year amplified the criticism by endorsing this call to reconsider separate schooling.[70] The published letters were a small fraction of all those sent to *Literaturnaia gazeta,* and additional letters are available to researchers at the Russian State Archive of Literature and the Arts.[71] Kolbanovskii's article, the editorial, the published letters, and especially the unpublished letters illustrate how the experience of separate schools provoked a resurgence of support for coeducation.

These interventions into educational discourse reverberated in multiple spaces for a prolonged period. International observers commented on the controversy unleashed by this article and letters, and comprehensive translations appeared in western publications.[72] Almost immediately, the published materials provoked anxiety, dissatisfaction, and concern among educators. In the spring and summer of 1950, Kolbanovskii's article was "hotly debated" at city-wide meetings of teachers, at the pedagogical councils within schools, and at special meetings involving parents and pupils.[73] After teachers at Stalingrad boys' school No. 8 discussed Kolbanovskii's article, they drafted a collective letter to *Literaturnaia gazeta* to convey their shared concerns.[74] Even parents responded to the articles by discussing problems in separate schools.[75] Copies of these materials circulated among policy makers, and a later report declared that growing preference for coeducation was "to a great extent" prompted by *Literaturnaia gazeta.*[76] Kolbanovskii's article and the ensuing discussion thus marked a turning point in the emerging debate over separate schools in the postwar Soviet Union.[77]

Kolbanovskii began by asserting that Soviet schools must educate "a *new* person."[78] Declaring that this education should occur in "an organized collective," where the child develops individual abilities, moral qualities, and personal character, Kolbanovskii then turned his attention to separate schools. Repeating language from the 1943 instructions, Kolbanovskii acknowledged the "serious" claims that coeducation did not devote sufficient attention to the particularities of boys and girls. Yet Kolbanovskii expressed a more critical perspective in the statement that "this innovation provoked a great deal of disagreement": "Proponents of coeducation— including many school directors, teachers, and parents—are convinced that in exchange for some difficulties and inconveniences, the new system of instruction has given rise to others, that are not any less, and perhaps even more, serious." Teachers and parents had thus spent six years asking, Which is better: coeducational or single-sex education? By offering two distinct perspectives on official policy, referring to critical views, and raising the question of which system was better, Kolbanovskii struck a remarkable tone, especially given the stultifying terms of postwar discourse where educational policies were rarely criticized from any perspective other than insufficient implementation of central decrees.[79]

After exposing the terms of this debate, Kolbanovskii proposed using "practice" as the "criterion of truth" to make a "parallel" evaluation of "both systems of education." The most "significant difficulties," according to "conversations" among experienced educators, was the tendency to "distort the basic principles of Soviet pedagogy" by differentiating between "masculine" and "feminine" types of education, thus encouraging "bifurcation" of Soviet schools. Examples of differentiation included the emphasis in boys' schools on math, physics, and chemistry, and in girls' schools on humanities disciplines such as literature, language, and history. Yet Kolbanovskii emphatically denied that these tendencies reflected the actual interests of pupils, and he charged instead that teachers had succumbed to the influence of defenders of separate schooling. After quoting Timofeev's statement from a 1945 article that the "particular qualities" of girls included softness of nature and "great sensitivity to other people," Kolbanovskii denied that these were "purely feminine qualities." He also rejected Timofeev's claim that girls' greater involvement in family relations, household management, and daily life meant they were less capable of studying geography, physics, chemistry, botany, zoology, and mathematics. Reviving political charges made in the 1930s against "bifurcation," Kolbanovskii reduced Timofeev's seemingly "innovative" position to the so-called law of fatalistic conditioning of children by biological and social circumstances that had been condemned by Soviet educators during the antipedology campaign. Accusing Timofeev of echoing "willingly or not (it is necessary to think unwillingly)" the bourgeois principle that women were inferior to men, Kolbanovskii implicitly questioned assertions that separate schooling would maintain women's equality. While others had raised similar questions, from the very first discussions of separate instruction in 1943, Kolbanovskii's intervention publicly challenged the claim that separate schooling could promote women's equality.[80]

Kolbanovskii also criticized the firsthand account by girls' school director Razvinova, which connected instruction in physics, chemistry, and other sciences to girls' domestic and maternal roles.[81] Declaring that "teaching girls to make soap" does not expose them to "the newest achievements in chemistry" Kolbanovskii asked, "Why is practical knowledge necessary only for women? Surely 'science in daily life' is not superfluous for men?" Declaring that pupils in girls' schools showed less interest in scientific fields with direct application in economic production, Kolbanovskii charged that Razvinova's seemingly "innocent" suggestions in effect prepared girls exclusively for service roles in the family and household. As further evidence of the "foul" effect of these views, Kolbanovskii warned that pupils in separate schools, especially girls' schools, were engrossed in "petty interests" and the pursuit of "vulgar happiness," such as those characteristic of middle-class women in capitalist or traditional societies, whose interests were limited to the family, physical appearance, and other personal concerns. Through these accusations that female pupils were displaying attitudes and behaviors that were incompatible with the ideal of a politically engaged and ideologically committed woman, Kolbanovskii indicted girls' schools as being antithetical to the Soviet ideology of gender equality.

After skewering both the historical justification for separate schools and the specific practices of girls' schools, Kolbanovskii conceded that some separate schools had made "substantial accomplishments." But, he quickly added, coeducational schools have made similar improvements, which meant that the "significant difficulties" of separate schools placed them at a disadvantage. Kolbanovskii particularly lamented the absence of the "restraining and ennobling influence" that boys and girls exerted upon each other in coeducational classrooms. Whereas "mutual estrangement" prevailed in separate schools, coeducation encouraged boys and girls to become "true friends," as they studied together, resolved common questions, created relationships built on "elevated ideological and cultural interests," and came to see each other as future comrades "in life and labor, and, if necessary, in battle." After praising the contributions of women and men in the war against Germany as well as to the Soviet economy, Kolbanovskii complained that meager efforts to organize extracurricular activities for pupils from boys' and girls' schools were ineffective, because they did not involve "the practice of daily comradely mutual interactions of male and female pupils." Kolbanovskii thus inverted the discursive pattern begun in 1941, which contrasted the observed deficiencies of coeducational schools with improvements anticipated in separate schools. Seven years of policy and practice provided ample evidence of the shortcomings of separate schools, which could now be unfavorably contrasted to an idealized situation in coeducational schools.

Kolbanovskii concluded that speaking "sharply" about separate schools was needed to provoke a public debate of this "troubling question." The editors of *Literaturnaia gazeta* apparently agreed, for his article appeared over the heading: "As a Matter for Discussion."[82] The flood of letters that followed provided a remarkably frank, frequently insightful, and generally critical assessment of separate schools.

Debating Separate Schools

Letters submitted to *Literaturnaia gazeta* provide a unique perspective on separate schools by exposing the tension between idealized goals and actual practices. Several correspondents expressed their gratitude for the opportunity to communicate with a broader audience. F. N. Bondarenna, an instructor in Stavropol, "enthusiastically welcomed" the article by Kolbanovskii and "with all my heart thanked the editors who raised this question on the pages of the progressive fighting newspaper *Literaturnaia gazeta*."[83] Leningrad boys' school teacher P. Prokhorova expressed her gratitude to Kolbanovskii for addressing "so sharply" a question that was "not just troubling, but even painful."[84] Two female eighth-graders in Ivanov declared that this question was "truly troublesome" for pupils.[85] The article's headline, "A Troubling Question," accurately expressed the experiences and perceptions of those involved in separate schools.

Less than a month after Kolbanovskii's article appeared, *Literaturnaia gazeta* published four letters, selected from a "large number" of submissions. Three of the four letters supported Kolbanovskii's position by criticizing separate instruction and arguing for coeducation.[86] As detailed below, the sole letter supporting separate schooling, from director Tiapkin, provoked a very strong reaction from readers, especially girls. A second set of responses, published in late June, represented approximately the same pattern: four letters critical of separate schools and just one letter defending current policies.[87] Reports on unpublished letters confirm this distribution of attitudes. *Literaturnaia gazeta* editors received more than 800 letters about separate schools, and just eighty favored separate instruction. But it would be wrong, the editors declared, to conclude that 10 percent of correspondents supported the current policy, because almost one-half of letters favoring coeducation were written collectively, expressing the views of a group of people. According to the editors, the 720 letters supporting coeducation actually reflected the views of approximately four thousand people, which meant that 98 percent of correspondents opposed the current policy.[88] In addition to demonstrating the breadth of support for coeducation, this emphasis on collective correspondence also acknowledged that the Soviet public was engaged in a critical debate about the legitimacy, effectiveness, and necessity of this official policy.[89] An examination of the content of letters, both published and unpublished, thus reveals how the experience of separate schools shaped perceptions of the relationship between gender and education.

Many correspondents contrasted practices in separate schools with their own experiences in coeducational schools. Published under the headline, "We are always together!" one letter was written "on behalf of" several hundred former teachers and pupils of a Moscow school, who described themselves as "greatly agitated" by the current policy, which they contrasted to the friendship and comradeship experienced in their coeducational school.[90] For L. Shevchenko, a member of the Ukrainian Supreme Court, memories of "studying together with boys" in a "wonderful school" where all pupils were treated "like equal comrades" led to charges that separate schools alienated children along gender lines, a pattern that could be remedied by "quickly restoring coeducational instruction everywhere."[91] A boys' school teacher recalled that coeducation fostered "the best and most comradely relations between boys and girls."[92] A woman recalled "wonderful relations" with classmates from her coeducational school, "a kind of friendship that boys and girls studying separately will never understand."[93] An even more poignant lamentation of this loss of interactions between the sexes came from L. E. Tomashpol'skii, who remembered sitting at the same desk for seven years with a girl named Dorisa, now a university student. Although they had arguments, Tomashpol'skii recalled, they always studied and played together, and they have maintained "comradely relations" as adults, "which did not in any way prevent her from getting married and raising a daughter."[94]

Other correspondents offered similarly personal evaluations of the positive effects of coeducation. Boys' school teacher Savochkina declared that her coeducational school "undoubtedly" had better discipline.[95] Another teacher asserted that discipline had never been a problem when she worked in coeducational schools, but during her one year in a boys' school, "the situation has become much worse."[96] Three women drew on their experience to deny that "any pernicious influence" came from coeducation.[97] Matekin remembered how the coeducational school encouraged children to develop mutual respect, while a mother recalled that coeducation taught her to "see boys as comrades."[98] Adopting an even more idealized rhetoric, educator Bondarenna declared that coeducation promoted "friendly comradely work" and "complete equality," while also eliminating the flirting that resulted from "unhealthy" curiosity toward the opposite sex.[99]

A different perspective, but with the same evaluations, came from parents concerned about the education of their sons and daughters. A. Zin'kovskii stated that this "troubling question" was a concern not only for teachers but also for parents.[100] A. Nedosekina, a Leningrad housewife, criticized separate schools for promoting contemptuous attitudes among boys, violating Soviet principles of equal education, and creating logistical difficulties. Her letter ended with this statement: "In conclusion, I want to repeat once more my opinion, a mother's opinion: let our children study together!" The phrase "a mother's opinion" became the headline in the published version.[101] Although Shevchenko was identified as a member of the Ukrainian Supreme Court, as cited above, her letter began with a different affiliation: "I, most certainly like the majority of parents, am dissatisfied" with separate education.[102] S. G. Miaspov, one of the few defenders of separate schools, listed "parent" under his signature, where others listed their rank, grade, or occupation.[103] Another collective letter, signed by dozens of residents from one Moscow apartment building, simply stated: "We, as parents, ask that male and female pupils all study together."[104]

Parents whose sons and daughters studied in separate schools called attention to the harmful effects, as in S. M. Makarovich's long account of how "separate instruction has brought nothing but damage."[105] His son, Vadim, began his studies in coeducational schools, where he succeeded academically and did not cause any disciplinary problems. In the fifth grade of a Baku boys' school, however, his achievement declined, his behavior worsened, and he was held back for a second year. After the family relocated, however, Vadim transferred to a coeducational school, where his grades and behavior improved, and he was easily promoted to the seventh grade. But when Makarovich was reassigned to Baku, his son returned to the same boys' school, and within two months, he had dropped out. Declaring that Vadim's trajectory was the "unfortunate" result of separate schooling, Makarovich ended with a strong statement of support for coeducation.[106]

The few letters defending separate schools offer further insights into both the appeal of this policy and the deficiencies in its actual practices. One of the most passionate supporters immediately became the most controversial. In a letter published under the headline "Separate Schooling Must be Preserved," Tiapkin, director of boys' school No. 32 in Rostov-on-Don, asserted that separate schools were introduced during the war for the most patriotic motives, all of which remained in force to the present day. Echoing official statements about the "specific character" of boys' schools, Tiapkin listed the desired traits of masculinity as discipline, hardiness, dexterity, and becoming "a good subordinate and an excellent leader."[107] Invoking Kolbanovskii's assertion that practice should be the basis for determining truth, Tiapkin drew on his own observations to claim that girls' schools had enjoyed "unquestioned success" in instruction, while female pupils had not suffered from the absence of the "restraining and ennobling" influences of boys. Tiapkin then described his own boys' school, where order was strict, demands on pupils were consistent and direct, considerable attention was devoted to physical education, the tone was appropriate, and discipline was good. After conceding that "certain difficulties" had "undoubtedly been overcome," and reminding the editors that coeducational schools had their own difficulties, Tiapkin charged that Kolbanovskii's article, and particularly his criticism of Razvinova, overlooked "a question of great importance—the question of a happy Soviet motherhood." Asserting that the education of "the future mother" was essential for happy family life, Tiapkin posed the question: "Why do we not offer this training to girls?" The published letter concluded that separate schools were natural, positive, and necessary in current Soviet conditions.

Tiapkin's letter provoked considerable outrage. Collective letters from female pupils provided the sharpest critique as well as the most sweeping repudiation. Ninth-grade pupils in a Leningrad girls' school were "especially offended and insulted," seventeen female pupils in Leningrad were "very indignant at the content of this article and completely reject it," eighth-grade pupils in Baku condemned this "very insulting" letter as a disturbing misrepresentation of female psychology, Moscow tenth-grade pupils were "greatly offended," eighth-grade pupils in Kazan were "indignant" at these "mistaken" views, and pupils in Gor'kii condemned Tiapkin for his backward, petit bourgeois assumption that girls needed a different kind of education.[108]

Beyond these expressions of outrage, however, these same letters went even further by denouncing the underlying assumptions involved in separate schools. Thus, Leningrad ninth-grade pupils questioned Tiapkin's claim that separate instruction was based on "deep patriotic motives" as they asked: "What is so patriotic about this?"[109] The same formulation came from tenth-grade Leningrad girls, who stated, "no matter how much we thought about it, we could not figure out" how separate schools could be justified by "patriotic" motives.[110] Several letters rejected Tiapkin's assertion that girls' schools should offer preparation for specifically feminine occupations or activities.[111] Moscow tenth-grade pupils declared that girls should acquire the same qualities as boys, because Soviet women, along with men, participated equally in economic, political, and cultural life.[112] Fifteen recent graduates of a Molotov girls' school declared indignantly that Tiapkin's views were a return to the past, to the era of finishing schools for girls and a barracks regime for boys.[113] Such "petit bourgeois" views completely ignored historical precedents familiar to all students, including scientists, prizewinning authors, and war heroines. Declaring that "these women certainly demonstrated their discipline" in the war, these graduates proclaimed their desire to serve the Motherland, without being confined, as Tiapkin urged, to the home and hearth.[114] Moscow ninth-grade pupils charged that this letter reminded them of a prerevolutionary "finishing school," preparing girls only for marriage and motherhood, whereas now Soviet girls dreamed of becoming useful to their country by acquiring physical strength and endurance, demonstrating their courage, and "never lagging behind boys by even a single step."[115] Invoking a particularly negative historical reference, female pupils in Gor'kii compared Tiapkin's appeal for more feminine training to the *Domostroi,* the seventeenth-century Russian homemaking guide, which progressives had long condemned for relegating women to narrow social roles. Asking why child care was only a girls' responsibility, why boys were not trained for fatherhood, and why training girls to be mothers was so essential, these pupils wrote that "until now, we, Soviet girls, thought that we were fully equal citizens of the USSR," but this premise was contradicted by Tiapkin's claim that girls must be trained for motherhood.[116]

Female pupils thus explicitly rejected Tiapkin's differentiation in the desirable traits of boys and girls. Leningrad tenth graders complained that educating girls for motherhood came at the expense of preparing them to become active members of society. Criticizing Tiapkin for being blind to Soviet reality, the girls concluded that a family built on "comradely relations between parents" was impossible to achieve through separate schools.[117] Tenth-grade pupil Popova declared that the attributes Tiapkin required of boys should also be considered "inherent qualities" of girls.[118] A different group of Leningrad pupils asked rhetorically whether Tiapkin actually believed that girls did not need discipline, could be out of touch, and did not require any ability to work.[119] These girls condemned Tiapkin's "un-Soviet view of women" for the insulting suggestion that kitchen and children were women's only concerns, and they concluded that "creating male and female educational profiles" contradicted the underlying principles of communism.[120] Asking if Tiapkin really believed that "a Soviet girl should be only a mother, and nothing more," Baku girls complained that a girl who spent ten years in a separate school would always "stand in a lower position relative to a boy!"[121] Eighth-grade pupils in a Kazan girls' school asked editors to publish their letter, "so that Tiapkin may read it, and realize his mistakes."[122]

Schoolgirls were not the only ones to reject Tiapkin's prescriptions. Several men, including Makarovich, the Baku father cited above, objected strongly to this assertion that girls should be trained primarily for motherhood.[123] Psychology student Idel'son, whose comparisons of boys' and girls' schools were discussed in the second chapter, asserted that girls should not be "limited" to giving birth and raising a family but, rather, should develop the same qualities Tiapkin expected of boys: discipline, physical health, intelligence, and the ability to issue and obey orders.[124] After quoting Tiapkin's phrase about the necessary qualities of boys, director Fedotov in Latvia declared that all pupils needed the same traits, "regardless of sex," and that therefore "Tiapkin is wrong."[125] Fedotov also dismissed Tiapkin's position as "old-fashioned, from the distant past," by declaring that only coeducational schools could prepare children to create happy families.[126] Pedagogical student Brodskii asked whether schools could really promote a spirit of mutual respect and comradeship, if "a boy knows that a girl is training to become a mother."[127]

Tiapkin thus became a lightning rod for growing dissatisfaction with separate schools. Female pupils reacted particularly bitterly to any implication that they should acquire different traits, prepare for a future as mothers, or yield in their educational accomplishments or patriotic contributions. Yet Tiapkin's views expressed official Soviet policy, which called for educators to address the particular needs of boys and girls as they prepared for their distinctive adult roles. Because the assumptions underlying educational policy contradicted the official rhetoric of gender equality, Tiapkin's expression provoked particularly bitter attacks, especially from adolescent girls, who invoked elements of Soviet propaganda, particularly the promise of equality in education, the family, and society. Focusing on this perceived denial of gender equality demonstrated how separate schools were undermined by tensions between educational practices and official ideology.

Tiapkin's letter was not the only defense of separate schools, although other expressions of this point of view provoked fewer and milder responses. In the only other published letter favoring the current policy, S. Nazarov, a teacher in a Yalta pedagogical institute, differentiated Soviet separate schools from prerevolutionary institutions, where pupils experienced crippled psyches, individualist aspirations, and social alienation. In the Soviet school, Nazarov declared, pupils actively participate in public life, as illustrated by the image of female pupils, "in their brown dresses," visiting voters and spreading election propaganda. Mutual alienation was avoided because boys and girls "meet each other in practical, comradely circumstances," including organizations such as the Komsomol. But, Nazarov affirmed, "equality" does not mean "leveling": "We must consider various subjects taught in schools according to whether they are being taught to boys or girls." In support of this argument for a more differentiated education, Nazarov described how a pedagogical institute had almost all women students while just one-third of students at an agriculture institute were women. Since the choice to enter these programs was completely free, Nazarov declared, this composition must reflect the actual interests of men and women. Echoing one of Tiapkin's more provocative claims, Nazarov also declared that Soviet girls "should be trained to fulfill the responsible duty of being a mother." Rather than debating which system was needed, the greater need was "carefully and urgently to develop programs appropriate for boys' and girls' schools." Nazarov's perspective was expressed in the final sentence, which was the headline for the published version: "The system of separate education should remain."[128]

Other defenders of separate schooling were less concerned about reconciling policy and practice with the promise of gender equality. In an unpublished letter two military aviators, Kobyzev and Lobanov, emphasized that separate schools should reinforce distinct gender roles. Given the true equality of communism, they claimed, all Soviet women could pursue "relatively masculine fields of activity," while also fulfilling the politically significant task of birthing, raising, and educating the next generation. Yet when these two men asked whether the existing system of nursery schools, cafeterias, and other domestic services really made it possible for an emancipated woman to work "in any field, side by side with a man," their answer was surprisingly blunt: "Of course not!" At this point, however, the authors exposed their self-interest more directly by declaring that women could not work in certain professions, such as military aviation, because their physiology preventing them from serving "at any time of year and at any time of the month." Invoking a formulation that contradicted Soviet gender ideology, and which certainly differed from wartime experience, the two men declared that women could be patriots, but not pilots. Kobyzev and Lobanov even invoked the historical example of Durova, who fought against Napoleon's army while disguised as a man, as proof of "the sterile and lusterless" outcome that came from denying gender differences. While conceding that coeducation encouraged friendship and "mutually ennobling influence" among girls and boys, Kobyzev and Lobanov concluded that the goal of training pupils for "specifically masculine and feminine purposes" justified the continued separation of schools.[129]

In their letter comparing academic results (as discussed in the second chapter), school directors Mushat and Remukhov denied that Soviet principles of equality meant that men and women should perform identical tasks and enter into the exact same professions. Their letter also took a more critical stance toward the article that prompted this public debate, as they charged that, although Kolbanovskii's support for coeducation was quite obvious, he did not present any "persuasive" evidence, "no facts" but, rather, general criticisms and allegations.[130] After charging Kolbanovskii with distorting the views of supporters of separate instruction, such as Timofeev, Mushat and Remukhov concluded that schools should continue to develop methods specific to the needs of male and female pupils.

Yet it was precisely this issue of gender differentiation that provoked the most vehement criticism of the existing policy. S. Platonov, a mother with two sons in Tashkent, declared that just as girls were future mothers as well as productive citizens, boys were going to be future fathers, and thus all pupils should be trained to bring up the next Soviet generation.[131] A letter written collectively by former pupils in Tbilisi condemned "false" notions of women as "the weaker sex," because the remarkable achievements of women proved their equality with "the stronger sex," even as they achieved "maternal happiness" by raising children to become politically aware and socially responsible communists.[132] Echoing Bocharova's unusual endorsement of changes in gender roles (as cited above), tenth-grade pupil Rototaev asserted that boys should be taught not only to use a hammer but also to darn a sock, cook a meal, and even, "when necessary," do laundry, just as girls must be able to shoot guns, throw grenades, and care for wounds.[133] Orlov, a father in Tbilisi, also stated that boys just as much as girls needed to learn domestic skills, such as cooking, sewing, and cleaning.[134] A. Fedorov responded to the claim of preparing girls for motherhood with a pointed question: "Yes, a girl is a future mother, but can a weak-willed mother raise strong-willed children?"[135] Bondarenna declared that while some Soviet families followed a traditional model, where the father earned more and the mother's "secondary position" allowed her to assume responsibility for household obligations, other families occupied a different situation, where the mother was the "main provider for the family." Bondarenna praised this blurring of gender roles as "an excellent model of family relations and complete mutual understanding and respect."[136] The debate on separate schools thus encouraged opponents to expand the definition of appropriate behaviors, roles, and attributes associated with defining masculine and feminine roles and relations.

The experience of the war, and especially the glorification of heroic women, was invoked by both advocates and opponents of separate schools. Ninth-grade pupils in Iaroslavl' credited prewar coeducational schools with producing "more than a few heroes," while other pupils invoked both the traits of individual soldiers and the collective spirit of the front as embodying the desired outcomes of educational processes.[137] An anonymous correspondent drew on her experience in an anti-aircraft unit to justify educating boys and girls to fulfill the same duties. After the war, this woman defied assumptions that the "proper technology for a woman is the saucepan and the iron" by entering an electronics institute and then designing electromagnetic instruments. Asserting that many women engineers and technicians were very successful, "yet this does not prevent them from being excellent mothers," she concluded that only coeducation prepared all pupils to work "shoulder to shoulder" to build communist society.[138] In a published letter, Fedorov charged that Tiapkin's list of essential male attributes were the same qualities demonstrated by Soviet women who fought on the front lines, "displaying unprecedented courage!"[139] Yet a proponent of separate schooling, Reiser, drew upon the same historical experience to argue that the school, "and most of all the system of coeducational instruction," failed to equip boys with the self-control necessary for military service. To prove the advantages of a gender-segregated environment, Reiser referred to the Suvorov military schools, where boys taught by "men teachers" and "without the presence of members of the opposite sex" received an excellent education.[140]

A few correspondents echoed Kolbanovskii's denunciation of "bifurcators," whose arguments were based on "unscientific" and "anti-Soviet" assumptions about innate gender differences. The letter from engineering student Chernogubovskaia appeared under the headline: "Where did the 'bifurcators' come from?" While her letter actually made no mention of bifurcators, she strongly challenged the assumptions of innate differences invoked by defenders of separate schools.[141] The term "bifurcators" also appeared in unpublished letters, demonstrating how pervasively this rhetoric penetrated Soviet discourse.[142] Even ninth-grade girls invoked this language by accusing supporters of separate schools, and Tiapkin in particular, for "bifurcating" views that assumed boys should be "masculine to the core" and girls should be "prim young ladies."[143] Denunciations of "bifurcators" led to broader explorations of gender boundaries. S. Kunanbaev, the secretary of the Komsomol Central Committee in Kazakhstan, criticized "bifurcators" for asserting that girls had fewer capabilities in math, physics, or chemistry. Building on highly charged rhetoric from before the war, Kunanbaev repudiated this view as a legacy of bourgeois ideology that relegated women to the inferiority expressed in the formula of "children, kitchen, clothing, and church" *(Kinder, Kuche, Kleider, Kirche)*. "Our woman is a great force," Kunanbaev declared, and "she should study *all* the sciences," and not just those defined as "merely feminine."[144] Ninth-grade female pupils used the same German phrase to challenge this emphasis on motherhood; these pupils argued that if Soviet women before the war had been trained only with domestic skills, they never would have withstood the suffering caused by the Nazi invasion.[145]

In contrast to the prevailing tone within the educational apparatus, these letters devoted comparatively little attention to disciplinary problems. Shevchenko stated that discipline in separate schools was not improving, but actually worsening,[146] but otherwise this issue remained mostly absent from letters, both published and unpublished, with the exception of those from some parents of male pupils. Many letters offered positive visions of proper relations in and out of the classroom. Kunanbaev declared that coeducational schools ensured that boys and girls had "an ennobling and deterrent" effect on each other: "In coeducation, boys and girls are familiar with each other, they know each other, they help each other, they see each other as comrades, and they create a united collective with common interests."[147] Opponents of separate schools criticized the ways that boys and girls interacted only in organized extracurricular activities or in "chance encounters," both of which fostered "mutual alienation."[148] Whereas separate schools produced undesirable yet unavoidable "ruptures" and "alienation," the goal of Soviet education should be the opposite, to ensure that boys and girls learned to work and live cooperatively.[149]

The effect of separate schools on the formation of a collective emerged as one of the strongest arguments for coeducation. Female tenth-grade pupils warned that separate schools made it difficult to "weld together strongly" the collective of pupils.[150] A letter from five men, all soldiers, declared that separate schooling was depriving youth of ten years of learning and working together, developing common interests, and forming the necessary Soviet collective. According to author Nikolai Atarov, who quoted the soldiers' letter in support of coeducation, this view was shared by hundreds of teachers and parents, who believed that separate schools could not form "a unified collective."[151] Invoking powerful ideals, correspondents promised that coeducation would "erase the border between girls and boys," promote the "most natural, friendly relations," and develop citizens "who will be comrades for their entire life."[152]

These idealized accounts of male–female interaction were challenged by defenders of separate schools, who drew on criticisms of coeducational schools made in the last seven years to reinforce their point of view. V. G. Marenkov declared that in the coeducational school, girls become coarser and boys become softer, thus interfering with their preparation for adult roles.[153] Reiser recalled his prerevolutionary coeducational school to assert that "nothing good came of this," as girls acquired "an unusual sharpness and crudeness," while "we boys looked down on them as weaker beings."[154] Even more pointedly, Kobyzev and Lobanov declared that educating boys in "a military spirit" was rendered impossible by coeducation's tendency toward "a cultivation of femininity."[155] Writing from a different perspective, housewife A. K. Uksusova supported separate instruction, based on her observations of her children's education: "In separate schools, teachers devote more attention to the inculcation of work habits in girls and the development and reinforcement of discipline among boys."[156]

Yet these defenders of the current arrangements were overwhelmed by those who invoked idealized visions of gender harmony in coeducational schools. According to Bondarenna, a coeducational school can teach boys and girls to be comrades throughout their lives, but "none of this could be achieved by a school which educates the sexes separately!"[157] A similar comparison came from Pavlov, who declared that coeducational schools never generated or tolerated the kinds of "sickly situations, distortions, or abnormalities" found in separate schools.[158] School girls listened "with envy" to the older generation talk about the "happy and strong comradeship" and "real comradely relations" in coeducational schools.[159]

All these letters demonstrate the breadth and depth of arguments for, and mostly against, separate schools. While a few letters defended the existing policies, the intense criticism found in most letters illustrates a shared view that separate schools did not offer any real improvement over coeducation but did foster undesirable attitudes, practices, and aspirations.

These criticisms revealed the potential importance of public opinion, particularly when correspondents openly called for the repudiation of the existing policy.

A Referendum on Separate Schools?

This chapter began with school director Disson's suggestion that if a referendum were held on separate schooling, most teachers would favor coeducation. According to the published transcript, this comment provoked laughter, suggesting that those in attendance were perhaps amused, or more likely astonished, at the idea of a popular referendum on a government policy that might lead to a negative assessment. But the letters described above in fact constituted a vigorous, thoughtful, and mostly critical referendum on this "troubling question." Although letters sent to *Literaturnaia gazeta* offered the most extensive evidence of these deliberations, other materials from this same time period revealed a broader dialogue on separate schools. In the spring of 1950, shortly after the publication of Kolbanovskii's article, an "overflowing" meeting of Leningrad teachers, school directors, and students listened to speakers "warmly and passionately" arguing for coeducation.[160] Declaring that "separate instruction has not justified itself in practice," director Kabash charged that "artificially isolated boys and girls" were unprepared to enter higher education and work together to build communism. Other speakers at this same meeting criticized separate schools for preventing "healthy competition and a mutually ennobling influence between boys and girls." Teacher A. A. Glazunova went even further by "sharply" criticizing the educational administration, including the Ministry of Education, the Academy of Pedagogical Sciences, and the newspaper *Uchitel'skaia gazeta,* for their "nonintervention" in discussions of separate schooling.[161]

This published report indicated that separate schools provoked negative assessments directed at the very basic claim that separating boys and girls would improve their educations. The fact that Leningrad had the second-highest proportion of separate schools suggests that these teachers drew upon a deep range of experience in boys' and girls' schools. Finally, and perhaps most importantly, these speeches—made in front of a professional gathering, with individuals identified by name, and published in a high-circulation newspaper—indicate some degree of official tolerance for dissenting opinions.

Other sources provide further evidence that the Soviet people were eager to talk about separate schools, even if their opinions differed from the consensus view reported from this meeting. Moscow director Pavlenko declared that "the question of coeducation" was raised primarily by teachers who could not control their classrooms, or by parents "who have memories of their time at school, when boys and girls sat together, dreamily passing notes back and forth." Pavlenko cited a rural school director's complaints about discipline as evidence that coeducation did not guarantee disciplined classrooms, he charged that "comrades who promote coeducation have forgotten what discipline was like before the schools were separated," and he warned that merging schools "in present-day conditions" would result in "a certain hardening of girls," while their supposed "ennobling" influence would have no influence on troublemakers, so "the situation would not change at all."[162]

Yet others drew on different experiences and perspectives to argue for coeducation. When a father, A. Baibakov, walked his daughter past a girls' school, she asked where the boys were, and so he turned to the editors of *Literaturnaia gazeta* for guidance: "How should I answer her question: Why?"[163] When the Kazan Communist Party committee scheduled a discussion on this topic, many teachers told their party colleagues to convey their dissatisfaction with separate schools.[164] Other accounts referred to "broad discussions" and even arguments among teachers.[165] Although most of these discussions occurred "only in private conversations among themselves," as recalled by a former teacher,[166] the available evidence reveals a striking willingness to offer frank evaluations of the current policy.

Some letters reviewed the available evidence and then reached conclusions explicitly for or against separate schools. Miaspov initially complained that proponents of separate instruction saw only the negatives in coeducation, while proponents of coeducation saw only the negatives in separate instruction, whereas he could see both arguments. Having considered all aspects of the debate, however, Miaspov "ended up on the side of separate instruction" and actually asked that his letter appear under the headline "In Favor of Separate Instruction."[167] Reiser began his letter even more emphatically, by stating, in capital letters: "I DO NOT AGREE" with advocates of coeducation, whose arguments were "completely unconvincing" and "proved nothing"; and then he declared emphatically, "I am in favor of separate instruction!"[168]

Yet most correspondents who expressed an opinion spoke in favor of coeducation. Stalingrad boys' teachers listed the many negatives observed in separate schools and then concluded: "We are in favor of coeducation."[169] Zin'kovskii's letter began with the heading "In Favor of Coeducation."[170] A teacher with almost forty years of experience, V. Mogachov, declared, "I favor coeducation, and I cannot think otherwise." Mogachov warned that separate schools encouraged pupils to emulate the nobility ("cavaliers and baronesses"), whereas coeducational schools taught pupils to think of themselves as comrades, standing together, "shoulder to shoulder," to defend the Motherland.[171] Leningrad boys' school teacher Prokhorova ended by declaring that separate instruction "was in essence profoundly mistaken."[172]

Former pupils from Tbilisi directly challenged proponents of separate schooling to engage the Soviet present, rather than an imagined past. To prove this point, their letter quoted Tbilisi boys' school No. 2 director Tabadze, who, when pressed for reasons to support separate schools, could only say, "it is better" or "that's how it used to be." The former pupils drew their own conclusions: "Tabadze had not thought about this question, and did not want to think about it. He says, that is how it 'used to be.' This 'used to be' relates to the old Tsarist regime, but surely the comrade director does not think that we want to return to this 'used to be'?" Declaring that "our Soviet schools are truly for the people and have nothing in common" with prerevolutionary institutions, these former pupils declared that "inequality had been eliminated," and "as we move ever closer to a communist society, we will not go back for any reason."[173] The arguments for separate schools were thus challenged by showing that inertia, rather than any productive vision, maintained a form of schooling associated with a reactionary historical period. These former pupils obviously felt comfortable not only questioning school officials about the justifications for policies but even mocking those opinions in a letter to a central newspaper, which included their names and quite possibly could have appeared in print.

Perhaps the most interesting contributions to this debate were letters written collectively by girls. These pupils drew upon personal experience in girls' schools, as discussed in chapter 3, to advocate for the complete restoration of coeducation. A letter from ninth-grade pupils in Leningrad girls' school No. 103 began with the heading "We Are Opposed!" After praising Kolbanovskii's article for exposing the problems of separate schools, they reaffirmed their position: "We are all against it."[174] Pupils in a Sverdlovsk girls' school, who had studied separately since the third grade, denounced separate schools for promoting "unhealthy relations" between boys and girls. This negative judgment was particularly revealing, because just a few years earlier, their Sverdlovsk school was the subject of a flattering report emphasizing the advantages of separate education. The letter was signed by six girls, with a note indicating that "a total of" thirty-five girls endorsed the statement and a further postscript asking the editors to publish this letter, because "it expresses the opinion of many girls in our school."[175]

Seventh-grade pupil Tat'iana Goriaeva began her letter by thanking Kolbanovskii for raising this question, and expressed "my gratitude, and also the gratitude of *many thousands of my friends*," that "Soviet society is now taking up the question of coeducation." Goriaeva ended her letter with this rhetorical question: "Why do we study separately, and not together?"[176] Seventeen female pupils from a Leningrad girls' school wrote to "call attention to the fact that the majority of boys and girls support the coeducational instruction of pupils," yet they also made the unusual request that their letter not appear in print.[177] Ninth-grade pupils in Ramen girls' school No. 1, who had studied separately since the fourth grade, declared "the separation of schools has not led to anything positive," whereas coeducation would "raise achievement" for all pupils and improve discipline among boys. Conceding that it was unusual to debate policy issues, these girls considered it "necessary" to express their opinion, which was shared by all of the class.[178] A letter signed by more than twenty female pupils, from an unidentified school, declared that "separate instruction has done great harm to Soviet youth." Urging consideration of how pupils could now benefit from "the most rapid resolution of this question in favor of coeducational instruction," these pupils concluded: "But, happily for Soviet pupils, public opinion is on the side of coeducation."[179] Almost forty pupils from a Moscow girls' school tenth grade stated that since they had studied separately since the fourth grade, "we can judge for ourselves the advantages and shortcomings of separate instruction." These girls warned that "only coeducational instruction" can produce healthy, friendly, and equal relations between boys and girls.[180] Ninth-grade pupils in Iaroslavl' wrote that "the question of coeducational instruction affects us directly," they "fully agree" with proponents of coeducation, and the newspaper should publish "the voices" of pupils on this question.[181] Eighth-grade girls in Leningrad declared that "we, female pupils of the Soviet school," supported coeducation and believed the proper solution would "follow from listening to the voices of pupils themselves."[182]

Conclusion

Whereas previous chapters examined the policies and practices of separate schools, this chapter seeks to "listen" to school directors, teachers, pupils, and the general public as they struggled not only to make sense of the new educational policy but to realize its promises and potential in their own schools. Some participants may have always been opposed to separate schooling, but a more common trajectory involved the accumulation of questions, concerns, and doubts about the effects of separate schooling on gender identities, dynamics, and boundaries. The failure of separate schools to fulfill their promised outcomes, the persistent tension between gender separation in schools and integration throughout society, the vigilance for any compromises in the promised equality of women, and finally, the hope that persistent problems could actually be addressed more effectively in coeducational schools all signaled a significant change in public opinion. Even within the constraints of postwar Stalinism, these critical voices effectively communicated broad dissatisfaction to policy makers. In reviewing the flood of letters received after the publication of Kolbanovskii's article, *Literaturnaia gazeta* editors concluded that proponents of separate instruction were unable to provide any substantive arguments in favor of this system. By contrast, this editorial asserted, arguments for coeducation were becoming broader and more thoughtful and convincingly demonstrated that only a change in policy could fulfill the ideals of the socialist system, improve the position of women, and address practical considerations.[183]

This change in Soviet public opinion bears directly on discussions of separate schooling in other contexts. Although the initial introduction of separate schooling tends to generate positive attention, notwithstanding the opposition and resistance of determined defenders of coeducation, the real test of this policy—as with any kind of educational reform—comes three, five, or seven years later.[184] By this time, the aura of newness has worn off, proponents of change have moved on to other innovations, and school officials, teachers, pupils, and parents are left to deal with the same curriculum and textbooks in the same classrooms. In the case of separate schools, the decision to make the gender of pupils into the most important boundary often comes without any substantive or durable explanations of how this variable can be incorporated into schooling without compromising educational objectives or ideological principles. In this context, confirmed supporters of coeducation, like Kolbanovskii and his many defenders among these correspondents, find new opportunities to press their case, for they could contrast the evident problems of separate schools with the possibilities of an idealized structure of coeducation. Yet the comments of director Disson, as cited in the chapter's introduction, are perhaps a better guide to understanding this trajectory. She was initially attracted to the promises of separate schools as a strategy yet quickly acknowledged the limitations of the new policy and thus ended up embracing a renewed faith in coeducation. As will be seen in the final chapter, this commitment to further reform would be realized only four years later, when coeducation was fully restored in the summer of 1954.

6 Restoring Coeducation
The End of an Experiment

IN THE LATE SUMMER OF 1950, at the same time as
the publication of the letters cited in the previous chapter, the Soviet
periodical *Krokodil* published an illustration under the heading, "As
a Matter for Discussion: The Question of Separate Instruction in the
Schools" (see figure 10). The top panels showed a boys' school and a girls'
school, with a similar layout of children leaving the building in pairs. The
bottom panels showed the same two schools, but now boys and girls walk
out together. The caption reads: "How two secondary schools . . . will be
made into two excellent schools." The meaning was obvious yet still quite
remarkable in its context. The transition from separate to coeducational
schools will take place, this cartoon affirmed, but the question was how to
do so in ways that improve education. Raising this question of restoring
coeducation "as a matter for discussion" (the same heading used to frame
the article by Kolbanovskii) anticipated a decision that had not yet been
made by policy makers yet certainly reflected prevailing trends in public
opinion, at least as expressed in the statements and letters discussed in
the previous chapter.

Of course, this illustration presented an idealized version of schooling,
with no hint of the acute disciplinary problems of boys' schools or the
intense social relations of girls' schools, as discussed in the third and
fourth chapters. Yet even with this idealized representation, the cartoon

10. "As a Matter for Discussion: The Question of Separate Instruction in Schools." "V poriadke diskussii," *Krokodil*, no. 21 (1950): 4.

illustrated the response of Soviet authorities to the emerging debate on separate schools. As discussed in the first two chapters, separate schools were never implemented universally or even consistently across the Soviet Union. Understanding how extensively schools were separated—and particularly the significant shifts even while the policy was still in place—provides some evidence of fluctuations in administrative support. In the early stages, educational departments were seemingly so enthusiastic that they exceeded instructions issued by central authorities. As the policy failed to deliver on its promises, however, this enthusiasm faded, leading some authorities to take the initiative to convert separate schools back to coeducational facilities or, equally important, to open new coeducational schools. Although central authorities offered some resistance to these deviations, this de facto repudiation of separate schooling contributed to the further erosion of the policy at the very time that critics were becoming increasingly more vocal.

Policy makers evaluated separate schools at the same time this question was being debated in letters sent to *Literaturnaia gazeta* or in meetings of school directors. As was the case in 1943, the actual decision-making process is difficult to interpret, given both the opacity of deliberations among the elite and the lack of reliable source materials. Educational leaders were certainly attentive to public opinion, as demonstrated most extensively in late spring 1954, when they convened meetings with parents, teachers, and school directors to discuss separate schools. Held in cities across the Soviet Union these meetings, in a public venue, raised many of the same issues, and reached the same conclusions, as the letters submitted four years earlier. Although the decision to eliminate separate schools had already been made by this time, the significance of these meetings lay in this resounding proclamation of support for coeducation. As will be discussed in the final section of this chapter, the restoration of coeducation in September 1954 involved significant logistical challenges, but the broad repudiation of separate schools by the general public, and eventually by policy makers, ensured general acceptance of this return to "normal" gender relations.

The elimination of separate schools took place during an era of extreme political turmoil. As policy makers deliberated over separate schools, they were also consumed by political conflicts and crisis.[1] Stalin's death in March 1953 almost immediately lessened the paranoia and suspicion that had characterized the past quarter century, even as the struggle for succession added new layers of tension. The willingness of educational policy makers to acknowledge the failures of this policy, as well as the years of delay that followed the substantive push for change in 1950, both reflected the conditions of late Stalinism and anticipated the transition to post-Stalinism. When coeducational schools opened in September 1954, the Soviet political system had entered the new stage that followed Stalin's death. The process of repudiating separate schools thus provides insights into the transition in the political sphere as well as new perspectives on the articulation, practice, and representation of gender in education.

Soviet repudiation of separate schools provides important lessons for educators, parents, and policy makers in other contexts. The most familiar narratives involving gender and education involve the transition from single-sex (especially all-male) to coeducational schools.[2] More recently educators and parents have described, often in heroic terms, their efforts to establish single-sex schools as alternatives to coeducational schools.[3] The narrative told in this chapter—the elimination of separate schooling and the reintegration of boys and girls into coeducational schools—follows a less familiar trajectory.[4] This lack of attention can be explained partially by the controversial status of separate schooling, but it also reflects a more fundamental tension in the gendering of schools. As long as separate schools are new, they seem to offer solutions to a myriad of problems and thus receive mostly positive public attention as well as the enthusiastic support of proponents.[5] After gender separation has been in place for a prolonged period, existing problems have not been eliminated, and new deficiencies have become undeniable, the attractiveness of this educational alternative diminishes significantly.[6] Although less familiar, this counternarrative matters a great deal, not just to explain the Soviet experiment but for all educators, parents, and pupils contemplating the option of single-sex schooling, who should also contemplate whether proposed solutions may actually turn out worse than the perceived problem. Advocates often depict separate schools as "a universal panacea," in the dismissive phrase used by Soviet editors reviewing the mostly critical letters discussed in the previous chapter.[7] As this chapter will argue, the repudiation of separate schools did not mean that coeducation was a panacea either but, rather, that careful attention to educational practices can illuminate the complicated and contested meanings of gender in schools.

Trajectories in Separate Schooling

The strong support for separate schools in the first stages found expression in the requests from local and regional authorities to expand implementation to even more cities. Already by December 1943, republic authorities in Uzbekistan requested and received approval from Moscow to extend separate schooling to four more cities, with further expansion planned for the following year.[8] The Sverdlovsk regional educational department requested similar permission to separate schools in five more cities, also by September 1944.[9] While these proposals did not explain the reasons for expanding separate instruction, focusing instead on the logistics of assignments, it seems likely that educators expected that more separate schools would produce positive outcomes for more pupils in more cities.[10]

The same trajectory was evident in the overall increase in cities with at least some separate schools, which more than doubled from the 72 cities listed in the 1943 instructions to a total of 169 cities by 1954. Whereas Narkompros approved separate schools in more than a hundred cities, the impetus for separation in one-quarter of the cities listed in 1954 came from district- or regional-level officials, apparently without approval from the center.[11] It was possible that these decisions were simply imposed from above or were blatant attempts to curry favor with superiors by overfilling policies, but the absence of rhetorical embellishment and the emphasis on logistics suggest that lower-level educational departments genuinely believed that separate schools delivered real results.

Within just a few years, however, this trend was completely reversed. Regional and urban educational departments began requesting permission to combine single-sex schools or open new coeducational schools. In Ufa, the location for the exemplary boys' and girls' schools described in the first chapter, six separate schools had been converted to coeducation by 1953, a year before the policy was repudiated.[12] The Ministry of Education report listed sixteen cities where "separate schools have been almost completely eliminated."[13] This rhetoric was somewhat hyperbolic, as separate schools still existed in most of these cities, but they did account for less than one-quarter of schools. Just one city, Armavir, had only coeducational schools.[14] Yet similar evidence of declining numbers of separate schools came from other cities.[15] In Alma-Ata, the number of separate schools declined from thirty-five in the first year to just twenty-three a decade later, even as total enrollment increased significantly.[16] Already by 1950, this trend toward coeducational schools was cited as evidence that educators "on the ground" had "repudiated" separate schools, even if this meant "assuming the risk" of defying established policy.[17]

The declining proportion of separate schools also resulted from the opening of new coeducational schools, especially on the peripheries of cities, where most of the new urban population settled.[18] When school No. 35 opened in 1948 on the edge of Iaroslavl', the nearest school was more than four kilometers away, so district authorities allowed the enrollment of both boys and girls.[19] But still central authorities resisted this trend toward converting separate schools. In fact, the Ministry of Education charged that in too many cities separate schools were being reorganized into coeducational schools "without sufficient justification," "without permission and without authorization," and "in contradiction to government resolutions."[20] Of the eighty-five requests to convert to coeducation that the Ministry of Education received, sixty were granted yet the others did not merit "yielding" on the established policy.[21] In an exceptional case, however, the Ministry of Education granted permission in 1951 to Iakutsk to combine all of the boys' and girls' schools.[22] According to a later report, as soon as the Iakutsk schools completed this transition, educators were convinced of the "indisputable" advantages of coeducation.[23] But even as late as 1953, the Ministry of Education endorsed new boys' and girls' schools. In Molotov, school No. 21 was converted to a boys' school, and school No. 92 was converted to a girls' school for the 1953/1954 school year.[24]

Just as the initial enthusiasm for separating schools should be seen as evidence for support among school officials and the general public, so too the pressure from below to combine separate schools revealed a growing preference for coeducational schools, despite the Ministry of Education's resistance. Although comprehensive data are not available, it seems that a declining number of separate schools educated a diminishing proportion of Soviet children. These shifts in school numbers certainly reinforced the growing perception among educators (to be discussed in the next section) that separate schools were not delivering desired improvements.

Debates within the Educational Apparatus

Even before the discussion unfolded in the *Literaturnaia gazeta*, education policy makers engaged in a parallel discussion of the advantages and disadvantages of single-sex schooling. Because this discussion remained less visible, while most published reports (with the notable exception of Kolbanovskii's article and subsequent letters) were unfailingly positive, the educational establishment was increasingly criticized for ignoring problems in separate schools. Two girls' school directors expressed "dismay" that *Uchitel'skaia gazeta* had ignored this "provocative question,"[25] while a *Literaturnaia gazeta* editorial condemned the rival newspaper for its "persistent silence."[26] This same editorial offered an even more pointed criticism of minister of education Kairov, based on an incident at a teachers' meeting shortly after the publication of Kolbanovskii's article. According to the editorial, Kairov responded to a teacher's question about separate schools by declaring, first, that his ministry was not examining these schools, because no one had raised any questions, and second, that no one knew whether coeducational or single-sex schooling resulted in higher achievement. Declaring that hundreds of letters sent to *Literaturnaia gazeta* certainly demanded attention to this question, the editors dismissed Kairov's response with the simple phrase: "What a strange position!"[27]

The responses within the educational apparatus to Kolbanovskii's article and subsequent letters demonstrated that the policy was now under active deliberation. Some responses were simply defensive, stating that it was "easy" to criticize this policy with some kind of "cursory remarks," but only "solid studies" constituted a serious basis for discussion.[28] A revealing account of how policy makers responded to public criticism came from Kairov four years later, when coeducation was fully restored. Although public opinion was already opposed to separate schools, according to Kairov's recollections, "once the article appeared, then people began to think about it and were allowed to talk about it." More pointedly, the public also began to ask why the minister of education did not speak out on this question. Kairov recalled that when Kolbanovskii's article appeared, he wrote to "the government" asking for permission to respond but was told that it was not possible, as the ministry's duty was to uphold the law and not engage in debates with newspapers. When Kairov requested that the newspapers not be permitted to write about this topic, the government replied, "Why not?" In fact, according to Kairov, the government invoked "freedom of speech" as a justification for allowing criticism to appear in the press. As a result, ministry representatives could not even discuss separate schools: "We might have spoken, but it would have been strange to announce that we were just following Soviet law." Kairov further justified the ministry's inaction by saying, "You can imagine what would happen if every government organ did not fulfill the law but decided to discuss it."[29] In other words, under pressure from public opinion, the Ministry of Education was prevented from either restoring coeducation, offering a vigorous defense of separate schooling, or censoring critics.

The Academy of Pedagogical Sciences also began a more systematic study of separate schools in response to discussion taking place "in broad circles of Soviet society," among educators, "and also on the pages of *Literaturnaia gazeta*."[30] Yet this report reached strikingly ambivalent conclusions. A survey of arguments for and against separate schools led to a cautious conclusion that coeducational instruction was "more advisable."[31] But the report also claimed that "the Academy of Pedagogical Sciences does not presently have any grounds for negatively assessing separate schools," because educational authorities did not have "at their disposal the necessary fully scientific and grounded materials for a competent judgment about the pedagogical results of the introduction of separate schools." In other words, the most important voice for the theory and practice of Soviet education could not state unequivocally which system was better. Implicitly acknowledging Kolbanovskii's charge that educational administrators neglected basic research, the report recommended further "scholarly study" that could produce a "substantial evaluation."[32]

Further efforts to gather information illustrated the continued erosion of support for separate schools at the regional level. During meetings held in the Chuvash region, teachers at girls' and boys' schools "unanimously" supported coeducation, with a desired implementation as soon as the next school year, a position endorsed by the regional educational department as "correct and well-founded."[33] The Smolensk educational department concluded that "separate instruction has not achieved sufficient pedagogical effectiveness," with specific problems related to the distribution of pupils, travel distances, the size of schools, poor discipline in boys' schools, and inadequate teacher training on the particular requirements of separate schools.[34]

Eroding support for separate schools among policy makers led to increasing criticism of educational administration. The Ministry of Education and the Academy of Pedagogical Sciences in particular were blamed for failing to provide adequate guidance, explanations, and instructions.[35] One defender of separate schools went so far as to denounce their "criminal indifference."[36] Stalinist rituals of self-criticism often included the assertion that policy failures resulted from implementation, thus displacing blame from the decision-making leadership. One example of this pattern came from Kairov, who declared that "things seem bad to us now" because the original instructions were only partially implemented. If Soviet educators had done everything that the decree required, Kairov declared in April 1954, "then we would not need to have the conversations that we are having now."[37]

Yet these statements were significant in part because they were so unusual. Most evaluations of separate schools focused on substantive problems, such as unbalanced enrollments, children from the same family attending different schools, and the long travel distances required of some pupils. These logistical complications meant that separate schools wasted government funds.[38] School director Velitskii advocated the conversion of separate schools to coeducational schools on the basis of "simple arithmetic": it would be easier for a school director to deal with 700 boys in a coeducational school, rather than 1,400 boys in a separate school, or for a teacher to work in a coeducational classroom, as "20 boys will make less of a nuisance than will 40 boys."[39]

Even as they wavered in their support for separate schools, policy makers sought to downplay the significance of this issue by declaring that the current policy "was not a political question" but, rather, an issue to be addressed "from a pedagogical and life perspective," without any polemical elements or arguments.[40] Yet when Kairov later echoed this perception that coeducation was "only pedagogical and practical," because full equality for women allowed for an experiment with separate schools, he was challenged by educator Zolotova who cited Lenin's views on women and then declared that the real question was what kind of school was most progressive. Zolotova's answer was clear: only coeducation was consistent with communist ideology.[41] Yet Kairov's concluding remarks again denied that separate schools were contrary to women's equal rights.[42]

The increasing criticism of separate schools within the educational apparatus did not, however, produce an immediate change in policy. In fact, a draft proposal from 1951 called for strengthening, rather than eliminating, separate schools. Promising "to eliminate deficiencies" in girls' and boys' schools, the proposal called on educational organizations to review the number of separate schools, strengthen the cadres appointed to boys' schools, examine "the particularities of instruction and upbringing in boys' and girls' schools," improve equipment and facilities, provide more methods literature for teachers, and control more closely this matter of "great government significance."[43] Yet perhaps the most significant aspect of this proposal was the absence of any justification of separate schools in terms of the "particular needs" of boys and girls. Even though the policy remained unchanged, educational officials were unable or unwilling to explain separate schools in terms of gender boundaries, as they had when the experiment began.

The gap between increasing awareness of deficiencies and the refusal to make substantive changes fully demonstrated the ways that the Stalinist system suppressed initiative, denied problems, and fostered stagnation. Kairov's recollections of being silenced by "the government" illustrated these powerful forces, even as his own attempted censorship disclosed the repressive impulses inherent in this system at every successive level. Policy deliberations took place in an intensified political climate. Kolbanovskii's article and the critical responses appeared in the immediate aftermath of the Leningrad Affair. For the next three years, until Stalin's death in March 1953, Soviet leaders feared the potential return of devastating cycles of repression, as experienced in the prewar decade.[44] Although neither the deliberations of policy makers nor the public discussion acknowledged this political context, the continued delay of any substantial reform until 1954, more than a year after the dictator's death, revealed both the stultifying effects of Stalin's last years and the potential for new initiatives that followed his demise.

Challenging Gender Boundaries

Even as policy makers delayed any substantive changes in schools, arguments for a restoration of coeducation continued to accumulate. In addition to critical assessments of separate schooling (as discussed in the previous chapter), a more affirmative argument emerged in favor of coeducation. Whereas the introduction of separate schools in 1943 prompted deliberate efforts to reinforce gender boundaries, the emphasis now was on minimizing distinctions between genders and emphasizing the common objectives. Critics of separate schools often pointed to the fact that every other level of education remained fully coeducational. An experienced teacher, A. V. Cherpakova, listed all the daily activities not separated by gender: children lived together in families, kindergartens combined boys and girls, most schools had not been separated, and higher education remained coeducational. Cherpakova then concluded that separating urban schools was inconsistent with Soviet education as a whole.[45] A housewife in Leningrad asked why boys and girls were segregated in schools, but together in children's homes or summer camps: "Isn't it somewhat illogical that spending several hours a day together at a school desk is harmful, but living and playing together is beneficial?"[46] Stalingrad teachers argued that when boys and girls educated together in the kindergarten were separated for the first grade, they began a "natural" alienation that escalated into mutual hostility.[47] Perhaps the most lyrical criticism came from teacher Mogachov's evocation of how young boys and girls "together take pleasure in their first toys," play and sing together, and "take pleasure in life together." These children would become adults struggling together for their homeland and their personal happiness. It was only in their school years, "that most valuable time" of learning about the human condition "when the young organism is full of happiness," that they were not permitted to study together.[48]

Yet this same anomaly provoked Miaspov to argue that separate schools did not encourage "isolation," because boys and girls spent time together in preschools as well as summer camps. Given that coeducation prevailed throughout children's lives, Miaspov argued, separate schools became their only opportunity to experience a single-sex grouping.[49] This affirmative position was overwhelmed, however, by increasingly emphatic arguments for the advantages of coeducation. In direct contrast to rhetoric used a decade earlier, now educators declared that separate schools failed to "distract" pupils from "unhealthy attractions" and to "concentrate attention on studies" and actually promoted "unhealthy manifestations of interest" in pupils of the opposite sex.[50] Often these arguments for coeducation invoked the "ennobling" influences that boys and girls could "exert upon each other."[51] Arguing for multiple potential benefits, Mogachov declared that only in a coeducational classroom would girls become "active" and "lively," while boys "would restrain themselves" in their use of crude words and ugly expressions.[52]

Other reports more specifically emphasized the "ennobling and restraining" influence that *girls* exerted upon *boys*.[53] An experienced and honored teacher, P. Novikova, described how more than twenty boys, deemed "completely hopeless" and "failures" in their separate school, all earned promotion after being transferred to her coeducational classroom: "You cannot imagine how the girls in my class have exerted a positive influence on the boys—even the most good-for-nothing ones!"[54] Boys' school director B. Fukalov praised the "hidden competition" in a coeducational school: "It might not even be noticed, but girls do not want to fall behind boys and they are embarrassed to get a bad grade."[55] A 1950 report stated that coeducation promoted "healthy, comradely, and cooperative relations between boys and girls," thus making "the life of the school" more interesting by allowing the greater energy, courage, and wit of boys to introduce brilliance and fascination into the school collective and enabling the entire collective to demonstrate morality, cleanliness, neatness, and achievement.[56] Underlying all these observations and predictions was the shared belief that, in the coeducational school, girls should serve the instrumental purpose of disciplining boys. Only rarely was this perception challenged, as in director Savchenko's warning that it was "incorrect" to devise disciplinary strategies at the expense of girls.[57]

The increasingly critical perception of separate schools also led to increasingly skeptical evaluations of claims of differences between boys and girls. Whereas educators had initially justified separate schools by the need to address the "particular" development of boys and girls, now critics warned that attempts to fabricate a "scientific-theoretical grounding" for gender differences undermined the equality of men and women. A 1951 report offered the following blunt assessment: "Separate education divided the school into two camps: a camp of boys and a camp of girls, with nothing connecting them and without any common interests." Boys became more crude and tactless, while girls grew more surly and unsociable or the opposite, too free and overly familiar. Even as boys and girls developed an "unhealthy interest" in each other, separate schools prevented the development of real friendships, a strong sense of comradeship, or any kind of simple and spontaneous mutual relationships. Gender separation was "unnatural" and inconsistent with Soviet society, where people of different nations, social positions, and personal backgrounds lived and worked together.[58]

Summarizing these increasingly critical evaluations, a 1953 article charged that biological differences between the sexes were assigned more significance than were the shared obligations of men and women, leading to "a noticeable decline" in the teaching of mathematics, physics, and chemistry in girls' schools. The emphasis on female responsibilities for family, housekeeping, and maternity encouraged a so-called parasitical mentality, distracting girls from their future roles in employment and public service. The feminization of schools was even leading boys to judge a girl on physical attributes, such as "the length of her braids!"[59]

This accumulating dissatisfaction was summarized in temperate, yet revealing, phrases: "Separate education has not proven itself," and separate schools did not deliver "any tangible benefits."[60] Although educators had initially been open to arguments in favor of gender boundaries, these criticisms reveal that the experiences, outcomes, and effects of separate schools produced increasing support for coeducation. After describing the negative results of separate schools, the 1951 report called for "the introduction of normal coeducational instruction, which has been proven by many years of experience."[61]

Assessments of separate schooling in so-called backward regions, especially in Central Asia, followed a similar trajectory from early enthusiasm to accumulating dissatisfaction. Educators in these regions initially endorsed claims that the new policy would promote girls' enrollment (as discussed in the first chapter) because parents would more willingly permit daughters to attend separate schools.[62] A decade later, however, the terms of this discussion had changed. Critics now claimed that separate schools reinforced obstacles to equality in communities that "have not yet completely eliminated feudal survivals in attitudes toward women."[63] Recalling an earlier discourse that emphasized coeducation as a step toward women's emancipation, Platonova warned that separate schools allowed "backward elements" in Tashkent to further "the alienation of girls from boys." Blaming girls' schools for worsening chronic problems such as attrition, early marriage, and even reveiling, Platonova concluded that "there should *only be coeducational schools for boys and girls*" in Central Asia.[64]

This same position was echoed, also in a letter to *Literaturnaia gazeta*, by Komsomol instructor Bort, who declared emphatically that separate instruction was fundamentally wrong for the "eastern republics," where the Communist Party and Russian people were emancipating women from repression and inequality. Warning that these schools replicated traditional forms of gender segregation, such as compulsory veiling or requiring women to sit separately at meals, Bort reported that many Uzbek pupils in girls' schools actually pulled on veils when men entered their classrooms. In a coeducational school, by contrast, "the well-known fact that girls are more diligent, persistent, and attentive during lessons" would encourage girls' confidence in their own abilities and also influence boys to see girls as equals, even as they moderated their behavior to become more disciplined and cultured. When boys and girls compete academically, "only good will come from coeducation" as schools become more consistent with the rhetoric of gender equality.[65]

As these remarks indicate, Central Asian educators responded to regional concerns (such as veiling), yet they also evaluated separate schools based on the same criteria as colleagues across the Soviet Union. The striking comments of Shelepov, an official in the Pavlodarsk educational department in Kazakhstan speaking at a teachers' meeting in March 1951, demonstrated the spread of critical views among educators. Raising "the possibility of a transition to coeducation," Shelepov told a regional education conference: "Girls' schools are in pretty good shape in terms of discipline, and everyone knows that good discipline produces achievement and order, but it is no secret that discipline is much worse and work is more difficult in boys' schools." Warning that the "comradely friendship" between boys and girls that developed in coeducational schools had been "disrupted," Shelepov declared that "it is time to raise the question of the possibility of a transition to coeducational instruction."[66] Even as this statement revealed the striking gap between a positive view of girls' schools and a negative appraisal of boys' schools, Shelepov also demonstrated that educators at the regional level were willing to call for policy changes at a time when the leadership was unwilling to take this step.

These criticisms of separate schools as harmful to children and incompatible with Soviet ideology thus found expression in public statements by educators. A 1951 report from the Chuvash regional educational department included a lengthy quoted statement from an honored teacher, N. M. Tiumedova, who asserted: "I consider the introduction of separate schooling to be unnatural for a socialist society."

Using rhetoric drawn from communist ideology, Tiumedova declared that Soviet women and men work together "equally" in all fields of labor, yet separate schools place boys and girls in an unnatural situation. As a result, boys become more coarse. Coeducation is preferred, Tiumedova concluded, because the experience of learning together is correct from a communist point of view.[67] The inclusion of Tiumedova's statement in this 1951 report illustrated the willingness of educators to speak out against established educational policy. If this comment was made at a teachers' meeting, as suggested by the report, Tiumedova may have believed that her perspective was broadly shared by her colleagues.

An even more pointed rhetorical strategy emerged in an August 1953 article by Atarov, an editor of *Literaturnaia gazeta* and a prominent author, who emphasized both the failure of separate schools to achieve their promised results and a sense of frustration that public discussion of shortcomings had not resulted in meaningful change. Atarov's article began with a long quotation, allegedly from Moscow teachers, who described a coeducational school that opened two years earlier in their outlying district. According to these teachers, forming a collective out of pupils reassigned from separate schools, "where they were not used to being together," required considerable effort, with particular attention to "violators of order," but gradually the situation improved: "boys and girls grew accustomed to studying together," discipline was strengthened, "respect and real comradeship" developed, and achievement rose. Yet in the fall of 1953, "everything was in danger," because of plans to build a new school in the same district. If the new school were coeducational, everything could remain the same. But if the new building housed a girls' school, then the current coeducational school would transition to a boys' school; if the new school were just for boys, then the existing school would be just for girls. Faced with these undesirable possibilities, a new coeducational school was the clear preference of parents, pupils, and educators, at least according to the teachers' collective letter.[68]

The article did not describe the outcome of this dilemma but, rather, cited the incident as a justification for dispatching correspondents to inspect boys' and girls' schools in Moscow as well as in Kazan', Molotov, Kuibyshev, and Iakutsk. Even as this article depicted "almost unanimous opposition" to separate schools (including many statements cited elsewhere in this chapter), the few cited comments from supporters for the current policy mostly served to underscore their seemingly feeble position. Of all the educators interviewed by these correspondents, only school director A.

Makarov openly opposed coeducation, on the grounds that "boys should be educated in a masculine spirit and girls in a feminine spirit," including the ability "to cook, do needlework, and be a mother." Even as Atarov stated that "this solitary voice needs to be taken into consideration," he also denounced these views for reinforcing the subordinate status of women. The cited claim by Kazan' boys' school director A. Avkent'ev that separate schools would "do no great harm" was undermined by his further pronouncement that boys' schools should have better facilities and more qualified teachers, a statement mocked as evidence that current policies undermined women's equality: "And this was a defense of separate education!"[69]

In another case, correspondents were allegedly surprised, and delighted, when a young woman teacher openly declared her support for separate schooling, because they wanted someone to "prove" the advantages of the current system. Yet the published account mostly served to undermine her position, as her references to biological differences between boys and girls were so vague and contradictory as to appear nonsensical. Her claim that boys behaved better when left to themselves, that girls spoke up more freely in their own classroom, and that it was easier to teach certain subjects, such as biology, to single-gender classes (precisely the same arguments used to justify separate schools in 1943) were now turned into objects of derision. And when this self-professed advocate for separate schooling was asked which school she preferred, "without even taking a second to think about it," she replied, "a girls' school, of course." When asked "what's so bad about a boys' school," she responded, "Hey, you're joking," and told a story about her friend who could not maintain any control in a boys' school, was subjected to insulting and harassing comments, and generally had "horrible" experiences.[70]

After referring to constitutional guarantees of equality as well as the practical experiences of millions of Soviet women who combined employment and maternity, Atarov declared that separate schools "as proven in practice" contradicted the equality between men and women and "thus introduce discord into the structures of our life." Invoking a romanticized vision of gender roles and relations, Atarov called for the restoration of coeducation, starting with the first grade in September 1953, so boys and girls could enter the school for the first time "holding hands tightly with each other."[71]

By the early 1950s, even as Ministry of Education officials denied that it was time for "serious" deliberations on ending separate schools,[72] the terms of this discussion had shifted almost entirely in favor of coeducation. Responding to a Ministry of Education survey, Penza boys' school teachers declared that coeducational classrooms were more disciplined and provided better instruction, because the "positive influence" of girls made boys more conscientious, industrious, and polite.[73] A 1951 report on Moscow boys' schools was prefaced by the author's "positive assessment of coeducation."[74] A 1951 report from the Smolensk educational department stated unequivocally that all schools should become coeducational.[75] Recalling the 1950 article by Kolbanovskii, the "absolute majority" of letters that "spoke against separate instruction," and critical conclusions by inspectors, Atarov declared emphatically that separate schools "do not deliver anything positive and do not serve any purpose" and thus offer "nothing to gain and much to lose."[76]

Even the rare remaining defenders of separate schools expressed their views in ways that demonstrated the growing dissatisfaction with the current situation. In 1950, boys' school director Liukhin declared, "I am not an opponent of coeducation, nor am I an advocate of it, but I am for separate education." Invoking the "definite advantages" of the current system, he warned against "the hasty merger of boys' and girls' schools."[77] At the same meeting, Moscow director Khrushchev stated, "Girls and boys do not lose anything by studying separately, because they cover the same program." Yet Khrushchev's evaluations, as suggested by his comments cited in earlier chapters, revealed a strong bias in favor of boys' schools. His dismissive statement that girls' schools were "simply getting lost," because of excessive attention to "private lives," while boys' schools, even with their "great difficulties," encouraged the development of more "inquisitive, energetic, and active" pupils illustrated this preference for a masculine emphasis in education.[78] Given the concerns about excessively feminine girls' schools and excessively disorderly boys' schools (as discussed in previous chapters), these comments were unlikely to convince others of the advantages of the current system. Yet still some educators remained loyal to separate schools. In early 1954, just months before the policy was repudiated, Moscow director Il'in declared his opposition to coeducation and proposed instead greater efforts to improve boys' and girls' schools, "thus leaving everything in place."[79]

Despite the caution of the Ministry of Education, these comments from educators illustrated the significant shift in the evaluation of separate schools. Whereas in the early 1940s, educators compared the observed shortcomings of coeducational schools to the anticipated advantages of separate schools, now the observed deficiencies experienced in separate schools could be compared to an idealized vision of gender equality and productive comradeship in coeducational schools. This trend in evaluations brought public opinion into the policy-making process. According to school director Gordunov, many teachers were asking for coeducation to be restored, only to be told "the government is deciding this question."[80] In his 1953 article, Atarov appealed to the Ministry of Education to listen to the "opinion of teachers," as "they have something to say" on this question.[81] As the next section argues, increased attention to the opinions of educators as well as to those of parents and even pupils played an important role in preparing for the elimination of separate schools.

Ending an Experiment

Although circumstances had changed significantly since Stalin's dictatorship had decreed separate schooling eleven years earlier, the combination of a secretive policy-making process, the flux of collective leadership, and the lack of reliable sources obscures efforts to determine the exact steps involved in this policy reversal.[82] As discussed above, draft proposals for restoring coeducation were prepared for the Council of Ministers as early as 1951, but it is not clear whether they were actually submitted, discussed, or approved. After a few more years of inaction, however, and a full year after Stalin's death, the Ministry of Education signaled its readiness in early 1954 to contemplate the repudiation of this policy. By this time, according to Kairov, separate schools, and especially the many "extraordinary incidents" at boys' schools, provoked "a great deal of alarm," and so the minister decided it was essential "to take this question to the government."[83]

Kairov's recognition of the urgent need for change was echoed and amplified by other speakers at the same April 1954 meeting. Moscow director Lebedev invoked a collective memory of coeducation as he confidently predicted meaningful improvements: "We remember our work in the past. At that time it was significantly easier. The bad things occurring now did not happen then and, I think, will not happen in the future when schools are combined together."[84] When Kairov spoke at another meeting later the same month, he outlined various options—but all involved the elimination of separate schooling, leaving open only the question of whether it was done gradually or immediately.[85] Even as the decision-making process remained obscured by the complex relationship among leaders and offices, Kairov was certainly responding to initiatives and opinions from directors, teachers, and parents rather than just demanding approval for a predetermined policy change. In fact, Kairov warned his colleagues against "simply taking up and uniting behind" any proposal for change.[86] Comments from school directors demonstrated this growing support for eliminating separate schools. Speaking directly, Zolotova declared that, for eleven years, "I have never understood the very idea of dividing boys and girls into separate schools." Rejecting the original purpose of separate schools, Zolotova charged that boy's schools offered inadequate programs in military instruction and that girls' schools did little more than put placemats and napkins in directors' offices.[87]

Even as they acknowledged the necessity of coeducation, directors also anticipated challenges in the formation of new collectives of pupils as well as in managing proper relations between boys and girls.[88] Moscow boys' school director Verbitskii warned that while "many place their hopes on coeducation," a decision he too supported, "it is wrong to say that this will completely solve" all problems in schools, which resulted from more fundamental deficiencies.[89] Boys' school director Il'in warned that a sudden shift to coeducation would produce a decline in discipline, as well as "unhealthy mutual relations" between boys and girls. Il'in was one of the very few participants at this April 1954 meeting to express support for "leaving things as they are" and for devoting efforts instead to improving boys' and girls' schools.[90] Other directors warned that girls' schools would "inevitably" encounter difficulties and that, therefore, "we must worry about girls' schools," with the clear implication that adding boys would worsen discipline.[91] Kul'nitskaia warned that girls who had spent ten years "only in a feminine environment" would encounter "all kinds of abnormalities" when they began to study with boys.[92] Even as they devoted attention to practical questions such as teacher assignments, drawing new school districts, and timing the transition the overwhelming sentiment of speakers favored coeducation.[93] In his conclusion, Kairov promised that "the government will review the question of coeducation and make a decision."[94]

Soviet policy makers took a more decisive—and certainly more public— step when they announced plans for meetings to allow parents, teachers, and the public "to express freely their judgment and to propose any solution desired on this question."[95] These meetings were widely reported, especially after the policy change was announced two months later, in ways that emphasized strong support for change. In Baku and other cities across

Azerbaijan, "people of the most varied professions—scientific employees, party and Komsomol officials, engineers, doctors, workers, employees, and housewives" attended meetings, where "the majority spoke in favor of coeducation of boys and girls."[96] In Moscow, where more than seventy thousand parents attended meetings, "almost all, with very few exceptions" of the more than six thousand speakers, called for coeducation.[97] In Leningrad, 94 percent of parents and 98 percent of teachers who spoke at meetings were in favor of coeducation.[98] These numbers were used to confirm claims that "broad discussions" at "well-attended meetings of parents and teachers" demonstrated that "coeducation met with unanimous approval."[99]

The main objections expressed at these meetings emphasized the "unjustified separation" of boys and girls at schools, in contradiction to the "correct comradely relations" that developed when both sexes lived together in families, attended nursery school and summer camp together, and studied in higher education and worked side by side as adults.[100] A parent at Moscow school No. 18 posed the question in a way that integrated diverse experiences and aspirations:

> Why is it that children are together everywhere, in the training schools, institutes, and camps, but not in school? As an old party member, I think a great deal about the upbringing of children. I have waited for 10 years for this experience to provide some kind of positive result, but it has not proven itself. . . . Everywhere in our country women stand together with men. When boys and girls studied together, they were accustomed from childhood to see each other as real comrades.[101]

Parents also complained that separate schools had a negative influence on children's behavior in the home, as girls were "aloof" and boys were "afraid" of female peers. One mother warned that since her son and daughter began attending separate schools, the boy was ashamed to be seen with his sister and also showed disdain for other girls.[102] The comments of a tiny minority of speakers supporting separate schools were dismissed as "unpersuasive," as in the case of the mother who warned that coeducation would not improve discipline, because boys would beat up girls, whereas tighter control could be exercised in separate schools.[103]

These meetings also provoked comparisons between the perceived crisis in boys' schools and the positive changes expected from coeducation. A school director in Ordzhonikidze described how converting to coeducation allowed his boys' school to overcome its reputation for poor discipline and become one of the city's best schools.[104] Speaking in Baku, a woman teacher, Abramian, made this emphatic comparison: "Discipline in the coeducational school is better than in separate schools, because of the beneficial influence of girls on boys and vice versa."[105] Drawing on their own experiences as well as an idealized vision of coeducation, teachers and parents predicted that boys who emulated the good examples set by girls would behave more appropriately, study more effectively, exercise "self-restraint," and act more "modestly."[106]

A report from the Alma-Ata city educational department in June 1954, just slightly before the policy was repudiated, amplified many criticisms made by parents and educators at these meetings, yet with more emphasis on the problems found in girls' schools. Created on the assumption that specifically feminine attributes, such as a soft character or greater sensitivity, would lead girls to show greater interest in subjects like literature and history as well as family responsibilities, separate schools were now seen to curtail girls' achievement in extracurricular activities such as technology groups and math competitions. With the repudiation of these "mistaken views" that seemed to discourage girls from pursuing advanced study and employment in agriculture and industry, the restoration of coeducation was now to be justified by the affirmed capacity of all pupils to cover the same program, prepare for the same adult roles, and acquire the same comradely relations.[107]

These criticisms of separate schools were consistent with the trajectory toward reform within the educational apparatus, yet they still offered public criticism of an established educational policy. The willingness of parents, teachers, and educators to articulate these critical perspectives was suggestive of a potential change in public discourse, just one year after Stalin's death, and was thus an early sign of the "thaw" that would emerge in the decade to follow.[108] This public criticism also demonstrated how separate schools had become thoroughly unpopular, as the failure to achieve promised improvements and a renewed commitment to gender equality had clearly persuaded the "overwhelming majority" of participants of the need for change.

A symbolic step toward the return of coeducation occurred during May Day 1954 celebrations in Tbilisi as pupils marched in a single formation, instead of separate columns for boys' and girls' schools as had been the practice for the last decade. According to the Georgian minister of education, pupils demonstrated an unusually high level of discipline, organization, and mutual respect. The orderly rows of boys and girls marching together reportedly evoked enthusiastic applause from the audience.[109]

Restoring Coeducation

In July 1954, less than two months before the new school year began, the eleven-year experiment with separate schools came to an end.[110] The decree, "On the introduction of coeducation in schools of Moscow, Leningrad, and other cities," echoed the formula used to introduce separate schools. The instructions were seemingly straightforward: coeducation would be restored in first through ninth grades beginning in September, while tenth-grade pupils would finish in their separate classes.[111] Yet the most interesting aspect of this decree was the opening line: "Taking into consideration the wishes of parents and the opinion of teachers . . ."[112] The complete repudiation of separate schooling that actually preceded this policy announcement, as discussed in the previous section, suggests that this invocation of a popular mandate was more than merely a propaganda slogan.

The justifications for this policy change echoed comments made by teachers, parents, and officials in their statements at meetings and letters to newspapers: separate schools did not improve achievement or discipline, interfered with "healthy comradely relations" between boys and girls, and were "artificial," "abnormal," and "not in harmony" with Soviet society.[113] Girls displayed "petit bourgeois attitudes," including undesirable bashfulness, fear, and alienation in regard to boys. Boys developed crude relations with comrades and teachers, a messy appearance, disorganization, "ostentatiously dashing behavior," and cynical attitudes toward girls.[114] The "unjustified" assumption that only separate schools could address the particular needs of boys and girls had produced "mistakes" and "distortions" that could now be corrected only by coeducation.[115] Echoing language used extensively before 1943, the educational newspaper declared: "Coeducation is a positive basis for forming a healthy children's collective and simple comradely relations between boys and girls."[116]

New instructions called for the implementation of coeducation "inclusively" and "simultaneously," thus setting aside more complicated transitions discussed just months earlier (to exempt the middle grades, for example, or to introduce changes by grade level).[117] Following the model set in 1943, regional educational departments were given tight deadlines to complete preparations for the new school year, now just over one month away.[118] New "micro-districts" ensured that pupils attended schools closest to their residence.[119] Despite the seeming simplicity of combining one boys' school and one girls' school to create two coeducational schools, authorities warned that preparing enrollment lists and reassigning pupils would be "complicated" and would require "serious and painstaking" efforts.[120] Some coeducational schools drew students from as many as eight different schools.[121] According to one Leningrad director, coordinating with three other school directors "seemed simple at first, yet turned out to be quite complicated."[122] School officials were explicitly warned against a "mechanical" transfer of pupils, as directors were supposed to "listen to the opinions of parents and the wishes of pupils themselves."[123] Schools earned praise if they managed this integration of pupils in an "orderly way."[124]

Educators identified the "main difficulty" as the formation of a strong pupils' collective in schools where one-half or more of pupils were "newcomers."[125] To achieve the goal of creating a strong, united, and "friendly collective of boys and girls," school directors and teachers planned outings, holiday celebrations, artistic creations, competitions, and campaigns to encourage boys and girls to embrace "their new collective life."[126] One logistical solution to the feared "breakup" of existing collectives was to transfer entire classes of boys or girls to a single coeducational school and then disperse the pupils into different classrooms.[127] Yet this method generated additional complications. Whereas the Ministry of Education in Azerbaijan initially permitted the transfer of "entire classes," just two weeks later Baku school officials were criticized because they transferred "entire classes from one school to another."[128] Vilnius school officials also transferred entire classes to other schools, even though some pupils actually lived closer to schools where they had studied the previous year.[129]

A visible step toward restoring gender balance included specifications that each school and classroom should have "an approximately equal number of boys and girls."[130] In some schools, however, boys and girls were unevenly distributed in classrooms.[131] Yet these same reports also tended to displace gender into the broader, yet also more ambiguous, categories of "strong and weak pupils." District officials issued instructions prohibiting assignment of all the strong pupils to one school and all the weak pupils to another school.[132] Despite these instructions, some directors, particularly of former girls' schools, reportedly tried to "hold on" to "their best pupils."[133] In Alma-Ata, the reluctance of school directors to "give up" their pupils led to unbalanced enrollment: a former boys' school had twenty boys and five girls in one classroom, while a former girls' school had thirteen boys and thirty-four girls in a sixth-grade classroom.[134] Teachers were also warned against any division into "our" and "their" pupils, which would re-create gender boundaries previously enforced by separate schools.[135] Some directors of former girls' schools even proposed that three-quarters of pupils in new coeducational schools be girls.[136] Even as the explicit attention to gender differences faded with the elimination of separate schools, certain underlying assumptions about girls and boys—now coded as strong or weak, well-behaved or undisciplined—shaped the practices and perceptions of educators.

The new policies required enthusiastic implementation, even as educators recognized the concerns of pupils and parents. School directors and teachers were expected to meet individually with pupils and parents to explain new assignments.[137] A photograph of a teacher at a former boys' school registering two siblings, a brother and sister, as pupils in the same school illustrated the new integrated ideals of the coeducational school.[138] Baku teacher Ryzhova planned "a series of conversations" about proper relations in coeducational schools: "It is important that children realize the necessity for friendship among Soviet people, the great efforts made by a cohesive, friendly collective and the weakness of the solitary person."[139] As late as the third week of August, an Erevan teacher complained that "not all parents understand the significance of coeducation."[140] Just a few days later, however, the same newspaper used virtually the same phrase to complain that "not all teachers" understood the meaning of coeducation.[141] Most concerns focused on the practical question of assignments. A few parents asked that their children be allowed to remain in the same school.[142] Pursuing the same end with a different method, some children asked parents to move to a different district, so they could attend the same school.[143] Even as they promised to show "sensitivity and tact," educational officials "explained patiently" that any deviations would lead to staffing problems and imbalances in enrollment, thus undermining the broader goal of universal education.[144]

The merger of girls' and boys' schools was expected to "preserve the basic composition of the pedagogical collective," meaning that most teachers remained in the same school.[145] Because of the prior preference for men teachers in boys' schools and women teachers in girls' schools, however, coeducational schools sometimes had "exclusively feminine" staffs or "a very large number of men teachers."[146] All teachers were expected to invest a great deal of effort in reviewing individual files, examination results, class journals, and evaluations by former teachers, in order to "get acquainted with pupils before the start of the new school year."[147]

Gender Boundaries in Coeducational Schools

The first day of school on September 1, 1954, was celebrated in Soviet newspapers and periodicals with numerous reports of boys and girls studying together, often for the first time in their lives.[148] Photographs and other illustrations depicted idealized forms of harmonious and egalitarian interactions between boys and girls (see figure 11), thus symbolically rejecting the last eleven years of gendered boundaries—even as the distinctive appearance of male and female pupils at different ages perpetuated awareness that equality did not mean the elimination of difference.

The complete restoration of coeducation was justified by both practical necessity and ideological principles. Coeducation eliminated the need for parallel classes, while simplifying the problem of staffing.[149] "One system" meant that "in all schools, without exceptions," pupils encountered "the same programs and textbooks, the same principles and methods" of instruction.[150] Coeducation would also promote the goals of establishing "a firm regime" in schools, because pupils showed "less restraint" in classes composed of the same sex. According to Kolbanovskii, whose 1950 article initiated a more public debate on separate schooling, greater "discretion" in mixed classrooms promised improvements in behavior and achievement.[151] The promise that coeducation would correct disciplinary problems found "especially in boys' schools" illustrated how particular dissatisfaction with male educational institutions shaped this change in policy. Coeducation was expected to lower attrition rates, as friendship and mutual respect would encourage boys and girls to participate "in the shared life of the school."[152] Educators drew upon "extensive experience" with coeducation to preserve healthy traditions while also building new communities.[153]

As the new school year began, educators acknowledged the difficulties of this transition. "Some pupils" who had displayed poor discipline in their boys' schools behaved badly in coeducational schools, which required additional disciplinary measures.[154] In some former girls' schools, including those considered the best in their districts, coeducation brought declines in academic achievement and worsening of discipline.[155] In Alma-Ata school No. 10, formerly a girls' school but now enrolling pupils from the former boys' school No. 25, deteriorating discipline in the fall of 1954 elicited numerous sanctions for bad behavior.[156] Making this same point more emphatically, but without explicit references to gender, Kolbanovskii declared that coeducational schools must deal decisively with "hooligans,"

11. "The Great Change." "Bol'shaia peremena," *Krokodil*, no. 24 (August 30, 1954): front cover.

whose indifference to academics and whose disruptive influence may have been tolerated in a previous school, but who now must be condemned, ridiculed, and corrected by teachers as well as classmates.[157]

The restoration of coeducation was hailed as a "great event in the life of schools" and a sign of "great changes."[158] Yet almost as soon as boys and girls entered coeducational classrooms, gender virtually disappeared from educational discourse. Policy goals were described in gender-neutral terms, to prepare youth for labor and to become good citizens, but without references to any specific features, roles, or obligations of either boys or girls.[159] Kolbanovskii declared emphatically that "there is no basis" for gender distinctions in academic instruction, because decades of coeducation had proven the equal capacity of all pupils; any differences resulted entirely from teachers' skills and pupils' abilities.[160] In an editorial, criticism of the "decline in discipline in many boys' schools" led to a pledge "to develop socialist discipline among all pupils," thus shifting from a gender-specific deficiency to a gender-inclusive remedy.[161] Declaring that "the introduction of coeducation into schools will undoubtedly bring positive results," published reports proclaimed that coeducation would create "simple, comradely relations between boys and girls," studying together in a "harmonious" collective, and contributing to successful educational work and strengthened discipline.[162]

Teachers and school directors were now encouraged to "use the advantages" of coeducational instruction, as boys and girls sharing the same classroom meant that "a variety of interests, inclinations, abilities, gifts, and talents" would make "the life of the collective especially rich in content and fully valued," and that pupils could develop "normal, comradely, and friendly relations."[163] A physics teacher, who presumably had previously taught only girls, praised boys who built a laboratory for her classroom.[164] Activities such as theater, choir, physical education, and other extracurricular functions were expected to be more interesting in coeducational schools.[165] The transition to coeducation thus involved deliberate efforts to eliminate the gender boundaries encouraged by separate schools. According to Kolbanovskii, separate schooling produced a whole range of undesirable attitudes among boys and girls: arrogance, superciliousness, alienation, misunderstanding, flirting, and courtship.[166] By carefully and sensitively fostering a sense of competition, the coeducational school exhorted boys and girls to strive toward "moral nobility."[167] This discourse revealed how previously gendered attributes, such as being orderly, disciplined, neat, and cooperative, once strongly associated with either a boys' or a girls' school, were now depicted in more neutral terms as desirable traits for all pupils.

The new advocates of coeducation acknowledged gender differences but directly challenged the assumptions that had previously justified separate schools: "Do not overestimate the significance of particularities in educational work, for individual differences among boys and girls are more significant than the differences between the sexes." Teachers could allow boys and girls to perform tasks suited to their interests. Reflecting the renewed emphasis on polytechnical education, the cited tasks mostly involved physical labor: cooking, child care, and laundry by girls, chopping wood, field work, and carrying water by boys. Yet this gendered division of labor, according to these same educators, should also be challenged and constrained in the coeducational school. Boys and girls should help each other in completing their tasks, and any suggestion of "survivals of the past," such as comments like "that's an old woman's task" or "girl work!" should be immediately corrected. Teachers should assign pupils to the same tasks, thus promoting a sense of complete gender equality between boys and girls, while also seeking to undermine stereotypes, such as boys' interest in technology or girls' inclinations to artistic expression.[168]

Returning to a pedagogical strategy recommended immediately after the revolution, teachers in coeducational schools were encouraged to seat a boy and a girl at the same desk. Although teachers were inclined to see this strategy as an effective measure to maintain order, they were explicitly cautioned against using this tactic to punish boys, through comments such as "You are making noise again! Now I am going to make you sit next to a girl!" Coeducational schools were also called upon to counter the negative influence of families on proper forms of friendship between boys and girls. These "incorrect views" could be countered by holding school assemblies, organizing book discussions, and working with school organizations.[169]

Coeducation thus produced new guidelines for managing romantic attachments, by ensuring that teachers guided sexual feelings to "emerge in such pure forms" and under such careful external restraint that they would not interfere with the work of the school. Teachers should hold discussions about the meaning of comradeship, friendship, and love, while also working to convince pupils of their obligations to comrades, parents, and the homeland.[170] Although this attention to managing adolescent sexuality involved some acknowledgment of gender differences, the dominant trajectory was now to deny that gender was even a factor in the education of boys and girls.

As suggested by the above description of tasks suited to boys and to girls, the new school year began with increased emphasis on teaching practical skills.[171] The number of hours devoted to chemistry and physics increased, while the hours assigned to literature, history, geography, logic, and other subjects decreased.[172] Renewed efforts to achieve universal education also dominated the new school year, in response to goals set by the Nineteenth Communist Party Congress in October 1952.[173] Although coeducation often disappeared from these discussions, both priorities were consistent with the new policy. The polytechnical curriculum was generally the same for all pupils, although girls still learned needlework and housekeeping.[174] Coeducation allowed children from the same family to attend the nearest school and strengthened connections between parents and schools, thus promoting universal education.[175]

In August 1954, the educational newspaper warned teachers and school directors to resist the temptation to think that all deficiencies resulted from separate instruction, and that thus the restoration of coeducation meant that everything would "straighten out and settle down."[176] Echoing this caution, teacher Aramian declared that coeducation would not eliminate all "disciplinary violations by boys," but that this change would make it easier to struggle against these violations.[177] A significant shift in discourse could be seen not only in prescriptive and propaganda texts but also in critical accounts. Thus, a report on the new school year at Baku school No. 189 recited a long list of familiar deficiencies: late assignments of pupils and teachers, overcrowded classrooms, shortages of staffing, and insufficient laboratory facilities.[178] These criticisms and complaints were most revealing, however, by the absence of any reference to the transition from single-sex to coeducational schooling. Gender had been removed as a consideration for evaluating the effectiveness and purpose of schooling.

Conclusion

For Amalrik, whose memoirs describing tense social relations in girls' schools were cited in chapter 3, the new school year in September 1954 also marked her first experience in a coeducational school:

> Of course, the boys introduced into the classroom a certain disorder and noise—anarchy, in short—but, to tell the truth, they also brought a certain amount of variety and freshness. The girls were generally of little interest

as I recall: they were strongly under the teacher's influence. The honours pupils acted primly, toadying to the teacher, and they were all nothing but tell-tales. But the boys had an element of fantasy and contradiction and they hardly ever told tales.[179]

This account emphasized the continuation of gender roles observed in separate schools, as boys were disorderly and girls were obedient. As Amalrik's dissenting perspective also indicates, however, separate schools could stimulate nonconformist behavior, most obviously as boys resisted school norms by their disorder and disobedience. Yet girls also deviated from the gender norms prescribed by separate schools, by "toadying," "petty," and "vulgar" behavior. Judging by the retrospective account of this first encounter between boys and girls, gender roles were more complicated than either the binary categories promoted by separate schools or the integrated collective desired by coeducation and resulted from a more complicated engagement of pupils with constructed norms of behavior and attitudes.

Amalrik's experiences in a coeducational school came at the end of a long process of repudiating separate schooling. The key turning points included meetings to discuss problems, "especially in boys' schools," the erosion of public support following the 1950 article by Kolbanovskii, criticism of and by educational administrators, and finally the extensive meetings with parents and teachers in late spring 1954. At each stage, arguments for separate schooling became less persuasive while the case for coeducation became more compelling. The end of separate schooling thus appeared almost as an anticlimax, for the established policy had been fully discredited even before it was finally repudiated. Setting aside Amalrik's dissenting views, many pupils, parents, and educators came to see coeducation as a "favorable moment" for establishing "comradely and friendly relations" among all pupils, "based on profound mutual respect and assistance."[180]

One of the most significant aspects of the process was the influence of those with direct experience in schools. The reports of school directors, the experiences of teachers, the statements of pupils, and the observations of parents created a strong impression of separate schools in a state of crisis. Poor discipline in boys' schools, excessive femininity in girls' schools, increased alienation between the sexes, logistical challenges, and tensions with a public ideology of gender equality combined to lead school officials, teachers, parents, and pupils to repudiate separate schooling. While the Communist Party and Soviet state maintained its monopoly on policy making, these decisions could respond to public opinion, so long as popular perceptions were consistent with political objectives. The phrase used to introduce the July 1954 Council of Ministers' decree, "taking into consideration the wishes of parents and the opinions of teachers," was a standard form of propaganda, but in this situation it also represented the growing sense among the Soviet public that the policy had failed and should be eliminated.

Conclusion
Learning Lessons from Soviet Separate Schools

According to a recent survey, three-quarters of Russians oppose separate schools for boys and girls. Published in early 2008, this poll of 1,500 respondents found that just 9 percent agreed that a system of separate schooling for boys and girls had "more advantages" than the existing system of coeducation. The advantages of coeducation, listed in order from most to least commonly cited, included the following: children learned necessary habits of social interactions and the norms of interacting with the opposite sex; they "get to know each other better"; instruction is better; children are better prepared for life; schools are "more lively, and more interesting"; any other system was inconceivable; first love occurs in an appropriate setting; and, finally, girls can assume more prominent roles in schools, as "girls discipline boys," "girls study better, and boys try to keep up with them," and "girls are smarter, and they influence boys." Among the small fraction of respondents supporting separate schools, the cited reasons included the following: children spend less time looking at each other and "more time devoted to their studies"; girls were not distracted by boys; education could better address the interests and inclinations of boys and girls; "more attention can be devoted to female attributes or to male attributes"; girls learned housekeeping skills and boys trained for the army;

schools would have "stricter discipline," "more order," "less conflict," and "less noise"; pupils would be less concerned with sexuality; schools would have less depravity and temptation, and more emphasis on chastity and morality; relations between boys and girls would improve if they were not in constant contact with each other; and boys would have more respect for girls if they learned to treat them like ladies.[1]

This poll articulated many of the themes raised by the Soviet experiment with separate schooling, even as the different context and life experiences of respondents shaped their overwhelming support for coeducation. Gender differences, behavioral norms, academic outcomes, social relations, and disciplinary strategies were all invoked by respondents in their comparisons of these two systems. The overall balance of opinion, much like the claim made in 1950 about the 98 percent of letters supporting coeducation, is perhaps less interesting from a research perspective than are the reasons cited for such views, which better reveal the nuanced relationship between gender identities, behaviors, and practices, on the one hand, and the policies and structures of coeducational or separate schools, on the other. More than five decades after the Stalinist experiment, the underlying promise of establishing and maintaining gender boundaries attracted some support as a means to improve education, prepare boys and girls for adult roles, and ensure the acquisition and display of appropriate gender identities. Yet the reasons cited for maintaining coeducation were also reflective of the similar perceptions shared by Soviet educators, parents, and pupils in the 1940s and 1950s, as their direct experience with separate schooling produced a strong opposition to this policy.

As illustrated by the previous chapters, separate schools were inextricably connected to underlying processes of marking and maintaining gender boundaries. According to a letter written by seventeen pupils enrolled in a Leningrad girls' school in 1950, separate instruction has established a "high border" between boys and girls. These pupils complained that even when boys' and girls' schools held combined events, pupils felt constrained and tended to separate "into two camps."[2] Zin'kovskii wrote in 1950 that the "experiment with separate instruction" had brought negative results, because "everyday Soviet reality is moving toward the rapid elimination of the border between feminine and masculine."[3] According to a 1950 letter signed by a collective of pupils from a Moscow girls' school, separate instruction had created "two camps," as boys and girls often seemed far apart from each other.[4] Brodskii, a pedagogical student, wrote, "as a future teacher and a graduate of prewar coeducational schools," that bringing boys and girls back together would contribute to "eliminating the centuries-old boundary between men and women."[5]

As these comments indicate, separate schools tended to reinforce a boundary that was otherwise being challenged, eroded, or diminished in Soviet society. One direct result of the decade-long experiment with separate schooling, in addition to the decline in public support for this option, was to diminish the relevance of this boundary.[6] Soviet educators, pupils, and society embraced coeducation as the preferred and more practical arrangement, and the history of separate schooling quickly receded from view, as coeducation resumed its previous status as an unquestioned truth of Soviet schooling.[7] Within a few years of 1954, visiting western observers praised the Soviet commitment to "complete equality between men and women," while an educational researcher contrasted the rapid and seemingly universal acceptance of coeducation in the Soviet Union to protracted and often inconclusive efforts under way elsewhere in the world.[8]

The significance of separate schooling, therefore, was not in the immediate historical impact, even for this generation that spent its school years in gender-segregated environments, but, rather, as a case study of the implications of social engineering by means of gender categories. Despite the absence of explicit discussion of gender differences, as explained above, Soviet urban school structures and educational discourse made gender into a primary category of identity—simply by separating boys and girls. Whereas in coeducational schools, educators could attribute disciplinary problems to all pupils and develop strategies aimed at the whole collective, separate schools more explicitly identified boys and girls as the subjects and objects of education. In this context, masculinity itself was increasingly defined in terms of this perception, now made concrete by the very structure of the school, of boys as disciplinary problems. Definitions of femininity, by contrast, were always more contested, as the perceived move toward lowering academic standards, emphasizing domestic skills, or narrowing girls' potential roles provoked criticism, resistance, and repudiations. Although a few educators responded favorably to the challenge of working with boys, far more common responses involved teachers who avoided boys' schools, directors who despaired of maintaining discipline, and pupils who studied in noisy, disruptive, and occasionally violent classrooms. Girls' schools, on the other hand, did not seem to have any trouble attracting and retaining teachers. These sources provide little information about the ways that boys themselves perceived these conditions, which makes it difficult to assess the impact of separate schooling on individual development or collective identity. Girls, by contrast, were consistently more vocal in challenging both the practical experience and the underlying purposes of separate schools, from the first questions in the summer of 1943 through the vehement denunciations in collectively written letters.

Evaluations of separate schools thus reinforced gender lines. Most important, gendered structures and a discourse of discipline suggests that separate schools validated, reinforced, and even deepened perceptions of boys as problems. This pattern in postwar Soviet schools thus anticipated recent research on American single-gender schools, which suggests that questions of discipline assume disproportionate importance in boys' schools, with the consequent lack of attention to other aspects of education.[9] Although Soviet boys' schools existed in a different set of conditions, similar experiments in other contexts may reinforce the same negative associations between discipline as a justification for separate schooling and perceptions of boys first and foremost as disciplinary problems. Eliminating single-sex schools was as much an effort to protect boys by reintegrating them with girls as it was a reaffirmation of communist ideology about gender equality. Where criticism of girls' schools revealed forms of behavior such as demands for equality and rigorous expectations that offered the potential of strengthening relative positions in restored coeducational schools, the accompanying expectation that coeducation would transform girls into part of the disciplinary regime for boys was difficult to reconcile with the claim that coeducation would make schooling more equal.

To the extent that postwar Soviet separate schooling confirmed gender categories, this historical example raises questions about current claims that single-gender programs can enhance the equality of boys and girls.[10] The underlying structures of Soviet schools, the practices of teachers, and even the behavior of pupils tended to confirm, rather than challenge or redefine, a pattern described in another context by Elisabeth Woody as "the inevitable privileges of being a boy."[11] While historians have tended to see Soviet separate schools as a diversion from the long-term (and never fully realized) project of achieving gender equality, a closer look indicates that girls' schools were "better" than boys' schools—in terms of academic achievement, classroom order, and the quality of the teachers. Yet this apparent advantage offered to and achieved by girls was both temporary, given the return of coeducation in 1954, and illusory, as administrators responded to problems in boys' schools by reallocating attention, facilities, and personnel away from girls' schools. Even the sharpest critics of boys' schools, in other words, inadvertently and simultaneously affirmed a privileged male position, because all this attention—even if it was "negative" attention—illustrated the ways that education, like other social and political institutions, primarily served the needs of boys rather than girls.

For all their discussion of the problems and possibilities of boys' and girls' schools, Soviet educators rarely connected these schools to other structures that maintained and legitimized other forms of gender inequality. As argued by Amanda Datnow and Lea Hubbard, achieving gender equity in schools "means not only providing equal opportunity to both genders but also acknowledging the power differences that exist between men and women in society and looking for ways that educational institutions can alter these taken-for-granted patterns that often place women on unequal footing to men and lead to restrictive notions of masculinity and femininity."[12] In the Stalinist context, the key assumptions of separate schooling—that boys were being trained as leaders, that boys had more energy and initiative, and that boys deserved better facilities and teachers, or that girls were easier to teach, girls were less accomplished, or girls were more tractable—tended to reinforce structural forms of gender inequality. The repudiation of separate schooling did not challenge this distribution of power and privilege but served instead to conceal shortcomings in boys' schools while also deploying girls as subjects, as well as objects, of educational structures.

Contemporary proponents of single-sex schooling need to address this question of how separating schools may privilege boys and penalize girls.[13] If it proves more difficult to recruit teachers for boys' schools, as was the case in the Soviet Union, how can the necessary human resources be allocated without subtracting from the education of girls?[14] If assumptions about the particular needs or interests of boys or girls lead to the provision of gender-specific facilities and services, what measures will be instituted to ensure that all schools receive equal shares of resources? Finally, to the extent that segregation makes girls' schools more celebrated as models of exemplary order and successful socialization, what mechanisms are in place to make sure that boys' schools receive comparable attention from administrators and the public? Even though Soviet educators claimed that separate schools were also equal, the underlying assumptions about boys' need for more experienced and effective teachers, as well as perceptions of girls as more successful and reliable, demonstrate how powerfully separate schools manufactured inequality.

The Soviet example should also provoke educators to ask the difficult question of what will come after the current proposals for single-sex programs have been implemented in public schools. As anyone involved in educational reforms should recognize, the passion and commitment of those advocating changes are often different from the persistence and engagement needed to sustain changes on a broad scale over a long period of time. Although separate schooling seemed to make sense to some Soviet educators in 1943, in the midst of a military emergency and after a decade of seemingly failed efforts to improve discipline, within a short period of time separate schooling had less and less support among any Soviet educators, who were then left with the challenge of first managing and then undoing a reform that had proven impractical, ineffective, and unsustainable. Without making claims for any kind of inevitability, the trajectory of the Soviet experiment suggests that whatever enthusiasm now exists for this policy may eventually ebb, as some proponents move on to other agendas, dedicated supporters become involved in the daily routines of schooling, and new research emerges suggesting the advantages of other approaches.[15]

More disturbing questions emerging from the Soviet case study also need to be addressed. What happens if educators in boys' schools see a worsening of the very disciplinary problems and instructional shortcomings that single-sex programs were supposed to eliminate? What if pupils in girls' schools embrace the separatism implicit in the structure of schools and withdraw from the obligations and expectations of equal citizenship? Will the solution be the further partition of the student population by assigning certain pupils to their own schools, or an effort to make the schools more "masculine" by placing greater emphasis on discipline or more "feminine" by emphasizing maternal duties, or a deliberate effort to reintegrate boys and girls into each other's programs—not for the sake of pupils themselves but as instruments to improve the education of others? All these scenarios emerged as responses to the problems that Soviet separate schools failed to resolve. To the extent that the "failure" of separate schools results from "structural" factors such as the distribution of resources and the functioning of a disciplinary regime, it is important that policies are not dependent on the passions and preferences of proponents to ensure effectiveness. Advocates of separate schooling need to ask—and be asked—about the long-term implications of positions advocated at the moment.

Perhaps most important, this case study is a reminder that discussion of single-sex education should always focus on the question of how best to educate boys *and* girls.[16] The Soviet experiment included three successive answers to this question: single-sex schools began as an attractive alternative to the coeducational status quo; were imposed as a policy regardless of preferences of teachers, pupils, or parents; and then were repudiated as a pedagogical failure. To a great extent, however, none of these stages ever resolved—or even addressed—the underlying issue of whether individuals and society were best served by schooling boys and girls toward the *same* or *different* ends. Soviet separate schools were structured around the latter within an ideological system that proclaimed the former, but the discourse on separate schooling never articulated how or what boys or girls should learn *differently* from each other. In fact, whenever Soviet educators, parents, and even pupils discussed how best to educate *all children,* their proposals and practices almost always gravitated toward coeducation as both an immediate remedy and a long-term ideal. Fifty years later, the strong support for coeducation in the poll cited above testified to the long-term persistence of these concerns about separate schooling. Promoting a dialogue around shared educational goals may avoid the false dichotomies made—and then repudiated—by Soviet educators as they sought unsuccessfully to provide the same education in separate schools.

Notes

Introduction

1. *Literaturnaia gazeta* (May 4, 1950): 2.

2. For the gendering of school spaces, see Barrie Thorne, "Girls and Boys together . . . but mostly Apart: Gender Arrangements in Elementary Schools," in *Men's Lives: Readings in the Sociology of Men and Masculinity*, 3rd ed., ed. Michael Kimmel and Michael Messner (New York: Macmillan, 1989), 61–73.

3. For a description of how the Soviet educational establishment demanded adherence to ideological principles in the postwar period, see George S. Counts and Nucia Lodge, *The Country of the Blind: The Soviet System of Mind Control* (Boston: Houghton Mifflin, 1949), 258–261. For a more nuanced discussion of public opinion in the postwar Soviet Union, see Elena Zubkova, *Russia after the War: Hopes, Illusions, and Disappointments, 1945–1957* (Armonk, NY: M. E. Sharpe, 1998). A decade earlier, proposed policy changes on abortion, marriage, and divorce were subjected to a broad range of public criticism, even as the outcome of the campaign was predetermined by Soviet leadership. Janet Evans, "The Communist Party of the Soviet Union and the Women's Question: The Case of the 1936 Decree 'In Defence of Mother and Child,'" *Journal of Contemporary History* 16 (1981): 757–775.

4. Kairov's concluding remarks were made at an open party meeting of the Communist Party of the Ministry of Education, September 11, 1950. TsAODM 1934/4/4/115–116. Kairov became minister of education in 1949 and remained in this position through the restoration of coeducation in 1954.

5. GARF A2306/72/72/3.

6. For discussion of gender roles in Stalinism, see Wendy Z. Goldman, *Women, the State, and Revolution: Soviet Family Policy and Social Life, 1917–1936* (Cambridge: Cambridge University Press, 1993); Goldman, *Women at the Gates: Gender and Industry in Stalin's Russia* (Cambridge: Cambridge University Press, 2002); Rebecca Balmas Neary, "Mothering Socialist Society: The Wife-Activists' Movement and the Soviet Culture of Daily Life, 1934–41," *Russian Review* 58 (July 1999): 396–412; David L. Hoffmann, "Mothers in the Motherland: Stalinist Pronatalism in Its Pan-European Context," *Journal of Social History* 34, no. 1 (2000): 35–54; E. Thomas Ewing, "Personal Acts with Public Meanings: Suicide by Soviet Women Teachers in the Stalin Era," *Gender & History* 14, no. 1 (2002): 117–137; Douglas Northrop, *Veiled Empire: Gender and Power in Stalinist Central Asia* (Ithaca: Cornell University Press, 2004); Marianne Kamp, *The New Woman in Uzbekistan: Islam, Modernity, and Unveiling under Communism* (Seattle: University of Washington Press, 2006).

7. "O vvedenii razdel'nogo obucheniia mal'chikov i devochek v 1943/44 uchebnom godu v nepolnykh srednikh i srednikh shkolakh oblastnykh, kraevykh gorodov, stolichnykh tsentrov soiuznykh i avtonomnykh respublik i krupnykh promyshlennykh

gorodov" (Resolution of the SNK SSSR, July 16, 1943), in *Narodnoe obrazovanie v SSSR. Obshcheobrazovatel'naia shkola: Sbornik dokumentov 1917–1973 gg* (Moscow: Prosveshchenie, 1973), 177.

8. For the shift in policy and rhetoric in 1943, see Catherine Merridale, *Ivan's War: Life and Death in the Red Army, 1939–1945* (London: Macmillan, 2007), 188–192; John Dunstan, *Soviet Schooling in the Second World War* (New York: St. Martin's Press, 1997), 149–150, 173; Jerry F. Hough, "Debates about the Postwar World," in *The Impact of World War II on the Soviet Union*, ed. Susan J. Linz (Totowa, NJ: Rowman and Allanheld, 1985), 253–254.

9. The war is the main explanation for the policy change offered by S. A. Chernik, *Sovetskaia obshcheobrazovatel'naia shkola v gody Velikoi Otechestvennoi Voiny* (Moscow: Pedagogika, 1984), 126–129.

10. For the gendering of identities as a result of the gradual militarization of Soviet society in the 1930s, see Anna Krylova, "Stalinist Identity from the Viewpoint of Gender: Rearing a Generation of Professionally Violent Women-Fighters in 1930s Stalinist Russia," *Gender & History* 16, no. 3 (November 2004): 626–653; Thomas G. Schrand, "Socialism in One Gender: Masculine Values in the Stalin Revolution"; and Karen Petrone, "Masculinity and Heroism in Imperial and Soviet Military-Patriotic Cultures," in *Russian Masculinities in History and Culture,* ed. Barbara Evans Clements, Rebecca Friedman, and Dan Healey (New York: Palgrave, 2002), 172–209.

11. Greta Bucher, *Women, the Bureaucracy and Daily Life in Postwar Moscow, 1945–1953* (Boulder, CO: East European Monographs, 2006), 12–15, 171–173; Bucher, "Struggling to Survive: Soviet Women in the Postwar Years," *Journal of Women's History* 12, no. 1 (Spring 2000): 144–148.

12. Gail Warshofsky Lapidus, *Women in Soviet Society: Equality, Development, and Social Change* (Berkeley and Los Angeles: University of California Press, 1978), 116; Richard Stites, *The Women's Liberation Movement in Russia: Feminism, Nihilism, and Bolshevism* (Princeton: Princeton University Press, 1978), 391. See also the discussion of separate schooling in the longer trajectory of women's expanding access to equal education in L. Dubrovina, *Women's Right to Education in the Soviet Union* (Moscow: Foreign Languages Publishing House, 1956), 16.

13. Bill Downs, "Revolution in Soviet School System Kills Coeducation for Youthful Reds," *Newsweek* (August 16, 1943): 76. One American editorial stated that the quest for "stability above anything else" led to a series of changes in women's status, including going "bourgeois to the point of abolishing coeducation in the schools." *New York Times* (July 13, 1944): 16. See also *New York Times* (August 5, 1943): 12; "Soldiering v. Mothering," *Time* 42 (August 16, 1943); "Soviet Reforms," *Times Educational Supplement* (October 30, 1943): 520. As the cold war hardened western perceptions of the Soviet Union, the military motives and implications of separate schools seemed to attract greater attention. George S. Counts, "Challenge of Soviet Education," *School Life* (1948): 23; *New York Times* (August 13, 1947): 21.

14. This study thus differs from approaches that see separate schooling primarily in terms of a restoration of more traditional forms of gender equality. Writing shortly after the new policy was implemented, émigré sociologist Nicholas Timasheff called the end of coeducation "an additional step toward the restoration of the pre-Revolutionary school order." Nicholas Timasheff, *The Great Retreat: The Growth and Decline of Communism* (New York: E. P. Dutton, 1946), 219. Echoing this interpretation, Ann Livschiz argues that this experiment in "gender socialization" was primarily a reflection of the "fundamental

social conservatism" of political leaders, and, even more emphatically, it was "the ultimate manifestation of the hypocritically-puritan attitude of Soviet establishment towards youth in general, and female sexuality in particular." Ann Livschiz, "Growing Up Soviet: Childhood in the Soviet Union, 1918–1958" (PhD diss., Stanford University, 2007), 692–693, 814–815. See also Ann Livschiz, "Pre-Revolutionary in Form, Soviet in Content? Wartime Educational Reforms and the Postwar Quest for Normality," *History of Education* 35, no. 4–5 (July–September 2006): 541–560. For a critical assessment of the "great retreat" interpretation of prewar Stalinism, see David L. Hoffmann, *Stalinist Values: The Cultural Norms of Soviet Modernity, 1917–1941* (Ithaca: Cornell University Press, 2003), 2–5.

15. Russian educational historian A. V. Pyzhikov also recognized that discipline was the main justification for both implementing and eliminating single-sex schooling, yet he does not acknowledge that it was discipline specifically in boys' schools that provoked an increasing sense of crisis in the late 1940s and early 1950s. A. V. Pyzhikov, "Razdel'noe obuchenie v sovetskoi shkole," *Pedagogika* 5 (2004): 78–84. John Dunstan states that the decision to implement separate education in urban schools was "advocated at this time on practical grounds," as expectations that schools prepare boys to be soldiers and girls to be mothers were accompanied by fears about family stability in the war and, most strikingly, the problem of maintaining order. Dunstan, *Soviet Schooling*, 170–176.

16. For discipline in the Stalinist school, see Larry E. Holmes, *Stalin's School: Moscow's Model School No. 25, 1931–1937* (Pittsburgh: University of Pittsburgh Press, 1999), 46–62; E. Thomas Ewing, *The Teachers of Stalinism: Policy, Practice, and Power in Soviet Schools of the 1930s* (New York: Peter Lang, 2002), 189–225; F. A. Fradkin and M. G. Plokhova, "Problemy distsipliny v sovetskoi shkole," *Sovetskaia pedagogika* 6 (1991): 91–98.

17. *New York Times* (October 17, 1943): 29.

18. Political concerns about youth attitudes and lack of discipline in postwar Stalinism are discussed in Zubkova, *Russia after the War*, 109–116; Juliane Furst, "Between Salvation and Liquidation: Homeless and Vagrant Children and the Reconstruction of Soviet Society," *Slavonic and East European Review* 86, no. 2 (April 2008): 232–258; Karl D. Qualls, *From Ruins to Reconstruction: Urban Identity in Soviet Sevastopol after World War II* (Ithaca: Cornell University Press, 2009), 121–122.

19. For this debate, see Juliane Furst, "Prisoners of the Soviet Self?—Political Youth Opposition in Late Stalinism," *Europe-Asia Studies* 54, no. 3 (2002): 353–375; Hiroaki Kuromiya, "'Political Youth Opposition in Late Stalinism': Evidence and Conjecture," *Europe-Asia Studies* 54, no. 4 (2003): 631–638; Juliane Furst, "Re-examining Opposition under Stalin: Evidence and Context—A Reply to Kuromiya," *Europe-Asia Studies* 55, no. 5 (2003): 789–802; Hiroaki Kuromiya, "Re-examining Opposition under Stalin: Further Thoughts," *Europe-Asia Studies* 56, no. 2 (2004): 309–314. On the "first shoots of political dissent" sprouting among youth, see Zubkova, *Russia after the War*, 109–111.

20. For the education of women and girls in Tsarist Russia, see N. A. Skvortsov, "Ocherednye voprosy zhenskago obrazovaniia," *Zhenskaia zhizn'* 16 (August 22, 1915): 1–2; Carol S. Nash, "Educating New Mothers: Women and the Enlightenment in Russia," *History of Education Quarterly* 21, no. 3 (1981): 301–316; L. D. Filippova, "Iz istorii zhenskogo obrazovaniia v Rossii," *Voprosy istorii* 2 (February 1963): 209–218; Christine Johanson, *Women's Struggle for Higher Education in Russia, 1855–1900* (Montreal: McGill-Queen's University Press, 1987); John Dunstan, "Coeducation and Revolution: Responses to Mixed Schooling in Early Twentieth-Century Russia," *History of Education* 26, no. 4 (1997): 275–393; Christine Ruane, *Gender, Class, and the Professionalization of Russian City Teachers, 1860–1914* (Pittsburgh: University of Pittsburgh Press, 1994).

21. For this shift in approaches to gender and education, see American Association of University Women, *The A.A.U.W. Report: How Schools Shortchange Girls* (Washington, DC: AAUW Educational Foundation, 1992); American Association of University Women, *Gender Gaps: Where Schools still Fail Our Children* (Washington, DC: AAUW Educational Foundation, 1998); Myra Sadker and David Sadker, *Failing at Fairness: How America's Schools Cheat Girls* (New York: Touchstone Books, 1994); Kathryn Herr and Emily Arms, "Accountability and Single-Sex Schooling: A Collision of Reform Agendas," *American Educational Research Journal* 41, no. 3 (Fall 2004): 530–533; Marcus Weaver-Hightower, "The 'Boy Turn' in Research on Gender and Education," *Review of Educational Research* 73, no. 4 (Winter 2003): 471–473; Cornelius Riordan, *Girls and Boys in School: Together or Separate?* (New York: Teachers College Press, 1990), 8–12.

22. For Soviet views on gender roles in education before this experiment with separate schools, see E. N. Evergetova, *Mal'chiki i devochki v sovetskoi shkole. K voprosu o sovmestnom vospitanii i obuchenii* (Moscow: Prosveshchenie, 1928); A. Gorchakov and I. Komarov, "Sovmestnoe obuchenie," *Shkola i zhizn* 10 (1927): 43–47; L. E. Raskin, "O mal'chikakh i devochkakh," *O nashikh detiakh* 2 (1929): 5–8; Raskin, "Eshche o sovmestnom vospitanii," *Na putiakh k novoi shkole* 6 (1929): 55–58; Frances L. Bernstein, "'The Dictatorship of Sex': Science, Glands, and the Medical Construction of Gender Difference in Revolutionary Russia," in *Russian Modernity: Politics, Knowledge, Practices,* ed. David L. Hoffmann and Yanni Kotsonis (New York: Macmillan, 2000), 138–160; Janet Hyer, "Managing the Female Organism: Doctors and the Medicalization of Women's Paid Work in Soviet Russia during the 1920s," in *Women in Russia and Ukraine,* ed. Rosalind Marsh (Cambridge: Cambridge University Press, 1996), 111–120. For the implications of these categories for historical analysis, see Denise Riley, "Does a Sex Have a History?" in *Feminism and History,* ed. Joan Scott (Oxford: Oxford University Press, 1996), 17–32.

23. *Pravda Severa* (August 22, 1943): 2

24. *Uchitel'skaia gazeta* (August 11, 1943): 2.

25. For discussion of the challenges of researching the history of postwar Soviet social policy in archival and published sources, see Bucher, *Women, the Bureaucracy and Daily Life,* 7–8; Juliane Furst, "Introduction: Late Stalinist Society: History, Politics, and People," in *Late Stalinist Russia: Society between Reconstruction and Reinvention,* ed. Juliane Furst (New York: Routledge, 2006), 16–17; Zubkova, *Russia after the War,* 5–8.

26. As part of his research during and after the war, L'vov spent considerable time traveling to different cities to meet with educators, although he also had access to reports and other internal documents. K. I. L'vov, "Zhenskoe obrazovanie v SSSR v proshlom i nastoiashchem" (V sviazi s problemoi sovmestnogo i razdel'nogo obucheniia devochek narodov SSSR) (Moscow: Scientific Scholarly Institute for Methods of Instruction of the Academy of Pedagogical Sciences, 1946). Citations are to the manuscript kept in the dissertation files at the Research Archive of the Russian Academy of Education. Before the war, L'vov studied girls' education in so-called non-Russian regions, and these materials, including firsthand school inspections, appeared in his dissertation as well as in published articles: K. I. L'vov, "Po shkolam Kirgizii," *Kommunisticheskoe prosveshchenie* 2 (1934): 134–138; L'vov, "Rovesnitsy Oktiabria," *Prosveshchenie natsional'nostei* 5 (1933): 43–46. L'vov died in 1950. *Uchitel'skaia gazeta* (October 25, 1950): 4.

27. L'vov's published articles on separate schools include "Pervyi god razdel'nogo obucheniia," *Uchitel'skaia gazeta* (June 7, 1944): 2; "Sovmestnoe obuchenie v proshlom i nastoiashchem," *Sovetskaia pedagogika* 10 (October 1945): 38–46; "Shkola v soiuznykh

respublikakh srednei azii i kavkaza v dni velikoi otechestvennoi voiny," *Sovetskaia pedagogika* 7 (July 1945): 48–54.

28. See the bibliography for a complete list of archives used in this study.

29. For the Stalinist decision-making process, particularly in the realms of economic, cultural, diplomatic, and security issues, see Yoram Gorlizki and Oleg Khlevniuk, *Cold Peace: Stalin and the Soviet Ruling Circle, 1945–1953* (Oxford: Oxford University Press, 2004), 46–59.

30. RGALI 634/4/96, 97. All RGALI citations refer to this collection of unpublished letters. The letters responded to an article published in *Literaturnaia gazeta* (April 8, 1950): 2. See below and in subsequent chapters for citations to specific letters. For analysis of letters sent to newspapers and journals as expressions of Soviet public opinion in the early 1950s, see Zubkova, *Russia after the War*, 38–39, 155–160; Juliane Furst, "In Search of Soviet Salvation: Young People Write to the Stalinist Authorities," *Contemporary European History* 15, no. 3 (2006): 327–345.

31. Published letters appeared in the May 4 and June 28, 1950, issues of *Literaturnaia gazeta*. Selections from additional letters, along with editorial commentary, appeared in *Literaturnaia gazeta* (August 24, 1950): 2, (August 6, 1953): 3–4. Analysis of these letters can be found in "The Pendulum Swings: Russia Reconsiders Co-education," *Times Educational Supplement* (August 25, 1950): 657; "The Discussion on Co-Education," *Soviet Studies* 5, no. 2 (1950): 180–192; "The Discussion on Co-education Re-opened," *Soviet Studies* 5, no. 3 (1953): 316–328; Pyzhikov, "Razdel'noe obuchenie," 82–83; Livschiz, "Growing Up Soviet," 774–781.

32. Emphasis in the original. RGALI 634/4/96/71–72.

33. RGALI 634/4/96/77–80.

34. RGALI 634/4/97/61–62.

35. RGALI 634/4/96/24–25.

36. RGALI 634/4/97/121–122. See further discussion of this letter in chapter 3.

37. Rosemary Salomone, *Same, Different, Equal: Rethinking Single-Sex Schooling* (New Haven: Yale University Press, 2003).

38. RGASPI 17/126/2/84.

39. TsAGM 528/1/872/49; L'vov, "Zhenskoe obrazovanie," 539. See the first chapter for further discussion of the initial responses to the announcement of the new policy.

40. For the transformation from single-sex to coeducational schooling in diverse contexts, see David Tyack and Elisabeth Hansot, *Learning Together: A History of Coeducation in American Public Schools* (New York: Russell Sage Foundation, 1992); James C. Albisetti, *Schooling German Girls and Women: Secondary and Higher Education in the Nineteenth Century* (Princeton: Princeton University Press, 1988).

41. The historical literature on the postwar period is growing quickly. See the following recent contributions: Zubkova, *Russia after the War;* Gorlizki and Khlevniuk, *Cold Peace;* Furst, *Late Stalinist Russia;* Juliane Furst, Polly Jones, and Susan Morrissey, "Introduction: The Relaunch of the Soviet Project, 1945–1964," *Slavonic and East European Review* 86, no. 2 (April 2008): 201–207; David Brandenberger, *National Bolshevism: Stalinist Mass Culture and the Formation of Modern Russian National Identity, 1931–1956* (Cambridge: Harvard University Press, 2002), 183–239.

42. In other twentieth-century European dictatorships, the elimination of coeducation has been identified as evidence of increasingly conservative social policies. See reports on the elimination of coeducation in Nazi Germany and Austria in *New York*

Times (April 5, 1934): 10, (February 12, 1938): 2, (September 2, 1938). For the restrictions on coeducation in Mussolini's Italy and Franco's Spain, see James C. Albisetti, "Catholics and Coeducation: Rhetoric and Reality in Europe before Divini Illius Magistri," *Paedagogica Historica* 35, no. 3 (1999): 687–688.

43. U.S. Department of Education, Office of Planning, Evaluation, and Policy Development, Policy and Program Studies Service, *Single-Sex versus Coeducational Schooling: A Systematic Review* (Washington: U.S. Department of Education, 2005), 1. One advocacy organization claims more than five hundred public schools in the United States either wholly separated by gender or offering at least some separate classes within a coeducational facility. National Association for Single-Sex Public Education, "Research," online: www.singlesexschools.org, accessed May 2009. As will be discussed in chapter 2, the number of single-sex schools remains an open question in the United States, just as it was in the Soviet Union.

44. In October 2006, U.S. Secretary of Education Margaret Spellings announced new guidelines in Title IX regulations designed to "give communities more flexibility in offering additional choices to parents in the education of their children," including gender-segregated classes, extracurricular activities, and schools, based on recognition "that some students learn better in a single sex class or school." Margaret Spellings, "Secretary Spellings Announces More Choices in Single Sex Education. Amended Regulations Give Communities More Flexibility to Offer Single Sex Schools and Classes," press Release, October 24, 2006, online: www.ed.gov.

45. For a discussion of how separate schools, especially for boys, are perceived primarily in terms of their disciplinary functions, see Herr and Arms, "Accountability and Single-Sex Schooling," 545–549; Elisabeth L. Woody, "Constructions of Masculinity in California's Single-Gender Academies," in *Gender in Policy and Practice: Perspectives on Single-Sex and Coeducational Schooling,* ed. Amanda Datnow and Lea Hubbard (New York: Routledge, 2002), 280–303.

46. Influential proponents of this position include Leonard Sax and Michael Gurian, whose books, presentations, and seminars have been praised by some educators for sparking their interest in separate schooling. Michael Gurian and Patricia Henley, *Boys and Girls Learn Differently! A Guide for Teachers and Parents* (San Francisco: Jossey Bass, 2001); Leonard Sax, *Why Gender Matters: What Parents and Teachers Need to Know about the Emerging Science of Sex Differences* (New York: Broadway Books, 2005). See discussion of their influence on principals, parents, and teachers in Elizabeth Weil, "Should Boys and Girls Be Taught Differently? Teaching to the Testosterone," *New York Times Magazine* (March 2, 2008): 38–45, 84–87.

47. For discussion of the need to plan for the implementation of separate schooling (and some revealing examples of a lack of such planning), see Michael Robert Younger and Molly Warrington, "Would Harry and Hermione Have Done Better in Single-Sex Classes? A Review of Single-Sex Teaching in Coeducational Secondary Schools in the United Kingdom," *American Educational Research Journal* 43, no. 4 (Winter 2006): 611–612.

48. Salomone, *Same, Different, Equal;* Amanda Datnow, Lea Hubbard, and Gilberto Conchas, "How Context Mediates Policy: The Implementation of Single-Gender Public Schooling in California," *Teachers College Record* 103, no. 2 (2001): 184–206; American Association of University Women, *Separated by Sex: A Critical Look at Single-Sex Education for Girls* (Washington, DC: AAUW Educational Foundation, 1998); Sadker and Sadker, *Failing at Fairness,* 226–250; Janice Streitmatter, *For Girls Only: Making a Case*

for Single-Sex Schooling (New York: State University of New York Press, 1999); Frances R. Spielhagen, ed., *Debating Single-Sex Education: Separate and Equal?* (Lanham, MD: Rowman and Littlefield Education, 2008); Linda J. Sax, *Women Graduates of Single-Sex and Coeducational High Schools: Differences in Their Characteristics and the Transition to College* (Los Angeles: UCLA Graduate School of Education and Information Studies, 2009), online: www.gseis.ucla.edu.

49. See the discussion of the scope of research projects in Streitmatter, *For Girls Only,* 5–6; Frances R. Spielhagen, "Single-Sex Classes: Everything That's Old Is New Again," in *Debating Single-Sex Education,* 3. Several major studies examined the single largest effort in recent U.S. education, the Single-Gender Academies in California, which involved schools in just six districts, with an enrollment of approximately five hundred pupils, during a period of less than three years. Datnow, Hubbard, and Conchas, "How Context Mediates Policy," 184–206; Amanda Datnow, Lea Hubbard, and Elisabeth Woody, *Is Single Gender Schooling Viable in the Public Sector? Lessons from California's Pilot Program* (Final report to the Ford Foundation and Spencer Foundation, 2001); Herr and Arms, "Accountability and Single-Sex Schooling," 527–555; Kathryn Herr and Emily Arms, "The Intersection of Educational Reforms: Single-Gender Academies in a Public Middle School," in *Gender in Policy and Practice* (New York: Routledge, 2002); Lea Hubbard and Amanda Datnow, "Are Single-Sex Schools Sustainable in the Public Sector?"; and Woody, "Constructions of Masculinity," 74–89, 109–132, 280–303; Salomone, *Same, Different, Equal,* 228–232.

50. U.S. Department of Education, *Single-Sex versus Coeducational Schooling,* x.

51. Sax, *Women Graduates,* 14; Gerald Bracey, "The Success of Single-Sex Education Is Still Unproven," *Education Digest* 72, no. 6 (February 2007): 22–26; Frances R. Spielhagen, "Does It All Add Up? Single-Sex Classes and Student Achievement," in *Debating Single-Sex Education,* 59; Frances R. Spielhagen, "Single-Sex Education: Policy, Practice, and Pitfalls," *Teachers College Record* (October 7, 2008), n.p; Valerie E. Lee, "Is Single-Sex Secondary Schooling a Solution to the Problem of Gender Inequity?" in *Separated by Sex,* 43; Weil, "Should Boys and Girls Be Taught Differently?" 38–45, 84–87; Herr and Arms, "Accountability and Single-Sex Schooling," 529.

52. Sax, *Women Graduates,* 52, 61–62, 64–65.

53. See the recommendations reported in Cornelius Riordan, "The Future of Single-Sex Schools," in *Separated by Sex,* 58–59; Mary Ellen Flannery, "No Girls Allowed," *NEA Today* (April 2006), online: www.nea.org; Herr and Arms, "Accountability and Single-Sex Schooling," 551; Sax, *Women Graduates,* 16.

54. For comparative analysis of single-gender schooling, see Salomone, *Same, Different, Equal,* 206–210, 219, 235–236, 239; Valerie E. Lee and Marlaine E. Lockheed, "The Effects of Single-Sex Schooling on Achievement and Attitudes in Nigeria," *Comparative Education Review* 34, no. 2 (May 1990): 209–231; David P. Baker, Cornelius Riordan, and Maryellen Schaub, "The Effects of Sex-Grouped Schooling on Achievement: The Role of National Context," *Comparative Education Review* 39, no. 4 (November 1995): 468–482; Carolyn Jackson and Ian David Smith, "Poles Apart? An Exploration of Single-Sex and Mixed-Sex Educational Environments in Australia and England," *Educational Studies,* 26, no. 4 (2000): 409–422; Younger and Warrington, "Would Harry and Hermione Have Done Better in Single-Sex Classes?" 579–620. For efforts to use this comparative research to shape the debate on American separate schools, see Ilana DeBare, *Where Girls Come First. The Rise, Fall, and Surprising Revival*

of Girls' Schools (New York: Penguin, 2004), 287–288; Riordan, *Girls and Boys in School,* 153–155; Sax, *Women Graduates,* 18–19.

55. See discussion of the need for more research in Amanda Datnow and Lea Hubbard, "Introduction"; Rosemary Salomone, "The Legality of Single-Sex Education in the United States"; and Cornelius Riordan, "What Do We Know about the Effects of Single-Sex Schools in the Private Sector? Implications for Public Schools," in *Gender in Policy and Practice,* 5, 27, 70; Salomone, *Same, Different, Equal,* 202–206, 227, 235–244.

56. Karen Stabiner, *All Girls: Single-Sex Education and Why It Matters* (New York: Riverhead Books, 2002); DeBare, *Where Girls Come First;* Diana Meehan, *Learning like a Girl: Educating Our Daughters in Schools of Their Own* (New York: Public Affairs, 2007).

57. These editorial and position statements provide a sense of the range of views: American Association of University Women, "AAUW Opposes Education Dept. Single-Sex Regulations," press release, October 24, 2006, online: www.aauw.org; National Organization for Women, "NOW Opposes Single-Sex Public Education as 'Separate and Unequal,'" press release, October 24, 2006, online: www.now.org; Leonard Sax, "The Promise and Peril of Single-Sex *Public* Education," *Education Week* 24, no. 25 (March 2, 2005): 34–35, 48, online: www.edweek.org.

58. National Coalition for Girls' Schools, "Research Shows: Girls' Schools Have an Edge," press release, 2009, online: www.ncgs.org; Archer School for Girls, "New Research Shows Girls' School Advantage," press release, April 6, 2009, online: www.archer.org.

59. *Christian Science Monitor* (May 25, 2004), online: www.csmonitor.com; Weil, "Should Boys and Girls Be Taught Differently?" 38–45, 84–87; Peter Meyer, "Learning Separately: The Case for Single-Sex Schools," *Education Next* (Winter 2008): 10–21; *Washington Post* (June 15, 2008): 1; *New York Times* (March 11, 2009): 24; Michelle Davis, "Department Aims to Promote Single-Sex Schools," *Education Week* 21, no. 36 (May 15, 2002): 24, 26, online: www.edweek.org.

60. See discussion of methods in Sadker and Sadker, *Failing at Fairness;* R. W. Connell, "Teaching the Boys: New Research on Masculinity, and Gender Strategies for Schools," *Teachers College Record* 98, no. 2 (Winter 1996): 206–235; Weaver-Hightower, "Boy Turn," 471–498.

61. Kathleen Canning, *Gender History in Practice: Historical Perspectives on Bodies, Class, and Citizenship* (Ithaca: Cornell University Press, 2006), 62.

62. Joan W. Scott, "Feminism's History," *Journal of Women's History* 16, no. 2 (2004): 21.

63. The editorial claim of 98 percent support for coeducation appeared in *Literaturnaia gazeta* (August 24, 1950): 2. See chapter 5 for discussion of this assessment.

64. For these statements, see L'vov, "Zhenskoe obrazovanie," 538; TsAGM 528/1/920/21.

65. *Pravda Ukrainy* (July 29, 1954): 3.

66. *Zaria Vostoka* (July 24, 1954): 2.

67. APRK 708/27/1487/160–169.

68. *Pravda* (July 18, 1954): 1.

1 — Disciplining Gender

1. *Krasnaia Bashkiriia* (September 3, 1943): 2.

2. Reading "for cracks, for dissonances" in official discourse can illuminate

strategic responses to contextual opportunities and situational constraints. Northrop, *Veiled Empire*, 87.

3. For administrative jurisdictions, see Chernik, *Sovetskaia obshcheobrazovatel'naia shkola*, 65–69.

4. For the Stalinist approach to educational administration, see Larry E. Holmes, *Stalin's School*; Holmes, *Grand Theater: Regional Governance in Stalin's Russia, 1931–1941* (Lanham, MD: Lexington Books, 2009); Ewing, *Teachers of Stalinism*; Dunstan, *Soviet Schooling.*

5. For analysis of the role of communist school directors and teachers in the prewar decade, see E. Thomas Ewing, "A Precarious Position of Power: Soviet School Directors in the 1930s," *Journal of Educational Administration and History* 41, no. 3 (August 2009): 253–266; Ewing, *Teachers of Stalinism*, 139–147.

6. By contrast, Stalin was directly involved in setting educational policy in the 1930s, as discussed in Holmes, *Stalin's School*, 72–75.

7. For an example of a positive report of "the first day of single-sex classrooms" at a Louisville school, see Bruce Schreiner, "Single-Sex Classes Could Become more Common as Obstacles Are Removed," Associated Press, August 20, 2002, accessed from Lexis-Nexis Academic.

8. Advocacy of separate schooling as a response to social or cultural change comes from different political or ideological perspectives. Conservatives may see separate schooling as a preferred alternative to a permissive culture or unstable social norms, while feminists may advocate girls' schools as an alternative to a sexist, or sexualized, mainstream culture. See discussion of these debates in DeBare, *Where Girls Come First*, 198–213; Salomone, *Same, Different, Equal*, 38–63.

9. For historical studies of separate schooling that look to the implementation stage for explanations of perceived failure and policy reversals, see Datnow, Hubbard, and Conchas, "How Context Mediates Policy," 184–206.

10. For analysis of the presence and absence of gender in Soviet educational discourse in the 1930s, see E. Thomas Ewing, "If the Teacher Was a Man: Masculinity and Power in Stalinist Schools," *Gender & History* 21, no. 1 (April 2009): 107–129; Ewing, "A Stalinist Celebrity Teacher: Gender and Professional Identities in the Soviet Union in the 1930s," *Journal of Women's History* 16, no. 4 (Winter 2004): 92–118; Ewing, "Personal Acts with Public Meanings," 117–137.

11. Dora Shturman, *The Soviet Secondary School* (London: Routledge, 1988), 60.

12. E. Merkhelevich, "Ideiia sovmestnogo obucheniia v istorii nashei shkoly i eia politicheskoe znachenie," *Soiuz Zhenshchin* 3 (1909): 6–7; N. Kabanov, "Sovmestnoe obuchenie," in *Sovmestnoe vospitanie i obrazovanie. Biblioteka Svobodnago Vospitaniia i Obrazovaniia i Zashchity Detei*, ed. I. Gorbunov-Posadov No. 88 (Moscow, 1913): 27–38; Dunstan, "Coeducation and Revolution," 275–393; Livschiz, "Growing Up Soviet," 656–660; Pyzhikov, "Razdel'noe obuchenie," 78.

13. Aleksandr Ostrogorskii, "O sovremennom sostoianii nachal'nogo obrazovaniia v Rossii," *Obrazovanie* 5, no. 7–8 (July–August 1896): 92–139.

14. Ben Eklof, *Russian Peasant Schools: Officialdom, Village Culture, and Popular Pedagogy, 1861–1914* (Berkeley and Los Angeles: University of California Press, 1986), 311.

15. "O vvedenii obiazatel'nogo sovmestnogo obucheniia," May 18, 1918, in *Sobranie uzakonenii i rasporiazhenii rabochego i krest'ianskogo pravitel'stva* 39 (June 4, 1918): 475.

16. L'vov, "Shkola v soiuznykh respublikakh," 48–54; P. S. Miloslavskii, "Natsional'nuiu shkolu Severnogo Kavkaza—na uroven' peredovykh shkol stran," *Severo-Kavkazskii uchitel'*

10 (1935): 8; E. Thomas Ewing, "Not One Girl outside the School! Educating 'Non-Russian' Girls in the Soviet Union in the 1930s" (unpublished paper, 2007).

17. *Uchitel'skaia gazeta* (June 22, 1928): 4. See also E. Thomas Ewing, "Gender Equity as Revolutionary Strategy: Coeducation in Russian and Soviet Schools," in *Revolution and Pedagogy: Interdisciplinary and Transnational Perspectives on Educational Foundations,* ed. E. Thomas Ewing (New York: Palgrave, 2005), 39–60.

18. L. E. Raskin, "Bor'ba za devochku kak odna iz problem vospitaniia," *Na putiakh k novoi shkole* 2 (1929): 53–54; Raskin, "O mal'chikakh i devochkakh," 5–8; Dunstan, "Coeducation and Revolution," 275–393; Livschiz, "Growing Up Soviet," 662–664.

19. *Zhenshchina v SSSR: Statisticheskii sbornik* (Moscow: Gosplan, 1936), 107.

20. A. Savich, "Trudnye voprosy sovmestnogo vospitaniia i obucheniia v shkole," *Sredniaia shkola* 5 (1939): 23–32. See also analysis of this article in Ewing, "Gender Equity," and a broader discussion of adolescent sexuality in Livschiz, "Growing Up Soviet," 669–678.

21. TsAGM 528/1/678/1. See discussion of this shift in thinking among Soviet leaders in Pyzhikov, "Razdel'noe obuchenie," 78.

22. *Kul'turnoe stroitel'stvo* (Moscow: Gosizdat, 1940), 37–39.

23. For analysis of ethnicity and language in Stalinist education, see Peter Blitstein, "Nation-Building or Russification? Obligatory Russian Instruction in the Soviet Non-Russian School, 1938–1953," in *A State of Nations: Empire and Nation-Making in the Age of Lenin and Stalin,* ed. Ronald Grigor Suny and Terry Martin (New York: Oxford University Press, 2001), 253–274; E. Thomas Ewing, "Ethnicity at School: Educating the 'Non-Russian' Children of the Soviet Union, 1928–1939," *History of Education* 35, no. 4–5 (2006): 499–519.

24. Dunstan, *Soviet Schooling,* 55–57; Pyzhikov, "Razdel'noe obuchenie," 78–79.

25. Potemkin was appointed as minister of education in 1940 and served until his death in 1946. Vladimir Petrovich Potemkin, "Ob uluchshenii kachestva obucheniia i vospitaniia v shkole. Doklad na vserossiiskom soveshchanii po narodnomu obrazovaniiu, 15 avgusta 1944 g.," in *Stat'i i rechi po voprosam narodnogo obrazovaniia* (Moscow: Izdatel'stvo APN RSFSR, 1947), 192. See also Dunstan, *Soviet Schooling,* 65–67, 118–121. On militarization and masculinity in the 1930s, see Petrone, "Masculinity and Heroism," 172–193.

26. For discipline in Stalinist schools, see Fradkin and Plokhova, "Problemy distsipliny," 91–98; Ewing, *Teachers of Stalinism,* 189–225; Dunstan, *Soviet Schooling,* 67–69.

27. NA RAO 15/1/214/3.

28. RGASPI 17/3/1039/11. See also Livschiz, "Growing Up Soviet," 684–690; Pyzhikov, "Razdel'noe obuchenie," 79.

29. RGASPI 17/126/2/79.

30. The Gor'kii city educational department endorsed proposals to separate schools starting with the first grade. NA RAO 15/1/214/46–47.

31. TsGARU 94/5/4042/23–24, 30–31. See also discussion of the implications of gender separation in these regions in Livschiz, "Growing Up Soviet," 703; Chernik, *Sovetskaia obshcheobrazovatel'naia shkola,* 129, and chapter 5. For the broader relationship between gender and education in Soviet Central Asia, see Gregory Massell, *The Surrogate Proletariat: Moslem Women and Revolutionary Strategies in Soviet Central Asia, 1919–1929* (Princeton: Princeton University Press, 1974), 139–141, 280, 299–300; Adrienne Lynn Edgar, *Tribal Nation: The Making of Soviet Turkmenistan* (Princeton: Princeton University Press, 2004), 70–71, 227, 231–232; Marianne Kamp, *The New*

Woman in Uzbekistan: Islam, Modernity, and Unveiling under Communism (Seattle: University of Washington Press, 2006), 85–93, 150–214; Shoshana Keller, *To Moscow, Not Mecca: The Soviet Campaign against Islam in Central Asia, 1917–1941* (Westport, CT: Praeger, 2001), 39–40, 74, 89, 95–96, 124, 209–210, 234; Northrop, *Veiled Empire*, 109–115, 182, 195–196, 322, 329, 332; Ewing, "Not One Girl."

32. According to the School Section, even as all educational organizations approved of separate instruction "in principle," most of them did not provide concrete and grounded proposals for implementation. RGASPI 17/126/2/79–80.

33. RGASPI 17/126/2/80–81. In the summer of 1941, an American journal article offered this revealing prediction: "In recent Russian wave of morality, co-education may be discontinued because it is thought distracting." "A Life Photographer Looks at Moscow a Week before the Nazi Invasion Began," *Life* 11, no. 6 (August 11, 1941): 24.

34. For *gymnasia* and *progymnasia* in prerevolutionary Russia, see Livschiz, "Pre-Revolutionary in Form," 542–546; E. Thomas Ewing, "From an Exclusive Privilege to a Right and an Obligation: Modern Russia," in *Girls' Secondary Education in the Western World: From the 18th to the 20th Century,* ed. James C. Albisetti, Joyce Goodman, and Rebecca Rogers (New York: Palgrave, 2010), 165–179.

35. RGASPI 17/126/2/86. See similar qualifications in TsGARU 94/5/4042/26, 31.

36. According to 1943 reports, 503 cities had populations above twenty thousand, including 187 cities with populations above fifty thousand. *Itogi vsesoiuznoi perepisi naseleniia 1970 goda* (Moscow: Statistika, 1972), 61.

37. RGASPI 17/126/2/91.

38. For the war's impact on Soviet schools, see Dunstan, *Soviet Schooling;* Chernik, *Sovetskaia obshcheobrazovatel'naia shkola.*

39. Livschiz, "Growing Up Soviet," 687–694; Livschiz, "Pre-Revolutionary in Form," 531–560.

40. For examples of liberal and feminist educators embracing single-sex schooling, see Meehan, *Learning like a Girl;* DeBare, *Where Girls Come First.*

41. RGASPI 17/126/2/80.

42. Population estimates are from *Itogi vsesoiuznoi perepisi,* 1, 61–62. For other examples of Stalinist policy making that set national policies based on limited experiments, see Holmes, *Stalin's School,* 10–12, 131–132.

43. At least nine Moscow schools took part in these experiments. NA RAO 15/1/214/9, 14. See also brief mention of these experiments in V. N. Markov, "O razdel'nom obuchenii," *Vozhatyi* 8–9 (August 1943): 4; L'vov, "Zhenskoe obrazovanie," 521; Livschiz, "Growing Up Soviet," 690; Chernik, *Sovetskaia obshcheobrazovatel'naia shkola,* 127.

44. Extensive discussions occurred in February and April 1943, as recorded in meetings organized by the Scientific Research Institute for Schools. Transcripts of these meetings are preserved in the Archive of the Russian Academy of Education. Participants in these meetings included inspectors who observed lessons in separate classrooms as well as leading pedagogical researchers. The inspectors' reports included descriptions of classroom behavior as well as comments from school directors, teachers, and even pupils. The archival materials also include reports on coeducational and separate schooling in prerevolutionary Russia and in western countries. Both meetings were convened by B. V. Vsesviatskii, director of the institute. Citations to NA RAO 15/1/214/21–22 refer to the meeting on February 4, 1943; and to NA RAO 15/1/214/3–16, the meeting on April 6, 1943.

45. NA RAO 15/1/214/7–8, 10.

46. NA RAO 15/1/214/9–10.

47. NA RAO 15/1/214/3, 4, 7.

48. NA RAO 15/1/214/8.

49. Orlov's comments are cited in Livschiz, "Growing Up Soviet," 707–708.

50. Markov, "O razdel'nom obuchenii," 4.

51. For a firsthand account of gender groupings in a prewar school, see Nina Lugovskaya, *The Diary of a Soviet Schoolgirl, 1932–1937,* trans. Joanne Turnbull (Moscow: Glas, 2003).

52. See evaluations cited in Weil, "Should Boys and Girls," 38–45, 84–87.

53. Vladimir Petrovich Potemkin, "Rech' na sobranii aktiva uchitelei g. Moskvy," February 7, 1943, in *Stat'i i rechi po voprosam narodnogo obrazovaniia,* 163–164. The speech was apparently first published in *Sovetskaia pedagogika* 5–6 (1943): 1–9.

54. For the division of household labor in Soviet ideology and practice, see H. Kent Geiger, *The Family in Soviet Russia* (Cambridge: Harvard University Press, 1968), 176–187; Goldman, *Women, the State, and Revolution,* 130–133.

55. See further remarks from Moscow educators involved in this experiment during a May 1943 discussion, as cited in Livschiz, "Growing Up Soviet," 696–701.

56. NA RAO 15/1/214/ 17–18. See also discussion of the transition from 1941 drafts to the 1943 decree in Pyzhikov, "Razdel'noe obuchenie," 79; Livschiz, "Growing Up Soviet," 690, 695–696.

57. An editorial published on July 22, 1943, under a headline referring to preparations for the coming school year, made no mention of separate schools. *Izvestiia* (July 22, 1943): 1.

58. RGASPI 17/3/1048/21; L'vov, "Zhenskoe obrazovanie," 522. See a slightly different time line for approval and announcement in Pyzhikov, "Razdel'noe obuchenie," 79–80.

59. GARF A2306/70/2835/1; "O vvedenii razdel'nogo obucheniia," in *Narodnoe obrazovanie v SSSR,* 177–178.

60. For Stalinist maternalism, see Hoffmann, "Mothers in the Motherland," 35–54.

61. This recollection came from minister of education Kairov almost a decade later, as educators were deliberating on the restoration of coeducation. GARF A2306/72/3680/48. This statement is cited by Livschiz to support her argument that separate schools resulted to a great extent from the "fundamental social conservatism of the majority of the top political leadership of the country and their great fear of youth, and particularly female, sexuality, as a force that could not be overcome, controlled, or fully harnessed for the service of the state, the main criteria for the permissibility of a certain phenomenon." Livschiz, "Growing Up Soviet," 691–692. The powerful appeal of separate schools as a device for controlling adolescents was not unique to the Stalinist context, as suggested by the comments from educators cited in Weil, "Should Boys and Girls," 38–45, 84–87, and the arguments developed in Sax, *Why Gender Matters.*

62. GARF A2306/70/2835/1.

63. *Pravda* (August 6, 1943): 4. At about this same time, foreign reports cited statements by Moscow school director Solokhin, but the source of these statements was not identified. Downs, "Revolution in Soviet School System," 76; *New York Times* (August 5, 1943): 12. As is discussed in the next chapter, the first extended defense of separate schooling was published by the educational newspaper just a week later. *Uchitel'skaia gazeta* (August 11, 1943): 2.

64. L'vov, "Zhenskoe obrazovanie," 524; GARF A2306/70/2835/5–9.

65. GARF A2306/70/2835/5–6. In fact, some schools did divide boys and girls within the same building, in effect creating separate schools in coeducational spaces. As late as 1950, a boys' school and a girls' school were located in the same building in Stalinabad, led by the same director and operating in shifts. RGALI 634/4/97/125–130. According to historian Chernik, the Soviet Union actually had three kinds of urban secondary schools: separate, coeducational, and "combined" (separate classes in one school). Chernik, *Sovetskaia obshcheobrazovatel'naia shkola,* 129. For arguments that separate classrooms within the same building provide the same instructional advantages as separate schools, but without additional logistical challenges, see *New York Times* (March 11, 2009): 24.

66. GARF A2306/70/2835/6–9.

67. These instructions also specified further steps to ensure conformity to the new policies and assess their implementation. During the first days, the "entire pedagogical collective" should carry out "intensified observation of pupils," with the stated goal of strengthening order. Two weeks after the start of school, the pedagogical council should discuss "revealed mistakes and shortcomings," develop plans for improvements, and send reports to the district educational department, where they would be combined into summary accounts sent to regional educational departments and finally to Narkompros. All reports were due by October 15, 1943, six weeks after schools opened. GARF A2306/70/2835/9.

68. See explanation in *Leningradskaia pravda* (August 4, 1943): 1; GARF A2306/70/2957/51; Pyzhikov, "Razdel'noe obuchenie," 80. The school-entering age was eight until 1944 but then was lowered to seven. Dunstan, *Soviet Schooling,* 176–178.

69. GARF A2306/70/2835/6.

70. GARF A2306/70/2835/6–7.

71. GARF A2306/70/2835/7.

72. GARF A2306/70/2835/8.

73. George Z. F. Bereday, William W. Brickman, and Gerald H. Read, *The Changing Soviet School* (Boston: Houghton Mifflin, 1960), 83.

74. See discussion of these reforms in *Pravda* (August 6, 1943): 4; *Kazakhstanskaia pravda* (September 1, 1945): 1; *Uchitel'skaia gazeta* (August 11, 1943): 2; Potemkin, "Ob uluchshenii kachestva," 189–190; Dunstan, *Soviet Schooling,* 170–179; Bereday, *Changing Soviet School,* 83; Chernik, *Sovetskaia obshcheobrazovatel'naia shkola,* 125; Livschiz, "Pre-Revolutionary in Form," 546–552. For an American case study of an experiment with separate schooling that was complicated, and eventually undermined, by multiple changes in school policies, mostly associated with high-stakes testing, see Herr and Arms, "Accountability and Single-Sex Schooling," 527–555.

75. Shturman, *Soviet Secondary School,* 60.

76. NA RAO 15/1/214/17.

77. *New York Times* (August 5, 1943): 12; Downs, "Revolution in Soviet School," 76.

78. GARF A2306/72/3680/48–50. See discussion of several critical comments by educators in May 1943, prior to the announcement of the new policy, in Livschiz, "Growing Up Soviet," 698–700. The expansion of separate schooling beyond the parameters of the original instruction is discussed more fully in chapter 5.

79. GARF A2306/72/3680/33.

80. GARF A2306/70/3016/9–10.

81. *Krasnaia Tatariia* (July 30, 1943): 4, (August 15, 1943): 4.

82. *Kirovskaia pravda* (August 11, 1943): 1, (August 18, 1943): 2; *Pravda Severa*

(August 22, 1943): 2; Markov, "O razdel'nom obuchenii," 4; *Uchitel'skaia gazeta* (August 7, 1943): 3.

83. GARF A2306/70/3016/2, 7; *Uchitel'skaia gazeta* (June 7, 1944): 2. As is discussed in chapter 5, gender separation took place at a time of acute shortages of all educational resources, including teachers and buildings.

84. GARF A2306/70/2835/8.

85. The proportion of men among secondary school directors declined slightly from 86 percent in 1939 to 80 percent in 1950; these figures included all secondary schools, including those in rural areas and smaller cities not subject to gender separation. *Kul'turnoe stroitel'stvo SSSR* (1940), 90; *Cultural Progress in the U.S.S.R.* (Moscow: Foreign Languages Publishing House, 1956), 184–185.

86. GARF A2306/70/3016/2, 12–16, 18.

87. GARF A2306/70/3016/12–16.

88. GARF A2306/70/3016/5.

89. *Uchitel'skaia gazeta* (September 8, 1943): 2.

90. *Uchitel'skaia gazeta* (December 8, 1943): 2.

91. *Izvestiia* (January 8, 1944): 4.

92. *Uchitel'skaia gazeta* (February 4, 1944): 2–3.

93. *Uchitel'skaia gazeta* (June 7, 1944): 2.

94. L'vov, "Zhenskoe obrazovanie," 527. See reports in Livschiz, "Growing Up Soviet," 715.

95. *Pravda Severa* (August 22, 1943): 2; GARF A2306/70/3016/2.

96. NA RAO 15/1/214/10.

97. TsAGM 528/1/872/61.

98. Potemkin, "Ob uluchshenii kachestva," 191–192.

99. *Kul'turnoe stroitel'stvo SSSR* (1940), 90.

100. *Cultural Progress,* 184–185.

101. NA RAO 15/1/214/11.

102. TsGARU 94/4/4797b/110.

103. *Kommunist* (August 21, 1954): 3.

104. *Kul'turnoe stroitel'stvo SSSR. Statisticheskii sbornik* (Moscow: Gosudarstvennoe Statisticheskoe Izdatel'stvo, 1956), 186–187.

105. *Bakinskii rabochii* (August 21, 1943): 1; GARF A2306 70/2957/50.

106. TsGARU 94/4/4797b/112.

107. L'vov, "Zhenskoe obrazovanie," 527; APRK 708/8/1555/8. For enrollment policies and practices in Russian and "non-Russian" schools, see Ewing, "Ethnicity at School," 499–519.

108. By contrast, Kazakh schools made up almost one-half of rural schools in the Alma-Ata region. APRK 708/8/1550/3.

109. *Kirovskaia pravda* (August 18, 1943): 2; *Krasnaia Tatariia* (August 29, 1943): 1; *Leningradskaia pravda* (August 20, 1943): 3; *Pravda Severa* (September 1, 1943): 2, (September 7, 1943): 2; *Uchitel'skaia gazeta* (November 3, 1943): 3.

110. TsAGM 528/1/872/49.

111. RGASPI 17/3/1048/21; Markov, "O razdel'nom obuchenii," 4; *Pravda Vostoka* (September 1, 1943): 1.

112. *Kirovskaia pravda* (August 18, 1943): 2; TsAGM 528/1/878/26; GARF A2306 70/2957/50, 3016/2, 6, 18; L'vov, "Zhenskoe obrazovanie," 534–535.

113. Markov, "O razdel'nom obuchenii," 5.

114. See reports of teachers' conferences in *Leninskii put'* (August 29, 1943): 1; GARF A2306 70/2957/50; TsAGM 528/1/878/26; *Bakinskii rabochii* (August 31, 1943): 2.

115. *Krasnaia Bashkiriia* (August 17, 1943): 1, (August 20, 1943): 2.

116. GARF A2306/70/3016/18.

117. L'vov, "Zhenskoe obrazovanie," 536–537.

118. *Uchitel'skaia gazeta* (February 4, 1944): 3.

119. TsAGM 528/1/872/48, 50.

120. TsAGM 528/1/872/56.

121. *Bakinskii rabochii* (August 31, 1943): 2.

122. *Ural'skii rabochii* (September 3, 1943): 4.

123. TsAGM 528/1/872/49.

124. Ibid.

125. *Uchitel'skaia gazeta* (June 7, 1944): 2.

126. L'vov, "Zhenskoe obrazovanie," 538–539.

127. *Uchitel'skaia gazeta* (September 3, 1943): 3.

128. *Krasnaia Tatariia* (September 3, 1943): 4.

129. *Kazakhstanskaia pravda* (September 3, 1943): 2.

130. *Krasnaia Bashkiriia* (September 3, 1943): 2.

131. *Uchitel'skaia gazeta* (September 3, 1943): 1.

132. *Krasnaia Tatariia* (September 3, 1943): 4.

133. *Leningradskaia pravda* (September 2, 1943): 4.

134. *Uchitel'skaia gazeta* (September 8, 1943): 2.

135. *Pravda Vostoka* (October 3, 1943): 3.

136. L'vov, "Zhenskoe obrazovanie," 530. See the accounts of war damage to schools in Leningrad, Stalingrad, Kursk, Smolensk, and other cities in *Uchitel'skaia gazeta* (September 3, 1943): 1, as well as Potemkin, "Rech' na sobranii aktiva," 153–170.

137. *Leningradskaia pravda* (August 20, 1943): 3, (October 1, 1943): 1; *Pravda Severa* (September 1, 1943): 2; *Pravda Vostoka* (September 1, 1943): 1, (October 3, 1943): 3.

138. *Leninskii put'* (August 29, 1943): 1.

139. TsAGM 528/1/872/20–21. On the welfare functions of schools in wartime, see Dunstan, *Soviet Schooling,* 105–112.

140. TsAGM 528/1/920/1; NA RAO 15/1/214/11; GARF A2306/70/3016/5; *Uchitel'skaia gazeta* (September 8, 1943): 2; L'vov, "Zhenskoe obrazovanie," 530.

141. See affirmations of the need to build a strong collective in separate schools in E. A. Parsanova, "Kollektiv klassa uchashchikhsia muzhskoi shkoly," *Nachal'naia shkola* 2–3 (1945): 33; GARF A2306/70/3016/3; TsAGM 528/1/920/6. On the importance of the collective in Soviet pedagogy, see Dunstan, *Soviet Schooling,* 16–18.

142. I. K. Novikov, *Organizatsiia uchebno-vospitatel'noi raboty v shkole. Iz opyta raboty 110-i muzhskoi srednei shkoly Moskvy* (Moscow: Izdatel'stvo APN, 1950), 381.

143. Markov, "O razdel'nom obuchenii," 4.

144. L'vov, "Zhenskoe obrazovanie," 531. For efforts to educate orphaned children, see A. M. Arsen'ev et al., *Ocherki istorii shkoly i pedagogicheskoi mysli narodov SSSR 1941–1961 gg.* (Moscow: Pedagogika, 1988), 22–23. See also discussion of a "wild kind of childhood" experienced by Soviet children during and immediately after the war, in Catherine Merridale, *Night of Stone: Death and Memory in Twentieth-Century Russia* (New York: Viking, 2001), 246–247. For official statements about parents' roles in disciplining children, see Catriona Kelly, *Children's World: Growing Up in Russia, 1890–1991* (New

Haven: Yale University Press, 2007), 127–128.

145. L'vov, "Zhenskoe obrazovanie," 532.

146. Ibid., 531. 147. NA RAO 15/1/214/11. Compare this initially positive impression to the statement made by the mother of a middle-school pupil in a separate boys' classroom in New York City: "Now I never hear a word from teachers about behavior problems, and when he talks about school, he is actually talking about work." *New York Times* (March 11, 2009): 24.

148. TsGARU 94/4/4797b/99, 116; APRK 708/7/1/713/6; GARF A2306/70/2957/52.

149. Potemkin, "Ob uluchshenii kachestva," 192.

150. L'vov, "Zhenskoe obrazovanie," 538, 540.

151. TsAGM 528/1/920/21. See similar assessments from Moscow teachers reported in *Uchitel'skaia gazeta* (June 14, 1944): 1.

152. L'vov, "Zhenskoe obrazovanie," 538–539.

153. GARF A2306/70/3016/18.

154. TsGARU 94/4/4797b/110.

155. L'vov, "Zhenskoe obrazovanie," 542. See chapter 3 for more comments from girls about conditions in separate schools.

156. *Uchitel'skaia gazeta* (December 8, 1943): 2. See chapter 4 for discussion of this meeting.

157. Ibid.

158. *Uchitel'skaia gazeta* (September 8, 1943): 2.

159. NA RAO 15/1/214/5.

160. Existing distinctions in education included rural-urban schools, languages of instruction, different levels of schools, and fees charged for senior grades. See discussion of status differences in Stalinist education in Holmes, *Stalin's School,* 31–45; Dunstan, *Soviet Schooling,* 51–52, 188–195; Livschiz, "Growing Up Soviet," 693–694; Livschiz, "Pre-Revolutionary in Form," 549–552.

161. In the words of one proponent, separating boys and girls "so they can get their work done" can seem "so logical." Meyer, "Learning Separately," 11. See teachers' conflicting assessments of the initial period of implementation in Herr and Arms, "Accountability and Single-Sex Schooling," 544–545.

162. The first stages of the Soviet experiment also anticipated patterns in other contexts, where separate schooling has been implemented with limited public discussion, on short notice, and with little advance preparation of teachers, pupils, or parents. In New York City, public school No. 140 implemented separate classrooms for boys and girls with "no special training or monitoring," after the principal heard that a school in North Carolina with girls' classes had produced improved test results: "it was as simple as that." *New York Times* (March 11, 2009): 24. See also the description of one faculty meeting, a one-day teachers' seminar, and one parents' meeting that preceded the introduction of separate classrooms in an Alabama middle school. Weil, "Should Boys and Girls," 40–43. For discussion of the rushed implementation and almost as sudden termination of California's single-sex academies, see DeBare, *Where Girls Come First,* 271. See also cautions against "hasty implementation" and recommendations for "a year for general planning" in Spielhagen, "Single-Sex Education."

163. See accounts of new separate schools and classrooms in Meehan, *Learning like a Girl,* 88–91; DeBare, *Where Girls Come First,* 1–2; Schreiner, "Single-Sex Classes."

2 — Teaching and Learning in Separate Schools

1. Perstova was director of Moscow girls' school No. 18. These comments were made at a November 1948 meeting, on the "peculiar features" of teaching in boys' and girls' schools, convened by a Moscow institute for teacher training. GARF A2306/71/721/6–7.

2. See discussion of "what is better" when it comes to evaluating coeducational and single-sex schools: academic results—such as test scores, graduation rates, and college admissions—or "less empirical criteria—such as graduates' self-esteem, creativity, or happiness." DeBare, *Where Girls Come First,* 8–9; Sax, *Women Graduates,* 13–18, 37–38.

3. This chapter focuses on the articles published during the first two years of this policy, including newspaper articles by professor M. Tsuzmer, "O razdel'nom obuchenii," *Uchitel'skaia gazeta* (August 11, 1943): 2; psychologists A. Smirnov and N. Levitov, "O psikhologicheskikh osobennostiakh mal'chikov i devochek," *Uchitel'skaia gazeta* (September 22, 1943): 2–3; and K. L'vov, "Pervyi god razdel'nogo obucheniia," *Uchitel'skaia gazeta* (June 7, 1944): 2; as well as two articles in the main educational journal, the first by M. G. Timofeev, "Sovmestnoe i razdel'noe obuchenie v proshlom i nastoiashchem," *Sovetskaia pedagogika* 4 (1945): 6–13; and a critical response, L'vov, "Sovmestnoe obuchenie," 38–46.

4. For research on Stalinist educational practices that makes extensive use of similar kinds of archival materials, see Holmes, *Stalin's School;* Ewing, *Teachers of Stalinism.*

5. For the conclusion that "academic research is inconclusive," see *New York Times,* (March 1, 2009): 24. See also the statement that "not much" of the research on separate schools "holds up to close scrutiny," in Bracey, "Success of Single-Sex Education," 22–26.

6. For a defense of separate schools emphasizing social interactions, see Sax, *Why Gender Matters,* 214–216. For an argument in favor of separate schooling that emphasizes academics, see Meyer, "Learning Separately," 10–21.

7. GARF A2306/71/721/3.

8. See the balance between same and different in Salomone, *Same, Different, Equal,* 188–236.

9. This estimate is based on partial figures in GARF A2306/72/75/83. Similar estimates were reported in *Pravda* (July 20, 1954): 2. Total enrollment figures are from *Cultural Progress,* 86–91.

10. The main postwar compilation of school statistics was published in 1956 and did not include any mention of separate schools. *Kul'turnoe stroitel'stvo SSSR* (1956).

11. This uncertainty about numbers is not confined to the postwar Stalinist situation, although the dictatorial conditions certainly contributed to the lack of data. In the contemporary United States, neither federal nor state educational agencies appear to maintain records of separate schools or classrooms even in the public sector. As a result, most published estimates of the number of public boys' or girls' schools or schools offering gender-separated classrooms come from advocacy groups, such as the National Association for Single Sex Public Education, which have an obvious interest in providing ever higher estimates. No published reports have been located estimating the number of American public separate schools from any other source. For examples of these estimates in published reports, see Meyer, "Learning Separately," 19; *New York Times* (March 11, 2009): 24; DeBare, *Where Girls Come First,* 278; Weil, "Should Boys and Girls," 38–45, 84–87; *USA Today* (March 26, 2008).

12. *Cultural Progress*, 86–87. During the 1940s, the number of births (30 million) was less than in either the 1930s (closer to 40 million) or the 1950s (more than 45 million), according to later statistical reports on the Soviet population. *Itogi vsesoiuznoi perepisi naseleniia 1970 goda*, 12.

13. At the end of the war, 90 percent of all Soviet schools were classified as "rural." *Kul'turnoe stroitel'stvo* (1956), 80–86. See statements acknowledging the impracticality of separating rural schools in TsAGM 528/1/678/1; RGASPI 17/126/2/86, 94–95.

14. These policies were not unique to postwar Soviet education, as separate schools have generally been concentrated in systems serving dense populations. Only recently have any rural schools in the United States begun implementing separate schools or separate classrooms. *USA Today* (March 26, 2008).

15. Urban enrollment also fluctuated in response to conditions, declining from almost 11 million in 1941 to just under 8 million in 1946, returning gradually to prewar levels, and then exceeding 12 million by 1954. *Cultural Progress*, 83, 88–89.

16. *Kul'turnoe stroitel'stvo* (1956), 83

17. L'vov, "Zhenskoe obrazovanie," 524.

18. GARF A2306/72/2707/1–43.

19. GARF A2306/72/2839/12–14. Slightly different totals are provided in Chernik, *Sovetskaia obshcheobrazovatel'naia shkola*, 128; Arsen'ev et al., *Ocherki istorii shkoly*, 26. One historical account claims that the "overwhelming majority" of separate schools were located in eighty-one cities in the Russian Republic, as only ten cities in the other republics had separate schools. No documentation or explanation is provided for this claim. Pyzhikov, "Razdel'noe obuchenie," 80. As will be discussed below, a much larger number of cities implemented separate schooling than Pyzhikov estimated.

20. *Pravda Vostoka* (July 21, 1954): 1; *Turkmenskaia iskra* (July 30, 1954): 1, (September 1, 1954): 1; *Kazakhstanskaia pravda* (July 30, 1954): 2; L'vov, "Shkola v soiuznykh respublikakh," 51.

21. TsGARU 94/4/4797b/112; *Pravda Vostoka* (July 31, 1954): 2.

22. Chernik, *Sovetskaia obshcheobrazovatel'naia shkola*, 128.

23. *Bakinskii rabochii* (August 3, 1954): 1, (August 21, 1943): 1, (July 22, 1954): 2; Chernik, *Sovetskaia obshcheobrazovatel'naia shkola*, 128; L'vov, "Shkola v soiuznykh respublikakh," 51.

24. *Zaria Vostoka* (July 24, 1954): 2; *Kul'turnoe stroitel'stvo* (1956), 126–127, 150–151.

25. *Sovetskaia Kirgiziia* (July 29, 1954): 1; *Kul'turnoe stroitel'stvo* (1956), 152–153.

26. *Pravda Ukrainy* (July 29, 1954): 3.

27. GARF A2306/72/75/83.

28. GARF A2306/72/2707/1–43.

29. *Uchitel'skaia gazeta* (June 14, 1944): 1.

30. GARF A2306/71/1074/7.

31. *Vecherniaia Moskva* (July 21, 1954): 3

32. A report on the Stalingrad schools on September 1, 1943, describes the extensive damage of the military campaigns but makes no mention of separate schools. *Uchitel'skaia gazeta* (September 3, 1943): 1. For wartime conditions in Soviet cities, including Sevastopol and Stalingrad, see Arsen'ev, *Ocherki istorii shkoly*, 16–19, 27; Chernik, *Sovetskaia obshcheobrazovatel'naia shkola*, 25; Qualls, *From Ruins to Reconstruction*, 119–120.

33. The letter suggests that the formation of separate schools in Stalingrad

occurred only in 1947, although more confirmation of this timing is needed. RGALI 634/4/96/121–125. See also GARF A2306/72/2707/13.

34. *Literaturnaia gazeta* (August 6, 1953): 3–4.

35. GARF A2306/72/2707/3.

36. See reports on war damage and children's experiences in *Uchitel'skaia gazeta* (September 3, 1943): 1; Dunstan, *Soviet Schooling*, 90–93, 165–166, 190.

37. GARF A2306/71/1175/13.

38. GARF A2306/72/2707/31.

39. The percentage of pupils in separate schools was 47 percent in Novosibirsk, 54 percent in Krasnoiarsk, 60 percent in Kazan, 52 percent in Omsk, and 60 percent in Irkutsk. GARF A2306/72/2707/6, 7, 23, 28, 43. In Iakutsk, located almost five thousand kilometers from Moscow, the regional government requested approval to eliminate separate schools in 1951, as discussed in chapter 6.

40. GARF A2306/72/2707/19, 40.

41. GARF A2306/70/2957/52; 72/2707/19.

42. APRK 708/7/1/713/6. Total enrollment is estimated from *Kul'turnoe stroitel'stvo* (1956), 62.

43. TsGARU 94/5/4797b/112.

44. *Uchitel'skaia gazeta* (August 4, 1954): 1.

45. GARF A2306/72/2707/13–14.

46. GARF A2306/72/2707/36.

47. GARF A2306/72/2707/1.

48. GARF A2306/72/2707/9.

49. GARF A2306/72/2707/8.

50. For ideological proclamations of women's equality in the postwar era, as well as the contradictions and complications associated with policy and practice, see Bucher, *Women, the Bureaucracy and Daily Life*, 39–40. For discussion of women's equality in earlier stages of Soviet history, see Goldman, *Women, the State, and Revolution;* Choi Chatterjee, *Celebrating Women: Gender, Festival Culture, and Bolshevik Ideology, 1910–1939* (Pittsburgh: University of Pittsburgh Press, 2002).

51. Dubrovina, *Women's Right to Education.*

52. *Uchitel'skaia gazeta* (June 22, 1928): 4.

53. For discussion of equity issues in American single-sex schooling, see Spielhagen, "Single-Sex Education"; Herr and Arms, "Accountability and Single-Sex Schooling," 528–533, 547; U.S. Department of Education, *Single-Sex versus Coeducational Schooling,* 85; Weaver-Hightower, "Boy Turn," 476.

54. RGASPI 17/126/2/83, 87–88, 96–98. See also discussion of the achievement of women's equality in Pyzhikov, "Razdel'noe obuchenie," 79; Livschiz, "Growing Up Soviet," 701–702.

55. Markov, "O razdel'nom obuchenii," 3.

56. *Uchitel'skaia gazeta* (August 11, 1943): 2. One of the first public statements in defense of separate schooling, this article by M. Tsuzmer appeared in August 1943 in the main educational newspaper, *Uchitel'skaia gazeta,* less than one month after the new policy was announced. Several versions of Tsuzmer's manuscript are preserved in the NA RAO 15/1/215. Little additional information is available about the author, whose byline refers to "Prof. M. Tsuzmer"; there is no further indication of his academic position or even geographical location.

57. TsAGM 528/1/872/49.

58. In this case, the particular objectives of girls' schools were not mentioned. *Leningradskaia pravda* (August 20, 1943): 3.

59. Timofeev, "Sovmestnoe i razdel'noe obuchenie," 9.

60. L'vov, "Zhenskoe obrazovanie," 544; *Uchitel'skaia gazeta* (June 7, 1944): 2. For a similar promise that separate schools would prepare "fully equal and all-around developed citizens," see Timofeev, "Sovmestnoe i razdel'noe obuchenie," 10.

61. *Uchitel'skaia gazeta* (August 11, 1943): 2.

62. Ibid.

63. *Pravda Severa* (August 22, 1943): 2. These maternalist arguments were widely repeated by foreign observers, who connected the elimination of coeducation to other conservative policies on gender roles and family status during the war. See Downs, "Revolution in Soviet School System," 76; *New York Times* (August 5, 1943): 12; "Soldiering v. Mothering," 44.

64. TsAGM 528/1/872/49.

65. TsAGM 528/1/920/1.

66. L'vov, "Zhenskoe obrazovanie," 538. The term she used for "tower" *(terem)* comes from the Muscovite era tradition of secluding elite women. See historical analysis in Natalia Pushkareva, *Women in Russian History: From the Tenth to the Twentieth Century* (Armonk, NY: M. E. Sharpe, 1997), 89, 121–130.

67. GARF A2306 70/2957/51.

68. Emphasis in the original. *Literaturnaia gazeta* (August 24, 1950): 2.

69. GARF A2306/72/72/6.

70. See review of political, legal, and educational debates in Meyer, "Learning Separately," 10–21; DeBare, *Where Girls Come First,* 6–9.

71. For perceptions of gender differences shared by teachers in single-gender academies, see Herr and Arms, "Intersection of Educational Reforms," 88; Meyer, "Learning Separately," 18. See also the statement that "traditional sex-role development" is one of the arguments in favor of single-sex schools, in Riordan, *Girls and Boys,* 52. For a statement that invokes ideas about innate sex differences to justify separate schooling, see Christina Hoff Sommers, "Give Same-Sex Schooling a Chance," *Education Week* 21, no. 4 (September 26, 2001): 26, online: www.edweek.org. See also the critical evaluation of how such views inform current debates in Wayne Martino and Deborah Berrill, "Boys, Schooling, and Masculinities: Interrogating the 'Right' Way to Educate Boys," *Educational Review* 55, no. 2 (2003): 104–106; Woody, "Constructions of Masculinity," 285–286.

72. Frances L. Bernstein, *The Dictatorship of Sex: Lifestyle Advice for the Soviet Masses* (DeKalb: Northern Illinois University Press, 2007), 42–43.

73. *Izvestiia* (January 8, 1944): 4.

74. For the Marxist foundations of Soviet views on women, see Goldman, *Women, the State,* 31–43. In education, the primacy of social explanations and the categorical rejection of innate causes reached a most destructive level with the 1936 denunciation of pedology as a false science linked to fascist arguments about racial inferiority. E. Thomas Ewing, "Restoring Teachers to Their Rights: Soviet Education and the 1936 Denunciation of Pedology," *History of Education Quarterly* 41, no. 4 (Winter 2001): 471–493.

75. *Pravda Severa* (August 22, 1943): 2.

76. *Krasnaia Tatariia* (August 29, 1943): 1; *Leningradskaia pravda* (August 4, 1943): 1, (October 1, 1943): 1; Timofeev, "Sovmestnoe i razdel'noe obuchenie," 9–10; *Uchitel'skaia gazeta* (June 7, 1944): 2.

77. Timofeev, "Sovmestnoe i razdel'noe obuchenie," 10. For examples of American teachers holding views about gender segregation that are different from the policies of their schools, see Gurian and Henley, *Boys and Girls Learn Differently!* 209–212.

78. *Uchitel'skaia gazeta* (September 22, 1943): 4. Anatolii Smirnov and Nikolai Levitov were specialists in developmental and educational psychology, members of the Academy of Pedagogical Sciences in the 1940s, and prominent figures in Soviet psychology from the 1920s through the 1970s. See their biographies in *Psykhologicheskii leksikon. Entsiklopedicheskii slovar' v shesti tomakh,* ed. L. A. Karpenko (Moscow: PER SE, 2005), online: slovari.yandex.ru.

79. *Uchitel'skaia gazeta* (September 22, 1943): 4.

80. Ibid.

81. Ibid.

82. TsGARU 94/5/4797/99.

83. GARF A2306/70/3016/18.

84. *Izvestiia* (January 8, 1944): 4; GARF A2306/71/721/27.

85. For the hope that brain research can "come up with an empirical answer to that tantalizing question" of whether single-sex or coeducational schooling is "better," see DeBare, *Where Girls Come First,* 286. See also favorable statements about the uses of brain research for advancing learning in Meehan, *Learning like a Girl,* 128, 205. The most emphatic argument for using gender differences in learning to justify expanded access to separate schools is found in Sax, *Why Gender Matters,* as well as the "research" section of the National Association for Single Sex Public Education website, www.singlesexschools. org. By contrast, Rosemary Salomone, who has made legal arguments in favor of separate schools, offers this strong opposition: "Every time I hear of school officials selling single-sex programs to parents based on brain research, my heart sinks." This statement is quoted in Weil, "Should Boys and Girls," 41.

86. GARF A2306/71/772/10. See also discussion of "the murky world of physiological and biological determinism," in Livschiz, "Growing Up Soviet," 699–700.

87. L'vov, "Sovmestnoe obuchenie," 43–44.

88. *Uchitel'skaia gazeta* (August 11, 1943): 2.

89. L'vov, "Sovmestnoe obuchenie," 44; *Uchitel'skaia gazeta* (August 11, 1943): 2. See Soviet scientists' discussion of sexual maturation in Dan Healey, *Bolshevik Sexual Forensics: Diagnosing Disorder in the Clinic and Courtroom, 1917–1939* (DeKalb: Northern Illinois University Press, 2009), 37–82.

90. *Uchitel'skaia gazeta* (September 22, 1943): 4.

91. Ibid.

92. L'vov, "Sovmestnoe obuchenie," 38–39.

93. Ibid., 43.

94. For analysis of how assumptions about gender shape debates on separate schools, see Patricia B. Campbell and Ellen Wahl, "What's Sex Got to Do with It? Simplistic Questions, Complex Answers," in *Separated by Sex,* 63–68.

95. For the "formal curriculum" in Soviet schools, see Dunstan, *Soviet Schooling,* 113–117.

96. For Stalinist classroom strategies, see Ewing, *Teachers of Stalinism;* Holmes, *Stalin's School.*

97. For gender in classrooms, see Connell, "Teaching the Boys," 206–235.

98. Markov, "O razdel'nom obuchenii," 4; *Uchitel'skaia gazeta* (August 11, 1943): 2; *Krasnaia Tatariia* (August 15, 1943): 4; L'vov, "Zhenskoe obrazovanie," 568.

99. *Leninskii put'* (September 4, 1943): 3.

100. *Pravda Severa* (September 7, 1943): 2.

101. *Bakinskii rabochii* (August 21, 1943): 1.

102. TsGARU 94/4/4797b/116.

103. GARF A2306/70/3016/18; TsAGM 528/1/878/4, 26; APRK 708/8/1522/31; NA RAO 15/1/214/12, 23; TsGARU 94/4/4797b/99.

104. TsAGM 528/1/878/4.

105. APRK 708/8/1522/31–32.

106. GARF A2306/70/2957/51.

107. L'vov, "Zhenskoe obrazovanie," 613–615. For contemporary descriptions of separate schools that emphasize how gender differences produce different classroom behaviors as well as responses from teachers, see *New York Times* (March 11, 2009): 24.

108. NA RAO 15/1/214/21. See also Chernik, *Sovetskaia obshcheobrazovatel'naia shkola,* 127.

109. L'vov, "Zhenskoe obrazovanie," 600–601, 606.

110. *Uchitel'skaia gazeta* (November 3, 1943): 3.

111. L'vov, "Zhenskoe obrazovanie," 561.

112. Ibid., 582.

113. Kosmodem'ianskaia was an eighteen-year-old Communist activist tortured and executed by German forces in late 1941; she became one of the most publicized heroines of the anti-Nazi resistance. *Uchitel'skaia gazeta* (April 29, 1948): 3.

114. Virtually the same observations of the same Lermontov poem were described by observers of Sverdlovsk boys' school No. 37 and girls' school No. 12 and Alma-Ata girls' school No. 10 and boys' school No. 56. *Uchitel'skaia gazeta* (June 7, 1944): 2; APRK 708/8/1522/32.

115. L'vov, "Zhenskoe obrazovanie," 576. See chapter 3 for more examples from this school.

116. L'vov, "Zhenskoe obrazovanie," 576.

117. Ibid., 575–576. See similar reports in APRK 708/8/1522/32.

118. L'vov, "Zhenskoe obrazovanic," 560–561.

119. Potemkin, "Ob uluchshenii kachestva," 191–192.

120. For descriptions of how teachers in contemporary American schools adapt their approaches to gender-segregated classrooms, see *New York Times* (March 11, 2009): 24.

121. The necessity for enhanced military training for boys was cited by Soviet historians as the main reason for separate schooling. Chernik, *Sovetskaia obshcheobrazovatel'naia shkola,* 127; Arsen'ev, *Ocherki istorii,* 26.

122. Potemkin, "Ob uluchshenii kachestva," 192.

123. TsAGM 528/1/872/49.

124. TsAGM 528/1/872/65; L'vov, "Zhenskoe obrazovanie," 608.

125. NA RAO 15/1/214/12; APRK 708/8/1522/31.

126. NA RAO 15/1/214/21–22. These comments were made at the February 1943 meeting, as described in the previous chapter.

127. NA RAO 15/1/214/23.

128. Ibid.

129. NA RAO 15/1/214/22–23.

130. Rives was an important Soviet pedagogue, who began researching and writing about pedagogy during the 1920s. NA RAO 15/1/214/23.

131. NA RAO 15/1/214/21.

132. NA RAO 15/1/214/23.

133. For a contemporary American debate over the proper outcomes of girls' schooling, see DeBare, *Where Girls Come First*, 71–72.

134. TsAGM 528/1/872/49–50.

135. Emphasis in the original. Timofeev, "Sovmestnoe i razdel'noe obuchenie," 6.

136. NA RAO 15/1/214/14.

137. GARF A2306/71/721/43.

138. GARF A2306/72/3680/1.

139. Markov, "O razdel'nom obuchenii," 4.

140. See the reports on examination results by city in Arsen'ev et al., *Ocherki istorii shkoly*, 28.

141. *Pionerskaia pravda* (May 8, 1951): 1.

142. *Kul'turnoe stroitel'stvo SSSR* (1940), 172–173. See evaluations of school systems based on achievement rates in *Pravda Vostoka* (July 31, 1954): 2.

143. *Uchitel'skaia gazeta* (April 29, 1948): 3. See similarly high rates of promotion in *Uchitel' Kazakhstana* (May 22, 1953): 3, (May 29, 1953): 3.

144. By contrast, American researchers have devoted considerable attention to measuring educational outcomes in order to compare single-sex and coeducational classrooms, even as the results of such quantitative research remain ambivalent. *New York Times* (March 11, 2009): 24; DeBare, *Where Girls Come First*, 8–9, 282–300; Spielhagen, "Single-Sex Education"; Weaver-Hightower, "Boy Turn," 485–486; Salomone, *Same, Different, Equal*, 24–25, 31, 180–181, 206–210, 238–244; Salomone, "Legality of Single-Sex Education," 62–63; U.S. Department of Education, *Single-Sex versus Coeducational Schooling*.

145. *Uchitel'skaia gazeta* (August 11, 1943): 2.

146. GARF A2306/70/2957/52.

147. GARF A2306/71/807/19.

148. Pyzhikov, "Razdel'noe obuchenie," 83–84.

149. Cited in Livschiz, "Growing Up Soviet," 760.

150. GARF A2306/71/807/19.

151. NA RAO 15/1/214/l.

152. TsAGM 528/1/1308/93.

153. RGALI 634/4/97/125–130. As is discussed in chapter 5, the letter from these directors responded to a critical article in the newspaper *Literaturnaia gazeta*.

154. GARF A2306/72/2839/9–10.

155. *Uchitel'skaia gazeta* (June 7, 1944): 2.

156. Mostovoi's comments were made at an October 1950 meeting of school directors convened by the Ministry of Education. GARF A2306/71/772/31–32.

157. GARF A2306/71/772/34.

158. For the lack of reliable quantitative measures of academic outcomes in separate schools, see U.S. Department of Education, *Single-Sex versus Coeducational Schooling*.

159. Potemkin, "Ob uluchshenii kachestva," 191.

160. NA RAO 15/1/214/3–4.

161. NA RAO 15/1/214/11–12.

162. Expressing even greater ambivalence, the Academy of Pedagogical Sciences concluded that "a rather mixed picture" characterized the relative achievement of boys', girls', and coeducational schools: "But in a significant number of boys' schools, the

general achievement level of pupils is significantly lower than in girls' schools, which can be explained by the unsatisfactory state of discipline." GARF A2306/72/72/7.

163. GARF A2306/71/772/4.

164. RGALI 634/4/97/125–130.

165. Ibid.

166. For similar assessments of the tension between academic and emotional factors involved in advocating for separate schools, see Meehan, *Learning like a Girl;* Weil, "Should Boys and Girls," 44–45, 87.

167. TsAGM 528/1/878/27.

168. See the thoughtful discussion of the implications of researching separate schools in Lee, "Is Single-Sex Secondary Schooling a Solution," 41–61.

169. *Kazakhstanskaia pravda* (September 4, 1943): 2.

170. TsAGM 528/1/878/4; GARF A2306/70/3016/18; APRK 708/8/1522/31–32; NA RAO 15/1/214/4; TsGARU 94/4/4797b/114; *Uchitel'skaia gazeta* (June 7, 1944): 2, (August 11, 1943): 2; *Pravda Severa* (August 22, 1943): 2.

171. L'vov, "Zhenskoe obrazovanie," 565–566, 599–600. See observations of a biology lesson in an American girls' school, as discussed in Meyer, "Learning Separately," 10–12. For sexuality in Soviet discourse, see Bernstein, *Dictatorship of Sex.*

172. TsAGM 528/1/872/49.

173. *Uchitel'skaia gazeta* (June 7, 1944): 2.

174. L'vov, "Zhenskoe obrazovanie," 634–635.

175. Quoted in ibid., 540.

176. Ibid., 564.

177. RGALI 634/4/96/156–157.

178. RGALI 634/4/96/146–153. For further concerns about femininity in girls' schools and masculinity in boys' schools, see chapters 3 and 4.

179. Out-of-school behavior was a particular concern of Soviet pedagogy, and in fact one of the "rules" for pupil behavior specifically addressed the need for polite behavior outside the school. Markov, "O razdel'nom obuchenii," 5.

180. TsAGM 528/1/872/66; NA RAO 15/1/214/16; GARF A2306/70/3016/3.

181. Markov, "O razdel'nom obuchenii," 5. See similar arguments in GARF A2306/72/72/5; TsGARU 94/4/4797b/116; *Bakinskii rabochii* (August 31, 1943): 2.

182. GARF A2306/71/721/13, 16, 46.

183. NA RAO 15/1/214/5, 9.

184. RGALI 634/4/96/13–14.

185. Timofeev, "Sovmestnoe i razdel'noe obuchenie," 12.

186. Datnow, Hubbard, and Conchas, "How Context Mediates Policy," 184–206; Riordan, *Girls and Boys in School;* Meyer, "Learning Separately," 10–21; Woody, "Constructions of Masculinity," 280–303.

3 — Clean, Warm, and Calm

1. *Uchitel'skaia gazeta* (August 10, 1949): 3. Durova was an early-nineteenth-century noblewoman who passed as a cavalry officer; Krupskaia was Lenin's widow and a socialist educator; and Kovalevskaia was a nineteenth-century mathematician. See chapter 5 for a different invocation of Durova's lessons for gender roles.

2. Lapidus, *Women in Soviet Society,* 116; Stites, *Women's Liberation Movement,*

391; Timasheff, *Great Retreat*, 219; Livschiz, "Growing Up Soviet," 656–657, 750–751, 814–816. For a contemporary U.S. account emphasizing the position of Soviet women, see Downs, "Revolution in Soviet School," 76.

3. For Soviet women during and after the war, see Bucher, *Women, the Bureaucracy and Daily Life*; Bucher, "Struggling to Survive," 144–148.

4. For this emphasis, see Livschiz, "Growing Up Soviet," 814–815.

5. NA RAO 15/1/214/21. See further discussion of equality in chapter 2.

6. Rebecca Rogers, "Schools, Discipline, and Community: Diary-Writing and Schoolgirl Culture in Late Nineteenth-Century France," *Women's History Review* 4, no. 4 (1995): 525–555; DeBare, *Where Girls Come First*; Johanson, *Women's Struggle*; Benita Blessing, *The Antifascist Classroom: Denazification in Soviet-Occupied Germany, 1945–1949* (New York: Palgrave Macmillan, 2006), 106–120.

7. Meehan, *Learning like a Girl*; Stabiner, *All Girls*; DeBare, *Where Girls Come First*.

8. For methodological issues involved in reading Stalinist sources, particularly about gender, see Northrop, *Veiled Empire*, 86–87; Hoffmann, *Stalinist Values*, 79.

9. For the emphasis on "listening to the voices" of current and past pupils of girls' schools, see DeBare, *Where Girls Come First*, 300.

10. Emphasis in the original. Angela Woollacott, *Gender and Empire* (New York: Palgrave Macmillan, 2006), 3.

11. *Pravda* (November 17, 1948): 2.

12. *Uchitel'skaia gazeta* (August 10, 1949): 3.

13. See chapter 1 for additional discussion of the first days of separate schools in September 1943. Contemporary accounts of American girls' schools also call attention to changes in classroom tone and behavior as a result of gender separation. See, for example, the introduction to DeBare, *Where Girls Come First*, 1–2, and the comments from girls cited in Meyer, "Learning Separately," 12. According to Diana Meehan, the common traits of successful American girls' schools are "small, inclusive, innovative, girl-nurturing societies." Meehan, *Learning like a Girl*, 213.

14. L'vov, "Zhenskoe obrazovanie," 542. This girl's remarks anticipate many of the themes in assessments of a girls' school cited in Meyer, "Learning Separately," 12.

15. For the argument that separate schools provide girls with "a place they can 'own,'" see Meehan, *Learning like a Girl*, xvi.

16. L'vov, "Zhenskoe obrazovanie," 542, 635. For a contemporary American report that identifies the three keys to success in girls' school as focusing on academics, emphasizing discipline, and eliminating the distraction of boys, see Meyer, "Learning Separately," 16.

17. See chapter 2 for the context of Perstova's comments at a November 1948 meeting of Moscow school directors. GARF A2306/71/721/5.

18. TsGARK 1692/1/1904/183; GARF A2306/72/72/7.

19. *Uchitel'skaia gazeta* (June 7, 1944): 2.

20. GARF A2306/71/818/249.

21. *Uchitel'skaia gazeta* (April 29, 1948): 3.

22. TsAGM 528/1/920/5–6.

23. L'vov, "Zhenskoe obrazovanie," 643–644. For the argument that separate schools can promote the self-confidence of girls, especially in difficult stages of adolescence, see Debare, *Where Girls Come First*, 4, 12; Meyer, "Learning Separately," 12.

24. L'vov, "Zhenskoe obrazovanie," 644.

25. GARF A2306/70/3016/18. Compare to descriptions of girls' classrooms emphasizing mutual support, self-confidence, and collaborative activities in DeBare, *Where*

Girls Come First, 279–282; Meehan, *Learning like a Girl*, 172–173, 187. For arguments that girls' schools should focus on "the connections girls have (a) with the content, (b) with each other, and (c) with the teacher," see Weil, "Should Boys and Girls," 38–45, 84–87.

26. APRK 708/12/1440/78.

27. *Uchitel'skaia gazeta* (April 29, 1948): 3.

28. *Uchitel'skaia gazeta* (September 8, 1943): 2.

29. *Pravda Vostoka* (September 1, 1949): 1.

30. *Uchitel'skaia gazeta* (February 4, 1944): 3.

31. L'vov, "Zhenskoe obrazovanie," 646–647. See similar comments in GARF A2306/71/721/11.

32. TsAGM 528/1/920/9–10.

33. GARF A2306/71/721/27.

34. GARF A2306/71/772/31–32, 846/315, 1175/457; *Uchitel'skaia gazeta* (April 29, 1948): 3. While some city educational departments required uniforms, even these officials admitted that not all students wore the same clothing, often due to a shortage of materials. See chapter 4 for the clothing and appearance of boy pupils.

35. L'vov, "Zhenskoe obrazovanie," 556.

36. *Izvestiia* (January 8, 1944): 4.

37. APRK 708/8/1550/23.

38. GARF 2306/71/818/248–249.

39. *Uchitel'skaia gazeta* (April 29, 1948): 3.

40. APRK 708/8/1522/33.

41. L'vov, "Zhenskoe obrazovanie," 556.

42. GARF A2306/71/1175/456–457.

43. This image of peaceful conversation is strikingly different from this father's descriptions of his sons' school, which emphasize noise, chaos, running, and disobedience, as will be discussed in the following chapter. RGALI 634/4/96/11–12.

44. *Izvestiia* (January 8, 1944): 4.

45. GARF A2306/71/721/25.

46. GARF A2306/71/772/19. See the following chapter for Khrushchev's dismissive attitude toward teaching in a girls' school.

47. "Pervye shkol'nye gody," *SSSR na stroike* 4 (1949): 7. For more on this teacher, see Ewing, "Stalinist Celebrity Teacher," 92–118.

48. NA RAO 15/1/214/7–8.

49. TsAGM 528/1/920/25.

50. TsAGM 528/1/878/26.

51. *Izvestiia* (January 8, 1944): 4.

52. *Uchitel'skaia gazeta* (September 22, 1943): 4.

53. Emphasis in the original. Timofeev, "Sovmestnoe i razdel'noe obuchenie," 10. For American girls' schools responding to "mixed messages," see DeBare, *Where Girls Come First*, 11, 98.

54. Timofeev, "Sovmestnoe i razdel'noe obuchenie," 12. Compare Timofeev's statement to the emphasis in American girls' schools on empathy, connection, egalitarianism, and nonauthoritarian styles of learning and teaching. Meehan, *Learning like a Girl*, 89, 227.

55. For the efforts by American girls' schools to counter this perception that girls have limited interests, capacities, and potential in math and science subjects, see Meehan, *Learning like a Girl*, 221–227; Sax, *Women Graduates*, 9.

56. *Izvestiia* (January 8, 1944): 4.

57. These letters are quoted in L'vov, "Zhenskoe obrazovanie," 549–550.

58. Ibid., 553–554.

59. Ibid., 568–570.

60. *Uchitel'skaia gazeta* (April 29, 1948): 3.

61. L'vov, "Zhenskoe obrazovanie," 568–570.

62. TsAGM 528/1/920/6–7.

63. *Uchitel'skaia gazeta* (September 8, 1943): 2.

64. *Uchitel'skaia gazeta* (February 4, 1944): 3. For evidence that women graduates of single-sex schools demonstrate "greater academic engagement," see Sax, *Women Graduates*, 7–8, 44.

65. *Uchitel'skaia gazeta* (September 8, 1943): 2.

66. *Uchitel'skaia gazeta* (May 31, 1944): 2.

67. L'vov, "Zhenskoe obrazovanie," 646.

68. This report was prepared by an official of the Kazakh Narkompros and read to a regional conference of educational administrators in July 1944. APRK 708/8/1522/31. Compare these evaluations to the comments by an American teacher in a girls' school, who stated that her female pupils are "louder socially and more fearless than girls I've taught in coed schools." Cited in Meyer, "Learning Separately," 16. See also this statement from another teacher about teaching topics with any kind of sexual connotations in an American girls' school: "I'm freer. I'm more able to be bold in my statements." Weil, "Should Boys and Girls," 86–87.

69. L'vov, "Zhenskoe obrazovanie," 644.

70. Ibid., 645. Daybooks *(dnevniki)* were used by teachers to maintain a constant record of pupils' disciplinary and academic grades.

71. *Uchitel'skaia gazeta* (June 7, 1944): 2.

72. *Uchitel'skaia gazeta* (September 8, 1943): 2.

73. For the "shortchanging" of girls, see AAUW, *The A.A.U.W. Report*.

74. GARF A2306/71/721/3. See chapter 2 for discussion of the ideological commitment to equal education in separate schools.

75. For this emphasis in girls' schools, see DeBare, *Where Girls Come First*, 190–198.

76. *Uchitel'skaia gazeta* (August 10, 1949): 3.

77. L'vov, "Zhenskoe obrazovanie," 552.

78. *Uchitel'skaia gazeta* (February 4, 1944): 3.

79. TsAGM 528/1/920/17–18.

80. L'vov, "Zhenskoe obrazovanie," 577–578.

81. APRK 708/8/1522/32.

82. *Uchitel'skaia gazeta* (February 4, 1944): 3.

83. Timofeev, "Sovmestnoe i razdel'noe obuchenie," 10–11.

84. L'vov, "Zhenskoe obrazovanie," 571–572.

85. *Uchitel'skaia gazeta* (February 4, 1944): 3. See chapter 2 for more discussion of how history lessons symbolized the different approaches of boys' and girls' schools. For American girls' schools that call attention to female role models, see *New York Times* (March 11, 2009): 24; Meehan, *Learning like a Girl*, 147, 219; Riordan, *Girls and Boys in School*, 49–50.

86. For Soviet labor education, see Larry E. Holmes, "The Decline of Labor Education in Soviet Russia's Schools, 1931–1937," *Russian Review* 51, no. 4 (1992): 545–565.

87. TsAGM 528/1/872/59; 878/26; *Uchitel'skaia gazeta* (April 1, 1950): 2; Livschiz, "Growing Up Soviet," 754–755.

88. *Leninskii put'* (August 29, 1943): 1.

89. GARF A2306/71/721/8–9.

90. *Uchitel'skaia gazeta* (April 1, 1950): 2.

91. GARF A2306/70/2957/51–52, 71/721/25–26.

92. GARF A2306/71/721/9.

93. L'vov, "Zhenskoe obrazovanie," 554–555.

94. *Uchitel'skaia gazeta* (April 1, 1950): 2.

95. GARF A2306/71/721/39.

96. *Uchitel'skaia gazeta* (September 22, 1943): 4.

97. *Uchitel'skaia gazeta* (December 10, 1952): 3.

98. *Izvestiia* (January 8, 1944): 4.

99. *Uchitel'skaia gazeta* (June 7, 1944): 2. A similar combination of domestic crafts and academic circles was reported in Alma-Ata girls' schools. APRK 708/8/1522/32.

100. *Uchitel'skaia gazeta* (September 8, 1943): 2.

101. TsGARK 1692/1/1564/102.

102. *Uchitel'skaia gazeta* (April 29, 1948): 3

103. For the meaning of maternity in Stalinist ideology, policy, and practice, see Bucher, *Women, the Bureaucracy and Daily Life,* 17–22, 45–46; Melanie Ilic, *Women Workers in the Soviet Interwar Economy: From "Protection" to "Equality"* (London: Macmillan, 1999); Neary, "Mothering Socialist Society," 396–412; Hoffmann, *Stalinist Values,* 88–117; Hoffmann, "Mothers in the Motherland," 35–54; Thomas G. Schrand, "The Five-Year Plan for Women's Labour: Constructing Socialism and the 'Double Burden', 1930–1932," *Europe-Asia Studies* 51, no. 8 (1999): 1455–1478.

104. For maternalism as a political strategy, see Seth Koven and Sonya Michel, "Womanly Duties: Maternalist Politics and the Origins of Welfare States in France, Germany, Great Britain, and the United States, 1880–1920," *American Historical Review* 95, no. 4 (1990): 1077–1079; Gisela Bock and Pat Thane, eds., *Maternity and Gender Policies: Women and the Rise of the European Welfare States* (London: Routledge, 1991).

105. GARF 2306/72/72/5; *Uchitel'skaia gazeta* (June 7, 1944): 2.

106. *Uchitel'skaia gazeta* (September 8, 1943): 2.

107. Potemkin, "Ob uluchshenii kachestva," 191.

108. L'vov, "Sovmestnoe obuchenie," 44; L'vov, "Zhenskoe obrazovanie," 561.

109. *Uchitel'skaia gazeta* (September 3, 1943): 1, (November 29, 1944): 4.

110. TsAGM 528/1/920/17–18. Teacher training programs in girls' schools continued the efforts begun in some Central Asian republics, where women's pedagogical institutes trained female teachers for villages where girls' enrollment remained low. See discussion in Ewing, "Not One Girl."

111. TsAGM 528/1/872/59; TsGARU 94/4/4797b/99; *Uchitel'skaia gazeta* (February 4, 1944): 3.

112. GARF A2306/71/721/24.

113. *Uchitel'skaia gazeta* (September 8, 1943): 2. For the ambivalence about sports in girls' schools, see DeBare, *Where Girls Come First,* 95–98.

114. *Uchitel'skaia gazeta* (February 4, 1944): 3.

115. RGALI 634/4/97/87–88.

116. *Uchitel'skaia gazeta* (February 4, 1944): 3.

117. GARF A2306/71/721/23–24.

118. *Uchitel'skaia gazeta* (September 22, 1943): 4.

119. NA RAO 15/1/214/21.

120. TsGARU 94/4/4797b/114.

121. TsAGM 528/1/920/22.

122. For "sex differences in curriculum opportunities," see Riordan, *Girls and Boys in School,* 53–54.

123. TsAGM 528/1/920/6–7.

124. GARF A2306/71/721/40.

125. GARF A2306/71/772/20. For Khrushchev's argument that the very best teachers should be assigned to boys' schools, see chapter 4.

126. *Izvestiia* (January 8, 1944): 4.

127. L'vov, "Zhenskoe obrazovanie," 562.

128. *Uchitel'skaia gazeta* (June 7, 1944): 2; TsGARU 94/4/4797b/116.

129. L'vov, "Zhenskoe obrazovanie," 564–565.

130. GARF A2306/71/721/30.

131. GARF A2306/71/807/29–30.

132. For science lessons in girls' schools, see DeBare, *Where Girls Come First,* 1–2, 279–282.

133. GARF A2306/71/846/189.

134. TsGARU 94/5/4749b/99; *Uchitel'skaia gazeta* (June 7, 1944): 2.

135. APRK 708/8/1522/31.

136. *Kazakhstanskaia pravda* (September 2, 1953): 2.

137. *Uchitel'skaia gazeta* (February 4, 1944): 3.

138. *Uchitel'skaia gazeta* (May 31, 1944): 2.

139. L'vov, "Zhenskoe obrazovanie," 584–585.

140. Ibid., 560.

141. *Uchitel'skaia gazeta* (June 7, 1944): 2.

142. GARF A2306/71/721/6–8.

143. L'vov, "Zhenskoe obrazovanie," 589–590.

144. GARF A2306/71/772/25.

145. RGALI 634/4/97/238–243. See chapter 4 for further discussion of boys' perceptions of female pupils and girls' schools.

146. L'vov, "Zhenskoe obrazovanie," 604.

147. *Uchitel'skaia gazeta* (February 4, 1944): 3.

148. *Uchitel'skaia gazeta* (May 31, 1944): 2.

149. GARF A2306/71/721/21–22. The tendency to assume that all girls' classrooms are the same is also criticized in DeBare, *Where Girls Come First,* 308–309.

150. Timofeev, "Sovmestnoe i razdel'noe obuchenie," 11.

151. GARF A2306/71/721/6–7. For this teacher's comparison of working in a girls' and a boys' school, see chapter 2.

152. *Uchitel'skaia gazeta* (April 29, 1948): 3.

153. *Izvestiia* (January 8, 1944): 4.

154. *Uchitel'skaia gazeta* (August 10, 1949): 3.

155. *Uchitel'skaia gazeta* (June 7, 1944): 2.

156. L'vov, "Zhenskoe obrazovanie," 541.

157. RGALI 634/4/96/30–31. The complaints cited in this paragraph were included in letters submitted to the newspaper *Literaturnaia gazeta* in the spring and summer of 1950, as is discussed more fully in chapter 5.

158. RGALI 634/4/96/167–168. See a similar complaint about estrangement in RGALI 634/4/97/81–82.

159. RGALI 634/4/96/145.

160. RGALI 634/4/96/156–157.

161. RGALI 634/4/97/100.

162. APRK 708/27/1487/165.

163. L'vov, "Zhenskoe obrazovanie," 543; GARF A2306/72/3680/44.

164. GARF A2306/72/3680/27.

165. RGALI 634/4/96/202–205; GARF A2306/72/3680/38.

166. *Literaturnaia gazeta* (August 24, 1950): 2.

167. GARF A2306/71/789/16; *Literaturnaia gazeta* (June 28, 1950): 2.

168. *Literaturnaia gazeta* (August 24, 1950): 2. See discussion of efforts to regulate virtue in girls' schools in Livschiz, "Growing Up Soviet," 756. For the influence on American girls' schools of community anxieties about female sexuality, see Weil, "Should Boys and Girls," 86–87. For Soviet perceptions of sexual maturation in terms of gender differences, see Healey, *Bolshevik Sexual Forensics,* 49–51.

169. TsAGM 528/1/920/6–7.

170. GARF A2306/72/3680/42.

171. A later speaker reported that the "sexual question" prompted the most concern from parents, who sought more guidance from schools. GARF A2306/71/721/13, 47. Perstova's comments suggest the tension inherent in Soviet ideology, which recognized adolescent sexuality as natural and normal yet restricted expressions of desire or pleasure. Bernstein, *Dictatorship of Sex.*

172. GARF A2306/71/721/13.

173. *Literaturnaia gazeta* (May 4, 1950): 2.

174. RGALI 634/4/96/11–12. These parents sent letters to the newspaper *Literaturnaia gazeta* in 1950, in response to an article critical of separate schools, as is discussed in chapter 5.

175. RGALI 634/4/96/12.

176. RGALI 634/4/96/32.

177. GARF A2306/71/721/43.

178. GARF A2306/71/721/33–34. See also a father's warning that girls spent their time after school trying to meet up with boys. RGALI 634/4/96/65–66. For the ways that girls in separate schools tended to view male peers in terms of masculine stereotypes, see Woody, "Constructions of Masculinity," 290–291.

179. RGALI 634/4/96/13–14.

180. GARF A2306/71/721/45.

181. NA RAO 15/1/214/5; GARF A2306/71/721/15; TsAGM 528/1/920/20; Livschiz, "Growing Up Soviet," 717–718. For American teachers' preferences for working in girls' schools, see DeBare, *Where Girls Come First,* 273; Herr and Arms, "Accountability and Single-Sex Schooling," 547.

182. *Izvestiia* (January 8, 1944): 4.

183. TsAGM 528/1/920/20.

184. TsAGM 528/1/920/16, 26–27. For teachers' differing views of "which gender is tougher to teach," see DeBare, *Where Girls Come First,* 273.

185. APRK 708/8/1522/33; 1550/17.

186. L'vov, "Zhenskoe obrazovanie," 655.

187. *Uchitel'skaia gazeta* (November 3, 1943): 3.

188. TsGARK 1692/1/1575/59.

189. TsAGM 528/1/920/6–7, 10. For a similar call to educate "real Soviet women," not characters from Turgenev novels, see GARF 2306/72/3680/43.

190. NA RAO 15/1/214/7.

191. GARF A2306/71/721/37–38. For the greater "intensity" and "drama" of relationships and interactions in girls' schools and classrooms, see DeBare, *Where Girls Come First,* 130–150, 303–307; *New York Times* (March 11, 2009): 24.

192. For tensions between obedience and identity in postwar Stalinism, see Juliane Furst, "The Importance of Being Stylish: Youth, Culture, and Identity," in *Late Stalinist Russia,* 209–230.

193. TsAGM 528/1/878/26. See also reports cited in Zubkova, *Russia after the War,* 111.

194. Timofeev, "Sovmestnoe i razdel'noe obuchenie," 13.

195. GARF A2306/71/721/13.

196. TsAGM 528/1/920/8–9.

197. GARF A2306/72/429/29, 818/249; L'vov, "Zhenskoe obrazovanie," 555; *Literaturnaia gazeta* (August 6, 1953): 3–4

198. GARF A2306/72/3680/41.

199. GARF A2306/71/721/4–5, 9–11.

200. Guzel Amalrik, *Memories of a Tatar Childhood* (London: Hutchinson, 1979), 49.

201. GARF A2306/71/721/22–23.

202. L'vov, "Zhenskoe obrazovanie," 559–560.

203. GARF A2306/71/721/15.

204. L'vov, "Zhenskoe obrazovanie," 559.

205. GARF A2306/71/721/36.

206. Potemkin, "Ob uluchshenii kachestva," 191.

207. GARF A2306/71/721/36, 39, 42.

208. L'vov, "Zhenskoe obrazovanie," 558.

209. Quoted in Zubkova, *Russia after the War,* 111.

210. See the emphasis on girls' voices in Meehan, *Learning like a Girl,* 13.

211. L'vov, "Zhenskoe obrazovanie," 541–542.

212. RGALI 634/4/96/35–36. These evaluations of separate schools were included in letters to the editors of *Literaturnaia gazeta,* as part of a broader wave of dissatisfaction with this policy, as is discussed in chapter 5.

213. RGALI 634/4/96/48–49. See also the desire to have boys as "school friends," as expressed by Kazan eighth-grade pupils. RGALI 634/4/97/87–88.

214. RGALI 634/4/97/27.

215. RGALI 634/4/96/174–175.

216. RGALI 634/4/96/67.

217. RGALI 634/4/96/108.

218. RGALI 634/4/96/167–168, 97/87–88, 100.

219. RGALI 634/4/97/212.

220. RGALI 634/4/96/185–187.

221. RGALI 634/4/96/12.

222. RGALI 634/4/96/44–45.

223. RGALI 634/4/96/178–181. See chapters 5 and 6 for additional discussion of how the perceived shortcomings of girls' schools reinforced support for a restoration of coeducation.

224. RGALI 634/4/96/48–49. See chapter 5 for a discussion of the latter quote from school director Tiapkin.

225. RGALI 634/4/96/156–157, 167–168.

226. RGALI 634/4/97/87–88.

227. RGALI 634/4/97/162.

228. RGALI 634/4/97/121–122. See the introduction for more statements from these girls.

229. RGALI 634/4/96/185–187.

230. See the claim that girls' schools create a "small bit of alternative reality," in which girls receive "an antidote to the dominant culture" in terms of academic achievement, social roles, and personal development. DeBare, *Where Girls Come First*, 324. Stabiner explains the renewed appeal of American girls' schools as "a progressive alternative to the documented prejudices of a coeducational classroom," with the goal of better preparing female students for adult roles. Stabiner, *All Girls*, 56. Meehan argues that girls' schools can be an "antidote" to the dominent elements in "female adolescent culture" that place girls at a disadvantage. Meehan, *Learning like a Girl*, xvi.

231. For the argument that American teachers believed single-sex schools worked better for girls than for boys, see Herr and Arms, "Accountability and Single-Sex Schooling," 547.

232. See normative (and gender neutral) school objectives in *Pravda* (November 17, 1948): 2.

233. *Uchitel'skaia gazeta* (April 29, 1948): 3.

4 — The Problem of Order

1. TsAGM 528/1/1308/93–94.

2. TsAGM 528/1/1308/94–97. Kholmogortsev worked as a history teacher and also served in the Moscow educational department before the war. Holmes, *Stalin's School*, 21–22, 60, 97.

3. TsAGM 528/1/1308/106–107.

4. TsAGM 528/1/1308/117–118.

5. This interpretation builds on arguments that boys and girls make different, and to some extent competing, demands on teachers' time, and thus the more attention that teachers devote to boys (even if the attention is negative), the less attention is available for girl pupils. Sadker and Sadker, *Failing at Fairness*, 42–65. See also the interpretation that in California single-gender academies, the fact that girls seemed to be doing so well inadvertently ceded attention to the boys, thus allowing the attention of teachers to focus on the question, "What do we do about the boys?" Herr and Arms, "The Intersection of Educational Reforms," 85–86.

6. For masculinity and Stalinism, see Petrone, "Masculinity and Heroism," 172–193.

7. See literature reviews in Woody, "Constructions of Masculinity," 284–285; Weaver-Hightower, "Boy Turn," 471–498; Martino and Berrill, "Boys, Schooling, and Masculinities," 99–106; Connell, "Teaching the Boys," 206–235; Nancy Lesko, "Introduction," in *Masculinities at School* (Thousand Oaks, CA: Sage, 2000): xi–xxx; Blye Frank, Michael Kehler, Trudy Lovell, and Kevin Davison, "A Tangle of Trouble: Boys, Masculinity, and Schooling—Future Directions," *Educational Review* 55, no. 2 (2003):

119–133; Salomone, *Same, Different, Equal,* 67–68, 80–83, 220–222.

8. Weaver-Hightower, "Boy Turn," 478. See also Martino and Berrill, "Boys, Schooling, and Masculinities," 99–106; Weil, "Should Boys and Girls," 45, 84–85.

9. AAUW, *The A.A.U.W. Report;* AAUW, *Gender Gaps;* AAUW, *Separated by Sex;* and AAUW, *Beyond the "Gender Wars": A Conversation about Girls, Boys, and Education* (Washington: AAUW Educational Foundation, 2001).

10. R. W. Connell comments (drily) that "more heat than light has been generated by these claims" that girls or boys are more or less disadvantaged. Connell's own work has successfully looked beyond this polemical rhetoric to identify some key issues involved in the relationship between gender and education. Connell, "Teaching the Boys," 207. See also Weaver-Hightower's view that research on the "boy turn" may "indeed have progressive ends, but it requires vigilant screening." Weaver-Hightower, "Boy Turn," 490. For even more recent discussion of the "boy crisis" in American education, Peter Meyer, "Learning Separately," 17–18; Meehan, *Learning like a Girl,* 234–235; Sara Mead, "The Evidence Suggests Otherwise: The Truth about Boys and Girls" (Washington: Education Sector, 2006).

11. Connell, "Teaching the Boys," 214.

12. For disciplinary strategies in Stalinist schools, see Holmes, *Stalin's School,* 46–62; Ewing, *Teachers of Stalinism,* 189–226; Fradkin and Plokhova, "Problemy distsipliny v sovetskoi shkole," 91–98. For broader concerns about lack of discipline among Soviet youth in the postwar period, see Zubkova, *Russia after the War,* 109–116.

13. Chernik, *Sovetskaia obshcheobrazovatel'naia shkola,* 172–176.

14. For examples of pupil misbehavior and disciplinary actions that responded to gendered perceptions and practices, see analysis in E. Thomas Ewing, "How Is Power Exercised in an Authoritarian School?" (unpublished paper, 2008).

15. NA RAO 15/1/214/7, 11.

16. *Uchitel'skaia gazeta* (December 8, 1943): 2.

17. *Uchitel'skaia gazeta* (June 7, 1944): 2.

18. Potemkin, "Ob uluchshenii kachestva," 189–208.

19. GARF A2306/71/1175/456, 458, 72/72/2–3, 446/9, 25; TsGARU 94/4/4797b/115.

20. This interpretation draws on an analysis of masculinity in California single-gender academies, which argues that perceptions of boys as needing strict discipline became a central factor in shaping school policies and practices. Woody, "Constructions of Masculinity," 286–289. See also the reference to school discipline as an example of "masculinizing practices governed by the gender regime of the school" in Connell, "Teaching the Boys," 215. For the significance assigned to disciplining boys as a factor in evaluating single-gender schooling, see Patricia B. Campbell and Jo Sanders, "Challenging the System: Assumptions and Data behind the Push for Single-Sex Schooling," in *Gender in Policy and Practice,* 39–40; Herr and Arms, "Intersection of Educational Reforms," 84–86. For a brief discussion of masculinity in Soviet boys' schools, see Livschiz, "Growing Up Soviet," 753–754. See also the description of the "serious discipline" in a New York City boys' school in Weil, "Should Boys and Girls," 45. For a contrary argument, emphasizing the potential for boys' schools to nurture "a broader definition of masculinity," see Meehan, *Learning like a Girl,* 240.

21. NA RAO 15/1/214/4.

22. GARF A2306/71/789/2, 15, 33.

23. RGALI 634/4/97/24–26.

24. GARF A2306/71/1175/456–458, 72/72/7, 285/26, 446/29, 2839/10; APRK 708/8/1550/17; *Literaturnaia gazeta* (August 24, 1950): 2; *Uchitel' Kazakhstana* (January 17, 1953): 3, (February 13, 1953): 1.

25. Emphasis in the original. GARF A2306/72/429/29.

26. TsAGM 667/1/80/102–103; GARF A2306/71/818/249–250, 1175/458, 72/285/26; TsGARK 1692/1/1575/60; Livschiz, "Growing Up Soviet," 758–759.

27. GARF A2306/72/3676/31.

28. GARF A2306/72/3676/10, 24, 47–48.

29. GARF A2306/72/3676/29. A historian's discussion of similar reports of pupils' misbehavior did not make any connection to gender-segregated schooling. Qualls, *From Ruins to Reconstruction,* 120–122. See the next chapter for connections between disciplinary problems and enrollment increases, especially in boys' schools.

30. This meeting of boys' school directors was convened in October 1950 by the Ministry of Education. GARF A2306/71/772/2–3, 14.

31. GARF A2306/71/772/2.

32. GARF A2306/71/772/13.

33. *Uchitel' Kazakhstana* (May 13, 1954): 3.

34. RGALI 634/4/96/11–12.

35. APRK 708/27/1487/164.

36. *Leningradskaia pravda* (April 13, 1950): 3. For further discussion of "disorganizers" and "hooligans," whom school officials blamed for causing disruptions yet whom classmates saw as "folk-heroes," see *Uchitel' Kazakhstana* (May 6, 1954): 3; APRK 708/27/1487/163; TsGARK 1692/1/1575/59–60; Timofeev, "Sovmestnoe i razdel'noe obuchenie," 11–12.

37. *Uchitel' Kazakhstana* (May 13, 1954): 3.

38. GARF A2306/72/3676/11.

39. *Uchitel'skaia gazeta* (December 8, 1943): 2.

40. TsAGM 528/1/878/4.

41. TsAGM 528/1/1308/101.

42. Transformational narratives were an essential feature of Stalinist educational discourse, as the path from delinquent hooligan to dedicated student reproduced the path from tsarism to communism. James Bowen, *Soviet Education: Anton Makarenko and the Years of Experiment* (Madison: University of Wisconsin Press, 1962).

43. GARF A2306/70/2957/50.

44. GARF A2306/71/818/250.

45. GARF A2306/71/772/7. This comment can be compared to teachers' perception that they "couldn't let up for a minute" in their boys' classrooms, or "things would careen wildly out of control," as reported in Herr and Arms, "Accountability and Single-Sex Schooling," 544. For a different interpretation, arguing that a boys' school is "too flexible, too comfortable, too nurturing to be martial," see Meehan, *Learning like a Girl,* 239. See also the suggestion that "problems of order and control might be considerably reduced by a policy of single-sex schooling," based on reports of decreased disciplinary violations in separate schools, in Riordan, *Girls and Boys in School,* 59.

46. GARF A2306/71/772/22.

47. GARF A2306/71/1175/457. For mechanisms of surveillance in school discipline, see Michel Foucault, *Discipline and Punish: The Birth of the Prison* (New York: Vintage, 1979), 170–177.

48. GARF A2306/71/1126/49–50.

49. GARF A2306/71/818/250.

50. GARF A2306/71/1175/458.

51. This pattern was also observed in an American school with all-male classrooms, where teachers adopted a strategy of "defensive teaching," in anticipation of resistance and misbehavior from pupils, which produced a "stifling" atmosphere in order to maintain control. Herr and Arms, "Accountability and Single-Sex Schooling," 545–546.

52. TsAGM 528/1/1308/97.

53. TsAGM 528/1/1308/97–98. For prohibitions on corporal punishment and other humiliating tactics, see Ewing, *Teachers of Stalinism,* 200–205.

54. *Uchitel'skaia gazeta* (February 4, 1944): 2.

55. Ibid. Emphasis in the original.

56. *Uchitel'skaia gazeta* (July 9, 1952): 3.

57. Parsanova, "Kollektiv klassa," 35. For similar transformative narratives involving schools where discipline had initially weakened but then gradually strengthened as school directors and teachers developed more appropriate and effective strategies for "dealing with boys," see APRK 708/8/1522/33; RGALI 634/4/96/113–114.

58. GARF A2306/72/3680/37–38.

59. GARF A2306/71/772/39.

60. For nurturing approaches in boys' schools, see Weil, "Should Boys and Girls," 44–45, 84–85; Meehan, *Learning like a Girl,* 233–242.

61. *Pionerskaia pravda* (May 8, 1951): 1.

62. *Uchitel'skaia gazeta* (June 7, 1944): 2.

63. APRK 708/8/1522/32; TsGARU 94/4/4797b/100.

64. GARF A2306/71/846/315–316.

65. GARF A2306/71/1175/457. See similar praise for Moscow boys' school No. 67 in TsAGM 528/1/1308/101.

66. *Pravda Vostoka* (September 1, 1949): 1.

67. TsAGM 528/1/1308/95–96.

68. *Kommunist* (August 21, 1954): 3.

69. GARF A2306/72/3676/10.

70. *Uchitel' Kazakhstana* (May 13, 1954): 3.

71. GARF 2306/71/818/249.

72. Parsanova, "Kollektiv klassa," 33–35.

73. TsAGM 667/1/80/100–108.

74. GARF A2306/71/1175/457.

75. TsAGM 528/1/1308/91.

76. *Literaturnaia gazeta* (August 6, 1953): 3–4. See chapter 5 for further discussion of this critical article.

77. GARF A2306/71/772/10, 22–23, 72/3680/1; *Uchitel'skaia gazeta* (June 7, 1944): 2; TsAGM 528/1/1319/2; Timofeev, "Sovmestnoe i razdel'noe obuchenie," 11.

78. GARF A2306/70/2957/51. Whereas girls' science lessons seemed diminished by emphasizing practical applications (as discussed in chapter 3), reports on boys' technology circles did not suggest any such concerns about diminished academic content.

79. GARF A2306/71/772/10.

80. TsAGM 528/1/1319/2.

81. GARF A2306/71/772/25, 72/446/31, 3680/6; Timofeev, "Sovmestnoe i razdel'noe obuchenie," 12.

82. For the opposite argument, that "competition creates ambivalence in most girls," see Meehan, *Learning like a Girl,* 95.

83. GARF A2306/72/3676/13. This word "ennobling" is significant, because later it was claimed that coeducational schools allowed girls to have an "ennobling" effect on boys. See chapters 5 and 6 for the implications of this emerging discourse.

84. TsAGM 528/1/878/4, 26, 528/1/1308/111–112, 528/1/1319/2, 667/1/80/107; GARF A2306/71/772/10, 39, 72/3676/23, 72/2839/3–4; APRK 708/8/1522/33; *Uchitel'skaia gazeta* (June 7, 1944): 2. For a discussion of boys' mobility as an innate characteristic of masculinity, see *Uchitel'skaia gazeta* (September 22, 1943): 4.

85. GARF A2306/71/772/19, 72/2839/5. For comparable statements in other contexts, see this statement by David Chadwell, coordinator of Single-Gender Initiatives at the South Carolina Department of Education: "You need to get them up and moving. That's based on the nervous system, that's based on eyes, that's based upon volume and the use of volume with the boys. . . . You need to engage boys' energy, use it, rather than trying to say, No, no, no." Cited in Weil, "Should Boys and Girls," 42, 43. See also a description of constant motion in a separate school, where "boys are blurs," in Meehan, *Learning like a Girl*, 235–238.

86. *Uchitel'skaia gazeta* (February 4, 1944): 2.

87. *Uchitel'skaia gazeta* (June 7, 1944): 2; GARF A2306/71/721/16.

88. GARF A2306/71/772/39, 72/2839/5; *Uchitel'skaia gazeta* (June 7, 1944): 2. The fact that the transition to coeducation resulted in complaints about inadequate physical education facilities and equipment in girls' schools indirectly confirms that boys' schools were better in this respect. Girls' schools received improvements in physical education facilities in the transition to coeducation. *Uchitel' Kazakhstana* (August 12, 1954): 1.

89. GARF A2306/71/772/28.

90. TsAGM 528/1/1308/110–112.

91. GARF A2306/71/772/16.

92. GARF A2306/71/772/39, 45–46. See also TsAGM 528/1/1319/6.

93. GARF A2306/72/2839/4, 10.

94. For the relative and autonomous influence of gender on schooling, see Woody, "Constructions of Masculinity," 285; Weaver-Hightower, "Boy Turn," 481–482; Salomone, "Legality of Single-Sex Education," 68–69.

95. GARF A2306/72/446/32.

96. This analysis draws on the arguments in Connell, "Teaching the Boys," 206–235.

97. *Literaturnaia gazeta* (May 4, 1950): 2. See chapter 5 for the controversial impact of this letter.

98. GARF A2306/71/789/18, 72/3676/35, 72/3680/27; *Uchitel' Kazakhstana* (January 17, 1953): 3.

99. Timofeev, "Sovmestnoe i razdel'noe obuchenie," 12.

100. Ibid.

101. Ibid., 13.

102. APRK 708/8/1550/17, 1522/32; GARF A2306/72/3680/27; *Uchitel'skaia gazeta* (June 7, 1944): 2.

103. For descriptions of how American separate schools encourage boys to study art, music, foreign languages, and other subjects often perceived as dominated by girls in coeducational settings, see Meehan, *Learning like a Girl*, 238. See also contrary examples, where boys in separate schools seem more anxious about "what was perceived to be a feminine activity." Woody, "Constructions of Masculinity," 294.

104. GARF A2306/71/772/19–20, 32, 36, 39.

105. NA RAO 15/1/214/7. For a contemporary argument from teachers and pupils who view single-sex classrooms as "liberating rather than confining," see Meyer, "Learning Separately," 14. See also the statement that boys "had more freedom to do what they wanted" in the absence of girls, yet they were not as free to "blur the lines of masculinity and femininity." Woody, "Constructions of Masculinity," 292–293.

106. GARF A2306/71/789/15–16.

107. GARF A2306/72/3680/33.

108. GARF A2306/71/721/16.

109. GARF A2306/71/772/7.

110. TsAGM 528/1/1319/3.

111. TsGARU 94/4/4797b/110.

112. GARF A2306/71/721/15.

113. *Uchitel'skaia gazeta* (November 3, 1943): 3.

114. See recommendations for transfers in GARF A2306/70/3016/5, 72/446/39; RGALI 634/4/97/125–130.

115. TsAGM 528/1/1319/3.

116. L'vov, "Zhenskoe obrazovanie," 562–563.

117. *Leningradskaia pravda* (August 20, 1943): 3.

118. GARF A2306/71/772/14.

119. GARF A2306/72/446/26.

120. TsAGM 528/1/1308/92–93.

121. GARF A2306/72/446/26.

122. GARF A2306/72/3676/48.

123. GARF A2306/72/446/9.

124. Pyzhikov, "Razdel'noe obuchenie," 83.

125. GARF A2306/72/3680/14.

126. GARF A2306/72/3680/9.

127. GARF A2306/71/772/20.

128. GARF A2306/72/3680/44.

129. GARF A2306/71/772/4; 72/3680/44. For similar perceptions of girls' schools as "relatively delightful" for teachers, see DeBare, *Where Girls Come First,* 227; Herr and Arms, "Accountability and Single-Sex Schooling," 547.

130. *Uchitel'skaia gazeta* (June 7, 1944): 2; L'vov, "Zhenskoe obrazovanie," 563.

131. TsAGM 528/1/1343/1–3; GARF A2306/71/772/3, 37, 789/3.

132. GARF A2306/71/772/32.

133. GARF A2306/71/772/36.

134. TsAGM 528/1/1308/121–122. These evaluations are similar to the positive assessments of teaching in all-boys' classrooms (mostly from male teachers) cited in *New York Times* (March 11, 2009): 24; Meehan, *Learning like a Girl,* 234–238.

135. GARF A2306/71/789/12.

136. TsAGM 528/1/878/26.

137. GARF A2306/72/3680/41.

138. Yet this same researcher also stated that other teachers preferred more "diligent" and consistent female pupils, while the majority said it made no difference whether they taught in boys', girls', or coeducational schools. NA RAO 15/1/214/4.

139. GARF A2306/71/772/36.

140. GARF A2306/71/772/25.

141. TsAGM 528/1/878/4. This observation anticipates the comment made by a teacher in an American boys' school: "I am so afraid of them, so afraid." Cited in Herr and Arms, "Accountability and Single-Sex Schooling," 546.

142. L'vov, "Zhenskoe obrazovanie," 563.

143. GARF A2306/72/446/26.

144. Ibid.

145. GARF A2306/72/446/39.

146. L'vov, "Zhenskoe obrazovanie," 529.

147. TsAGM 528/1/1308/106.

148. *Literaturnaia gazeta* (August 6, 1953): 3–4.

149. GARF A2306/71/772/16.

150. GARF A2306/72/429/29–30, 3676/18–19, 48, 65.

151. GARF A2306/71/772/14, 17, 72/3676/32.

152. GARF A2306/72/72/9–10.

153. GARF A2306/71/772/20.

154. GARF A2306/71/772/36.

155. GARF A2306/71/772/47.

156. GARF A2306/71/772/8.

157. GARF A2306/71/772/19.

158. GARF A2306/70/3016/16, 18.

159. L'vov, "Zhenskoe obrazovanie," 529.

160. GARF A2306/71/772/14.

161. GARF A2306/71/772/17.

162. L'vov, "Zhenskoe obrazovanie," 528.

163. GARF A2306/71/772/32.

164. GARF A2306/70/2957/50–51.

165. GARF A2306/71/818/249–250.

166. GARF A2306/72/3680/27.

167. GARF A2306/71/772/32.

168. TsAGM 528/1/1308/122.

169. *Pravda Vostoka* (September 1, 1949): 1.

170. Ibid.; TsGARU 94/4/4797b/100.

171. TsGARU 94/4/4797b/110.

172. RGALI 634/4/96/113–114.

173. By contrast, most recent profiles of American separate classrooms or schools have adhered to gender boundaries, with male teachers working with boys and female teachers working with girls. No reliable statistics have been located indicating the gender distribution in separate schools. See profiles maintaining gender boundaries in *New York Times* (March 11, 2009): 24; Meyer, "Learning Separately," 10–12. An article that begins with a gendered combination (a woman teaching girls and a man teaching boys) does refer to one woman teaching in a boys' school. Weil, "Should Boys and Girls," 41–45, 84–87.

174. GARF A2306/72/3680/35.

175. GARF A2306/71/772/32.

176. TsAGM 528/1/1319/3.

177. GARF A2306/72/2839/5.

178. TsAGM 528/1/1308/110–112.

179. L'vov, "Zhenskoe obrazovanie," 563–564.

180. GARF A2306/70/2957/51.

181. GARF A2306/72/3680/27.

182. GARF A2306/72/3680/42.

183. *Literaturnaia gazeta* (August 6, 1953): 3–4. For the argument that boys' schools may become "breeding grounds for virulent sexism," where girls complained about "persistent sexual harassment from their male peers," see Weaver-Hightower, "Boy Turn," 487; Woody, "Constructions of Masculinity," 288. Even a proponent of separate schooling conceded that boys in coeducational schools tended to have "more egalitarian attitudes toward the role of women in society." Riordan, *Girls and Boys in Schools,* 111. For the counterargument, that boys' schools promote more "egalitarian attitudes" toward girls, see Meehan, *Learning like a Girl,* 240.

184. RGALI 634/4/96/81–83.

185. NA RAO 15/1/214/16.

186. RGALI 634/4/96/121–125.

187. APRK 708/27/1487/166.

188. RGALI 634/4/96/178–181.

189. RGALI 634/4/96/113–114.

190. *Uchitel'skaia gazeta* (November 3, 1943): 3.

191. GARF A2306/71/772/31.

192. This account was provided in August 1954, after the Soviet government announced the full restoration of coeducation. *Kommunist* (August 21, 1954): 3.

193. GARF A2306/72/2839/4.

194. GARF A2306/72/3680/6.

195. *Leningradskaia pravda* (August 8, 1954): 3. This argument that coeducation would be an effective way to discipline boys actually revived arguments from the nineteenth century. DeBare, *Where Girls Come First,* 48–50.

196. *Uchitel'skaia gazeta* (December 8, 1943): 2, (February 4, 1944): 2; Parsanova, "Kollektiv klassa," 33–36.

197. GARF A2306/71/772/39, 52.

198. GARF A2306/71/772/13.

199. Ibid.

200. GARF A2306/71/772/17–18.

201. GARF A2306/71/772/19–20, 41, 51. See a similar argument that teacher training in the United States "rarely incorporates boys and their issues." Weaver-Hightower, "Boy Turn," 488.

202. GARF A2306/71/721/47.

203. Most books about separate schools emphasize girls' schools, with little or no discussion of the implications of separate schools for boys. Of three widely available books, only Meehan devotes even a single chapter to boys' schools. Meehan, *Learning like a Girl,* 23–242; DeBare, *Where Girls Come First;* Stabiner, *All Girls.* Two edited collections by educational researchers include examples and analysis from boys' and girls' classrooms, but only a single chapter (by Woody) is dedicated to analysis of boys' schooling. *Gender in Policy and Practice,* ed. Amanda Datnow and Lea Hubbard; *Debating Single-Sex Education,* ed. Frances Spielhagen.

204. Woody, "Constructions of Masculinity," 280–303.

205. GARF A2306/71/772/48–50.

5 — Debating Policy

1. This meeting, convened by Velichovskii in November 1948, included extensive comments from directors of boys' and girls' schools. See further discussion of this meeting in chapter 2. GARF A2306/71/721/48–51.

2. Ibid.

3. Merle Fainsod, *How Russia Is Ruled,* rev. ed. (Cambridge: Harvard University Press, 1965), 113–116; Merridale, *Night of Stone,* 248–249; Hough, "Debates about the Postwar World," 263.

4. Counts and Lodge, *Country of the Blind,* 244–280.

5. Furst, "Introduction: Late Stalinist Society," 5, 11, 13. For further analysis of changes in public opinion during and after the war, see Zubkova, *Russia after the War;* Furst, "In Search of Soviet Salvation," 327–345. The decision-making process is analyzed in Gorlizki and Khlevniuk, *Cold Peace.* See discussion of changing perspectives among educational leaders in Livschiz, "Growing Up Soviet," 769–771; Livschiz, "Pre-Revolutionary in Form," 541–560.

6. For analysis of "critical discussions" in the postwar context, see Alexei Kojevnikov, "Rituals of Stalinist Culture at Work: Science and the Games of Intraparty Democracy circa 1948," *Russian Review* 57 (January 1988): 27–28.

7. *Literaturnaia gazeta* (April 8, 1950): 2.

8. RGALI 634/4/97/33–34. The unpublished letters are available in the editorial files of the newspaper *Literturnaia gazeta,* specifically RGALI 634/4/96 and 97. The published letters include the following: L. Chernogubovskaia, "Otkuda berutsia 'bifurkatory,'" L. Shevchenko, "Uchest' opyt shkoly," V. Tiapkin, "Razdel'noe obuchenie neobkhodimo," "My–vsegda vmeste!" *Literaturnaia gazeta* (May 4, 1950): 2; A. Nedosekina, "Mnenie materi," A. Fedorov, "Tol'ko v obshchem trude," S. Kunanbaev, "'Bifurkatory'–oruzhenostsy pedologii," S. Nazarov, "Razdel'noe obuchenie nado sokhranit'," "Za sovmestnoe obuchenie!" *Literaturnaia gazeta* (June 28, 1950): 2. For analysis of letters as a source base for evaluating Stalinist public opinion, see Zubkova, *Russia after the War,* 36–39, 48–50, 147, 155–157; Furst, "In Search of Soviet Salvation," 327–345; Sheila Fitzpatrick, *Everyday Stalinism: Ordinary Life in Extraordinary Times: Soviet Russia in the 1930s* (New York: Oxford University Press, 1999), 175–178.

9. See brief mentions of school systems abandoning separate classrooms or schools in Weil, "Should Boys and Girls," 38–45, 84–87; *New York Times* (November 5, 2008): 24. For the process of ending the single-gender academies in California, see Woody, "Constructions of Masculinity," 281–282; Datnow, Hubbard, and Conchas, "How Context Mediates Policy," 184–206.

10. See the review of letters submitted to the U.S. Department of Education in DeBare, *Where Girls Come First,* 277–278.

11. *Leningradskaia pravda* (August 29, 1951): 2.

12. By contrast, enrollment in rural schools rose from 18 million to more than 21 million between 1945 and 1950 but then declined to 18 million by 1953/1954. *Kul'turnoe stroitel'stvo SSSR* (1956), 78–79.

13. GARF A2306/72/3676/58.

14. For complaints about over-age pupils in a boys' classroom, see *Leningradskaia pravda* (April 13, 1950): 3. For the effects of the war on school buildings, see Arsen'ev et al., *Ocherki istorii shkoly,* 16–17; Qualls, *From Ruins to Reconstruction,* 69–70, 119–120.

15. *Kul'turnoe stroitel'stvo SSSR* (1956), 82–83. As discussed in chapter 2, it is not clear what proportion of these students attended separate schools.

16. GARF A2306/71/789/38, 71/807/12–13, 72/72/10, 72/3680/6.

17. Novikov, *Organizatsiia uchebno-vospitatel'noi raboty v shkole,* 381, 415.

18. APRK 708/8/1522/31.

19. GARF A2306/70/3016/4–5, 71/846/19, 71/772/3–4; TsGARK 1692/1/1575/59; APRK 708/7/1/713/6–7, 12/1439/102; Chernik, *Sovetskaia obshcheobrazovatel'naia shkola,* 127.

20. GARF A2306/71/1074/7–9.

21. GARF A2306/71/772/26–27.

22. GARF A2306/72/3680/27.

23. GARF A2306/70/2957/50, 71/772/3–4, 39, 72/446/25, 72/2839/4, 72/3680/38, 44; *Pravda Vostoka* (September 1, 1949): 1; *Uchitel' Kazakhstana* (May 20, 1954): 3.

24. GARF A2306/72/3676/31.

25. GARF A2306/72/2839/4.

26. *Pravda Vostoka* (September 1, 1949): 1.

27. APRK 708/7/1/713/9, 12/1440/77.

28. GARF A2306/72/3676/8.

29. GARF A2306/71/772/19.

30. GARF A2306/72/3676/29.

31. GARF A2306/71/772/7.

32. GARF A2306/71/789/2–3. Beliaev's comments were repeated in a 1951 report on deficiencies in separate schools. GARF A2306/72/446/25–26.

33. GARF A2306/72/3680/23.

34. TsAGM 667/1/80/108; GARF A2306/71/846/17–19; 72/72/10.

35. GARF A2306/71/772/3, 10, 47; 72/3676/10–11, 20, 29.

36. GARF A2306/72/3680/6.

37. GARF A2306/71/721/16.

38. GARF A2306/71/772/26–27.

39. GARF A2306/71/772/4. In fact, three-quarters of these cities did have more girls' than boys' schools, but in most cases, the difference was just one or two schools. During the 1945/1946 school year, Moscow had twenty-four more girls' schools than boys' schools, but five years later, the gap had been reduced to ten. GARF A2306/71/846/17; 72/2707/1–43.

40. Figures for Leningrad schools when the policy began in September 1943 showed that girls' schools averaged more pupils, but this balance shifted over the years. Livschiz, "Growing Up Soviet," 711.

41. L'vov, "Zhenskoe obrazovanie," 524.

42. GARF A2306/72/2707/1–43.

43. Ibid.; L'vov, "Zhenskoe obrazovanie," 524.

44. GARF A2306/70/3016/2, 11, 72/446/39.

45. GARF A2306/72/2707/4.

46. GARF A2306/72/2707/1–43.

47. APRK 708/7/1/713/6–10.

48. GARF A2306/71/807/12–13.

49. GARF A2306/70/2933/62.

50. TsAGM 528/1/878/4, 27; GARF A2306/71/772/4, 19, 47.

51. GARF A2306/71/772/11.

52. *Literaturnaia gazeta* (June 28, 1950): 2.

53. GARF A2306/71/772/5.

54. The transcript has been preserved in the Russian state archive, but no evidence has been found of any published reports. GARF A2306/71/721/1–2.

55. GARF A2306/71/721/28, 34–35.

56. GARF A2306/71/721/38.

57. GARF A2306/71/721/46.

58. GARF A2306/71/721/15, 20.

59. GARF A2306/71/721/3, 8, 14–15.

60. Livschiz, "Growing Up Soviet," 773–774.

61. *Uchitel'skaia gazeta* (April 29, 1948): 3.

62. *Uchitel'skaia gazeta* (August 10, 1949): 3.

63. GARF A2306/71/847/1, 3–7, 204.

64. GARF A2306/71/809/1–2.

65. Parsanova, "Kollektiv klassa," 36.

66. Novikov, *Organizatsiia uchebno-vospitatel'noi raboty*, 454.

67. "School Principal Writes of Educators' Problems," *Current Digest of the Soviet Press* 3, no. 35 (October 13, 1951): 5–6, a translation of an article published in *Izvestiia* (September 1, 1951). See a similar silence in an annual report on schools. *Ob itogakh raboty shkol RSFSR v 1947/48 uchebnom godu i ocherednykh zadachakh na 1948/49 uchebnyi god. Prikaz Ministerstva prosveshcheniia RSFSR no. 434* (August 10, 1949): 1–15.

68. GARF A2306/72/72/11–12.

69. *Literaturnaia gazeta* (April 8, 1950): 2. For Kolbanovskii's contributions to discussions of gender in the postwar period, see Bucher, *Women, the Bureaucracy and Daily Life*, 175–177.

70. The article and letters were published under the same headline: "'Volnuiushchii vopros,'" *Literaturnaia gazeta* (May 4, 1950): 2, (June 28, 1950): 2.

71. Unpublished letters are preserved in RGALI 634/4/96, 97.

72. English translations include the following: "A Call to Reconsider Coeducation" [translation of Kolbanovskii's article], *Current Digest of the Soviet Press* 2, no. 14 (1950): 13–14, "The Discussion on Co-Education" [translations of Kolbanovskii's article and first set of letters]: 180–192, "The Discussion of Co-education Re-opened" [translations of second set of letters]: 316–328. See also comments in "The Pendulum Swings," 657; Livschiz, "Growing Up Soviet," 774–778; Pyzhikov, "Razdel'noe obuchenie," 82–83.

73. *Literaturnaia gazeta* (August 24, 1950): 2.

74. RGALI 634/4/96/121–125.

75. GARF A2306/72/3680/22–23.

76. GARF A2306/72/446/47, 2839/4; Livschiz, "Growing Up Soviet," 785; Pyzhikov, "Razdel'noe obuchenie," 83.

77. This article and the subsequent letters were written and published even as political leaders were becoming ever more restrained in their deliberations, following the Leningrad Affair. Gorlizki and Khlevniuk, *Cold Peace*, 10, 79–85, 94–95.

78. Emphasis in the original. *Literaturnaia gazeta* (April 8, 1950): 2. The term *novyi chelovek* is usually translated "new man," although the term *chelovek* is not gendered as male in same way as the English *man*.

79. Kolbanovskii's criticism of the "incomprehensible and absolutely unforgiveable neglect" of separate schools by the Ministry of Education and the Academy of Pedagogical

Sciences was more representative of this criticism of government agencies for failing to implement official policies. For a thoughtful examination of Stalinist educational discourse, see Larry E. Holmes, "Ascent into Darkness: Escalating Negativity in the Administration of Schools in the Kirov Region, 1931–1941," *History of Education* 35, no. 4–5 (2006): 521–540.

80. *Literaturnaia gazeta* (April 8, 1950): 2. The Central Committee denunciation of pedology in 1936 unleashed a campaign that challenged any assertions or assumptions that inherent physiological attributes determined, or even influenced, academic performance. See discussion of the tone and impact of these denunciations in Ewing, "Restoring Teachers to Their Rights," 471–493.

81. *Uchitel'skaia gazeta* (August 10, 1949): 3. See discussion of this director's celebration of girls' schools in chapter 3.

82. *Literaturnaia gazeta* (April 8, 1950): 2.

83. RGALI 634/4/96/13.

84. RGALI 634/4/97/24–26.

85. RGALI 634/4/97/27.

86. *Literaturnaia gazeta* (May 4, 1950): 2.

87. *Literaturnaia gazeta* (June 28, 1950): 2.

88. *Literaturnaia gazeta* (August 24, 1950): 2.

89. These letters thus do not follow the pattern observed for other topics, in which more conformist views were expressed in collectively written letters, while letters challenging official positions were "as a rule submitted by individuals." Zubkova, *Russia after the War,* 175.

90. *Literaturnaia gazeta* (May 4, 1950): 2.

91. Ibid.

92. GARF A2306/71/789/15–16.

93. RGALI 634/4/96/44–45.

94. RGALI 634/4/96/32.

95. GARF A2306/71/789/33.

96. GARF A2306/71/789/51.

97. RGALI 634/4/96/56.

98. RGALI 634/4/96/11–12.

99. RGALI 634/4/96/13.

100. RGALI 634/4/97/33–34.

101. *Literaturnaia gazeta* (June 28, 1950): 2.

102. *Literaturnaia gazeta* (May 4, 1950): 2

103. RGALI 634/4/96/99–101.

104. This letter is quoted in *Literaturnaia gazeta* (August 24, 1950): 2.

105. RGALI 634/4/96/65–66.

106. For a similarly negative judgment based on a son's experience in a coeducational and a boys' school, see RGALI 634/4/96/81–83.

107. *Literaturnaia gazeta* (May 4, 1950): 2.

108. RGALI 634/4/96/50, 67, 30–31, 188–189, 97/46, 87–88.

109. RGALI 634/4/96/30–31.

110. RGALI 634/4/96/35–36.

111. RGALI 634/4/96/56, 65–66.

112. RGALI 634/4/96/167–168.

113. RGALI 634/4/96/185–187.

114. Ibid.

115. RGALI 634/4/97/121–122.

116. RGALI 634/4/96/188–189. For the limited role of fathers in the postwar household, see Bucher, *Women, the Bureaucracy and Daily Life,* 104, 175.

117. RGALI 634/4/96/35–36.

118. RGALI 634/4/97/162.

119. RGALI 634/4/96/30–31.

120. Ibid.

121. RGALI 634/4/96/50.

122. RGALI 634/4/97/87–88.

123. RGALI 634/4/96/32–34, 65–66.

124. RGALI 634/4/96/146–153.

125. RGALI 634/4/96/24–25.

126. Ibid.

127. RGALI 634/4/97/61–62.

128. *Literaturnaia gazeta* (June 28, 1950): 2. In contrast to the scathing response to Tiapkin's defense of separate schools, a review of unpublished letters indicates that Nazarov provoked fewer critical responses (although his letter was published later, whereas most letters in the archive collection responded to the letters published in May). One former pupil, Zaitseva, denounced Nazarov's position that girls should "limit the circle of their activity to just the family." RGALI 634/4/97/212.

129. RGALI 634/4/96/77–80. See chapter 3 for an invocation of Durova as a role model for Soviet girls.

130. Emphasis in the original. RGALI 634/4/97/125–130.

131. RGALI 634/4/96/81–83.

132. RGALI 634/4/96/202–205.

133. RGALI 634/4/96/178–181.

134. RGALI 634/4/97/238–243.

135. *Literaturnaia gazeta* (June 28, 1950): 2.

136. RGALI 634/4/96/13.

137. RGALI 634/4/96/18–19, 24–25, 174–175, 178–181, 202–205, 97/81–82.

138. RGALI 634/4/96/44–45.

139. *Literaturnaia gazeta* (June 28, 1950): 2.

140. RGALI 634/4/96/71–72. For military academies for Soviet boys, see Dunstan, *Soviet Schooling,* 193, 202.

141. *Literaturnaia gazeta* (May 4, 1950): 2.

142. RGALI 634/4/96/13–14, 20–23.

143. RGALI 634/4/96/30–31.

144. The published letter used the German terms and then provided a Russian translation. *Literaturnaia gazeta* (June 28, 1950): 2.

145. RGALI 634/4/96/174–175.

146. *Literaturnaia gazeta* (May 4, 1950): 2

147. Kunanbaev was particularly critical of "separate boys' and girls' Komsomol organizations that lead to a distinct estrangement and to the manifestation of unnecessary and harmful 'particularities' in their work." *Literaturnaia gazeta* (June 28, 1950): 2.

148. GARF A2306/72/72/4. 149. *Literaturnaia gazeta* (May 4, 1950): 2; RGALI 634/4/96/202–205.

150. RGALI 634/4/97/46.

151. *Literaturnaia gazeta* (August 6, 1953): 3–4.

152. RGALI 634/4/96/32, 56, 81–83.

153. *Literaturnaia gazeta* (August 24, 1950): 2.

154. RGALI 634/4/96/71–72.

155. RGALI 634/4/96/77–80.

156. RGALI 634/4/96/211.

157. RGALI 634/4/96/13.

158. RGALI 634/4/96/20–23.

159. RGALI 634/4/96/30–31, 108.

160. *Literaturnaia gazeta* (June 28, 1950): 2.

161. Ibid. See the analysis of separate schools as the "forgotten reform" and the "stony silence" of educational bureaucracies in Livschiz, "Growing Up Soviet," 728, 779.

162. GARF A2306/71/772/32–36.

163. *Literaturnaia gazeta* (August 6, 1953): 3–4.

164. Ibid.

165. RGALI 634/4/96/18–19; *Bakinskii rabochii* (July 22, 1954): 2.

166. Shturman, *Soviet Secondary School*, 63.

167. RGALI 634/4/96/99–101.

168. RGALI 634/4/96/71–72.

169. RGALI 634/4/96/121–125.

170. RGALI 634/4/97/33–34.

171. RGALI 634/4/96/198.

172. RGALI 634/4/97/24–26.

173. RGALI 634/4/96/202–205.

174. RGALI 634/4/96/30–31. While these letters do not represent explicitly political challenges, they do seem more oppositional than the scope of practices recently identified as part of a quest for identity. These girls understood the relationship between official policy, school practices, and their own opportunities. Furst, "Introduction," 13.

175. RGALI 634/4/96/48–49. The positive account of this school appeared in *Uchitel'skaia gazeta* (June 7, 1944): 2.

176. RGALI 634/4/96/108. Emphasis in the original.

177. RGALI 634/4/96/67.

178. RGALI 634/4/96/145.

179. RGALI 634/4/96/156–157.

180. RGALI 634/4/96/167–168.

181. RGALI 634/4/97/81–82.

182. RGALI 634/4/97/100.

183. *Literaturnaia gazeta* (August 24, 1950): 2.

184. This analysis of the pace of school reforms and retrenchment draws upon David Tyack and Larry Cuban, *Tinkering toward Utopia: A Century of Public School Reform* (Cambridge: Harvard University Press, 1995).

6 — Restoring Coeducation

1. According to a recent account, Stalin's leadership in the final years consisted of "a crude toxic mixture of ideology and repression." Gorlizki and Khlevniuk, *Cold Peace*, 14.

2. Leslie Miller-Bernal, "Introduction: Coeducation: An Uneven Progression," in *Going Coed: Women's Experiences in Formerly Men's Colleges and Universities, 1950–2000,* ed. Leslie Miller-Bernal and Susan L. Poulson (Nashville: Vanderbilt University Press, 2004), 3–21.

3. See the stories of educators and parents in DeBare, *Where Girls Come First;* Meehan, *Learning like a Girl.*

4. A high-profile article about separate schools devoted just one paragraph to districts "that have started single-gender programs only to shut them down, as major logistical headaches outweighed the small academic gains." Weil, "Should Boys and Girls," 38–45, 84–87. An exception was the case in Greene County, Georgia, where an attempt to separate all pupils in all grades prompted national attention, as did the rapid reversal of this decision. "Ga. District under Fire for Plan to Separate Students by Gender," *Education Week* 27, no. 24 (February 20, 2008): 4, online: www.edweek.org.

5. For high-visibility profiles of the first years of separate schooling, see *New York Times* (March 11, 2009): 24; Schreiner, "Single-Sex Classes."

6. The exceptions to this pattern, of course, are well-established private schools that retained gender segregation when many similar schools went coeducational in the 1960s and now use this distinctive tradition as a form of recruiting pupils (and parents) attracted to the single-sex environment. Meyer, "Learning Separately," 10–21.

7. *Literaturnaia gazeta* (August 24, 1950): 2. For a caution against seeing separate schools as a "panacea," see Spielhagen, "Single-Sex Education."

8. TsGARU 94/4/4797b/110, 113; L'vov, "Shkola v soiuznykh respublikakh," 51.

9. GARF A2306/70/2933/19. Similar requests came from other regional educational departments. GARF A2306/70/2933/52, 62–63, 72/3680/49–50; RGASPI 17/126/7/47–48; Livschiz, "Growing Up Soviet," 709.

10. Potemkin's statement in August 1944 that separate schools should be expanded beyond the initial list of cities, as discussed in the first chapter, may have been a response to these requests "from below." Potemkin, "Ob uluchshenii kachestva," 192.

11. GARF A2306/72/2839/1.

12. *Literaturnaia gazeta* (August 6, 1953): 3–4. See similar reports of separate schools merging in GARF A2306/72/72/12; *Literaturnaia gazeta* (August 24, 1950): 2.

13. GARF A2306/72/2839/7–8.

14. Ibid.

15. GARF A2306/72/2707/11–12.

16. APRK 708/27/1487/161.

17. *Literaturnaia gazeta* (August 24, 1950): 2.

18. GARF A2306/70/2957/53, 72/2839/6, 72/3680/11–12.

19. This example was even more revealing of the bureaucratic dynamics of Soviet education, as the request to make just one school coeducational required approval from district, city, and regional educational departments and the Ministry of Education in Moscow. GARF A2306/72/2839/6.

20. Ibid.

21. GARF A2306/72/2839/8.

22. GARF A2306/72/2839/1.

23. *Literaturnaia gazeta* (August 6, 1953): 3–4.

24. Ibid.

25. RGALI 634/4/96/192–193. A former teacher also recalled that, in the 1950s, the specialized educational publications such as *Uchitel'skaia gazeta* and *Narodnoe*

prosveshchenie were "more boring, monotonous, and meagre in content" than publications, such as *Literaturnaia gazeta,* aimed at a broader audience and less constrained by official contributors and limited editorial policies. Shturman, *Soviet Secondary School,* 108–109.

26. *Literaturnaia gazeta* (August 24, 1950): 2.

27. *Literaturnaia gazeta* (August 24, 1950): 2. After Potemkin died in 1946, his successors as minister of education included A. G. Kalashnikov, A. A. Voznesenskii (who was later arrested and executed during the Leningrad Affair), and I. A. Kairov (who remained in this office through the restoration of coeducation). *Uchitel'skaia gazeta* (August 15, 1953): 2, (August 11, 1954): 2–4; *Pravda* (November 17, 1948): 2, (July 20, 1954): 2; Dunstan, *Soviet Schooling,* 79–80; Gorlizki and Khlevniuk, *Cold Peace,* 79–87; Livshiz, "Growing Up Soviet," 764, 774.

28. GARF A2306/71/772/11–12, 26, 52, 72/2839/4, 72/3680/1.

29. GARF A2306/72/3680/50–52.

30. GARF A2306/72/72/2–3. See also reference to this report in *Literaturnaia gazeta* (August 24, 1950): 2.

31. GARF A2306/72/72/6.

32. GARF A2306/72/72/3, 6–7, 13. The ambivalence in this report is suggestive of the conclusions reached five decades later by a research review commissioned by the U.S. government. U.S. Department of Education, *Single-Sex versus Coeducational Schooling.*

33. GARF A2306/72/446/31.

34. GARF A2306/72/446/29.

35. GARF A2306/72/72/7–8, 446/9, 39.

36. RGALI 634/4/96/77–80.

37. GARF A2306/72/3680/48. For rituals of self-criticism in postwar Stalinism, see Kojevnikov, "Rituals of Stalinist Culture," 25–52.

38. *Literaturnaia gazeta* (August 24, 1950): 2.

39. GARF A2306/72/3680/24.

40. GARF A2306/71/772/50, 72/446/28, 72/3680/5.

41. GARF A2306/72/3680/29, 34–35.

42. GARF A2306/72/3680/46.

43. GARF A2306/72/446/9–10.

44. On postwar repression, see Zubkova, *Russia after the War,* 109–111, 117–118, 129–131; Gorlizki and Khlevniuk, *Cold Peace,* 9–10.

45. GARF A2306/72/446/31. For similar claims that coeducational schools in villages, towns, and smaller cities proved the anomaly of separate schools, see RGALI 634/4/96/13–14, 73, 184.

46. *Literaturnaia gazeta* (June 28, 1950): 2.

47. RGALI 634/4/96/121–125.

48. RGALI 634/4/96/198.

49. RGALI 634/4/96/99–101.

50. *Literaturnaia gazeta* (August 6, 1953): 3–4.

51. GARF A2306/72/72/3; RGALI 634/4/96/202–205, 97/33–34; *Literaturnaia gazeta* (April 8, 1950): 2; L'vov, "Zhenskoe obrazovanie," 611. See similar comments heard in American single-sex schools, where one boy said about female classmates: "They keep us in check." Quoted in Herr and Arms, "Accountability and Single-Sex Schooling," 545.

52. RGALI 634/4/96/198.

53. NA RAO 15/1/214/5; APRK 708/27/1487/164, 166; GARF A2306/71/789/26, 32, 34, 36, 38, 44, 72/446/39; RGALI 634/4/96/192–193, 97/24–26.

54. *Literaturnaia gazeta* (August 6, 1953): 3–4.

55. Ibid.

56. GARF A2306/72/446/26–27.

57. GARF A2306/72/3680/44.

58. GARF A2306/72/446/27–28.

59. *Literaturnaia gazeta* (August 6, 1953): 3–4.

60. GARF A2306/72/72/3–4; 446/31, 39; *Bakinskii rabochii* (July 22, 1954): 2.

61. This report does not identify the author, but it was produced soon after the discussions among educators that took place in late 1950. GARF A2306/72/446/28.

62. TsGARU 94/4/4797b/112. For a historian's enthusiastic statement of separate schooling's potential to increase girls' enrollment, eliminate old traditions, and expand women's rights in Central Asia and the Caucasus, see Chernik, *Sovetskaia obshcheobrazovatel'naia shkola,* 129.

63. *Literaturnaia gazeta* (August 6, 1953): 3–4.

64. Emphasis in the original. RGALI 634/4/96/81–83.

65. RGALI 634/4/96/213–215.

66. TsGARK 1692/1/1904/183. According to an earlier report, six of the eight secondary schools in Pavlodar were converted to separate boys' or girls' schools. APRK 708/8/1555/5.

67. GARF A2306/72/446/30–31.

68. *Literaturnaia gazeta* (August 6, 1953): 3–4.

69. Ibid.

70. Ibid.

71. Ibid.

72. GARF A2306/71/772/52.

73. GARF A2306/71/789/16, 26, 30, 34, 36, 38, 44.

74. GARF A2306/72/446/32.

75. GARF A2306/72/446/29.

76. *Literaturnaia gazeta* (August 6, 1953): 3–4.

77. GARF A2306/71/772/4–5.

78. GARF A2306/71/772/25.

79. GARF A2306/72/3680/6, 9–10.

80. GARF A2306/72/3676/28.

81. *Literaturnaia gazeta* (August 6, 1953): 3–4.

82. For the decision-making process in the last years of Stalin's dictatorship, see Gorlizki and Khlevniuk, *Cold Peace,* 108–163.

83. GARF A2306/72/3676/65.

84. This meeting of Moscow school directors was convened by Kairov on April 17, 1954. GARF A2306/72/3676/51.

85. GARF A2306/72/3680/2.

86. GARF A2306/72/3680/1.

87. GARF A2306/72/3680/33–34. See chapter 1 for Zolotova's recollection of having a "very grim" feeling in 1943 when she heard Potemkin's enthusiasm for separate schools.

88. GARF A2306/72/3680/4, 11, 19.

89. GARF A2306/72/3676/31.

90. GARF A2306/72/3680/6, 9–10.

91. GARF A2306/72/3680/21, 27, 51.

92. GARF A2306/72/3680/41–42.

93. GARF A2306/72/3680/13, 15, 20, 25, 31.

94. GARF A2306/72/3680/52. According to a Leningrad educational official, the new Soviet leader, Nikita Khrushchev, announced that separate schools had been introduced without any popular consultation, and that "now is the time to correct that mistake" by discussing coeducation with the Soviet people. Cited in Livschiz, "Growing Up Soviet," 801.

95. *Pravda* (July 20, 1954): 2.

96. *Bakinskii rabochii* (July 22, 1954): 2.

97. *Vecherniaia Moskva* (July 21, 1954): 3; *Pravda* (July 20, 1954): 2; "O sovmestnom obuchenii v shkole," *Nachal'naia shkola* 9 (September 1954): 16–17.

98. The numbers come from Livschiz, "Growing Up Soviet," 801.

99. *Vecherniaia Moskva* (July 21, 1954): 3; *Uchitel'skaia gazeta* (July 21, 1954): 1.

100. *Bakinskii rabochii* (July 22, 1954): 2; *Vecherniaia Moskva* (July 21, 1954): 3. See also reports from Kiev, Tbilisi, and Alma-Ata cited in the introduction.

101. *Pravda* (July 20, 1954): 2.

102. "O sovmestnom obuchenii v shkole," 16–17.

103. APRK 708/27/1487/164.

104. *Pravda* (July 20, 1954): 2.

105. *Bakinskii rabochii* (July 22, 1954): 2.

106. *Kommunist* (August 21, 1954): 3; APRK 708/27/1487/164; *Pravda* (July 20, 1954): 2.

107. APRK 708/27/1487/162–163, 167–168.

108. On the "anticipation of some new ray of light" in the early 1950s, see Zubkova, *Russia after the War,* 147.

109. *Zaria Vostoka* (July 24, 1954): 2.

110. The Council of Ministers made the decision on July 1, the first public announcement came two weeks later, and the decree itself was published on July 18. *Leningradskaia pravda* (July 15, 1954): 3; *Pravda* (July 18, 1954): 1.

111. *Pravda* (July 18, 1954): 1. Councils of Ministers in other republics issued decrees with similar language specifying the restoration of coeducation in their cities. *Bakinskii rabochii* (July 22, 1954): 2; *Kommunist* (July 23, 1954): 1; *Zaria Vostoka* (July 24, 1954): 2; *Pravda Vostoka* (July 21, 1954): 1; *Uchitel' Kazakhstana* (July 15, 1954): 2; APRK 708/27/1487/164–166.

112. *Pravda* (July 18, 1954): 1.

113. *Kazakhstanskaia pravda* (July 30, 1954): 2; *Pravda* (July 20, 1954): 2; *Pionerskaia pravda* (July 23, 1954): 1; *Kommunist* (August 21, 1954): 3.

114. APRK 708/27/1487/163.

115. APRK 708/27/1487/161–162; "O sovmestnom obuchenii v shkole," 16; D. Petrikeev, "Perekhod na sovmestnoe obuchenie v shkolakh Leningrada," *Narodnoe obrazovanie* 1 (January 1955): 22.

116. *Uchitel'skaia gazeta* (July 21, 1954): 1. See also "O sovmestnom obuchenii v shkole," 16–17; "Coeducation in Russia," *Newsweek* (August 9, 1954): 78; *New York Times* (July 19, 1954): 4.

117. *Pravda* (July 20, 1954): 2; *Uchitel'skaia gazeta* (July 21, 1954): 1; B. P. Esipov and V. P. Shatskii, "Vospitatel'naia rabota v shkole sovmestnogo obucheniia," *Sovetskaia pedagogika,* no. 7 (July 1954): 12; *Bakinskii rabochii* (July 22, 1954): 2; *Sovetskaia Kirgiziia* (July 29, 1954): 1, (August 12, 1954): 2; *Kommunist* (July 23, 1954): 1; *Kazakhstanskaia pravda* (July 30, 1954): 2.

118. *Bakinskii rabochii* (July 22, 1954): 2; *Pravda Ukrainy* (July 29, 1954): 3; *Kazakhstanskaia pravda* (July 30, 1954): 2; *Leningradskaia pravda* (July 15, 1954): 3; *Vecherniaia Moskva* (July 21, 1954): 3.

119. *Pravda* (July 20, 1954): 2; *Uchitel'skaia gazeta* (July 21, 1954): 1; *Sovetskaia Kirgiziia* (July 29, 1954): 1; *Pravda Ukrainy* (July 29, 1954): 3; *Kazakhstanskaia pravda* (July 30, 1954): 2; Petrikeev, "Perekhod na sovmestnoe obuchenie," 21.

120. *Uchitel'skaia gazeta* (August 11, 1954): 1; *Bakinskii rabochii* (August 15, 1954): 2.

121. V. N. Kolbanovskii, *Vospitatel'naia rabota v shkole v usloviiakh sovmestnogo obucheniia* (Moscow: Izdatel'stvo Znanie, 1955), 4.

122. *Leningradskaia pravda* (August 8, 1954): 3.

123. *Uchitel'skaia gazeta* (August 4, 1954): 1; *Bakinskii rabochii* (August 3, 1954): 1; Kolbanovskii, *Vospitatel'naia rabota*, 14.

124. *Uchitel' Kazakhstana* (August 12, 1954): 1.

125. Esipov and Shatskii, "Vospitatel'naia rabota," 12; *Uchitel'skaia gazeta* (August 4, 1954): 1; *Bakinskii rabochii* (August 15, 1954): 2; *Uchitel' Kazakhstana* (September 9, 1954): 1; Petrikeev, "Perekhod na sovmestnoe obuchenie," 22; Livschiz, "Growing Up Soviet," 811–812.

126. Esipov and Shatskii, "Vospitatel'naia rabota," 12; *Uchitel'skaia gazeta* (July 21, 1954): 1; "O sovmestnom obuchenii v shkole," 17; *Uchitel' Kazakhstana* (September 2, 1954): 3.

127. *Uchitel'skaia gazeta* (July 21, 1954): 1, (August 4, 1954): 1.

128. *Bakinskii rabochii* (July 22, 1954): 2, (August 3, 1954): 1.

129. *Sovetskaia Litva* (August 15, 1954): 1.

130. *Uchitel'skaia gazeta* (July 21, 1954): 1; *Kommunist* (August 21, 1954): 3; *Kazakhstanskaia pravda* (July 30, 1954): 2; *Vecherniaia Moskva* (July 21, 1954): 3; "O sovmestnom obuchenii v shkole," 17; *Turkmenskaia iskra* (July 30, 1954): 1.

131. *Turkmenskaia iskra* (September 1, 1954): 1.

132. *Uchitel'skaia gazeta* (July 21, 1954): 1.

133. *Kommunist* (August 26, 1954): 2; *Uchitel' Kazakhstana* (September 9, 1954): 3.

134. *Uchitel' Kazakhstana* (August 12, 1954): 1, (November 18, 1954): 2.

135. *Uchitel'skaia gazeta* (August 11, 1954): 1; *Pravda Ukrainy* (July 29, 1954): 3; *Kommunist* (August 21, 1954): 3.

136. *Uchitel'skaia gazeta* (August 11, 1954): 1.

137. *Turkmenskaia iskra* (September 1, 1954): 2; *Sovetskaia Kirgiziia* (August 12, 1954): 2; *Uchitel'skaia gazeta* (August 11, 1954): 1. See also *Sotsialisticheskaia Karaganda* (September 1, 1954): 2; *Leningradskaia pravda* (July 15, 1954): 3, (August 8, 1954): 3; *Pravda Ukrainy* (July 29, 1954): 3; *Sovetskaia Litva* (August 3, 1954): 3, (August 20, 1954): 3.

138. *Uchitel' Kazakhstana* (July 29, 1954): 2.

139. *Bakinskii rabochii* (August 15, 1954): 2.

140. *Kommunist* (August 21, 1954): 3.

141. *Kommunist* (August 26, 1954): 2.

142. *Leningradskaia* pravda (August 8, 1954): 3; *Uchitel' Kazakhstana* (August 12, 1954): 1.

143. *Bakinskii rabochii* (August 15, 1954): 2.

144. *Sovetskaia Kirgiziia* (August 12, 1954): 2.

145. *Pravda* (July 20, 1954): 2; *Uchitel'skaia gazeta* (July 21, 1954): 1, (August 4, 1954): 1; *Bakinskii rabochii* (July 22, 1954): 2; *Zaria Vostoka* (July 24, 1954): 2; *Sovetskaia Kirgiziia* (August 12, 1954): 2.

146. Kolbanovskii, *Vospitatel'naia rabota*, 4.

147. *Leningradskaia pravda* (August 8, 1954): 3.

148. *Alma-Atinskaia pravda* (September 3, 1954): 1.

149. *Uchitel'skaia gazeta* (July 21, 1954): 1.

150. *Bakinskii rabochii* (July 22, 1954): 2; *Kazakhstanskaia pravda* (July 30, 1954): 2; *Kommunist* (August 21, 1954): 3.

151. Kolbanovskii, *Vospitatel'naia rabota*, 9–10.

152. *Zaria Vostoka* (July 24, 1954): 2; *Uchitel'skaia gazeta* (July 21, 1954): 1; *Bakinskii rabochii* (July 22, 1954): 2.

153. Petrikeev, "Perekhod na sovmestnoe obuchenie," 22–23.

154. Ibid., 22; Kolbanovskii, *Vospitatel'naia rabota*, 15.

155. Petrikeev, "Perekhod na sovmestnoe obuchenie," 28; *Uchitel' Kazakhstana* (November 18, 1954): 2.

156. *Uchitel' Kazakhstana* (November 18, 1954): 2. Although a published report attributed the misbehavior of boys to the absence of the technology clubs that used to keep them occupied, this same boys' school had prompted a father's bitter criticism, as discussed in chapter 4, of poor discipline, rude behavior, and lack of respect for teachers. See the father's comments in APRK 708/27/1487/164.

157. Kolbanovskii, *Vospitatel'naia rabota*, 22.

158. *Turkmenskaia iskra* (September 1, 1954): 2; *Pravda Vostoka* (July 31, 1954): 2; *Bakinskii rabochii* (July 22, 1954): 2, (August 15, 1954): 2; *Alma-Atinskaia pravda* (September 1, 1954): 1; Kolbanovskii, *Vospitatel'naia rabota*, 3.

159. *Uchitel'skaia gazeta* (July 21, 1954): 1; Petrikeev, "Perekhod na sovmestnoe obuchenie," 21–22; *Vecherniaia Moskva* (July 21, 1954): 3.

160. Kolbanovskii, *Vospitatel'naia rabota*, 10.

161. *Uchitel'skaia gazeta* (July 21, 1954): 1.

162. *Vecherniaia Moskva* (July 21, 1954): 3; *Sotsialisticheskaia Karaganda* (September 1, 1954): 2; Kolbanovskii, *Vospitatel'naia rabota*, 3–4.

163. Esipov and Shatskii, "Vospitatel'naia rabota," 12–13; Kolbanovskii, *Vospitatel'naia rabota*, 4.

164. *Uchitel' Kazakhstana* (September 9, 1954): 3.

165. Esipov and Shatskii, "Vospitatel'naia rabota," 13.

166. Kolbanovskii, *Vospitatel'naia rabota*, 25.

167. Esipov and Shatskii, "Vospitatel'naia rabota," 13.

168. Ibid., 16.

169. Ibid., 14.

170. Ibid., 14–15.

171. *Pravda* (July 20, 1954): 2; *Leningradskaia pravda* (September 1, 1954): 1; *Alma-Atinskaia pravda* (September 1, 1954): 1; *Sotsialisticheskaia Karaganda* (September 1, 1954): 2.

172. *Bakinskii rabochii* (August 15, 1954): 2.

173. *Sovetskaia Kirgiziia* (September 1, 1954): 2; *Kommunist* (July 24, 1954): 3; *Pravda Ukrainy* (July 29, 1954): 3; *Sovetskaia Litva* (August 20, 1954): 3; *Pravda* (July 20, 1954): 2.

174. Dubrovina, *Women's Right to Education*, 13–16.

175. *Kazakhstanskaia pravda* (July 30, 1954): 2.

176. *Uchitel'skaia gazeta* (August 11, 1954): 1.

177. *Kommunist* (August 21, 1954): 3.

178. *Bakinskii rabochii* (September 3, 1954): 2.

179. Amalrik, *Memories of a Tatar Childhood*, 103.

180. Kolbanovskii, *Vospitatel'naia rabota*, 31.

Conclusion

1. "Opros: 76% rossiian otritsatel'no otnosiatsia k vvedeniiu razdel'nogo obucheniia v srednei shkole," IA Regnum Poll, January 1, 2008. Online: www.regnum.ru/news, accessed September 2009; "Razdel'noe obuchenie v shkolakh: preimushchestva i nedostatki," Baza FOM, online: bd.fom.ru, accessed September 2009.

2. RGALI 634/4/96/ 67.

3. RGALI 634/4/97/33–34.

4. RGALI 634/4/97/46.

5. RGALI 634/4/97/61–62.

6. Dzhibladze, minister of education of Georgian SSR, conceded that a decade of separate schooling significantly decreased the number of supporters. *Zaria Vostoka* (July 24, 1954): 2.

7. Even historical accounts sought to downplay this experiment by underscoring how few pupils had enrolled in separate schools. Chernik, *Sovetskaia obshcheobrazovatel'naia shkola*, 126–129. Additional research is needed to understand the extent to which instruction, and especially discipline, were "gendered" in post-1954 Soviet coeducational schools.

8. *Soviet Commitment to Education: Report of U.S. Education Mission to the U.S.S.R.* (Washington: U.S. Office of Education, 1959), 2, 55; Walter B. Kolesnik, *Coeducation: Sex Differences and the Schools* (New York: Vantage, 1969). The one legacy of this experiment visible to western observers, even in the late 1950s, was that certain classes in the senior grades had more pupils of one sex or the other. When they asked for a reason, they were told that in some schools that had recently converted to coeducation, there remained a preponderance of one gender or the other, as boys' schools kept a majority of boys and girls' schools kept a majority of girls for a few more years. Bereday, Brickman, and Read, *Changing Soviet School*, 190.

9. Woody, "Constructions of Masculinity," 280, 287–288.

10. Salomone, *Same, Different, Equal*, 59–60, 162–165.

11. Woody, "Constructions of Masculinity," 280, 298.

12. Datnow and Hubbard, "Introduction," in *Gender in Policy and Practice*, 7–8.

13. For the distribution of school resources by gender, see Connell, "Teaching the Boys," 228–229; Salomone, *Same, Different, Equal*, 116–149.

14. For difficulties in recruiting and retaining the most qualified teachers for the single-gender academies during California's pilot program, see Herr and Arms, "Intersection of Educational Reforms," 81.

15. For the effects of eroding support for California's single-gender academies, see Lea Hubbard and Amanda Datnow, "Are Single-Sex Schools Sustainable in the Public Sector?" in *Gender in Policy and Practice*, 128–129. For "waves" of enthusiasm, acceptance, indifference, and opposition in educational reform, see Larry Cuban, *How Teachers Taught: Constancy and Change in American Classrooms, 1890–1980* (New York: Teachers College Press, 1988).

16. This point is raised in Lee, "Is Single-Sex Secondary Schooling a Solution," 58–61; Salomone, *Same, Different, Equal*, 38–42, 61–63, 101, 164, 183, 214, 236.

Bibliography

Primary Sources

Archives

Archive of the President of the Republic of Kazakhstan. Arkhiv Prezidenta Respublika Kazakhstana (APRK).

Central Archive of the City of Moscow. Tsentral'nyi Arkhiv Goroda Moskvy (TsAGM).

Central Archive for Public Movements in Moscow. Tsentral'nyi Arkhiv Obshchestvennykh Dvizhenii Moskvy (TsAODM).

Central State Archive of the Republic of Kazakhstan. Tsentral'nyi Gosudarstvennyi Arkhiv Respubliki Kazakhstana (TsGARK).

Research Archive of the Russian Academy of Education. Nauchnyi Arkhiv Rossiiskoi Akademii Obrazovaniia (NA RAO).

Russian State Archive for Literature and Art. Rossiiskii Gosudarstvennyi Arkhiv Literatury i Iskusstva (RGALI).

Russian State Archive of Social and Political History. Rossiiskii Gosudarstvennyi Arkhiv Sotsial'no-Politicheskoi Istorii (RGASPI).

Soviet Information Bureau Photographs, Davis Center, Harvard College Library.

State Archive of the Republic of Uzbekistan. O'zbekiston respublikasi markaziy davlat arkhivi (O'zRMDA) / Tsentral'nyi gosudarstvennyi arkhiv respubliki Uzbekistana (TsGARU).

State Archive of the Russian Federation. Gosudarstvennyi Arkhiv Rossiiskoi Federatsii (GARF).

[Archival citations are in the following format: 634/4/96/23–24, referring to fond/opis'/delo/listy.]

Newspapers

Alma-Atinskaia pravda
Bakinskii rabochii
Christian Science Monitor
Izvestiia
Kazakhstanskaia pravda
Kirovskaia pravda
Kommunist
Krasnaia Bashkiriia
Krasnaia Tatariia
Leningradskaia pravda
Leninskii put'

Literaturnaia gazeta
New York Times
Pionerskaia pravda
Pravda Severa
Pravda Ukrainy
Pravda Vostoka
Sotsialisticheskaia Karaganda
Sovetskaia Kirgiziia
Sovetskaia Litva
Turkmenskaia iskra
Uchitel' Kazakhstana
Uchitel'skaia gazeta
Ural'skii rabochii
USA Today
Vecherniaia Moskva
Washington Post
Zaria Vostoka

Articles and Books

Amalrik, Guzel. *Memories of a Tatar Childhood.* London: Hutchinson, 1979.
"Bol'shaia peremena." *Krokodil,* no. 24 (August 30, 1954): front cover.
"A Call to Reconsider Coeducation." *Current Digest of the Soviet Press* 2, no. 14 (1950): 13–14.
"Coeducation in Russia." *Newsweek* (August 9, 1954): 78.
Counts, George S. "Challenge of Soviet Education." *School Life* (1948): 18–19, 23.
Counts, George S., and Nucia Lodge. *The Country of the Blind: The Soviet System of Mind Control.* Boston: Houghton Mifflin, 1949.
Cultural Progress in the U.S.S.R. Moscow: Foreign Languages Publishing House, 1956.
"The Discussion on Co-education." *Soviet Studies* 5, no. 2 (1950): 180–192.
"The Discussion on Co-education Re-opened." *Soviet Studies* 5, no. 3 (1953): 316–328.
Downs, Bill. "Revolution in Soviet School System Kills Coeducation for Youthful Reds." *Newsweek* (August 16, 1943): 76.
Dubrovina, L. *Women's Right to Education in the Soviet Union.* Moscow: Foreign Languages Publishing House, 1956.
Esipov, B. P., and V. P. Shatskii. "Vospitatel'naia rabota v shkole sovmestnogo obucheniia." *Sovetskaia pedagogika,* no. 7 (July 1954): 12–17.
Evergetova, E. N. *Mal'chiki i devochki v sovetskoi shkole. K voprosu o sovmestnom vospitanii i obuchenii.* Moscow: Prosveshchenie, 1928.
Filippova, L. D. "Iz istorii zhenskogo obrazovaniia v Rossii." *Voprosy istorii* 2 (February 1963): 209–218.
Gorchakov, A., and I. Komarov. "Sovmestnoe obuchenie." *Shkola i zhizn,* no. 10 (1927): 43–47.
Itogi vsesoiuznoi perepisi naseleniia 1970 goda. Moscow: Statistika, 1972.
Kabanov, N. "Sovmestnoe obuchenie." In *Sovmestnoe vospitanie i obrazovanie. Biblioteka*

Svobodnago Vospitaniia i Obrazovaniia i Zashchity Detei, ed. I. Gorbunov-Posadov, no. 88 (Moscow, 1913): 27–38.

Kolbanovskii, V. N. *Vospitatel'naia rabota v shkole v usloviiakh sovmestnogo obucheniia*. Moscow: Izdatel'stvo Znanie, 1955.

Kul'turnoe stroitel'stvo SSSR. Statisticheskii sbornik. Moscow: Gosudarstvennoe Statisticheskoe Izdatel'stvo, 1956.

Kul'turnoe stroitel'stvo SSSR 1939. Statisticheskii sbornik. Moscow: Gosudarstvennoe Statisticheskoe Izdatel'stvo, 1940.

"A Life Photographer Looks at Moscow a Week before the Nazi Invasion Began." *Life* 11, no. 6 (August 11, 1941): 17–27.

Lugovskaya, Nina. *The Diary of a Soviet Schoolgirl, 1932–1937*. Translated by Joanne Turnbull. Moscow: Glas, 2003.

L'vov, K. I. "Po shkolam Kirgizii." *Kommunisticheskoe prosveshchenie* 2 (1934): 134–138.

———. "Rovesnitsy Oktiabria." *Prosveshchenie natsional'nostei* 5 (1933): 43–46.

———. "Shkola v soiuznykh respublikakh srednei azii i kavkaza v dni velikoi otechestvennoi voiny." *Sovetskaia pedagogika* 7 (July 1945): 48–54.

———. "Sovmestnoe obuchenie v proshlom i nastoiashchem." *Sovetskaia pedagogikia* 10 (October 1945): 38–46.

———. "Zhenskoe obrazovanie v SSSR v proshlom i nastoiashchem (V sviazi s problemoi sovmestnogo i razdel'nogo obucheniia devochek narodov SSSR)." Moscow: NII metodov obucheniia APN RSFSR, 1946.

Markov, V. N. "O razdel'nom obuchenii." *Vozhatyi* 8–9 (August 1943): 3–5.

Merkhelevich, E. "Ideiia sovmestnogo obucheniia v istorii nashei shkoly i eia politicheskoe znachenie." *Soiuz zhenshchin* 3 (1909): 6–7.

Miloslavskii, P. S. "Natsional'nuiu shkolu Severnogo Kavkaza na uroven' peredovykh shkol strany." *Severo-Kavkazskii uchitel'* 10 (October 1935): 3–9.

"Na puti k attestatu zrelosti." *SSSR na stroike*, 4 (1949): 10–11.

Narodnoe obrazovanie v SSSR. Obshcheobrazovatel'naia shkola: Sbornik dokumentov 1917–1973 gg. Moscow: Prosveshchenie, 1973.

Novikov, I. K. *Organizatsiia uchebno-vospitatel'noi raboty v shkole. Iz opyta raboty 110-i muzhskoi srednei shkoly Moskvy*. Moscow: Izdatel'stvo APN, 1950.

"O sovmestnom obuchenii v shkole." *Nachal'naia shkola* 9 (September 1954): 16–17.

"O vvedenii obiazatel'nogo sovmestnogo obucheniia." *Sobranie uzakonenii i rasporiazhenii rabochego i krest'ianskogo pravitel'stva* 39 (June 4, 1918): 475.

Ob itogakh raboty shkol RSFSR v 1947/48 uchebnom godu i ocherednykh zadachakh na 1948/49 uchebnyi god. Prikaz Ministerstva prosveshcheniia RSFSR 434 (August 10, 1949).

Ostrogorskii, Aleksandr. "O sovremennom sostoianii nachal'nogo obrazovaniia v Rossii." *Obrazovanie* 5, no. 7–8 (July–August 1896): 92–139.

Parsanova, E. A. "Kollektiv klassa uchashchikhsia muzhskoi shkoly." *Nachal'naia shkola* 2–3 (1945): 33–36.

"The Pendulum Swings. Russia Reconsiders Co-education." *Times Educational Supplement* (August 25, 1950): 657.

"Pervye shkol'nye gody." *SSSR na stroike* 4 (1949): 7.

Petrikeev, D. "Perekhod na sovmestnoe obuchenie v shkolakh Leningrada." *Narodnoe obrazovanie* 1 (1955): 21–28.

Potemkin, Vladimir Petrovich. *Stat'i i rechi po voprosam narodnogo obrazovaniia*. Moscow: Izdatel'stvo APN RSFSR, 1947.

Raskin, L. E. "Bor'ba za devochku kak odna iz problem vospitaniia." *Na putiakh k novoi shkole* 2 (1929): 53–54.

———. "Eshche o sovmestnom vospitanii." *Na putiakh k novoi shkole* 6 (1929): 55–58.

———. "O mal'chikakh i devochkakh." *O nashikh detiakh* 2 (1929): 5–8.

"The Road to a Big Life." *Soviet Union* (September 1950): 30.

Savich, A. "Trudnye voprosy sovmestnogo vospitaniia i obucheniia v shkole." *Sredniaia shkola* 5 (1939): 23–32.

"School Principal Writes of Educators' Problems." *Current Digest of the Soviet Press* 3, no. 35 (October 13, 1951): 5–6.

Skvortsov, N. A. "Ocherednye voprosy zhenskago obrazovaniia." *Zhenskaia zhizn'* 16 (August 22, 1915): 1–2.

"Soldiering v. Mothering." *Time* 42, no. 7 (August 16, 1943): 44.

"Soviet Reforms." *Times Educational Supplement* (October 30, 1943): 520.

Timofeev, M. G. "Sovmestnoe i razdel'noe obuchenie v proshlom i nastoiashchem." *Sovetskaia pedagogika* 4 (1945): 6–13.

"V poriadke diskussii." *Krokodil*, no. 21 (1950): 4.

Zhenshchina v SSSR: Statisticheskii sbornik. Moscow: Gosplan, 1936.

Secondary Sources

Studies of Soviet Education and History

Arsen'ev, A. M., V. I. Dodonov, M. N. Kolmakova, F. G. Panachin, and Z. I. Ravkin. *Ocherki istorii shkoly i pedagogicheskoi mysli narodov SSSR 1941–1961 gg.* Moscow: Pedagogika, 1988.

Bereday, George Z. F., William W. Brickman, and Gerald H. Read. *The Changing Soviet School.* Boston: Houghton Mifflin, 1960.

Bernstein, Frances L. *The Dictatorship of Sex: Lifestyle Advice for the Soviet Masses.* DeKalb: Northern Illinois University Press, 2007.

———. "'The Dictatorship of Sex': Science, Glands, and the Medical Construction of Gender Difference in Revolutionary Russia." In *Russian Modernity: Politics, Knowledge, Practices,* ed. David L. Hoffmann and Yanni Kotsonis, 138–160. New York: Macmillan, 2000.

Blitstein, Peter. "Nation-Building or Russification? Obligatory Russian Instruction in the Soviet Non-Russian School, 1938–1953." In *A State of Nations: Empire and Nation-Making in the Age of Lenin and Stalin,* ed. Ronald Grigor Suny and Terry Martin, 253–274. New York: Oxford University Press, 2001.

Bowen, James. *Soviet Education: Anton Makarenko and the Years of Experiment.* Madison: University of Wisconsin Press, 1962.

Brandenberger, David. *National Bolshevism: Stalinist Mass Culture and the Formation of Modern Russian National Identity, 1931–1956.* Cambridge: Harvard University Press, 2002.

Bucher, Greta. "Struggling to Survive: Soviet Women in the Postwar Years." *Journal of Women's History* 12, no. 1 (Spring 2000): 144–148.

———. *Women, the Bureaucracy and Daily Life in Postwar Moscow, 1945–1953.* Boulder, CO: East European Monographs, 2006.

Chatterjee, Choi. *Celebrating Women: Gender, Festival Culture, and Bolshevik Ideology, 1910–1939.* Pittsburgh: University of Pittsburgh Press, 2002.

Chernik, S. A. *Sovetskaia obshcheobrazovatel'naia shkola v gody Velikoi Otechestvennoi Voiny.* Moscow: Pedagogika, 1984.

Dunstan, John. "Coeducation and Revolution: Responses to Mixed Schooling in Early Twentieth-Century Russia." *History of Education* 26, no. 4 (1997): 275–393.

———. *Soviet Schooling in the Second World War.* New York: St. Martin's Press, 1997.

Edgar, Adrienne Lynn. *Tribal Nation: The Making of Soviet Turkmenistan.* Princeton: Princeton University Press, 2004.

Eklof, Ben. *Russian Peasant Schools: Officialdom, Village Culture, and Popular Pedagogy, 1861–1914.* Berkeley and Los Angeles: University of California Press, 1986.

Evans, Janet. "The Communist Party of the Soviet Union and the Women's Question: The Case of the 1936 Decree 'In Defence of Mother and Child.'" *Journal of Contemporary History* 16 (1981): 757–775.

Ewing, E. Thomas. "Ethnicity at School: Educating the 'Non-Russian' Children of the Soviet Union, 1928–1939." *History of Education* 35, no. 4–5 (July/September 2006): 499–519.

———. "From an Exclusive Privilege to a Right and an Obligation: Modern Russia." In *Girls' Secondary Education in the Western World: From the 18th to the 20th Century,* ed. James C. Albisetti, Joyce Goodman, and Rebecca Rogers, 165–179. New York: Palgrave, 2010.

———. "Gender Equity as Revolutionary Strategy: Coeducation in Russian and Soviet Schools." In *Revolution and Pedagogy: Interdisciplinary and Transnational Perspectives on Educational Foundations,* ed. E. Thomas Ewing, 39–59. New York: Palgrave Macmillan, 2005.

———. "How Is Power Exercised in an Authoritarian School?" Unpublished paper, 2008.

———. "If the Teacher Was a Man: Masculinity and Power in Stalinist Schools." *Gender & History* 21, no. 1 (April 2009): 107–129.

———. "Not One Girl outside the School! Educating 'Non-Russian' Girls in the Soviet Union in the 1930s." Unpublished paper, 2008.

———. "Personal Acts with Public Meanings: Suicide by Soviet Women Teachers in the Stalin Era." *Gender & History* 14, no. 1 (April 2002): 117–137.

———. "A Precarious Position of Power: Soviet School Directors in the 1930s." *Journal of Educational Administration and History* 41, no. 3 (August 2009): 253–266.

———. "Restoring Teachers to Their Rights: Soviet Education and the 1936 Denunciation of Pedology." *History of Education Quarterly* 41, no. 4 (Winter 2001): 471–493.

———. "A Stalinist Celebrity Teacher: Gender and Professional Identities in the Soviet Union in the 1930s." *Journal of Women's History* 16, no. 4 (Winter 2004): 92–118.

———. *The Teachers of Stalinism: Policy, Practice, and Power in Soviet Schools of the 1930s.* New York: Peter Lang, 2002.

Fainsod, Merle. *How Russia Is Ruled.* Cambridge: Harvard University Press, 1965.

Fitzpatrick, Sheila. *Everyday Stalinism: Ordinary Life in Extraordinary Times: Soviet Russia in the 1930s.* New York: Oxford University Press, 1999.

Fradkin, F. A., and M. G. Plokhova. "Problemy distsipliny v sovetskoi shkole." *Sovetskaia pedagogika* 6 (1991): 91–98.

Furst, Juliane. "Between Salvation and Liquidation: Homeless and Vagrant Children and the Reconstruction of Soviet Society." *Slavonic and East European Review* 86, no. 2 (April 2008): 232–258.

———. "The Importance of Being Stylish: Youth, Culture, and Identity." In *Late Stalinist Russia: Society between Reconstruction and Reinvention,* ed. Juliane Furst, 209–230. New York: Routledge, 2006.

———. "In Search of Soviet Salvation: Young People Write to the Stalinist Authorities." *Contemporary European History* 15, no. 3 (2006): 327–345.

———. "Prisoners of the Soviet Self?—Political Youth Opposition in Late Stalinism." *Europe-Asia Studies* 54, no. 3 (2002): 353–375.

———. "Re-examining Opposition under Stalin: Evidence and Context—A Reply to Kuromiya." *Europe-Asia Studies* 55, no. 5 (2003): 789–802.

Furst, Juliane, ed. *Late Stalinist Russia: Society between Reconstruction and Reinvention.* New York: Routledge, 2006.

Furst, Juliane, Polly Jones, and Susan Morrissey. "Introduction: The Relaunch of the Soviet Project, 1945–1964." *Slavonic and East European Review* 86, no. 2 (April 2008): 201–207.

Geiger, H. Kent. *The Family in Soviet Russia.* Cambridge: Harvard University Press, 1968.

Goldman, Wendy Z. *Women at the Gates: Gender and Industry in Stalin's Russia.* Cambridge: Cambridge University Press, 2002.

———. *Women, the State, and Revolution: Soviet Family Policy and Social Life, 1917–1936.* Cambridge: Cambridge University Press, 1993.

Gorlizki, Yoram, and Oleg Khlevniuk. *Cold Peace: Stalin and the Soviet Ruling Circle, 1945–1953.* Oxford: Oxford University Press, 2004.

Healey, Dan. *Bolshevik Sexual Forensics: Diagnosing Disorder in the Clinic and Courtroom, 1917–1939.* DeKalb: Northern Illinois University Press, 2009.

Hoffmann, David L. "Mothers in the Motherland: Stalinist Pronatalism in Its Pan-European Context." *Journal of Social History* 34, no. 1 (2000): 35–54.

———. *Stalinist Values: The Cultural Norms of Soviet Modernity, 1917–1941.* Ithaca: Cornell University Press, 2003.

Holmes, Larry E. "Ascent into Darkness: Escalating Negativity in the Administration of Schools in the Kirov Region, 1931–1941." *History of Education* 35, no. 4–5 (2006): 521–540.

———. "The Decline of Labor Education in Soviet Russia's Schools, 1931–1937." *Russian Review* 51, no. 4 (1992): 545–565.

———. *Grand Theater: Regional Governance in Stalin's Russia, 1931–1941.* Lanham, MD: Lexington Books, 2009.

———. *Stalin's School: Moscow's Model School No. 25, 1931–1937.* Pittsburgh: University of Pittsburgh Press, 1999.

Hough, Jerry F. "Debates about the Postwar World." In *The Impact of World War II on the Soviet Union,* ed. Susan J. Linz, 253–282. Totowa, NJ: Rowman and Allanheld, 1985.

Hyer, Janet. "Managing the Female Organism: Doctors and the Medicalization of Women's Paid Work in Soviet Russia during the 1920s." In *Women in Russia and Ukraine,* ed. Rosalind Marsh, 111–120. Cambridge: Cambridge University Press, 1996.

Ilic, Melanie. *Women Workers in the Soviet Interwar Economy: From "Protection" to "Equality."* London: Macmillan, 1999.

Johanson, Christine. *Women's Struggle for Higher Education in Russia, 1855–1900.* Montreal: McGill University Press, 1987.

Kamp, Marianne. *The New Woman in Uzbekistan: Islam, Modernity, and Unveiling under Communism.* Seattle: University of Washington Press, 2006.

Karpenko, L. A., ed. *Psykhologicheskii leksikon. Entsiklopedicheskii slovar' v shesti tomakh.* Moscow: PER SE, 2005.

Keller, Shoshana. *To Moscow, Not Mecca. The Soviet Campaign against Islam in Central Asia, 1917–1941.* Westport, CT: Praeger, 2001.

Kelly, Catriona. *Children's World: Growing Up in Russia, 1890–1991.* New Haven: Yale University Press, 2007.

Kojevnikov, Alexei. "Rituals of Stalinist Culture at Work: Science and the Games of Intraparty Democracy circa 1948." *Russian Review* 57 (January 1988): 25–52.

Kolesnik, Walter B. *Coeducation: Sex Differences and the Schools.* New York: Vantage, 1969.

Krylova, Anna. "Stalinist Identity from the Viewpoint of Gender: Rearing a Generation of Professionally Violent Women-Fighters in 1930s Stalinist Russia." *Gender & History* 16, no. 3 (November 2004): 626–653.

Kuromiya, Hiroaki. "'Political Youth Opposition in Late Stalinism': Evidence and Conjecture." *Europe-Asia Studies* 54, no. 4 (2003): 631–638.

——. "Re-examining Opposition under Stalin: Further Thoughts." *Europe-Asia Studies* 56, no. 2 (2004): 309–314.

Lapidus, Gail Warshofsky. *Women in Soviet Society: Equality, Development, and Social Change.* Berkeley and Los Angeles: University of California Press, 1978.

Livschiz, Ann. "Growing Up Soviet: Childhood in the Soviet Union, 1918–1958." PhD diss., Stanford University, 2007.

——. "Pre-Revolutionary in Form, Soviet in Content? Wartime Educational Reforms and the Postwar Quest for Normality." *History of Education* 35, no. 4–5 (July–September 2006): 541–560.

Massell, Gregory. *The Surrogate Proletariat: Moslem Women and Revolutionary Strategies in Soviet Central Asia, 1919–1929.* Princeton: Princeton University Press, 1974.

Merridale, Catherine. *Ivan's War: Life and Death in the Red Army, 1939–1945.* London: Macmillan, 2007.

——. *Night of Stone: Death and Memory in Twentieth-Century Russia.* New York: Viking, 2001.

Nash, Carol S. "Educating New Mothers: Women and the Enlightenment in Russia." *History of Education Quarterly* 21, no. 3 (1981): 301–316.

Neary, Rebecca Balmas. "Mothering Socialist Society: The Wife-Activists' Movement and the Soviet Culture of Daily Life, 1934–41." *Russian Review* 58 (July 1999): 396–412.

Northrop, Douglas. *Veiled Empire: Gender & Power in Stalinist Central Asia.* Ithaca: Cornell University Press, 2004.

"Opros: 76% rossiian otritsatel'no otnosiatsia k vvedeniiu razdel'nogo obucheniia v srednei shkole." IA Regnum, January 1, 2008. Online: www.regnum.ru/news.

Petrone, Karen. "Masculinity and Heroism in Imperial and Soviet Military-Patriotic Cultures." In *Russian Masculinities in History and Culture,* ed. Barbara Evans Clements, Rebecca Friedman, and Dan Healey, 172–193. New York: Palgrave, 2002.

Pushkareva, Natalia. *Women in Russian History: From the Tenth to the Twentieth Century.* Armonk, NY: M. E. Sharpe, 1997.

Pyzhikov, A. V. "Razdel'noe obuchenie v sovetskoi shkole." *Pedagogika* 5 (2004): 78–84.

Qualls, Karl D. *From Ruins to Reconstruction: Urban Identity in Soviet Sevastopol after World War II.* Ithaca: Cornell University Press, 2009.

"Razdel'noe obuchenie v shkolakh: preimushchestva i nedostatki." Baza FOM, January 10, 2008. Online: bd.fom.ru/.

Ruane, Christine. *Gender, Class, and the Professionalization of Russian City Teachers, 1860–1914.* Pittsburgh: University of Pittsburgh Press, 1994.

Schrand, Thomas G. "The Five-Year Plan for Women's Labour: Constructing Socialism and the 'Double Burden,' 1930–1932." *Europe-Asia Studies* 51, no. 8 (1999): 1455–1478.

———. "Socialism in One Gender: Masculine Values in the Stalin Revolution." In *Russian Masculinities in History and Culture,* ed. Barbara Evans Clements, Rebecca Friedman, and Dan Healey, 194–209. New York: Palgrave, 2002.

Shturman, Dora. *The Soviet Secondary School.* New York: Routledge, 1979.

Soviet Commitment to Education: Report of U.S. Education Mission to the U.S.S.R. Washington, DC: U.S. Office of Education, 1959.

Stites, Richard. *The Women's Liberation Movement in Russia. Feminism, Nihilism, and Bolshevism.* Princeton: Princeton University Press, 1978.

Timasheff, Nicholas. *The Great Retreat: The Growth and Decline of Communism.* New York: E. P. Dutton, 1946.

Weiner, Amir. "Robust Revolution to Retiring Revolution: The Life Cycle of the Soviet Revolution, 1945–1968." *Slavonic and East European Review* 86, no. 2 (April 2008): 208–231.

Zubkova, Elena. *Russia after the War: Hopes, Illusions, and Disappointments, 1945–1957.* Armonk, NY: M. E. Sharpe, 1998.

Studies of Gender and Education

Albisetti, James C. "Catholics and Coeducation: Rhetoric and Reality in Europe before Divini Illius Magistri." *Paedagogica Historica* 35, no. 3 (1999): 666–696.

———. *Schooling German Girls and Women: Secondary and Higher Education in the Nineteenth Century.* Princeton: Princeton University Press, 1988.

American Association of University Women. "AAUW Opposes Education Dept. Single-Sex Regulations." Press release, October 24, 2006. Online: www.aauw.org.

———. *The A.A.U.W. Report. How Schools Shortchange Girls.* Washington, DC: AAUW Educational Foundation, 1992.

———. *Beyond the "Gender Wars": A Conversation about Girls, Boys, and Education.* Washington, DC: AAUW Educational Foundation, 2001.

———. *Gender Gaps: Where Schools Still Fail Our Children.* Washington, DC: AAUW Educational Foundation, 1998.

———. *Separated by Sex: A Critical Look at Single-Sex Education for Girls.* Washington, DC: AAUW Educational Foundation, 1998.

———. *Where the Girls Are: The Facts about Gender Equity in Education.* Washington, DC: AAUW Educational Foundation, 2008.

Archer School for Girls. "New Research Shows Girls' School Advantage." Press release, April 6, 2009. Online: www.archer.org.

Baker, David P., Cornelius Riordan, and Maryellen Schaub. "The Effects of Sex-Grouped Schooling on Achievement: The Role of National Context." *Comparative Education Review* 39, no. 4 (November 1995): 468–482.

Blessing, Benita. *The Antifascist Classroom: Denazification in Soviet-Occupied Germany, 1945–1949.* New York: Palgrave Macmillan, 2006.

Bock, Gisela, and Pat Thane, eds. *Maternity and Gender Policies: Women and the Rise of the European Welfare States.* London: Routledge, 1991.

Bracey, Gerald. "The Success of Single-Sex Education Is Still Unproven." *Education Digest* 72, no. 6 (February 2007): 22–26.

Campbell, Patricia B., and Jo Sanders. "Challenging the System: Assumptions and Data behind the Push for Single-Sex Schooling." In *Gender in Policy and Practice: Perspectives on Single-Sex and Coeducational Schooling,* ed. Amanda Datnow and Lea Hubbard, 31–46. New York: Routledge, 2002.

Campbell, Patricia B., and Ellen Wahl, "What's Sex Got to Do with It? Simplistic Questions, Complex Answers." In *Separated by Sex: A Critical Look at Single-Sex Education for Girls.* Washington, DC: AAUW Educational Foundation, 1998.

Canning, Kathleen. *Gender History in Practice: Historical Perspectives on Bodies, Class, and Citizenship.* Ithaca: Cornell University Press, 2006.

Connell, R. W. "Teaching the Boys: New Research on Masculinity, and Gender Strategies for Schools." *Teachers College Record* 98, no. 2 (Winter 1996): 206–235.

Cuban, Larry. *How Teachers Taught: Constancy and Change in American Classrooms, 1890–1980.* New York: Teachers College Press, 1988.

Datnow, Amanda, and Lea Hubbard, eds. *Gender in Policy and Practice: Perspectives on Single-Sex and Coeducational Schooling.* New York: Routledge, 2002.

Datnow, Amanda, Lea Hubbard, and Gilberto Conchas. "How Context Mediates Policy: The Implementation of Single-Gender Public Schooling in California." *Teachers College Record* 103, no. 2 (2001): 184–206.

Datnow, Amanda, Lea Hubbard, and Elisabeth Woody. *Is Single Gender Schooling Viable in the Public Sector? Lessons from California's Pilot Program.* Final report to the Ford Foundation and Spencer Foundation, 2001.

Davis, Michelle. "Department Aims to Promote Single-Sex Schools." *Education Week* 21, no. 36 (May 15, 2002): 24, 26. Online: www.edweek.org.

DeBare, Ilana. *Where Girls Come First: The Rise, Fall, and Surprising Revival of Girls' Schools.* New York: Penguin, 2004.

Flannery, Mary Ellen. "No Girls Allowed." *NEA Today* (April 2006). Online: www.nea.org.

Foucault, Michel. *Discipline and Punish: The Birth of the Prison.* New York: Vintage, 1979.

Frank, Blye, Michael Kehler, Trudy Lovell, and Kevin Davison. "A Tangle of Trouble: Boys, Masculinity, and Schooling—Future Directions." *Educational Review* 55, no. 2 (2003): 119–133.

"Ga. District under Fire for Plan to Separate Students by Gender." *Education Week* 27, no. 24 (February 20, 2008): 4. Online: www.edweek.org.

Gurian, Michael, and Patricia Henley. *Boys and Girls Learn Differently! A Guide for Teachers and Parents.* San Francisco: Jossey-Bass, 2001.

Herr, Kathryn, and Emily Arms. "Accountability and Single-Sex Schooling: A Collision of Reform Agendas." *American Educational Research Journal* 41, no. 3 (Fall 2004): 527–555.

———. "The Intersection of Educational Reforms: Single-Gender Academies in a Public Middle School." In *Gender in Policy and Practice: Perspectives on Single-Sex and Coeducational Schooling,* ed. Amanda Datnow and Lea Hubbard, 74–89. New York: Routledge, 2002.

Hubbard, Lea, and Amanda Datnow. "Are Single-Sex Schools Sustainable in the Public Sector?" In *Gender in Policy and Practice: Perspectives on Single-Sex and Coeducational Schooling,* ed. Amanda Datnow and Lea Hubbard, 109–132. New York: Routledge, 2002.

Jackson, Carolyn, and Ian David Smith. "Poles Apart? An Exploration of Single-Sex and

Mixed-Sex Educational Environments in Australia and England." *Educational Studies* 26, no. 4 (2000): 409–422.

Koven, Seth, and Sonya Michel. "Womanly Duties: Maternalist Politics and the Origins of Welfare States in France, Germany, Great Britain, and the United States, 1880–1920." *American Historical Review* 95, no. 4 (1990): 1077–1079.

Lee, Valerie E. "Is Single-Sex Secondary Schooling a Solution to the Problem of Gender Inequity?" In *Separated by Sex: A Critical Look at Single-Sex Education for Girls,* 53–62. Washington, DC: AAUW Educational Foundation, 1998.

Lee, Valerie E., and Marlaine E. Lockheed. "The Effects of Single-Sex Schooling on Achievement and Attitudes in Nigeria." *Comparative Education Review* 34, no. 2 (May 1990): 209–231.

Lesko, Nancy, ed. *Masculinities at School.* Thousand Oaks, CA: Sage, 2000.

Martino, Wayne, and Deborah Berrill. "Boys, Schooling, and Masculinities: Interrogating the 'Right' Way to Educate Boys." *Educational Review* 55, no. 2 (2003): 99–106.

Martino, Wayne, Martin Mills, and Bob Lingard. "Interrogating Single-Sex Classes as a Strategy for Addressing Boys' Educational and Social Needs." *Oxford Review of Education* 31 (June 2005): 237–254.

Mead, Sara. "The Evidence Suggests Otherwise: The Truth about Boys and Girls." Washington, DC: Education Sector, 2006.

Meehan, Diana. *Learning like a Girl: Educating Our Daughters in Schools of Their Own.* New York: Public Affairs, 2007.

Meyer, Peter. "Learning Separately: The Case for Single-Sex Schools." *Education Next* (Winter 2008): 10–21.

Miller-Bernal, Leslie. "Introduction: Coeducation: An Uneven Progression." In *Going Coed: Women's Experiences in Formerly Men's Colleges and Universities, 1950–2000,* ed. Leslie Miller-Bernal and Susan L. Poulson, 3–21. Nashville: Vanderbilt University Press, 2004.

National Association for Single Sex Public Education. "Research." www.singlesexschools .org, accessed August 2009.

National Coalition for Girls' Schools. "Research Shows: Girls' Schools Have an Edge." Press release, 2009. Online: www.ncgs.org.

National Organization for Women. "NOW Opposes Single-Sex Public Education as 'Separate and Unequal.'" Press release, October 24, 2006. Online: www.now.org.

Riley, Denise. "Does a Sex Have a History?" In *Feminism and History,* ed. Joan Scott, 17–33. Oxford: Oxford University Press, 1996.

Riordan, Cornelius. "The Future of Single-Sex Schools." In *Separated by Sex: A Critical Look at Single-Sex Education for Girls,* 53–62. Washington, DC: AAUW Educational Foundation, 1998.

———. *Girls and Boys in School: Together or Separate?* New York: Teachers College Press, 1990.

———. "What Do We Know about the Effects of Single-Sex Schools in the Private Sector? Implications for Public Schools." In *Gender in Policy and Practice: Perspectives on Single-Sex and Coeducational Schooling,* ed. Amanda Datnow and Lea Hubbard, 10–30. New York: Routledge, 2002.

Rogers, Rebecca. "Schools, Discipline, and Community: Diary-Writing and Schoolgirl Culture in Late Nineteenth-Century France." *Women's History Review* 4, no. 4 (1995): 525–555.

Sadker, Myra, and David Sadker. *Failing at Fairness: How America's Schools Cheat Girls.* New York: Touchstone Books, 1994.

Salomone, Rosemary. "The Legality of Single-Sex Education in the United States: Sometimes 'Equal' Means 'Different.'" In *Gender in Policy and Practice: Perspectives on Single-Sex and Coeducational Schooling,* ed. Amanda Datnow and Lea Hubbard, 47–72. New York: Routledge, 2002.

———. *Same, Different, Equal: Rethinking Single-Sex Schooling.* New Haven: Yale University Press, 2003.

Sax, Leonard. "The Promise and Peril of Single-Sex *Public* Education." *Education Week* 24, no. 25 (March 2, 2005): 34–35, 48. Online: www.edweek.org.

———. *Why Gender Matters: What Parents and Teachers Need to Know about the Emerging Science of Sex Differences.* New York: Broadway Books, 2005.

Sax, Linda J. *Women Graduates of Single-Sex and Coeducational High Schools: Differences in Their Characteristics and the Transition to College.* Los Angeles: UCLA Graduate School of Education and Information Studies, 2009.

Schreiner, Bruce. "Single-Sex Classes Could Become More Common as Obstacles Are Removed." Associated Press, August 20, 2002, accessed from Lexis-Nexis Academic.

Scott, Joan W. "Feminism's History." *Journal of Women's History* 16, no. 2 (2004): 10–29.

Sommers, Christina Hoff. "Give Same-Sex Schooling a Chance." *Education Week* 21, no. 4 (September 26, 2001): 36. Online: www.edweek.org.

Spellings, Margaret. "Secretary Spellings Announces More Choices in Single Sex Education. Amended Regulations Give Communities More Flexibility to Offer Single Sex Schools and Classes." U.S. Department of Education press release, October 24, 2006. Online: www.ed.gov.

Spielhagen, Frances R., ed. *Debating Single-Sex Education. Separate and Equal?* Lanham, MD: Rowman and Littlefield Education, 2008.

———. "Single-Sex Classes: Everything That's Old Is New Again." In *Debating Single-Sex Education. Separate and Equal?* ed. Spielhagen, 1–7. Lanham, MD: Rowman and Littlefield Education, 2008.

———. "Single-Sex Education: Policy, Practice, and Pitfalls." *Teachers College Record* October 7, 2008. Online: www.tcrecord.org.

Stabiner, Karen. *All Girls: Single-Sex Education and Why It Matters.* New York: Riverhead Books, 2002.

Streitmatter, Janice. *For Girls Only: Making a Case for Single-Sex Schooling.* New York: State University of New York Press, 1999.

Thorne, Barrie. "Girls and Boys Together . . . But Mostly Apart: Gender Arrangements in Elementary Schools." In *Men's Lives: Readings in the Sociology of Men and Masculinity,* 3rd ed., ed Michael Kimmel and Michael Messner, 61–73. New York: Macmillan, 1992.

Tyack, David, and Larry Cuban. *Tinkering toward Utopia: A Century of Public School Reform.* Cambridge: Harvard University Press, 1995.

Tyack, David, and Elisabeth Hansot. *Learning Together: A History of Coeducation in American Public Schools.* New York: Russell Sage Foundation, 1992.

U.S. Department of Education, Office of Planning, Evaluation and Policy Development, Policy and Program Studies Service. *Single-Sex versus Coeducational Schooling: A Systematic Review.* Washington, DC: U.S. Department of Education, 2005.

Weaver-Hightower, Marcus. "The 'Boy Turn' in Research on Gender and Education." *Review of Educational Research* 73, no. 4 (Winter 2003): 471–498.

Weil, Elizabeth. "Should Boys and Girls Be Taught Differently? Teaching to the Testosterone." *New York Times Magazine,* March 2, 2008, 38–45, 84–87.

Woody, Elisabeth L. "Constructions of Masculinity in California's Single-Gender Academies." In *Gender in Policy and Practice: Perspectives on Single-Sex and Coeducational Schooling,* ed. Amanda Datnow and Lea Hubbard, 280–303. New York: Routledge, 2002.

Woollacott, Angela. *Gender and Empire.* New York: Palgrave Macmillan, 2006.

Younger, Michael Robert, and Molly Warrington. "Would Harry and Hermione Have Done Better in Single-Sex Classes? A Review of Single-Sex Teaching in Coeducational Secondary Schools in the United Kingdom." *American Educational Research Journal* 43, no. 4 (Winter 2006): 579–620.

Index